KAGUYA - SAMA
LOVE IS WAR
5

AKA AKASAKA

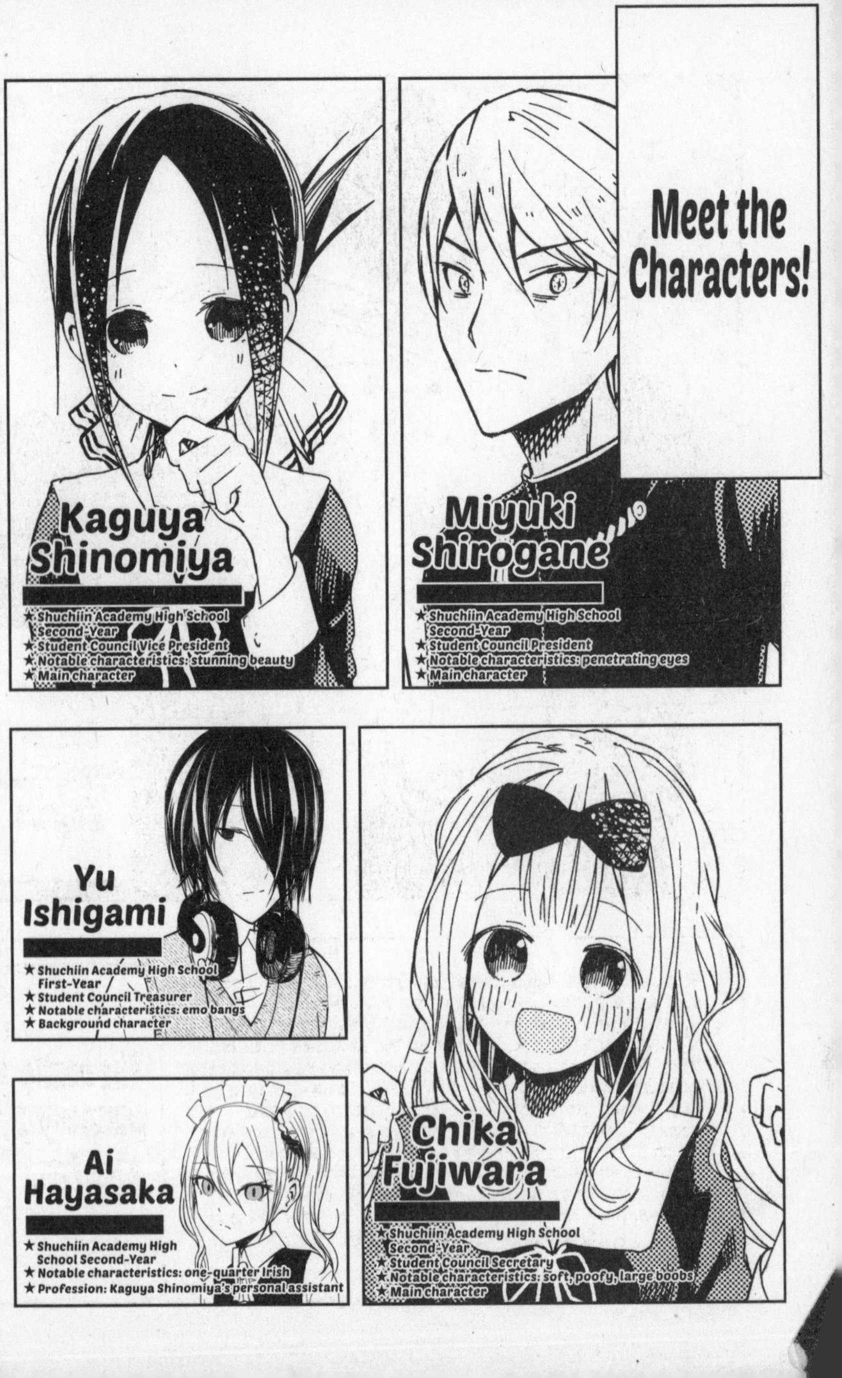
Meet the Characters!
Miyuki Shirogane
★Shuchiin Academy High School Second-Year
★Student Council President
★Notable characteristics: penetrating eyes
★Main character
Kaguya Shinomiya
★Shuchiin Academy High School Second-Year
★Student Council Vice President
★Notable characteristics: stunning beauty
★Main character
Chika Fujiwara
★Shuchiin Academy High School Second-Year
★Student Council Secretary
★Notable characteristics: soft, poofy, large boobs
★Main character
Yu Ishigami
★Shuchiin Academy High School First-Year
★Student Council Treasurer
★Notable characteristics: emo bangs
★Background character
Ai Hayasaka
★Shuchiin Academy High School Second-Year
★Notable characteristics: one-quarter Irish
★Profession: Kaguya Shinomiya's personal assistant

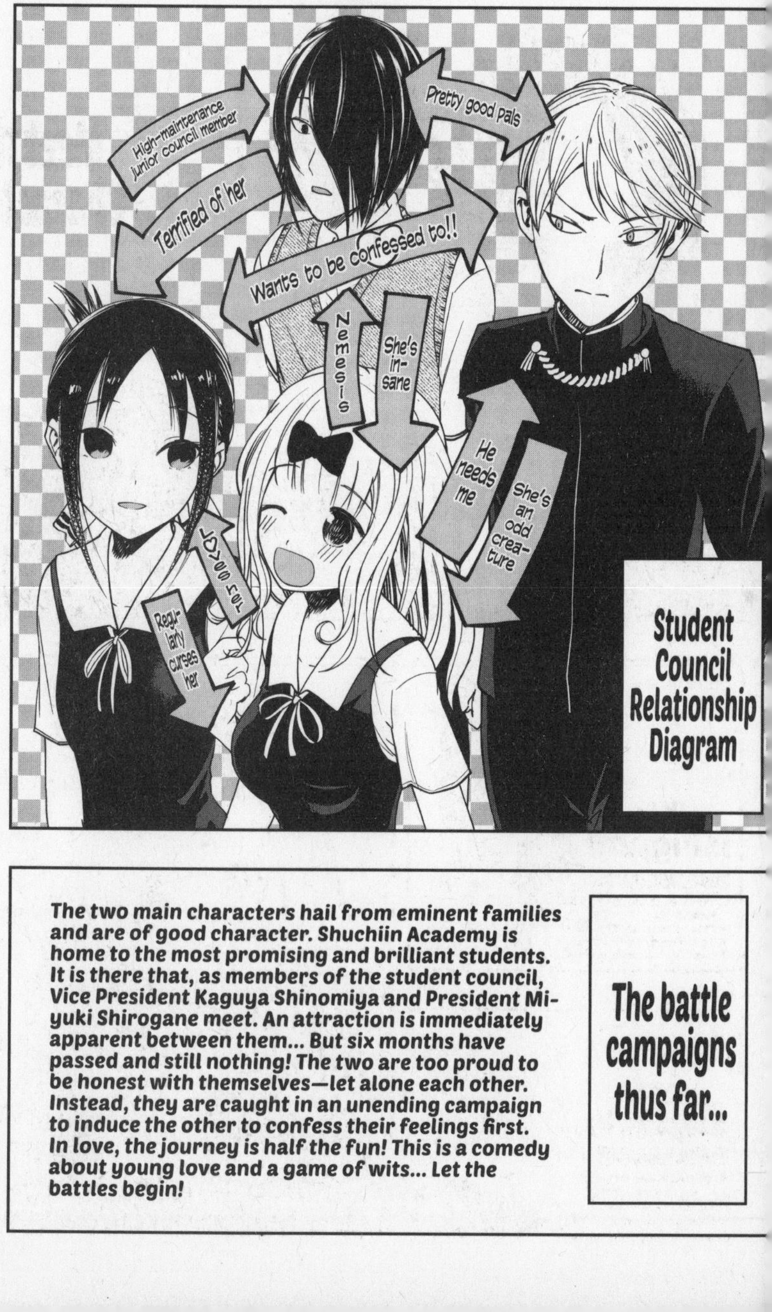
Student Council Relationship Diagram
Pretty good pals
High-maintenance junior council member
Terrified of her
Wants to be confessed to!!
Nemesis
She's insane
He needs me
She's an odd creature
Loves her
Regularly curses her

The battle campaigns thus far...

The two main characters hail from eminent families and are of good character. Shuchiin Academy is home to the most promising and brilliant students. It is there that, as members of the student council, Vice President Kaguya Shinomiya and President Miyuki Shirogane meet. An attraction is immediately apparent between them... But six months have passed and still nothing! The two are too proud to be honest with themselves—let alone each other. Instead, they are caught in an unending campaign to induce the other to confess their feelings first. In love, the journey is half the fun! This is a comedy about young love and a game of wits... Let the battles begin!

KAGUYA-SAMA LOVE IS WAR

5

BATTLE CAMPAIGNS

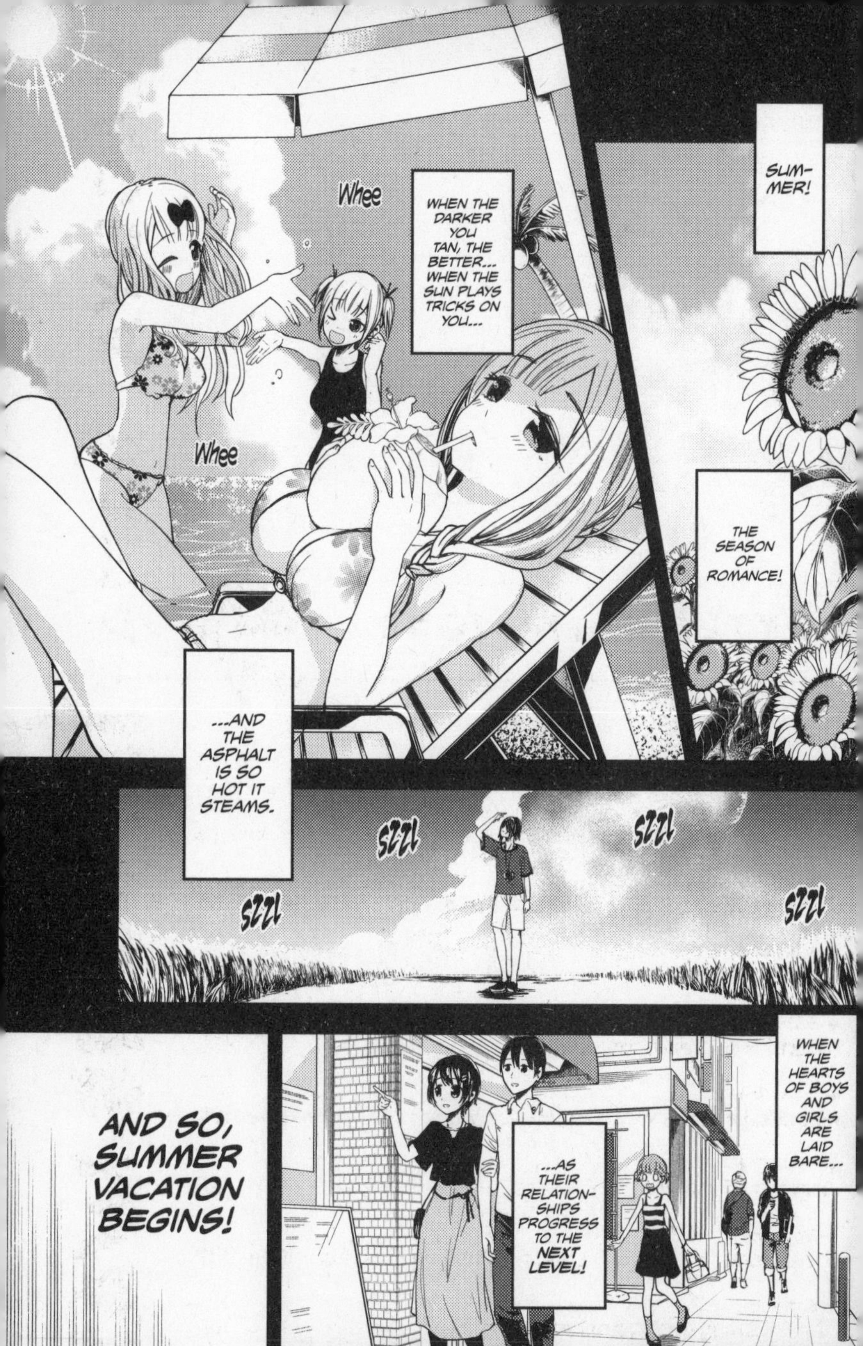
SUM-MER!
THE SEASON OF ROMANCE!
WHEN THE DARKER YOU TAN, THE BETTER... WHEN THE SUN PLAYS TRICKS ON YOU...
Whee
Whee
...AND THE ASPHALT IS SO HOT IT STEAMS.
SZZL
SZZL
SZZL
SZZL
WHEN THE HEARTS OF BOYS AND GIRLS ARE LAID BARE...
...AS THEIR RELATION-SHIPS PROGRESS TO THE NEXT LEVEL!
AND SO, SUMMER VACATION BEGINS!

Battle 41 Miyuki Shirogane Wants to See Y

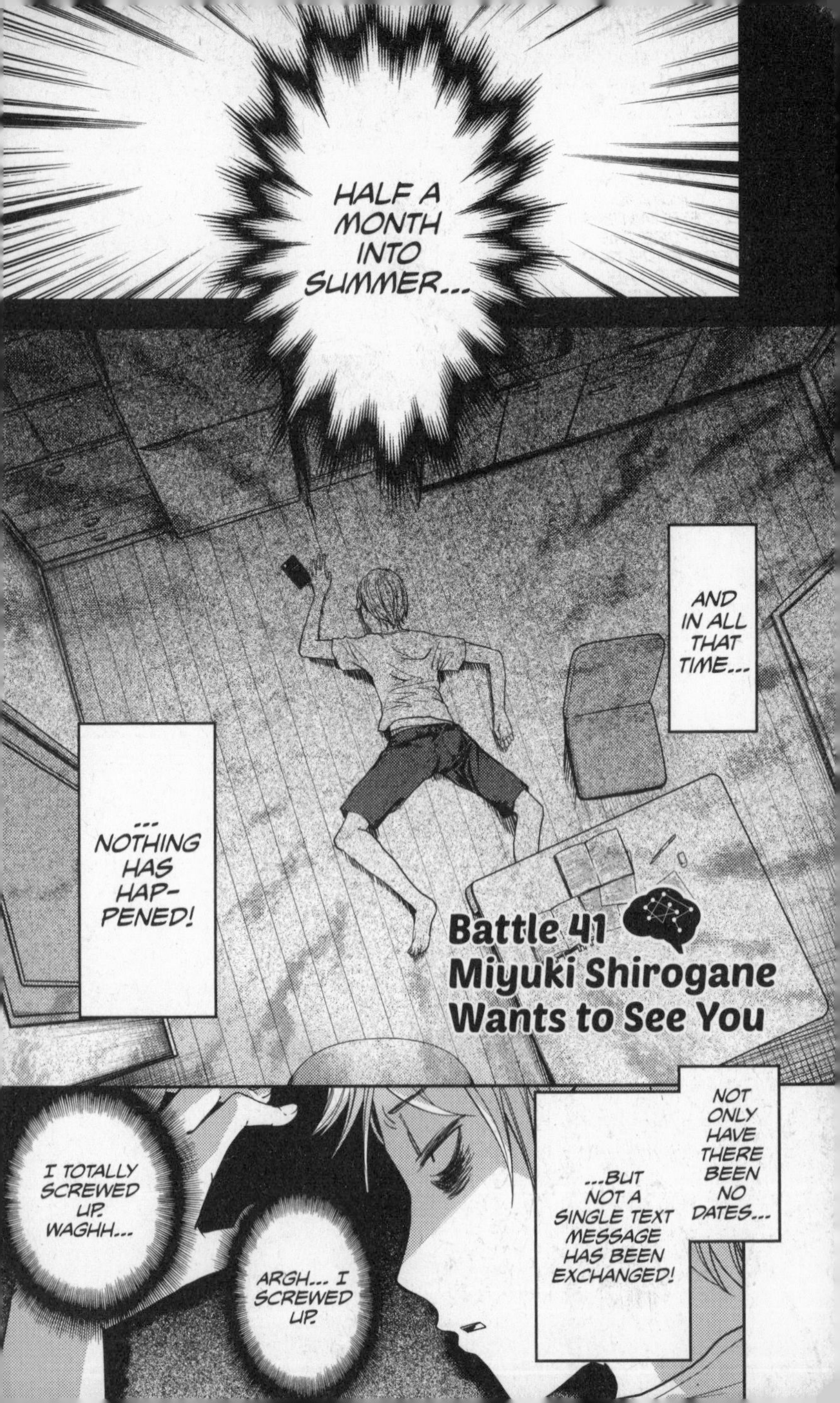
HALF A MONTH INTO SUMMER...
AND IN ALL THAT TIME...
...NOTHING HAS HAP-PENED!
Battle 41
Miyuki Shirogane Wants to See You
NOT ONLY HAVE THERE BEEN NO DATES...
...BUT NOT A SINGLE TEXT MESSAGE HAS BEEN EXCHANGED!
ARGH... I SCREWED UP.
I TOTALLY SCREWED UP. WAGHH...

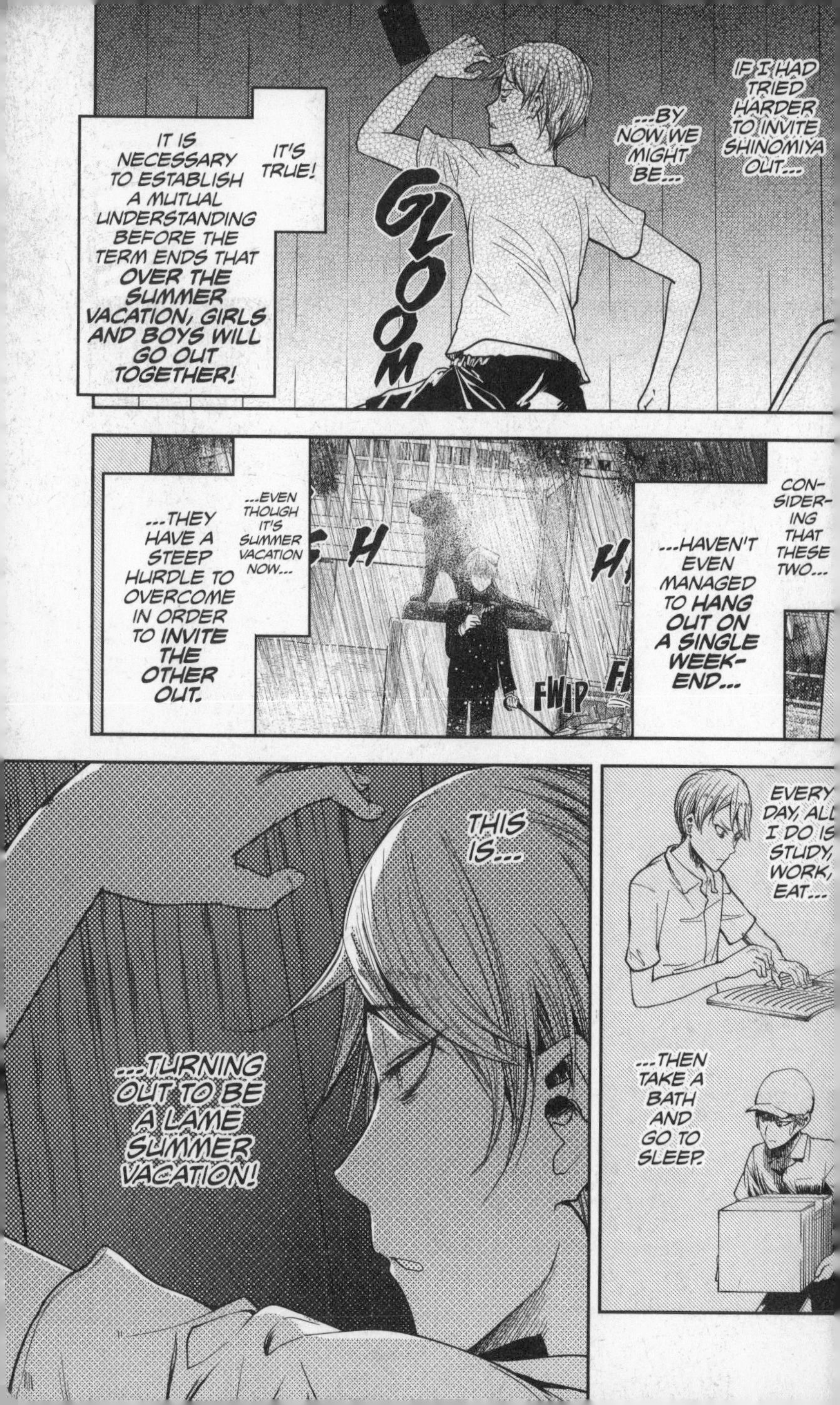
IF I HAD TRIED HARDER TO INVITE SHINOMIYA OUT...
...BY NOW WE MIGHT BE...
GLOOM
IT'S TRUE!
IT IS NECESSARY TO ESTABLISH A MUTUAL UNDERSTANDING BEFORE THE TERM ENDS THAT OVER THE SUMMER VACATION, GIRLS AND BOYS WILL GO OUT TOGETHER!
CON-SIDER-ING THAT THESE TWO...
...HAVEN'T EVEN MANAGED TO HANG OUT ON A SINGLE WEEK-END...
FWIP
...EVEN THOUGH IT'S SUMMER VACATION NOW...
...THEY HAVE A STEEP HURDLE TO OVERCOME IN ORDER TO INVITE THE OTHER OUT.
EVERY DAY, ALL I DO IS STUDY, WORK, EAT...
...THEN TAKE A BATH AND GO TO SLEEP.
THIS IS...
...TURNING OUT TO BE A LAME SUMMER VACATION!

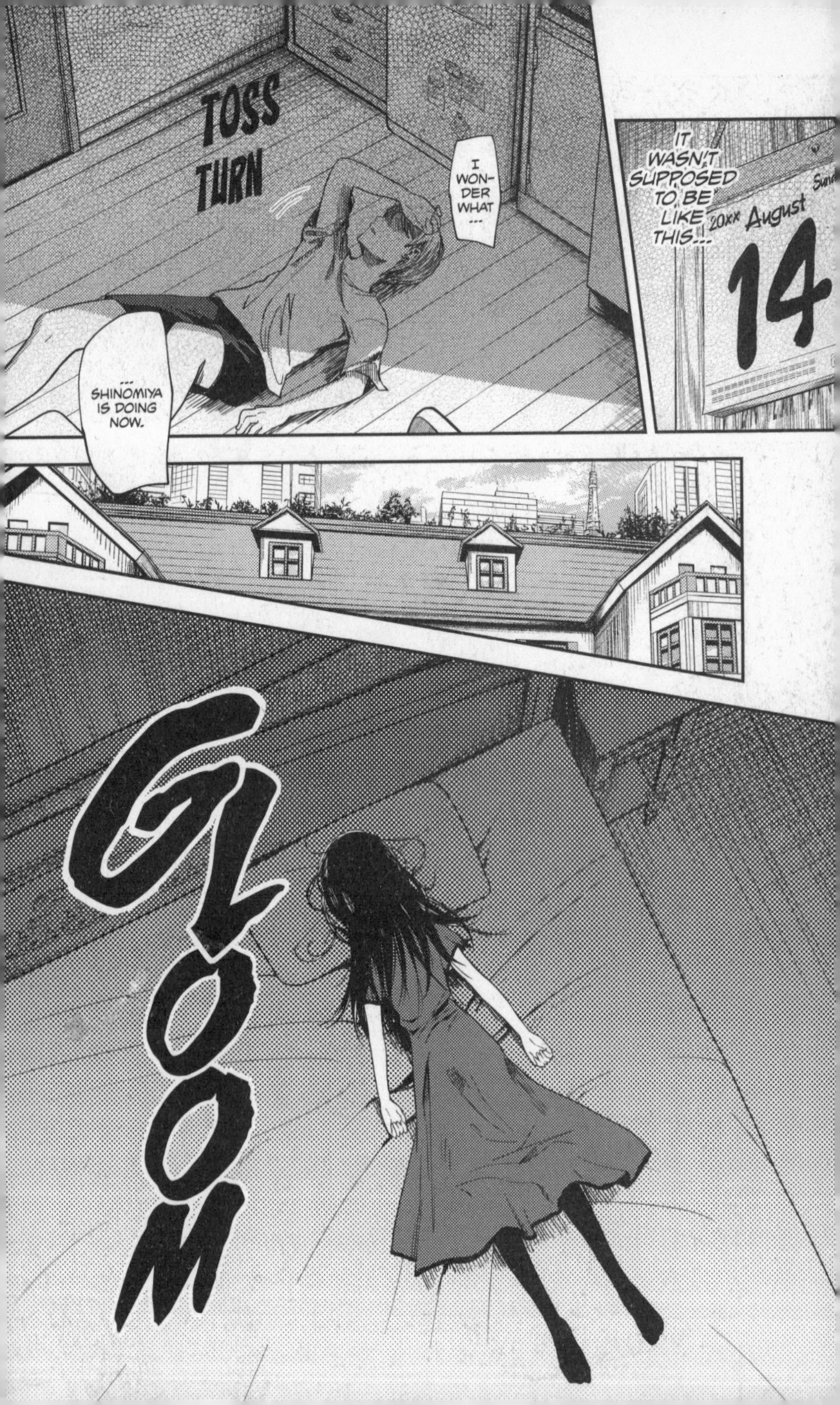
IT WASN'T SUPPOSED TO BE LIKE THIS...
20xx August
14
I WONDER WHAT ...
TOSS
TURN
... SHINOMIYA IS DOING NOW.
GLOOM

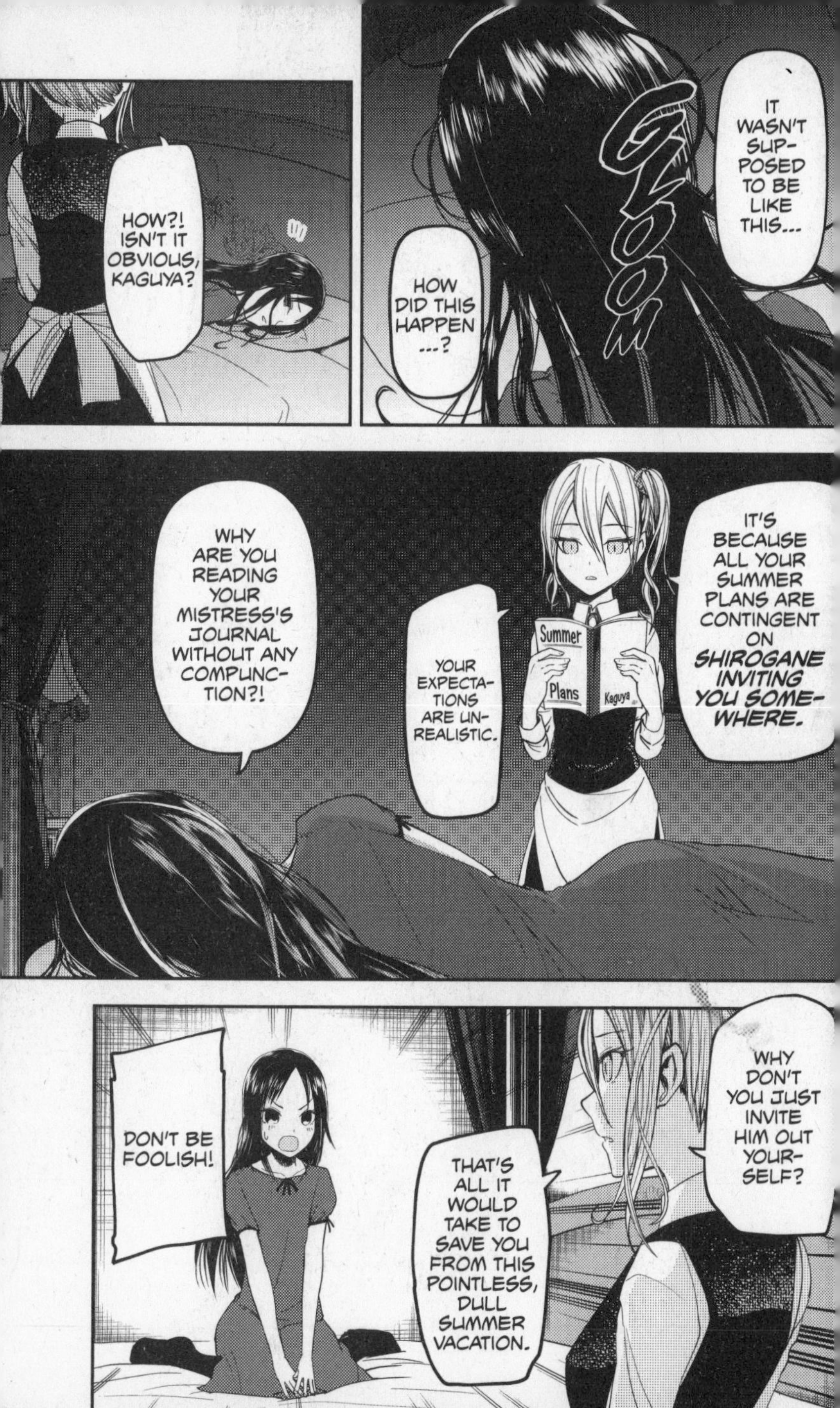
IT WASN'T SUP-POSED TO BE LIKE THIS...
GLOOM
HOW DID THIS HAPPEN ...?
HOW?! ISN'T IT OBVIOUS, KAGUYA?
IT'S BECAUSE ALL YOUR SUMMER PLANS ARE CONTINGENT ON ***SHIROGANE INVITING YOU SOME-WHERE.***
YOUR EXPECTA-TIONS ARE UN-REALISTIC.
Summer Plans Kaguya
WHY ARE YOU READING YOUR MISTRESS'S JOURNAL WITHOUT ANY COMPUNC-TION?!
WHY DON'T YOU JUST INVITE HIM OUT YOUR-SELF?
THAT'S ALL IT WOULD TAKE TO SAVE YOU FROM THIS POINTLESS, DULL SUMMER VACATION.
DON'T BE FOOLISH!

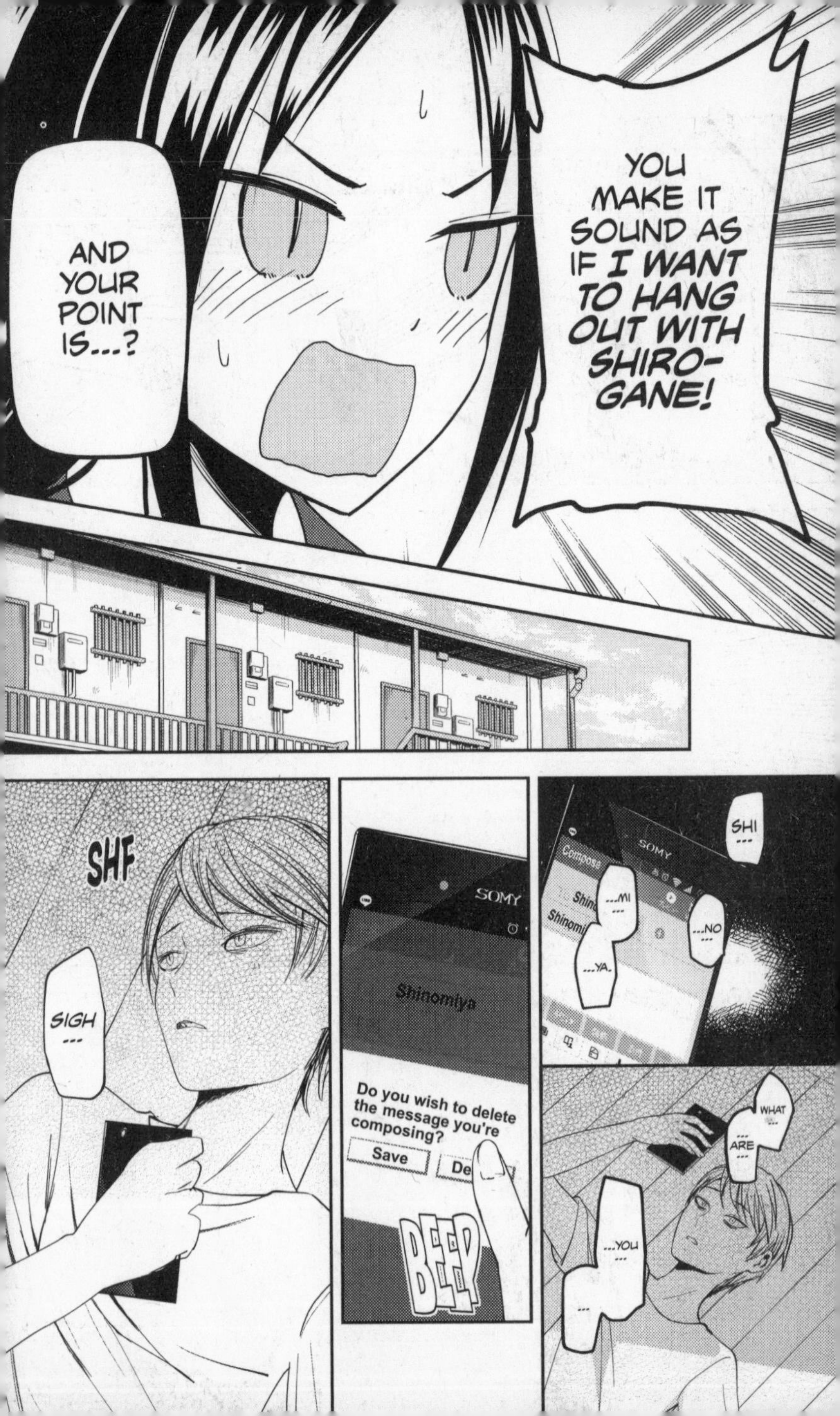

YOU MAKE IT SOUND AS IF I WANT TO HANG OUT WITH SHIRO-GANE!
AND YOUR POINT IS...?
SOMY
Compose
SHI...
...NO...
...MI...
...YA.
WHAT...
...ARE...
...YOU...
...
SOMY
Shinomiya
Do you wish to delete the message you're composing?
Save
De
BEEP
SHF
SIGH...

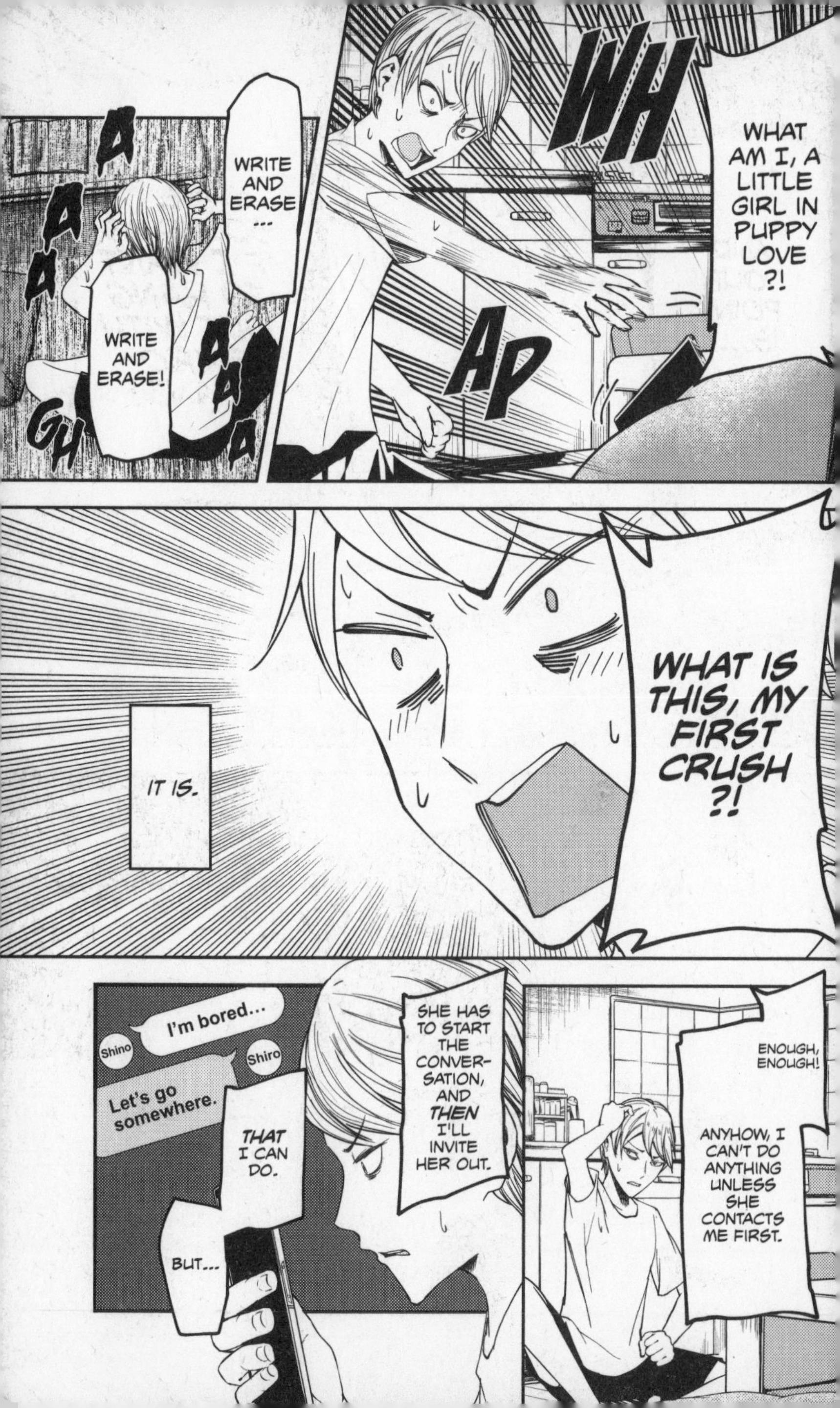

WHAT AM I, A LITTLE GIRL IN PUPPY LOVE ?!
WH
AP
WRITE AND ERASE ...
WRITE AND ERASE!
GH
WHAT IS THIS, MY FIRST CRUSH ?!
IT IS.
ENOUGH, ENOUGH!
ANYHOW, I CAN'T DO ANYTHING UNLESS SHE CONTACTS ME FIRST.
SHE HAS TO START THE CONVER-SATION, AND THEN I'LL INVITE HER OUT.
Shino
I'm bored...
Shiro
Let's go somewhere.
THAT I CAN DO.
BUT...

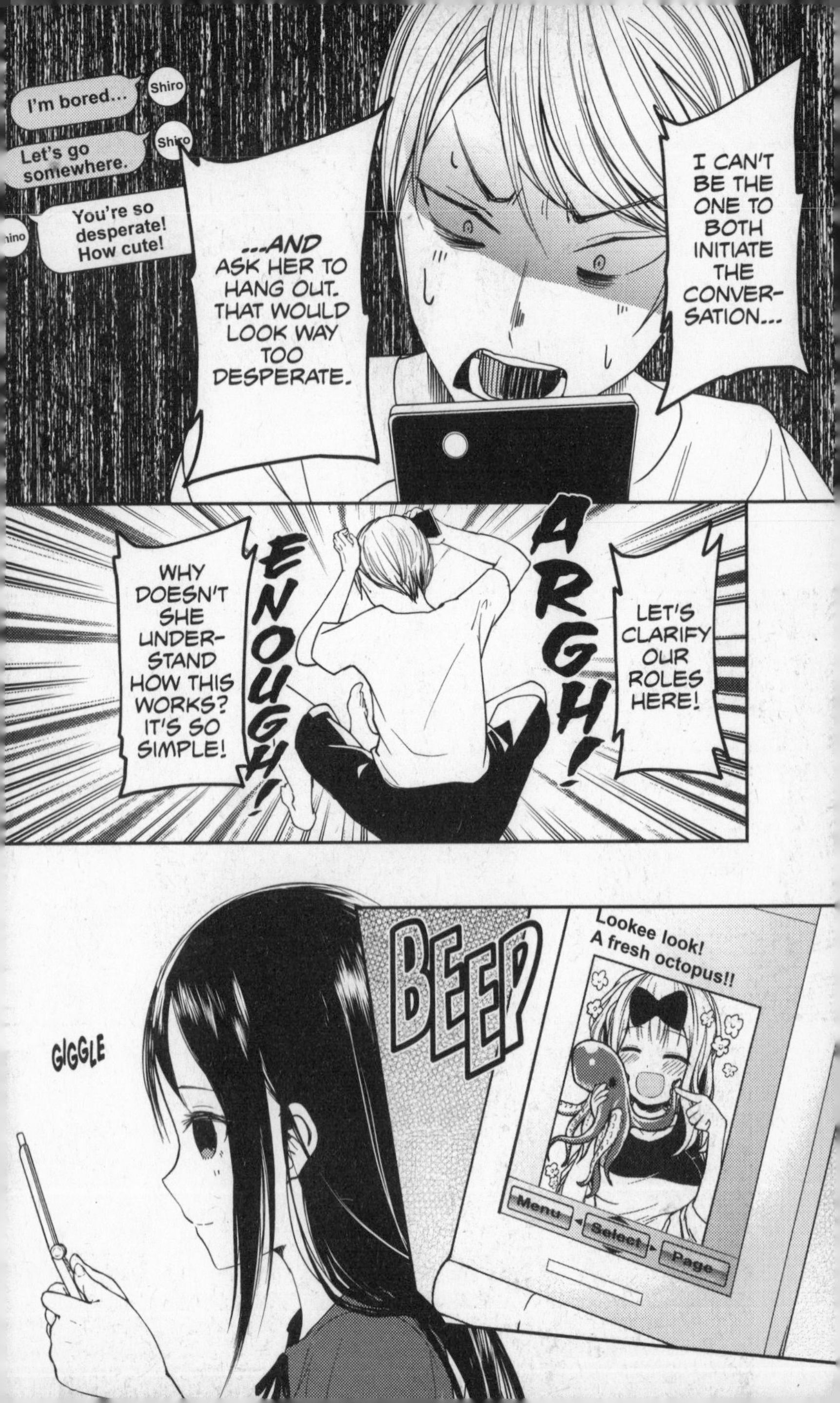

I CAN'T BE THE ONE TO BOTH INITIATE THE CONVERSATION...
...AND ASK HER TO HANG OUT. THAT WOULD LOOK WAY TOO DESPERATE.
Shiro
I'm bored...
Shiro
Let's go somewhere.
hino
You're so desperate! How cute!
LET'S CLARIFY OUR ROLES HERE!
ARGH!
ENOUGH!
WHY DOESN'T SHE UNDERSTAND HOW THIS WORKS? IT'S SO SIMPLE!
Lookee look! A fresh octopus!!
Menu
Select
Page
BEEP
GIGGLE

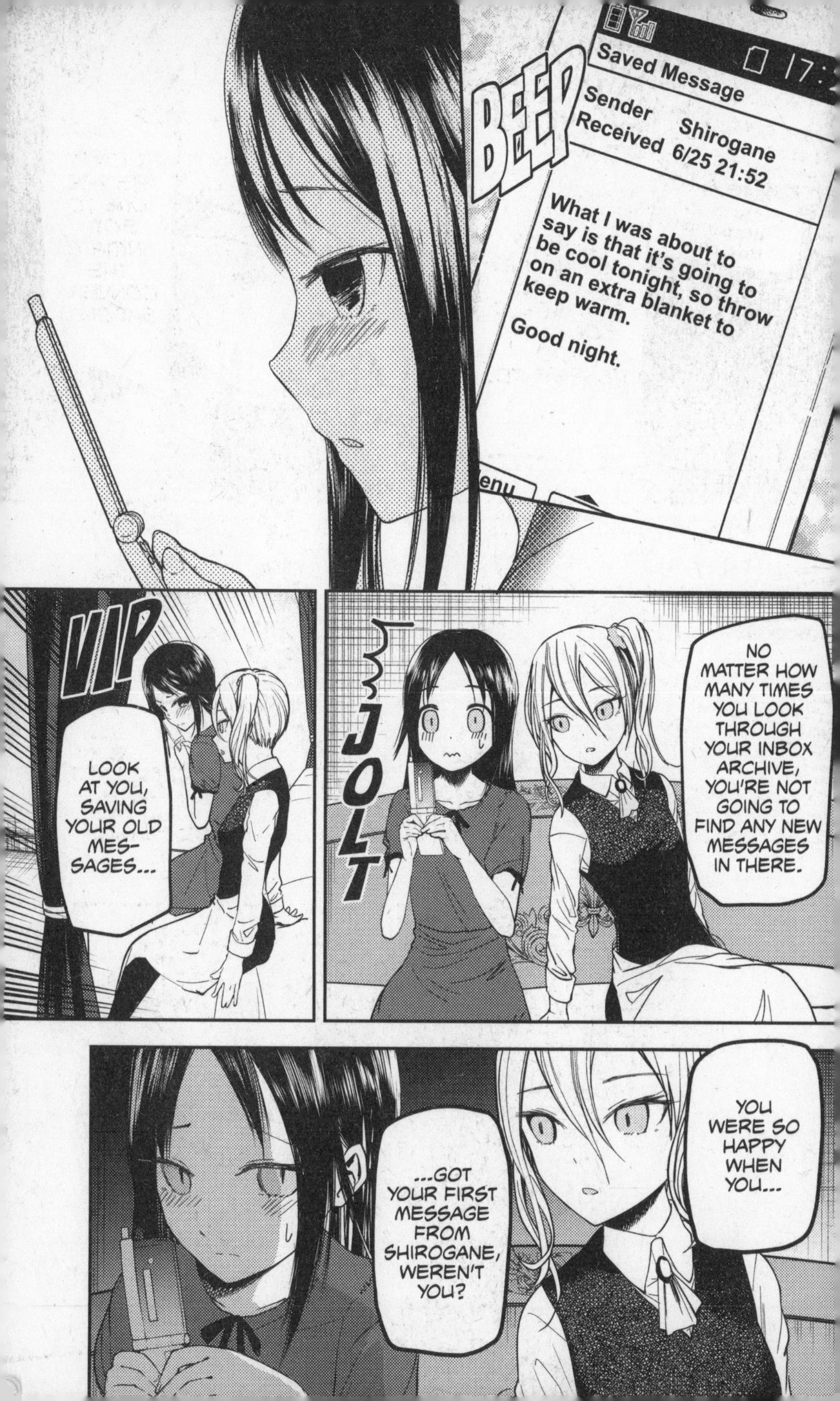
BEEP
Saved Message
Sender Shirogane
Received 6/25 21:52
What I was about to say is that it's going to be cool tonight, so throw on an extra blanket to keep warm.
Good night.
JOLT
NO MATTER HOW MANY TIMES YOU LOOK THROUGH YOUR INBOX ARCHIVE, YOU'RE NOT GOING TO FIND ANY NEW MESSAGES IN THERE.
VIP
LOOK AT YOU, SAVING YOUR OLD MES-SAGES...
YOU WERE SO HAPPY WHEN YOU...
...GOT YOUR FIRST MESSAGE FROM SHIROGANE, WEREN'T YOU?

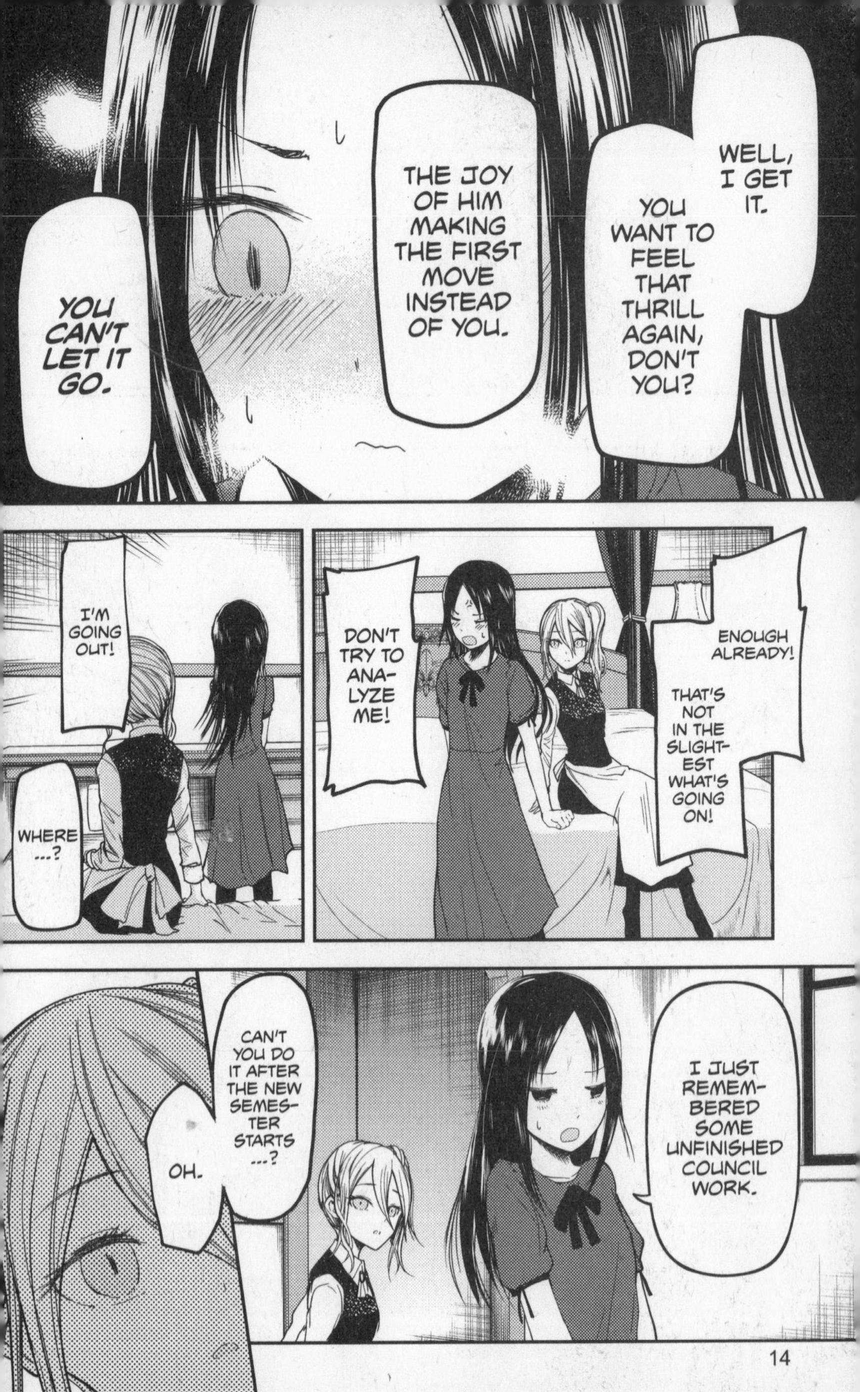
WELL, I GET IT.
YOU WANT TO FEEL THAT THRILL AGAIN, DON'T YOU?
THE JOY OF HIM MAKING THE FIRST MOVE INSTEAD OF YOU.
YOU CAN'T LET IT GO.
ENOUGH ALREADY!
THAT'S NOT IN THE SLIGHTEST WHAT'S GOING ON!
DON'T TRY TO ANALYZE ME!
I'M GOING OUT!
WHERE ...?
I JUST REMEMBERED SOME UNFINISHED COUNCIL WORK.
CAN'T YOU DO IT AFTER THE NEW SEMESTER STARTS ...?
OH.

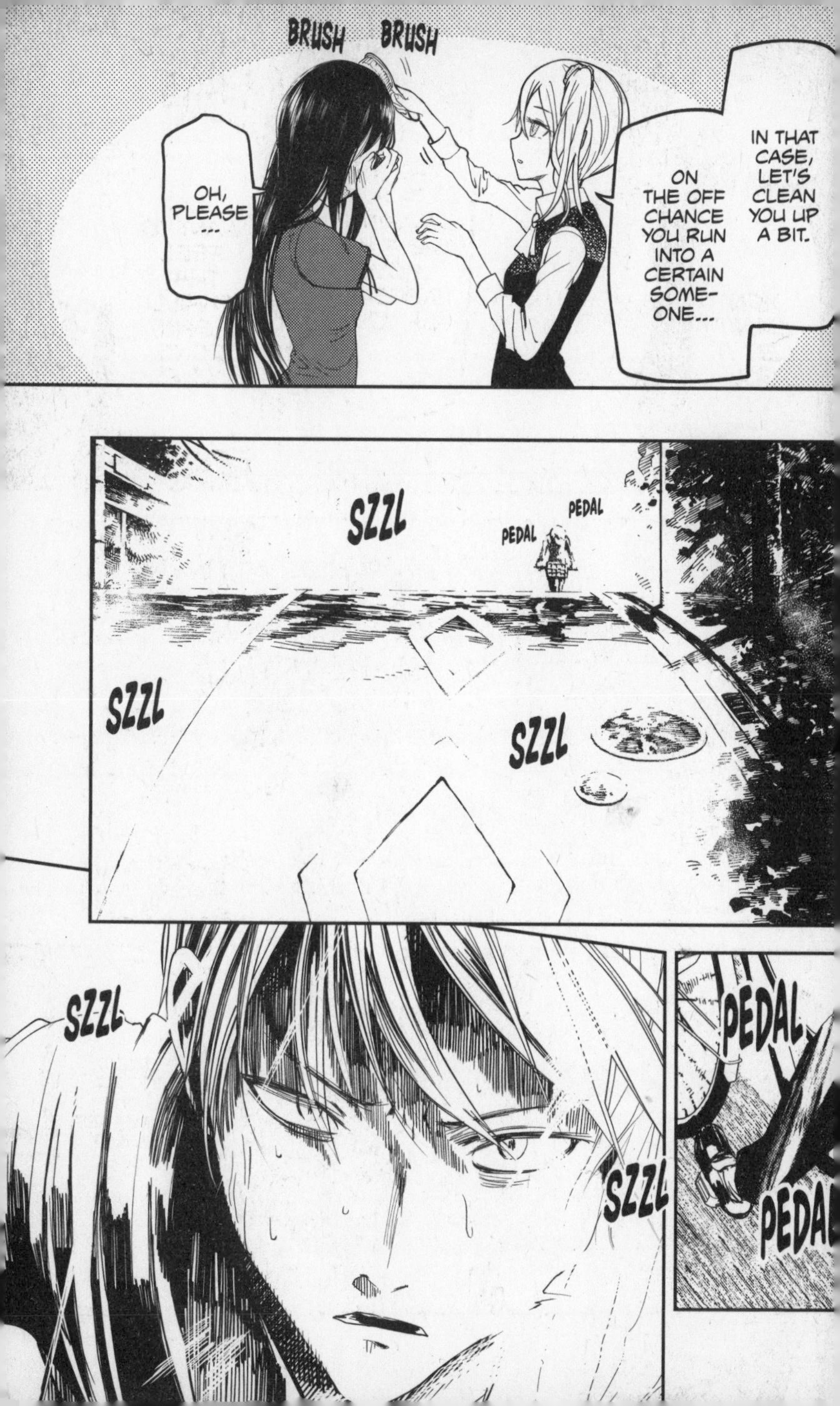
IN THAT CASE, LET'S CLEAN YOU UP A BIT.
ON THE OFF CHANCE YOU RUN INTO A CERTAIN SOME-ONE...
BRUSH BRUSH
OH, PLEASE ---
PEDAL
PEDAL
SZZL
SZZL
SZZL
PEDAL
PEDA
SZZL
SZZL

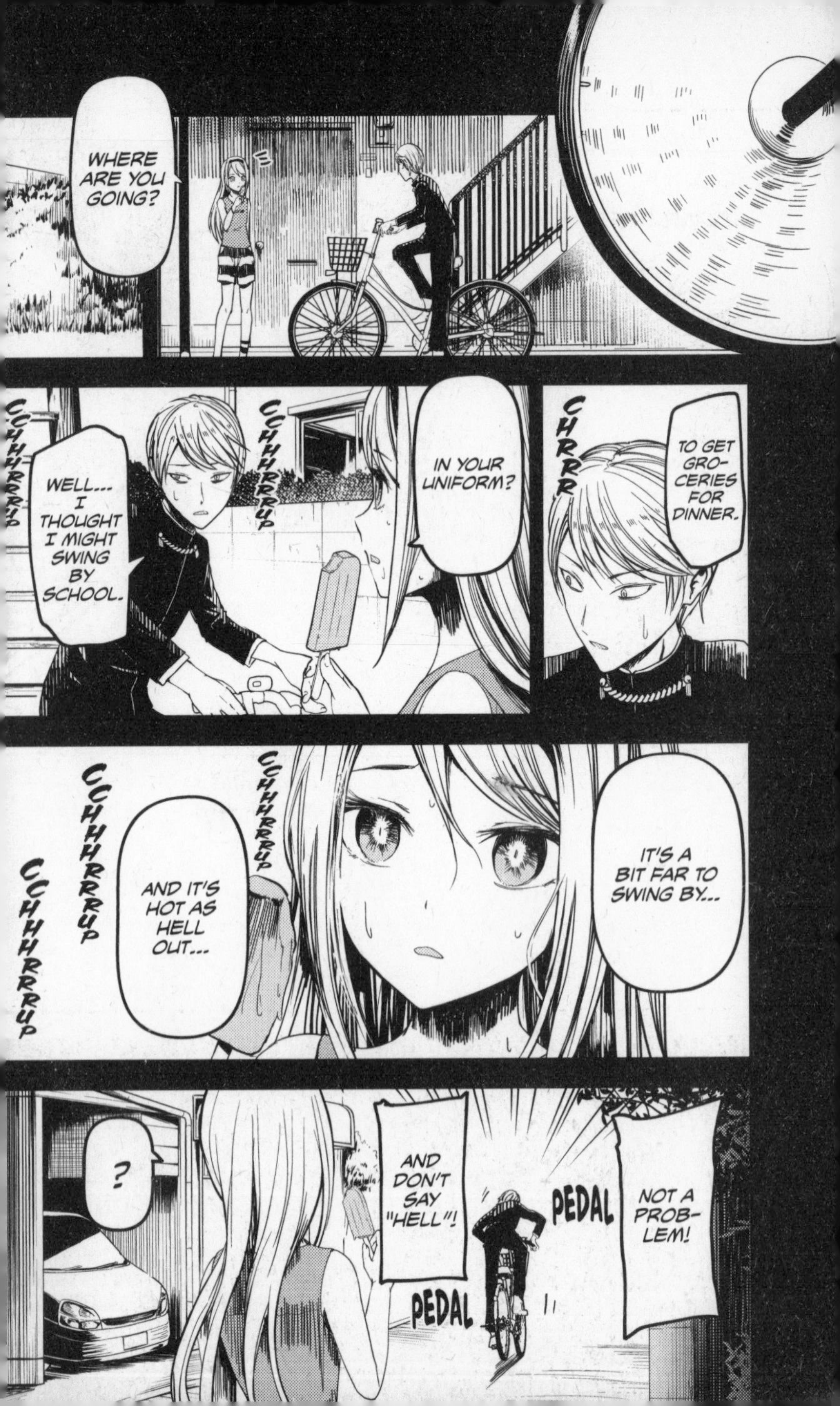
WHERE ARE YOU GOING?
CHRRR
TO GET GRO-CERIES FOR DINNER.
IN YOUR UNIFORM?
CCHHRRRUP
WELL... I THOUGHT I MIGHT SWING BY SCHOOL.
CCHHRRRUP
IT'S A BIT FAR TO SWING BY...
CCHHRRRUP
AND IT'S HOT AS HELL OUT...
CCHHRRRUP
CCHHRRRUP
NOT A PROB-LEM!
PEDAL
AND DON'T SAY "HELL"!
PEDAL
?

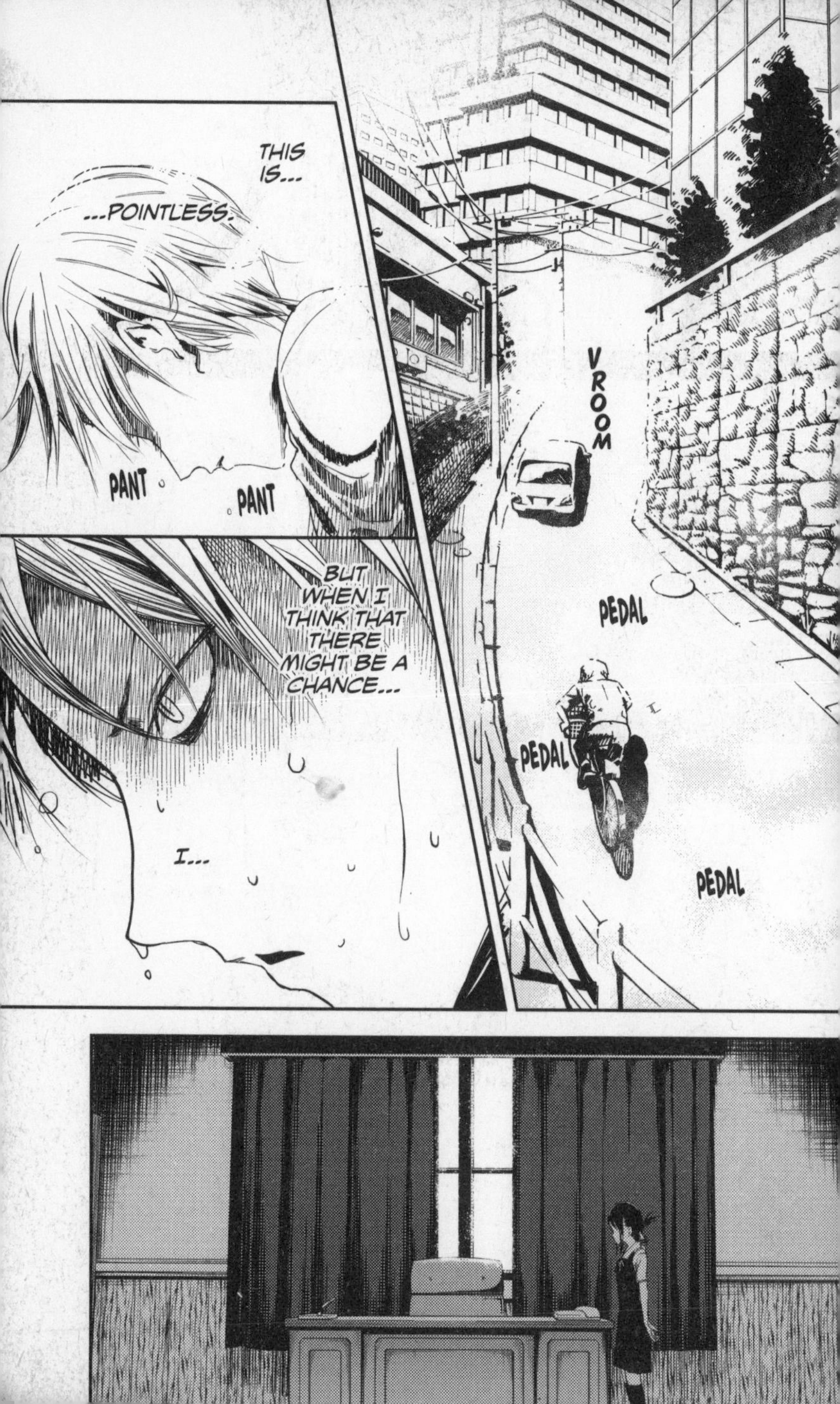
VROOM
PEDAL
PEDAL
PEDAL
THIS IS...
...POINTLESS.
PANT
PANT
BUT WHEN I THINK THAT THERE MIGHT BE A CHANCE...
I...

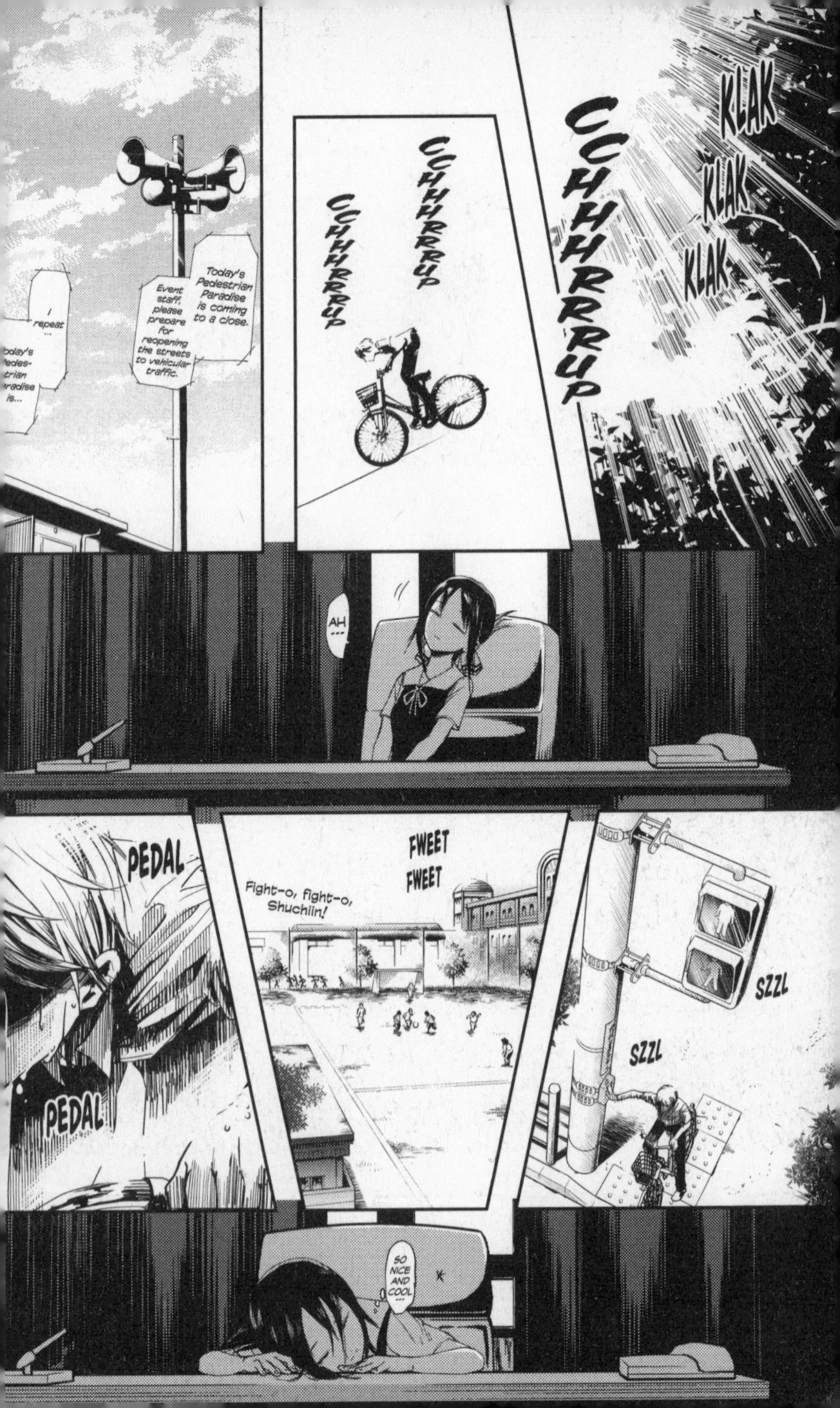
KLAK
KLAK
KLAK
CCHHHRRRRUP
CCHHHRRRUP
CCHHHRRRUP
Today's Pedestrian Paradise is coming to a close.
Event staff, please prepare for reopening the streets to vehicular traffic.
I repeat ...
oday's Pedes-trian aradise is...
AH ...
SZZL
SZZL
FWEET
FWEET
Fight-o, fight-o, Shuchiin!
PEDAL
PEDAL
SO NICE AND COOL ...

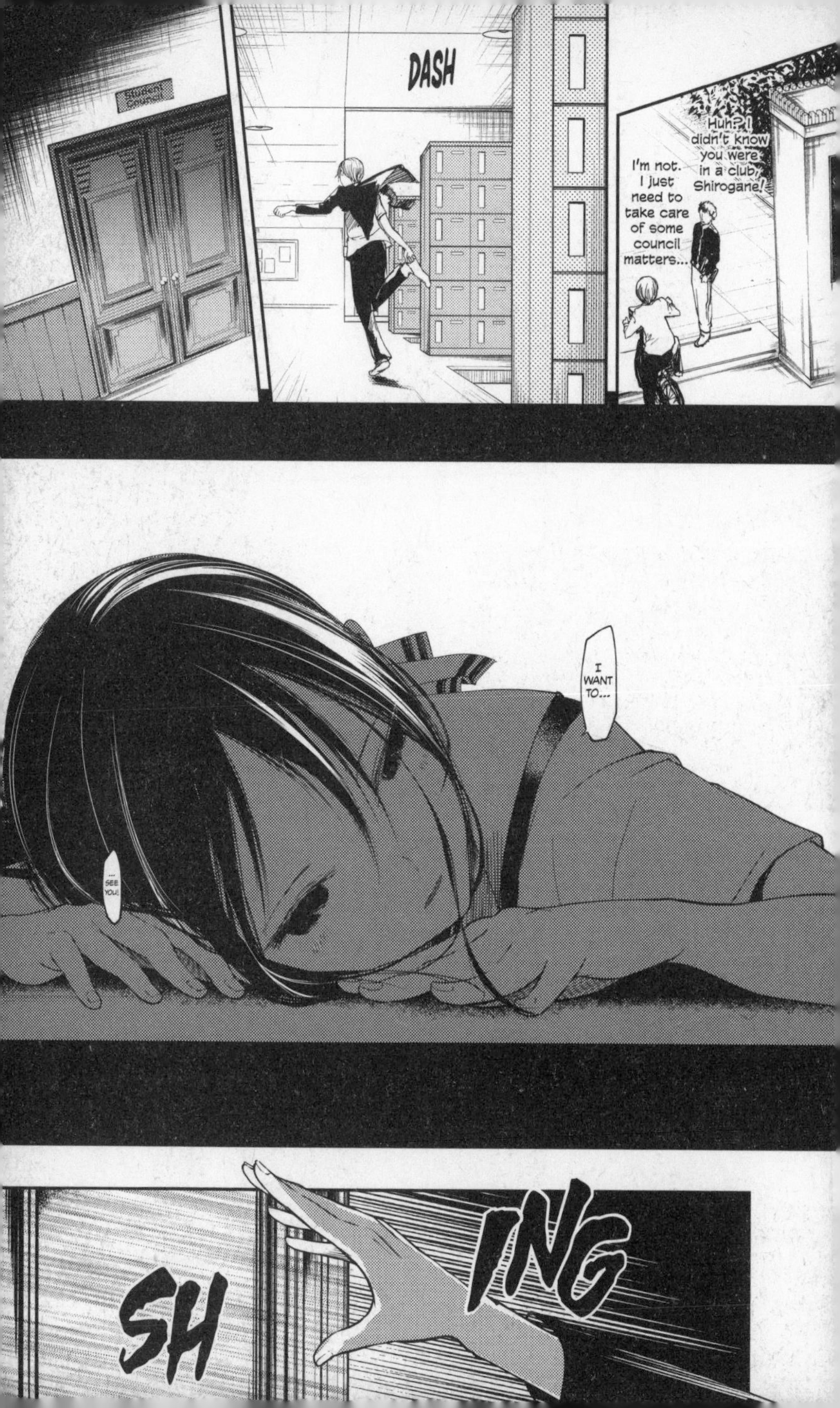
Huh? I didn't know you were in a club, Shirogane!
I'm not. I just need to take care of some council matters...
DASH
Student Council
I WANT TO...
...SEE YOU!
SH
ING

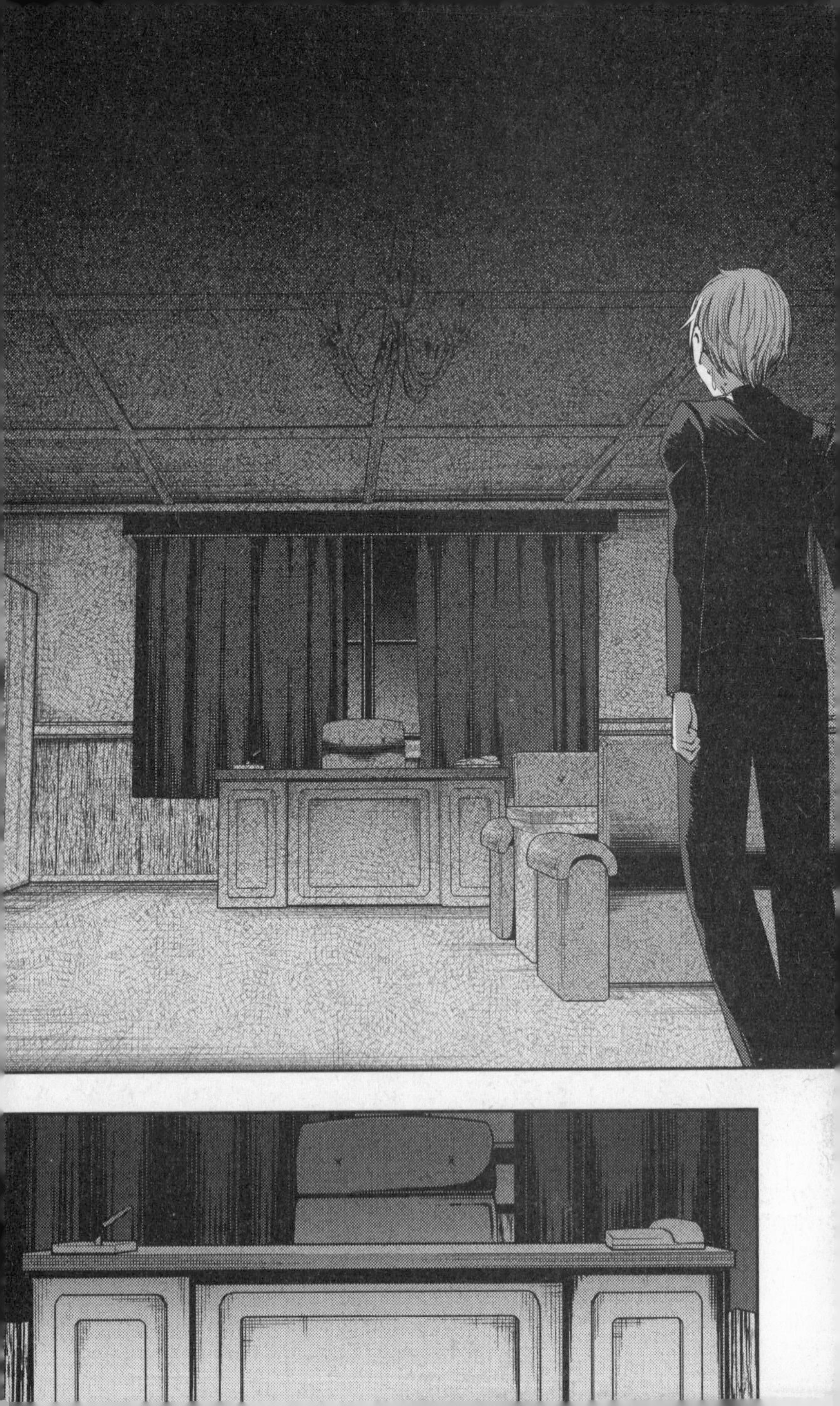

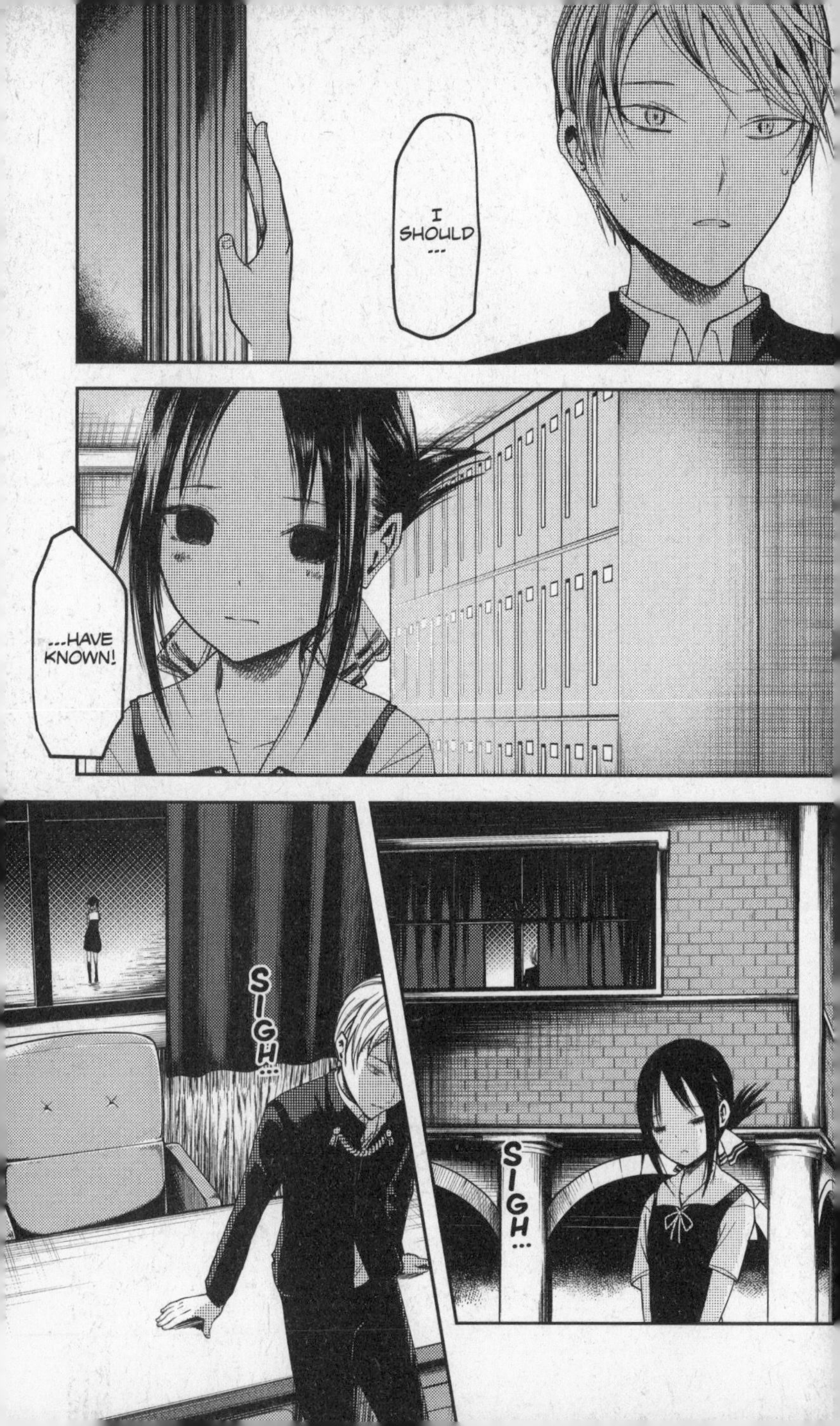
I SHOULD ---
---HAVE KNOWN!
SIGH...
SIGH...

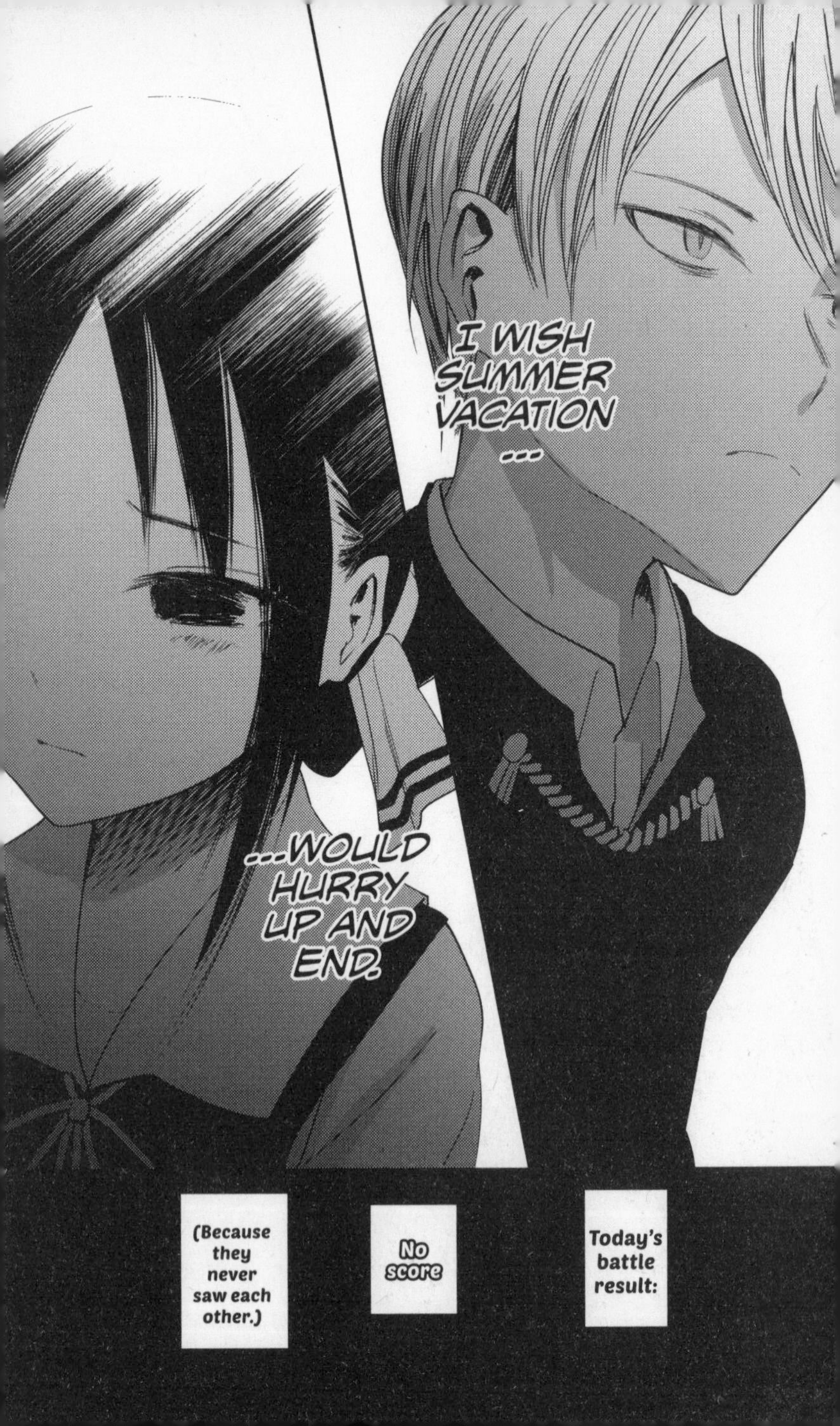
I WISH SUMMER VACATION...
...WOULD HURRY UP AND END.
Today's battle result:
No score
(Because they never saw each other.)

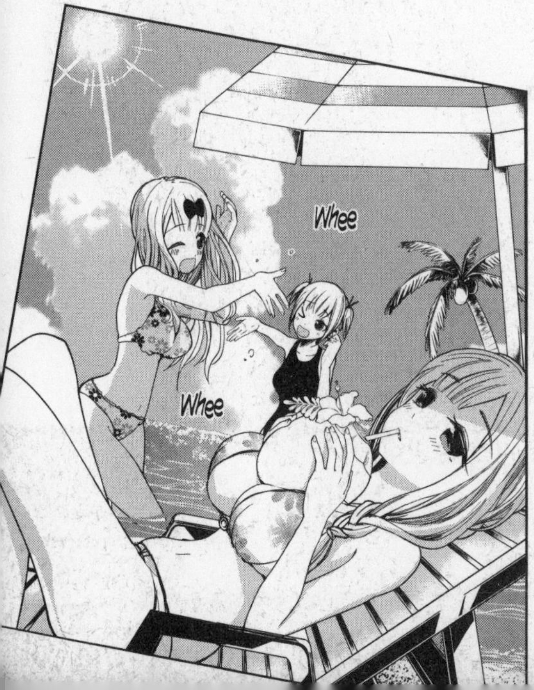
Whee
Whee

KAGUYA-SAMA
LOVE IS WAR

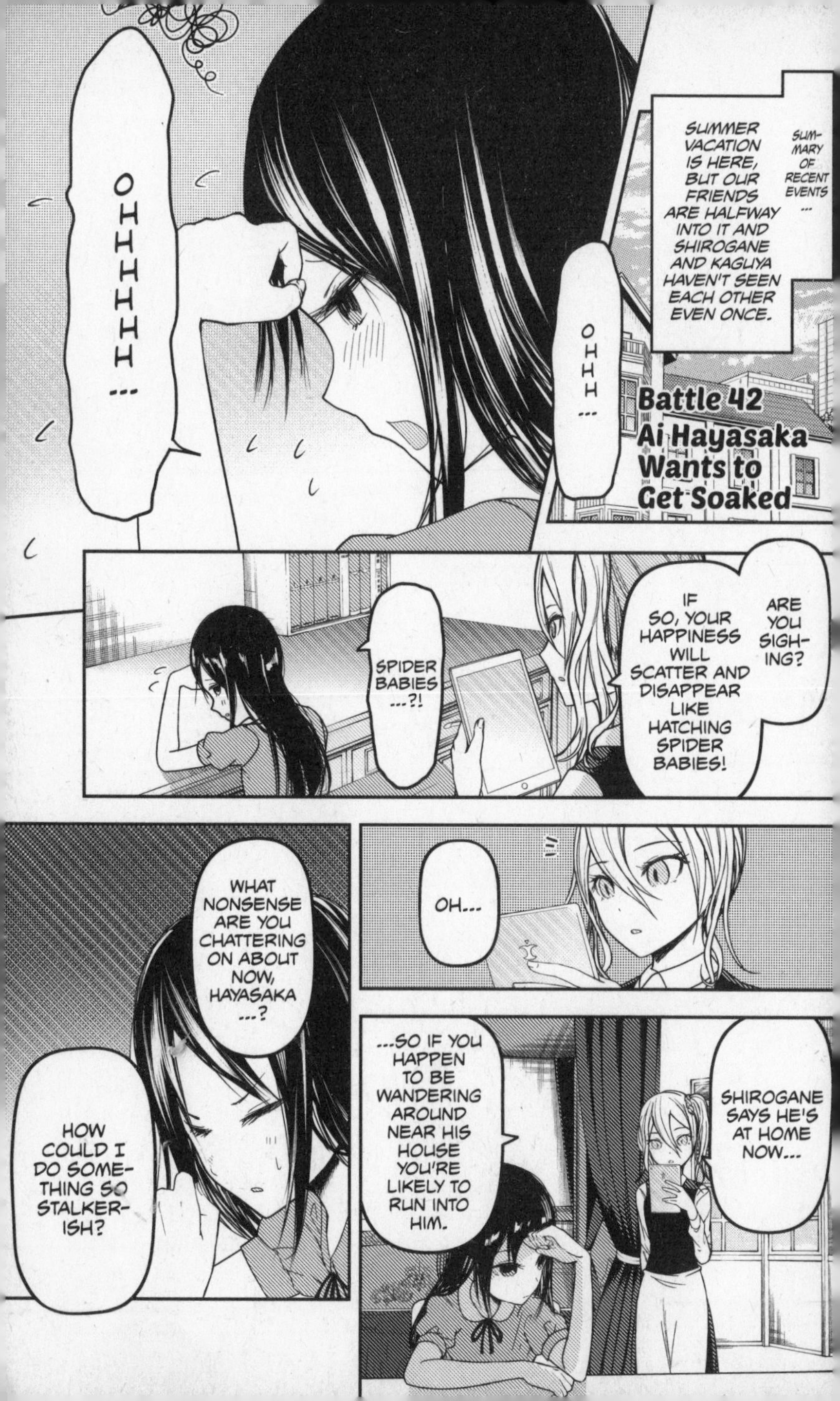
SUMMARY OF RECENT EVENTS...
SUMMER VACATION IS HERE, BUT OUR FRIENDS ARE HALFWAY INTO IT AND SHIROGANE AND KAGUYA HAVEN'T SEEN EACH OTHER EVEN ONCE.
Battle 42 Ai Hayasaka Wants to Get Soaked
OHHH...
OHHHHHH...
ARE YOU SIGHING?
IF SO, YOUR HAPPINESS WILL SCATTER AND DISAPPEAR LIKE HATCHING SPIDER BABIES!
SPIDER BABIES...?!
OH...
SHIROGANE SAYS HE'S AT HOME NOW...
...SO IF YOU HAPPEN TO BE WANDERING AROUND NEAR HIS HOUSE YOU'RE LIKELY TO RUN INTO HIM.
WHAT NONSENSE ARE YOU CHATTERING ON ABOUT NOW, HAYASAKA...?
HOW COULD I DO SOMETHING SO STALKER-ISH?

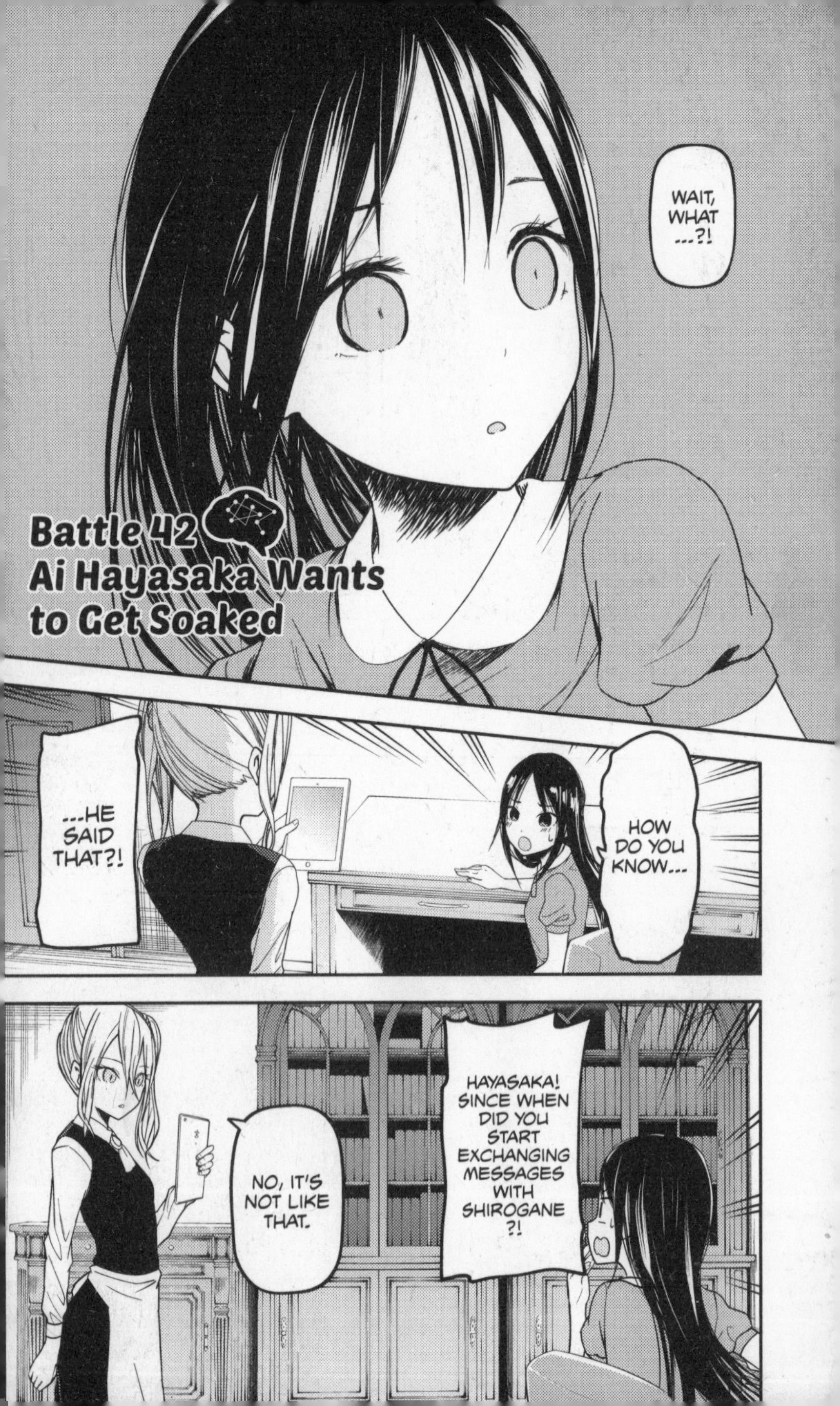
WAIT, WHAT ---?!
Battle 42 Ai Hayasaka Wants to Get Soaked
HOW DO YOU KNOW---
---HE SAID THAT?!
HAYASAKA! SINCE WHEN DID YOU START EXCHANGING MESSAGES WITH SHIROGANE ?!
NO, IT'S NOT LIKE THAT.

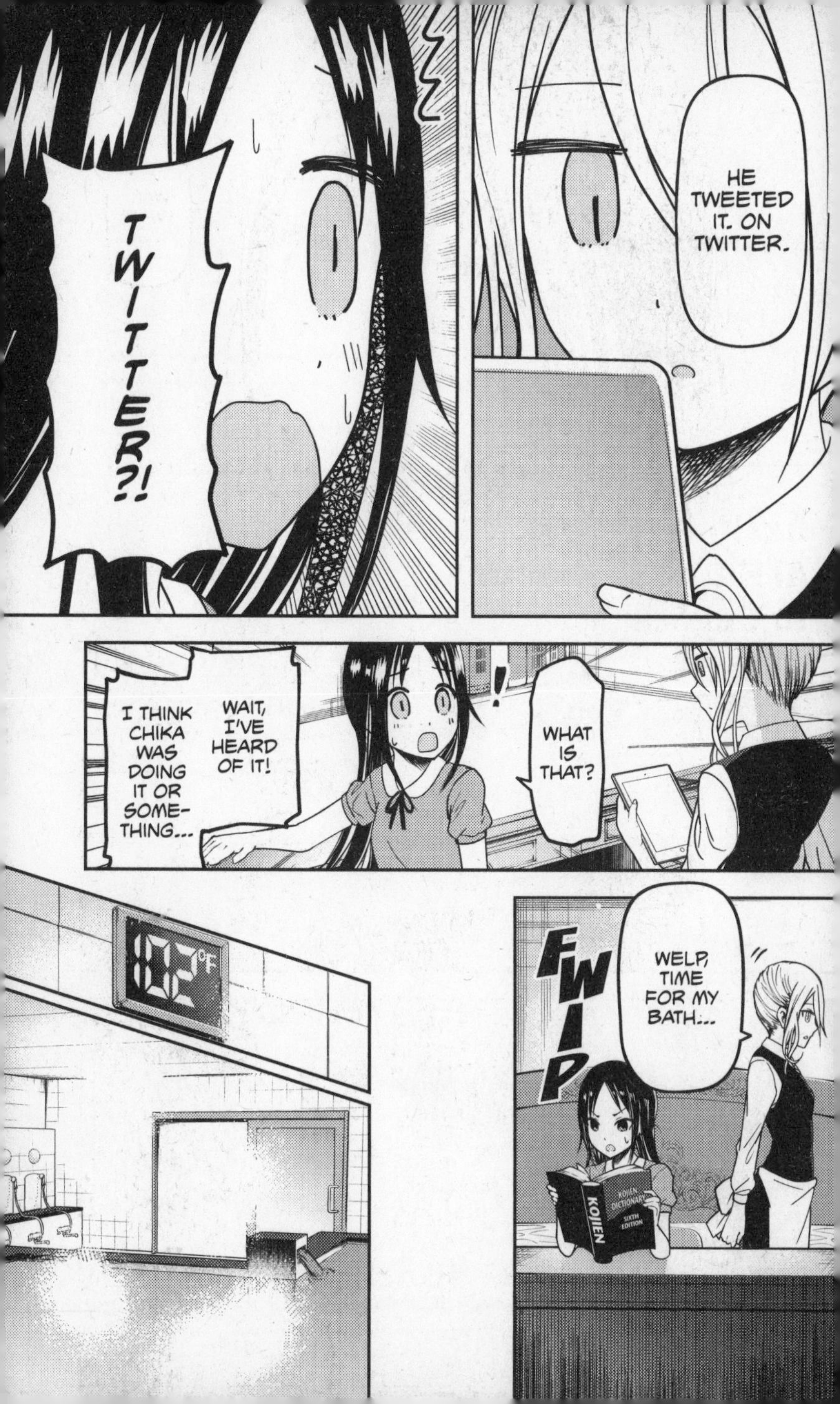
HE TWEETED IT. ON TWITTER.
TWITTER?!
WHAT IS THAT?
WAIT, I'VE HEARD OF IT!
I THINK CHIKA WAS DOING IT OR SOMETHING...
WELP, TIME FOR MY BATH...
FWIP
KOJIEN DICTIONARY
SIXTH EDITION
KOJIEN
102°F

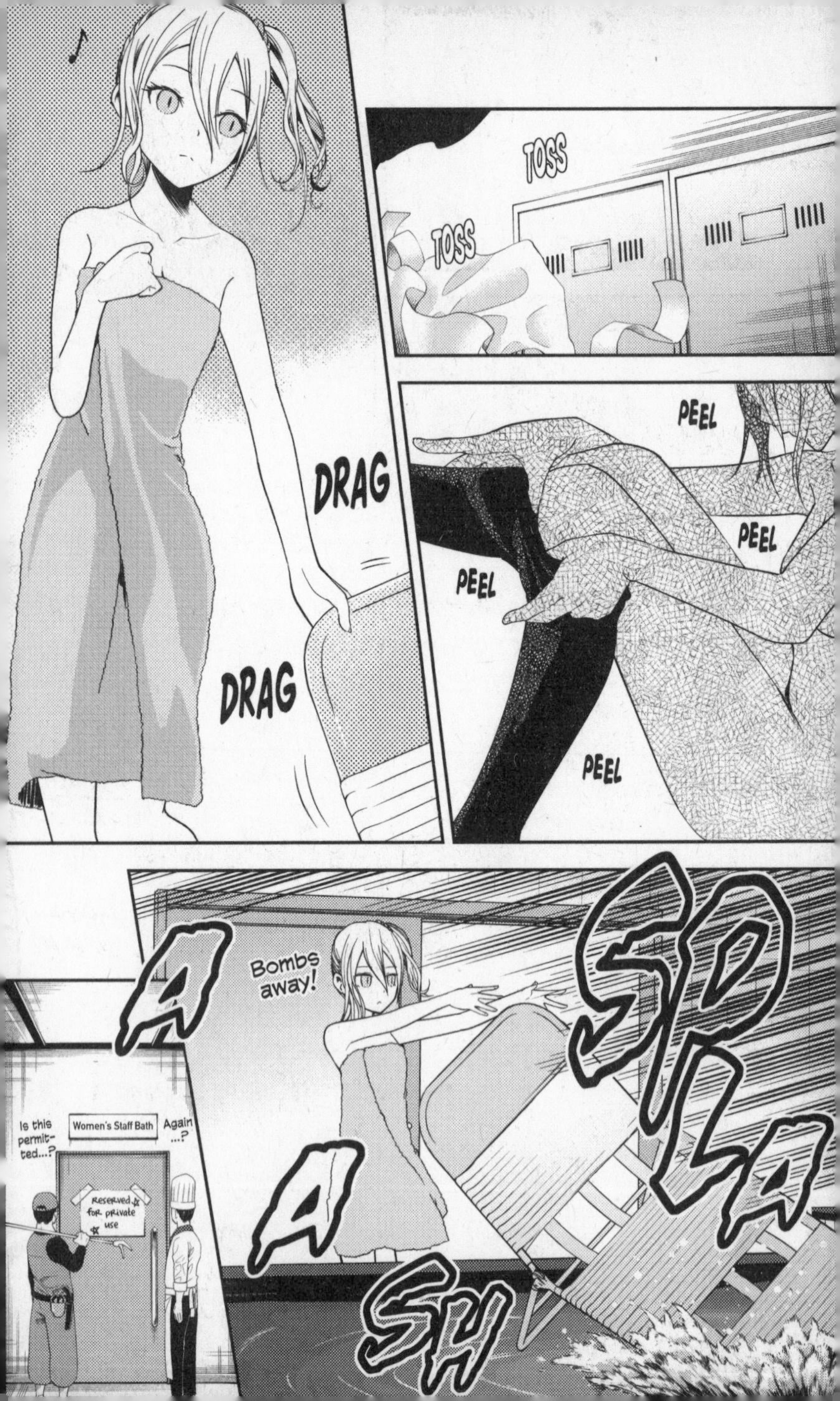

TOSS
TOSS
PEEL
PEEL
PEEL
PEEL
DRAG
DRAG
SPLA
SH
A
A
Bombs away!
Again ...?
Women's Staff Bath
Reserved for private use
Is this permitted...?

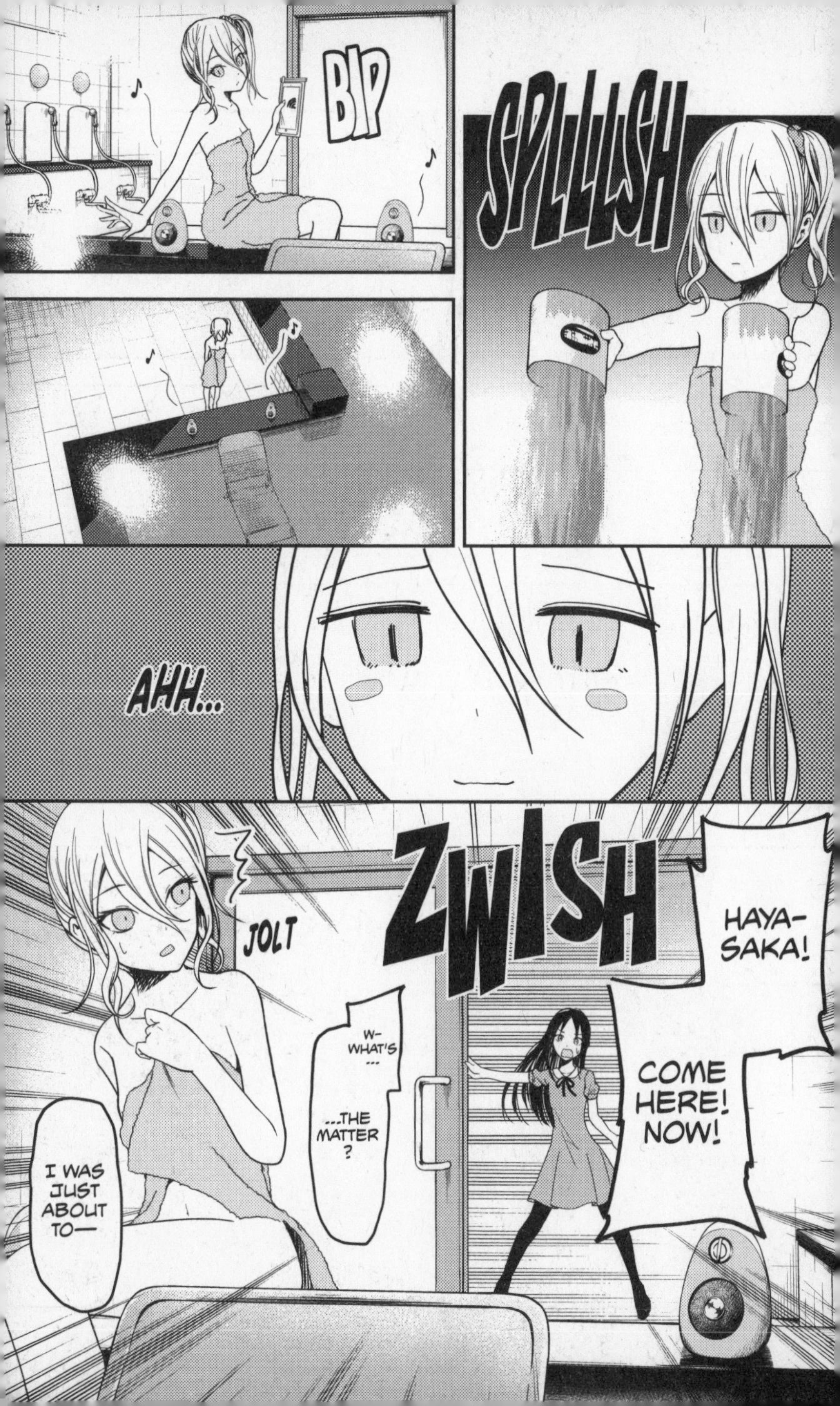
SPLLLSH
BIP
AHH...
ZWISH
HAYA-SAKA!
COME HERE! NOW!
JOLT
W-WHAT'S---
---THE MATTER?
I WAS JUST ABOUT TO—

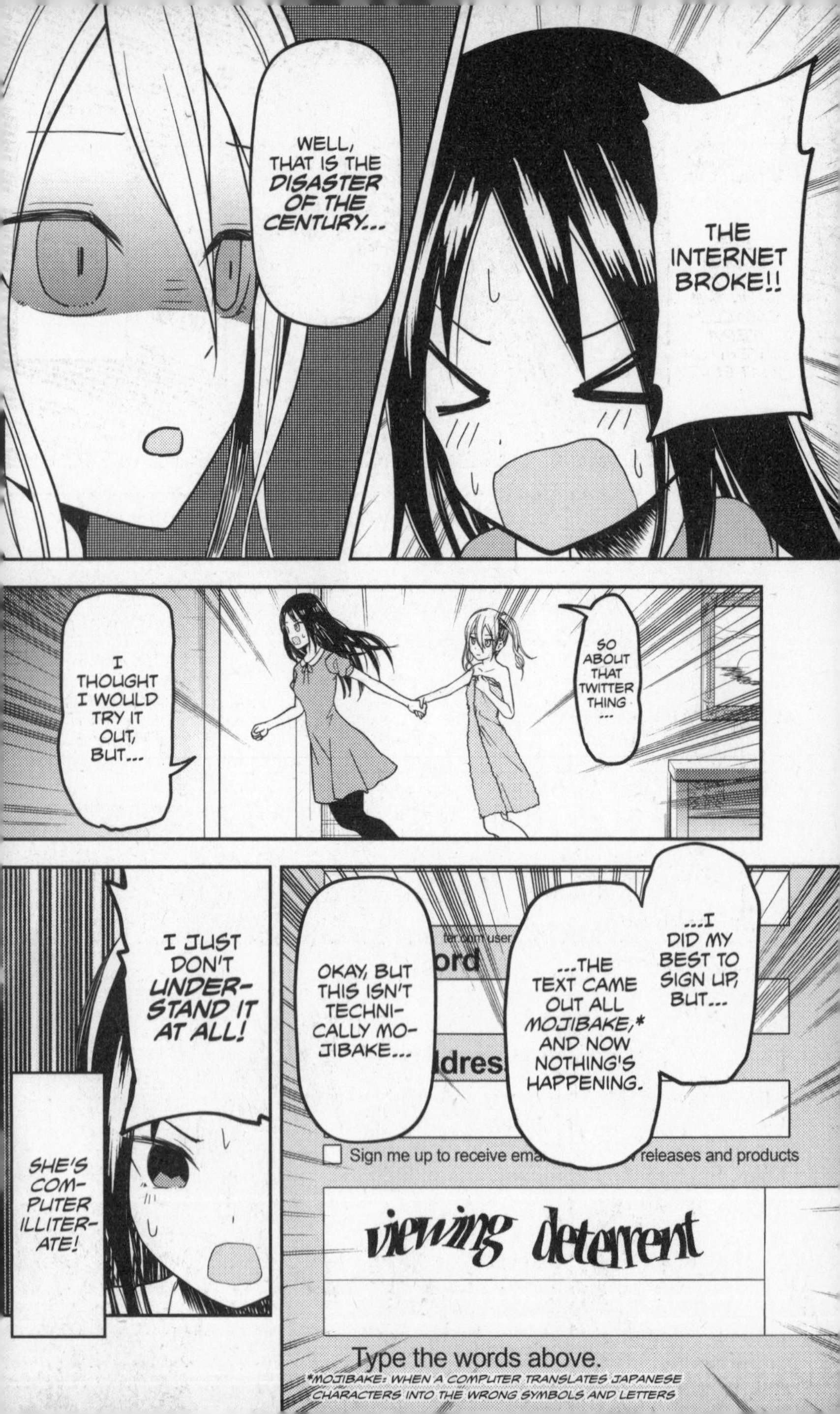
THE INTERNET BROKE!!
WELL, THAT IS THE *DISASTER OF THE CENTURY*...
SO ABOUT THAT TWITTER THING...
I THOUGHT I WOULD TRY IT OUT, BUT...
...I DID MY BEST TO SIGN UP, BUT...
...THE TEXT CAME OUT ALL *MOJIBAKE*,* AND NOW NOTHING'S HAPPENING.
OKAY, BUT THIS ISN'T TECHNICALLY MOJIBAKE...
viewing deterrent
Type the words above.
*MOJIBAKE: WHEN A COMPUTER TRANSLATES JAPANESE CHARACTERS INTO THE WRONG SYMBOLS AND LETTERS
I JUST DON'T *UNDERSTAND IT AT ALL!*
SHE'S COMPUTER ILLITERATE!

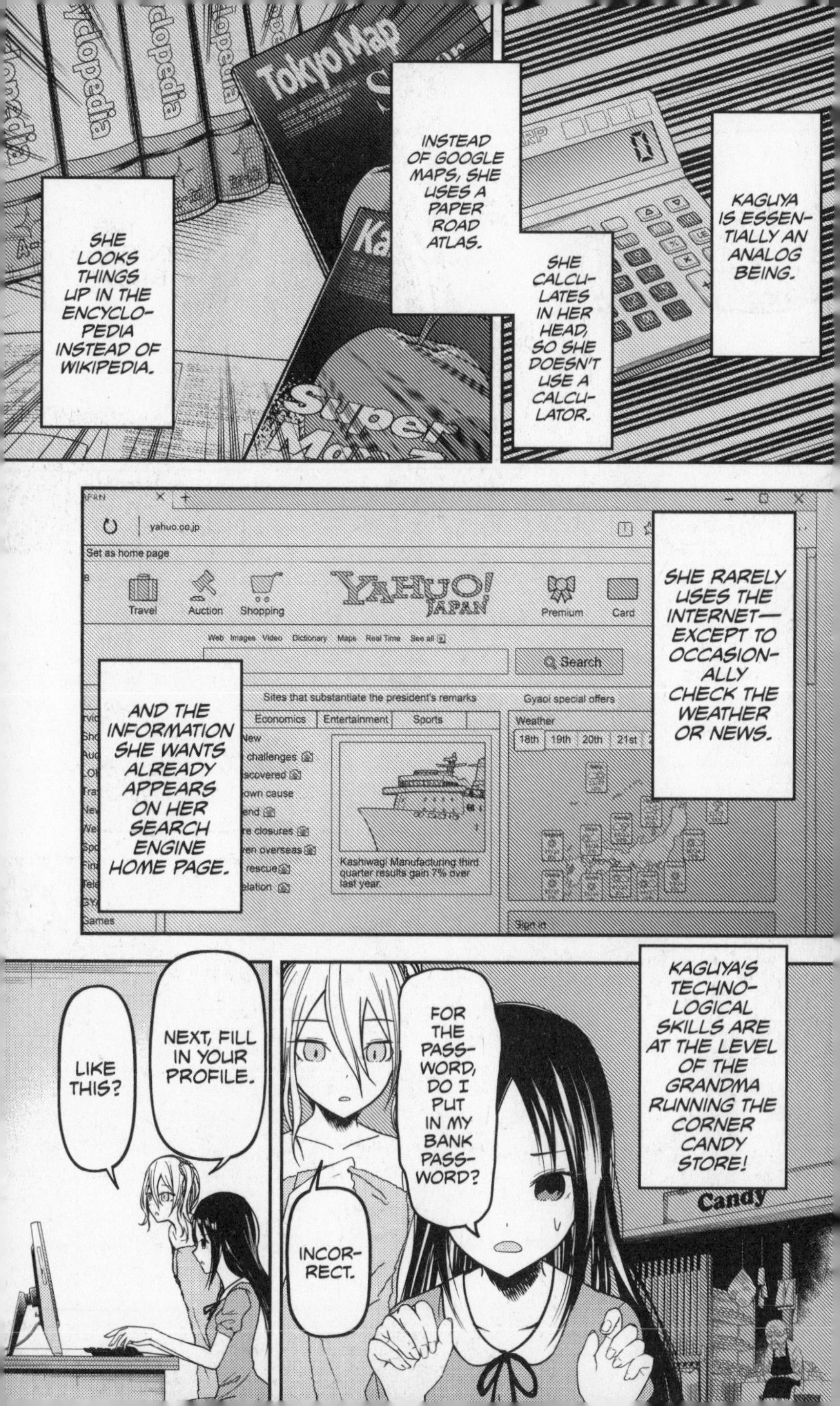
KAGUYA IS ESSENTIALLY AN ANALOG BEING.
SHE CALCULATES IN HER HEAD, SO SHE DOESN'T USE A CALCULATOR.
INSTEAD OF GOOGLE MAPS, SHE USES A PAPER ROAD ATLAS.
Tokyo Map
SHE LOOKS THINGS UP IN THE ENCYCLOPEDIA INSTEAD OF WIKIPEDIA.
Encyclopedia
SHE RARELY USES THE INTERNET—EXCEPT TO OCCASIONALLY CHECK THE WEATHER OR NEWS.
yahuo.co.jp
Set as home page
Travel
Auction
Shopping
YAHUO! JAPAN
Premium
Card
Web Images Video Dictionary Maps Real Time See all
Search
Sites that substantiate the president's remarks
Gyao! special offers
Economics
Entertainment
Sports
Weather
18th 19th 20th 21st
Kashiwagi Manufacturing third quarter results gain 7% over last year.
Games
Sign in
AND THE INFORMATION SHE WANTS ALREADY APPEARS ON HER SEARCH ENGINE HOME PAGE.
KAGUYA'S TECHNOLOGICAL SKILLS ARE AT THE LEVEL OF THE GRANDMA RUNNING THE CORNER CANDY STORE!
FOR THE PASSWORD, DO I PUT IN MY BANK PASSWORD?
INCORRECT.
Candy
NEXT, FILL IN YOUR PROFILE.
LIKE THIS?

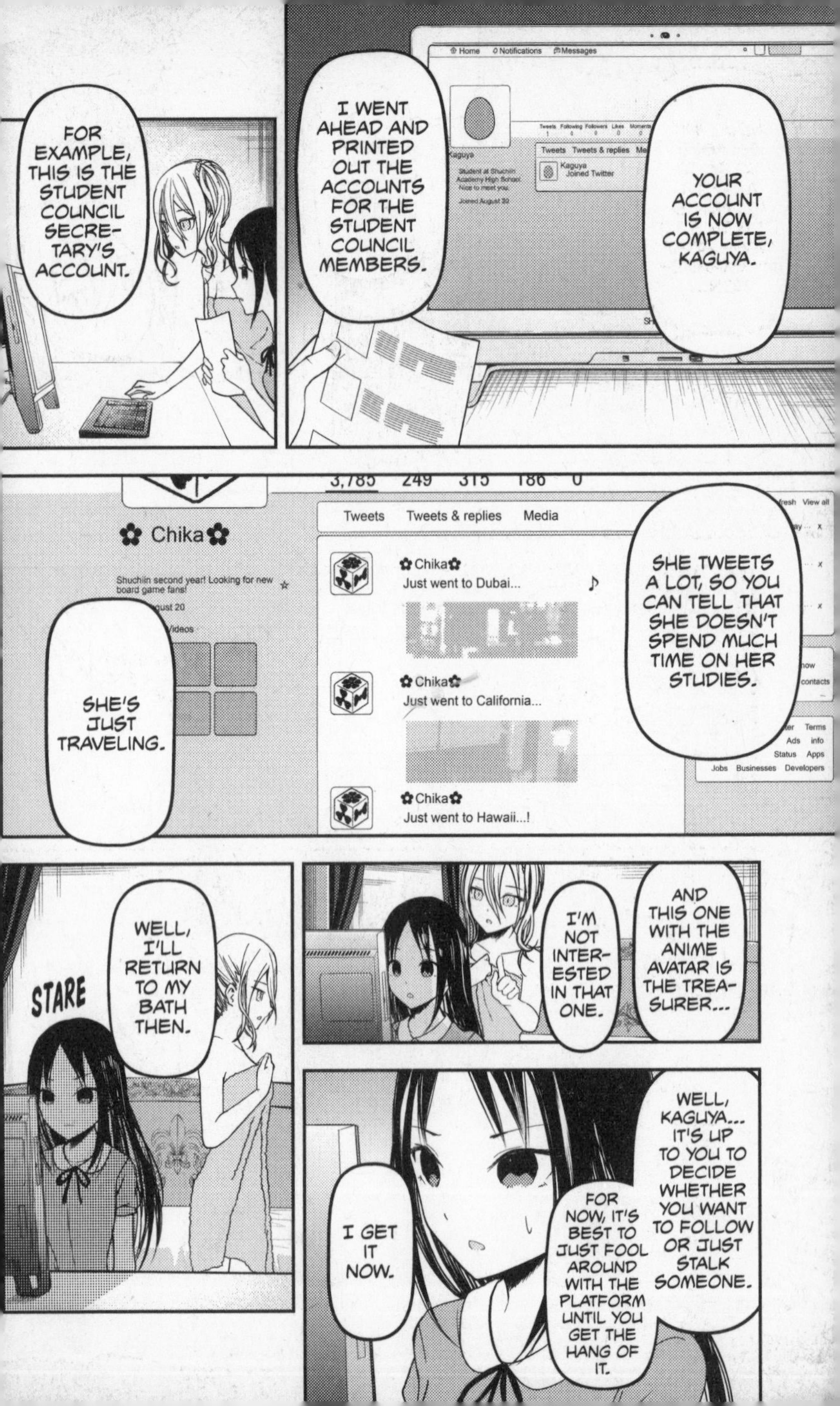
Home
Notifications
Messages
Kaguya
Student at Shuchiin Academy High School. Nice to meet you.
Joined August 20
Tweets
Tweets & replies
Kaguya
Joined Twitter
YOUR ACCOUNT IS NOW COMPLETE, KAGUYA.
I WENT AHEAD AND PRINTED OUT THE ACCOUNTS FOR THE STUDENT COUNCIL MEMBERS.
FOR EXAMPLE, THIS IS THE STUDENT COUNCIL SECRETARY'S ACCOUNT.
SHE TWEETS A LOT, SO YOU CAN TELL THAT SHE DOESN'T SPEND MUCH TIME ON HER STUDIES.
Tweets
Tweets & replies
Media
✿ Chika ✿
Just went to Dubai...
✿ Chika ✿
Just went to California...
✿ Chika ✿
Just went to Hawaii...!
✿ Chika ✿
Shuchiin second year! Looking for new board game fans!
SHE'S JUST TRAVELING.
AND THIS ONE WITH THE ANIME AVATAR IS THE TREASURER...
I'M NOT INTERESTED IN THAT ONE.
WELL, KAGUYA... IT'S UP TO YOU TO DECIDE WHETHER YOU WANT TO FOLLOW OR JUST STALK SOMEONE.
FOR NOW, IT'S BEST TO JUST FOOL AROUND WITH THE PLATFORM UNTIL YOU GET THE HANG OF IT.
I GET IT NOW.
STARE
WELL, I'LL RETURN TO MY BATH THEN.

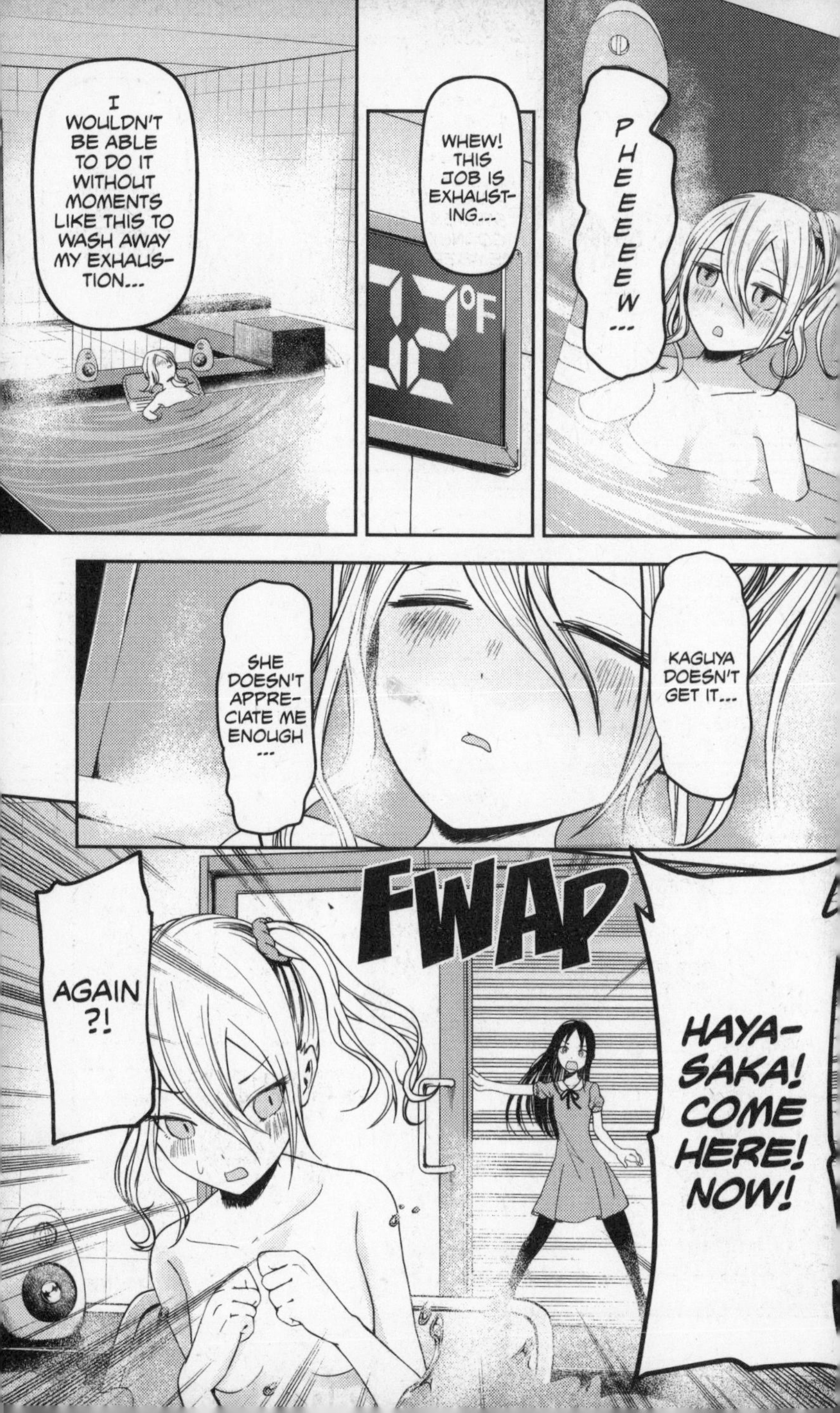
PHEEEEEW...
WHEW! THIS JOB IS EXHAUST-ING...
°F
I WOULDN'T BE ABLE TO DO IT WITHOUT MOMENTS LIKE THIS TO WASH AWAY MY EXHAUS-TION...
KAGUYA DOESN'T GET IT...
SHE DOESN'T APPRE-CIATE ME ENOUGH...
FWAP
HAYA-SAKA! COME HERE! NOW!
AGAIN?!

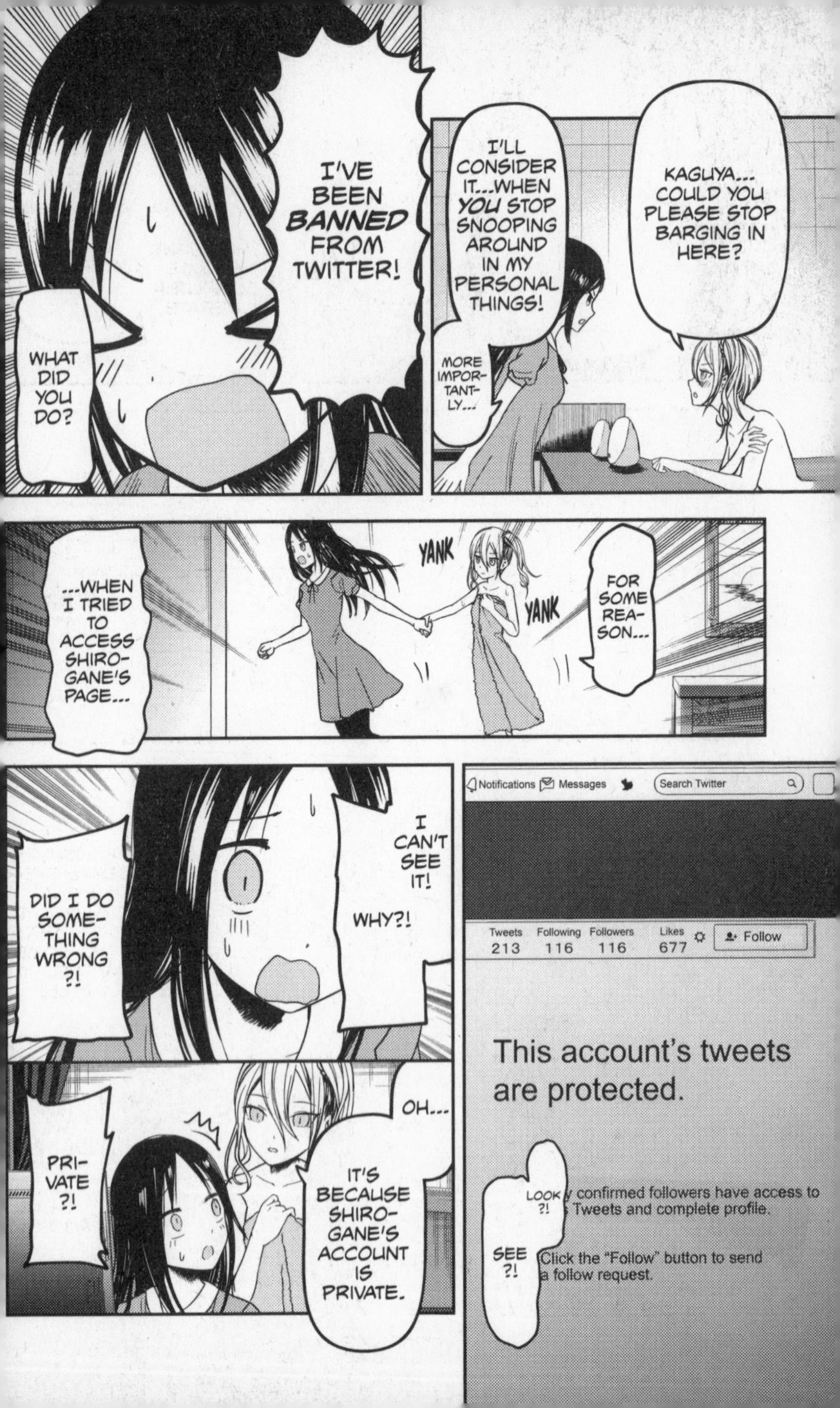
KAGUYA... COULD YOU PLEASE STOP BARGING IN HERE?
I'LL CONSIDER IT...WHEN *YOU* STOP SNOOPING AROUND IN MY PERSONAL THINGS!
MORE IMPOR-TANT-LY...
I'VE BEEN ***BANNED*** FROM TWITTER!
WHAT DID YOU DO?
FOR SOME REA-SON...
YANK
YANK
...WHEN I TRIED TO ACCESS SHIRO-GANE'S PAGE...
Notifications
Messages
Search Twitter
Tweets 213
Following 116
Followers 116
Likes 677
Follow
This account's tweets are protected.
LOOK?!
y confirmed followers have access to
s Tweets and complete profile.
SEE?!
Click the "Follow" button to send
a follow request.
I CAN'T SEE IT!
WHY?!
DID I DO SOME-THING WRONG?!
OH...
IT'S BECAUSE SHIRO-GANE'S ACCOUNT IS PRIVATE.
PRI-VATE?!

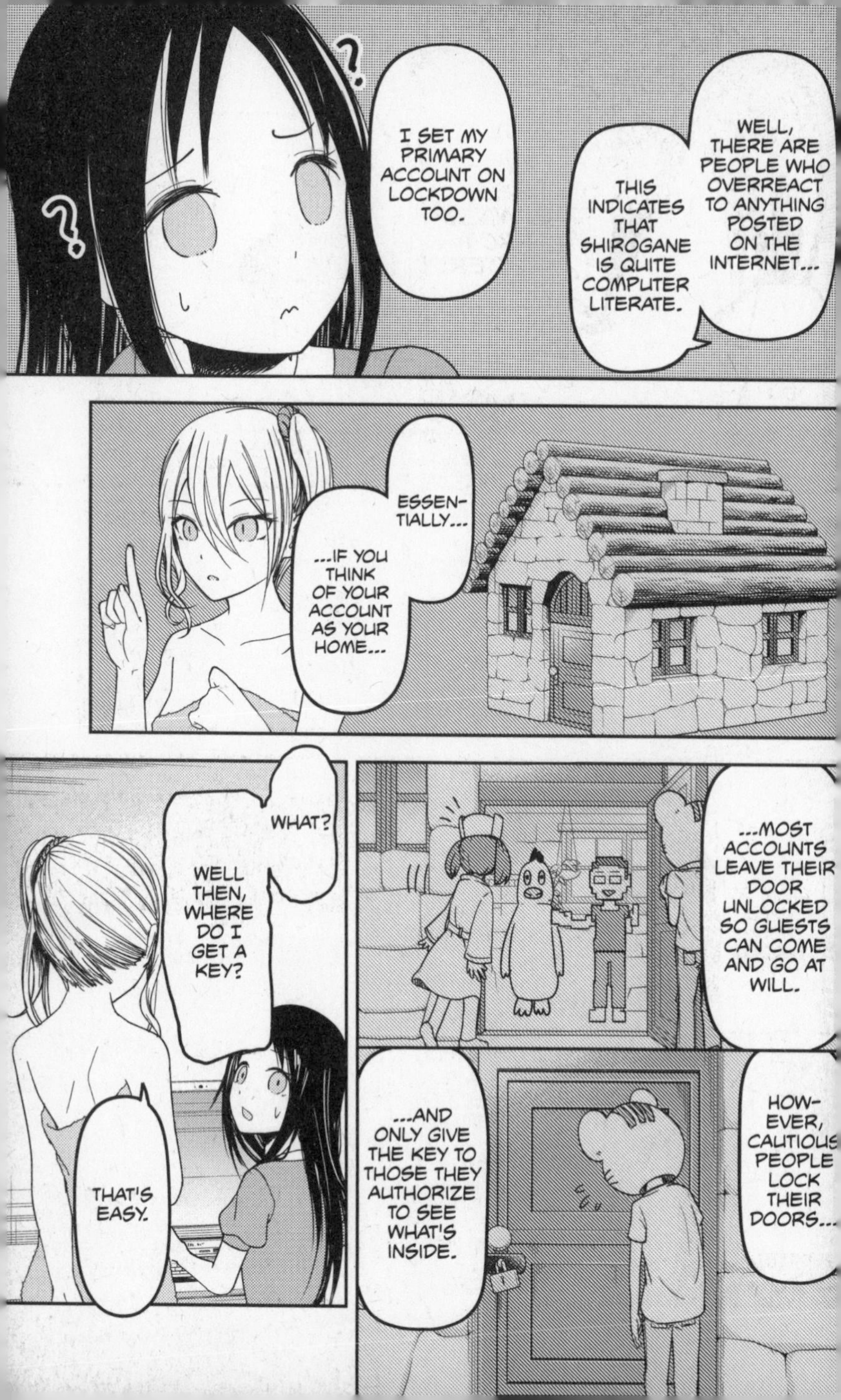
WELL, THERE ARE PEOPLE WHO OVERREACT TO ANYTHING POSTED ON THE INTERNET...
THIS INDICATES THAT SHIROGANE IS QUITE COMPUTER LITERATE.
I SET MY PRIMARY ACCOUNT ON LOCKDOWN TOO.
ESSEN-TIALLY...
...IF YOU THINK OF YOUR ACCOUNT AS YOUR HOME...
...MOST ACCOUNTS LEAVE THEIR DOOR UNLOCKED SO GUESTS CAN COME AND GO AT WILL.
HOW-EVER, CAUTIOUS PEOPLE LOCK THEIR DOORS...
...AND ONLY GIVE THE KEY TO THOSE THEY AUTHORIZE TO SEE WHAT'S INSIDE.
WHAT?
WELL THEN, WHERE DO I GET A KEY?
THAT'S EASY.

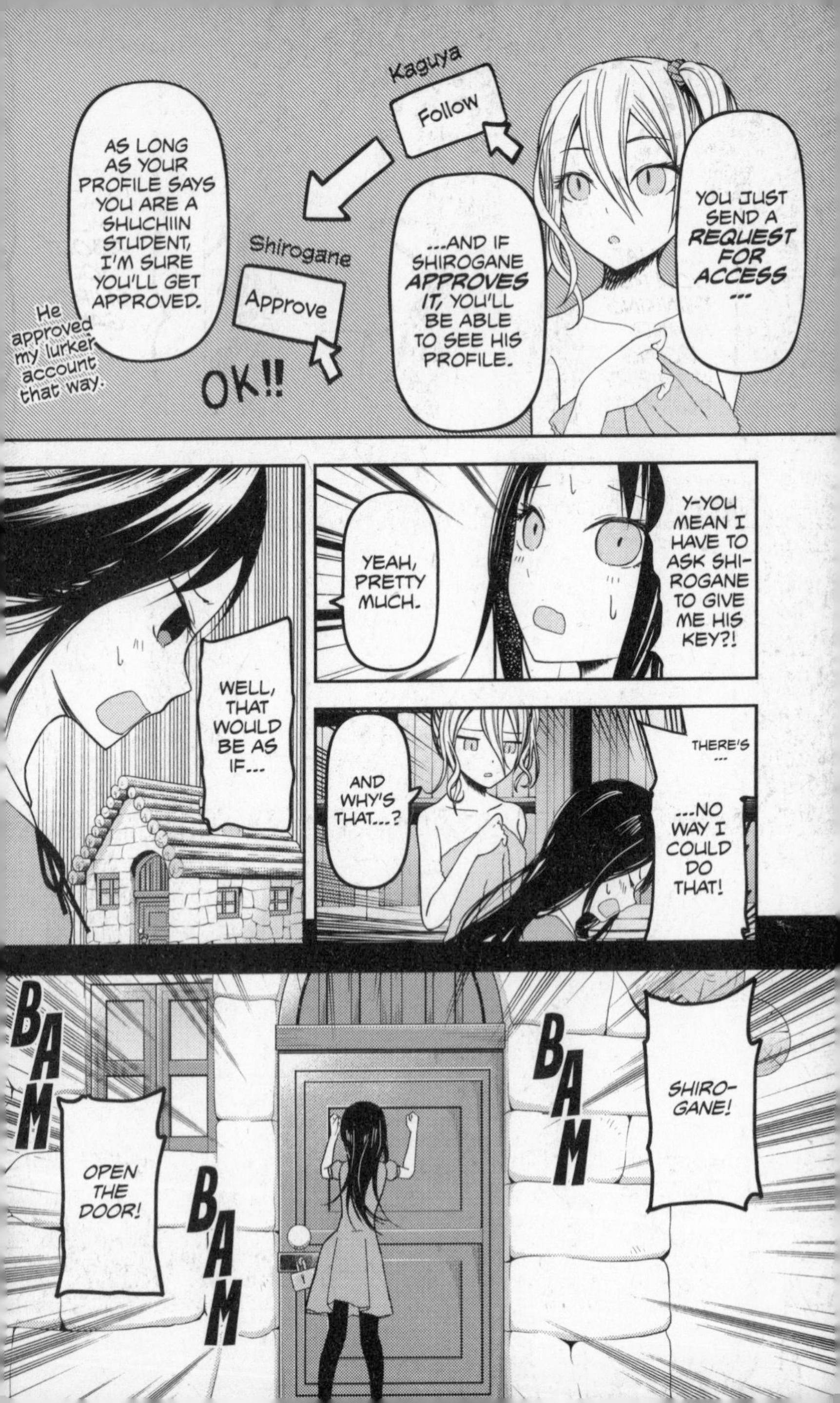
YOU JUST SEND A REQUEST FOR ACCESS...
...AND IF SHIROGANE APPROVES IT, YOU'LL BE ABLE TO SEE HIS PROFILE.
Kaguya
Follow
Shirogane
Approve
OK!!
AS LONG AS YOUR PROFILE SAYS YOU ARE A SHUCHIIN STUDENT, I'M SURE YOU'LL GET APPROVED.
He approved my lurker account that way.
Y-YOU MEAN I HAVE TO ASK SHIROGANE TO GIVE ME HIS KEY?!
YEAH, PRETTY MUCH.
THERE'S...
...NO WAY I COULD DO THAT!
AND WHY'S THAT...?
WELL, THAT WOULD BE AS IF...
BAM
SHIRO-GANE!
BAM
BAM
OPEN THE DOOR!
BAM

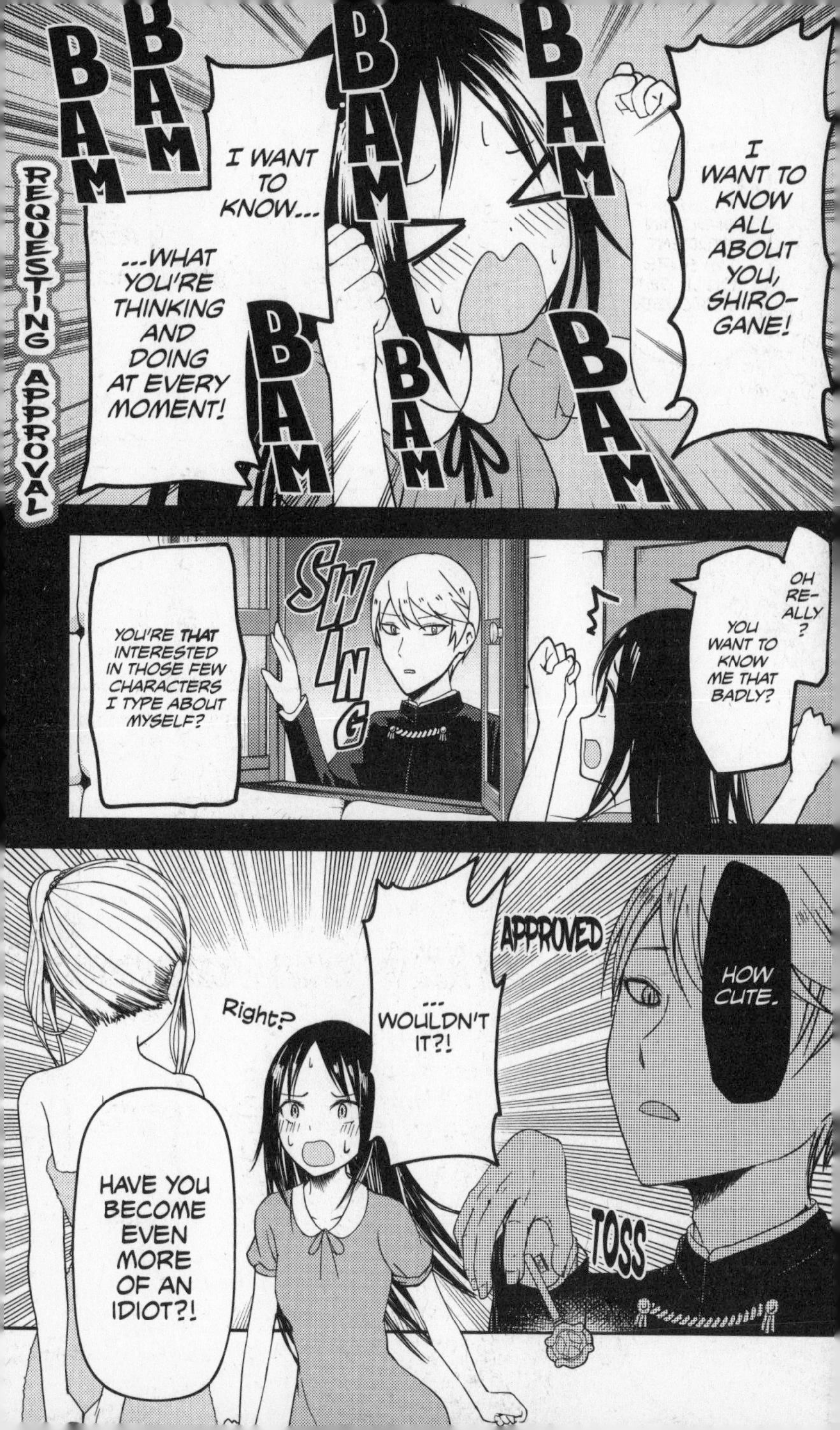
REQUESTING APPROVAL
I WANT TO KNOW ALL ABOUT YOU, SHIROGANE!
BAM BAM BAM BAM BAM BAM BAM
I WANT TO KNOW...
...WHAT YOU'RE THINKING AND DOING AT EVERY MOMENT!
OH REALLY?
YOU WANT TO KNOW ME THAT BADLY?
SWING
YOU'RE THAT INTERESTED IN THOSE FEW CHARACTERS I TYPE ABOUT MYSELF?
HOW CUTE.
APPROVED
TOSS
...WOULDN'T IT?!
Right?
HAVE YOU BECOME EVEN MORE OF AN IDIOT?!

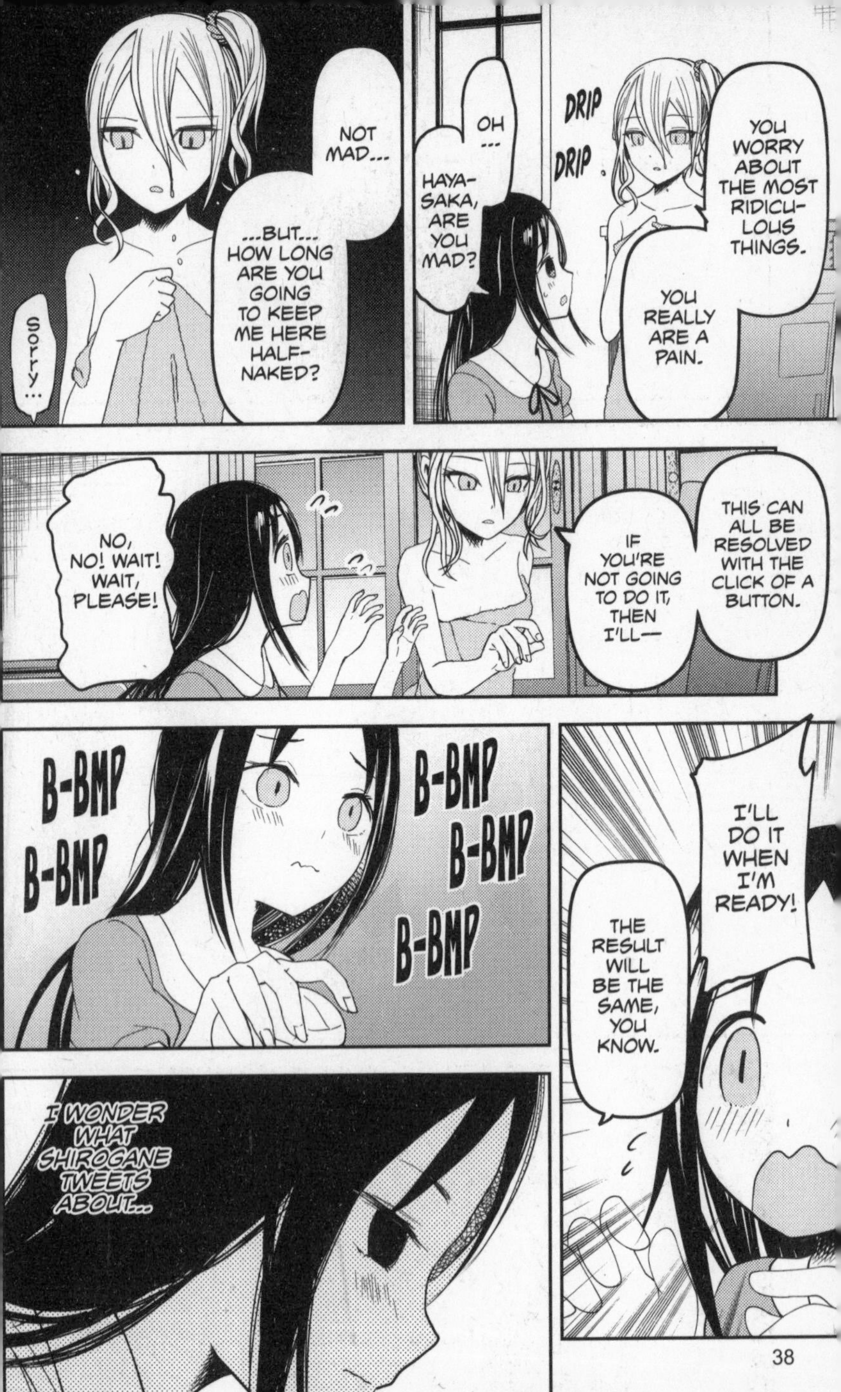
DRIP
DRIP
YOU WORRY ABOUT THE MOST RIDICULOUS THINGS.
YOU REALLY ARE A PAIN.
OH... HAYA-SAKA, ARE YOU MAD?
NOT MAD...
...BUT... HOW LONG ARE YOU GOING TO KEEP ME HERE HALF-NAKED?
Sorry...
THIS CAN ALL BE RESOLVED WITH THE CLICK OF A BUTTON.
IF YOU'RE NOT GOING TO DO IT, THEN I'LL—
NO, NO! WAIT! WAIT, PLEASE!
I'LL DO IT WHEN I'M READY!
THE RESULT WILL BE THE SAME, YOU KNOW.
B-BMP
B-BMP
B-BMP
B-BMP
B-BMP
I WONDER WHAT SHIROGANE TWEETS ABOUT...

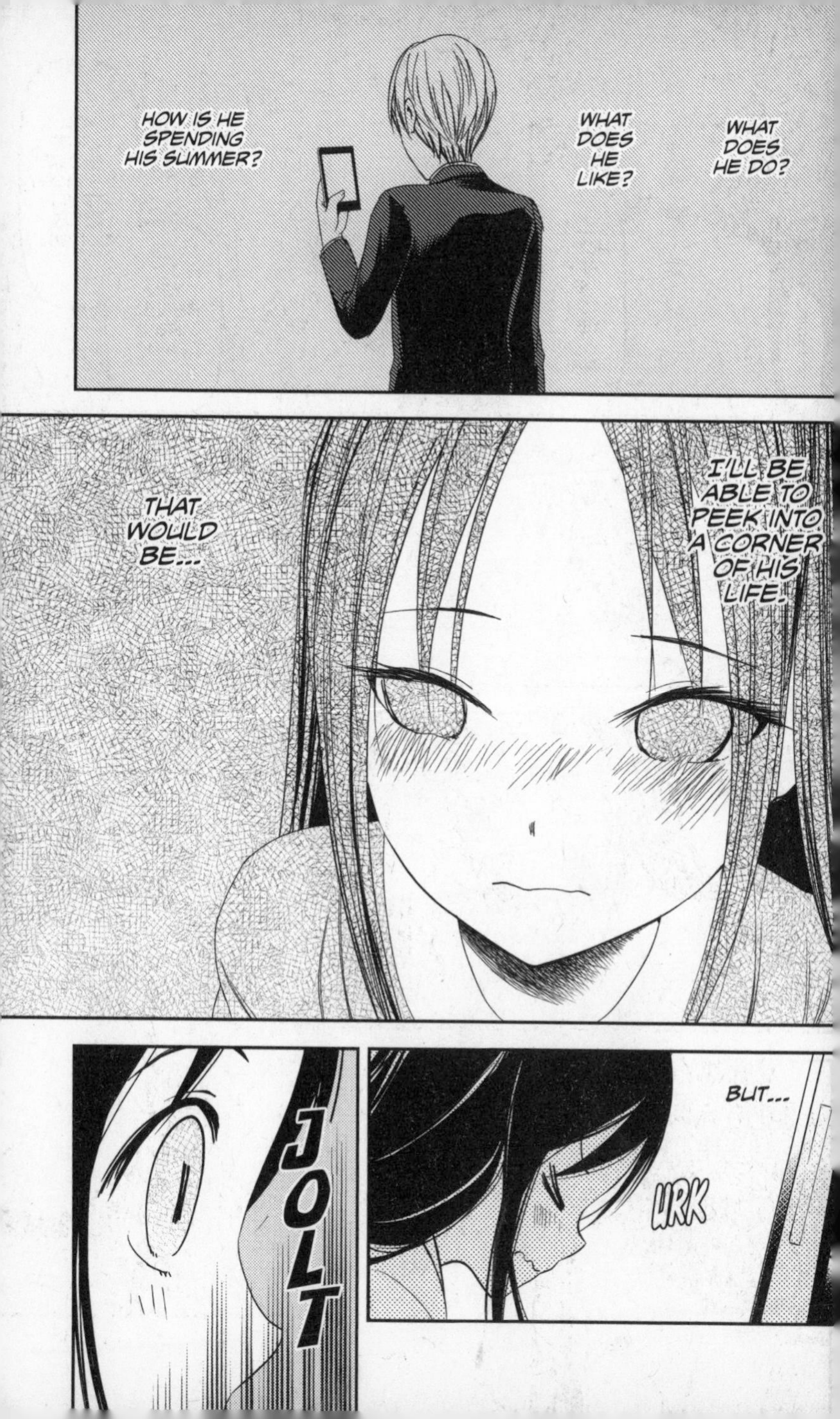
WHAT DOES HE DO?
WHAT DOES HE LIKE?
HOW IS HE SPENDING HIS SUMMER?
I'LL BE ABLE TO PEEK INTO A CORNER OF HIS LIFE.
THAT WOULD BE...
BUT...
URK
JOLT

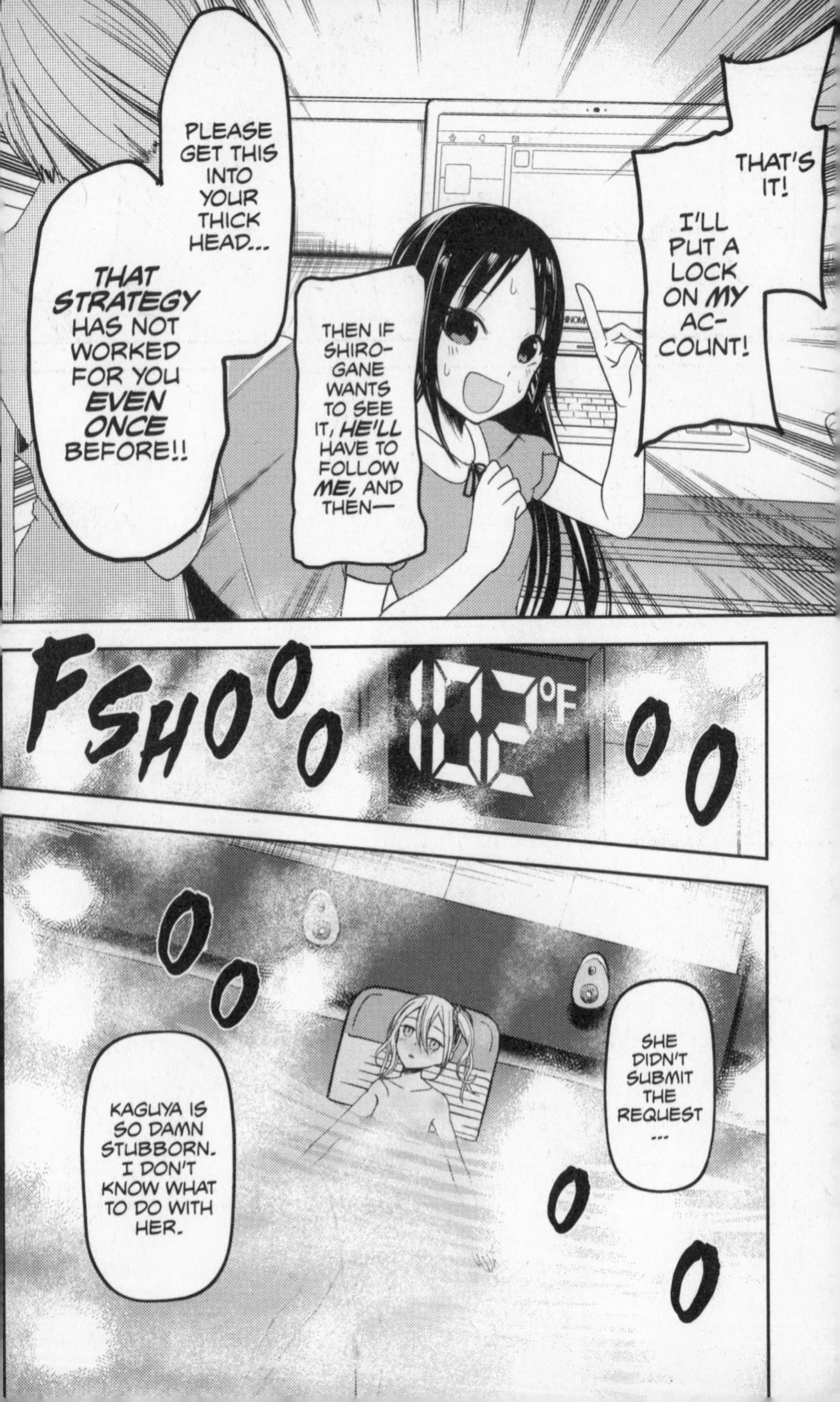
THAT'S IT!
I'LL PUT A LOCK ON MY AC-COUNT!
THEN IF SHIRO-GANE WANTS TO SEE IT, HE'LL HAVE TO FOLLOW ME, AND THEN—
PLEASE GET THIS INTO YOUR THICK HEAD...
THAT STRATEGY HAS NOT WORKED FOR YOU EVEN ONCE BEFORE!!
FSHOOOOOO
SHE DIDN'T SUBMIT THE REQUEST...
KAGUYA IS SO DAMN STUBBORN. I DON'T KNOW WHAT TO DO WITH HER.

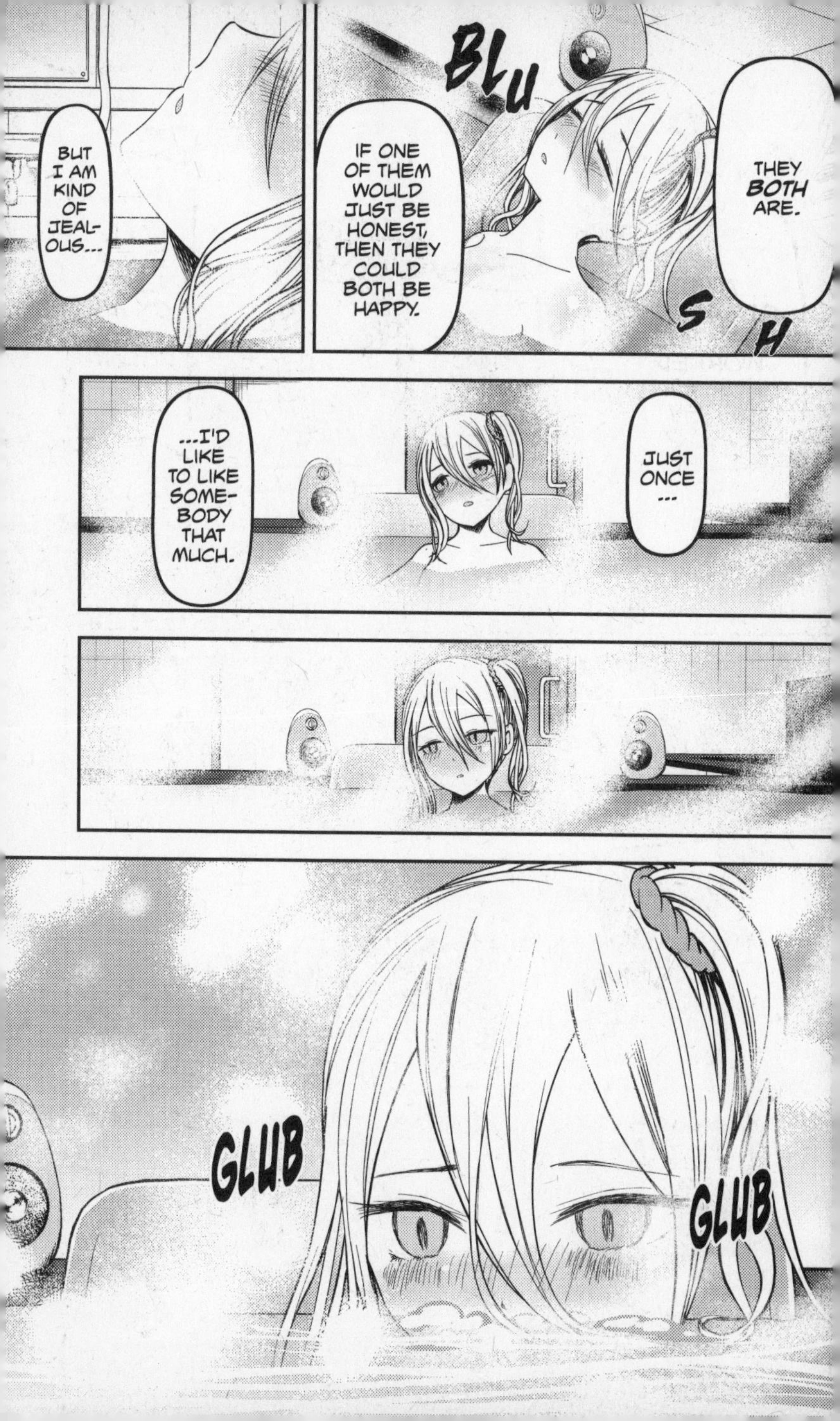

THEY BOTH ARE.
BLU
IF ONE OF THEM WOULD JUST BE HONEST, THEN THEY COULD BOTH BE HAPPY.
SH
BUT I AM KIND OF JEAL-OUS...
JUST ONCE...
...I'D LIKE TO LIKE SOME-BODY THAT MUCH.
GLUB
GLUB

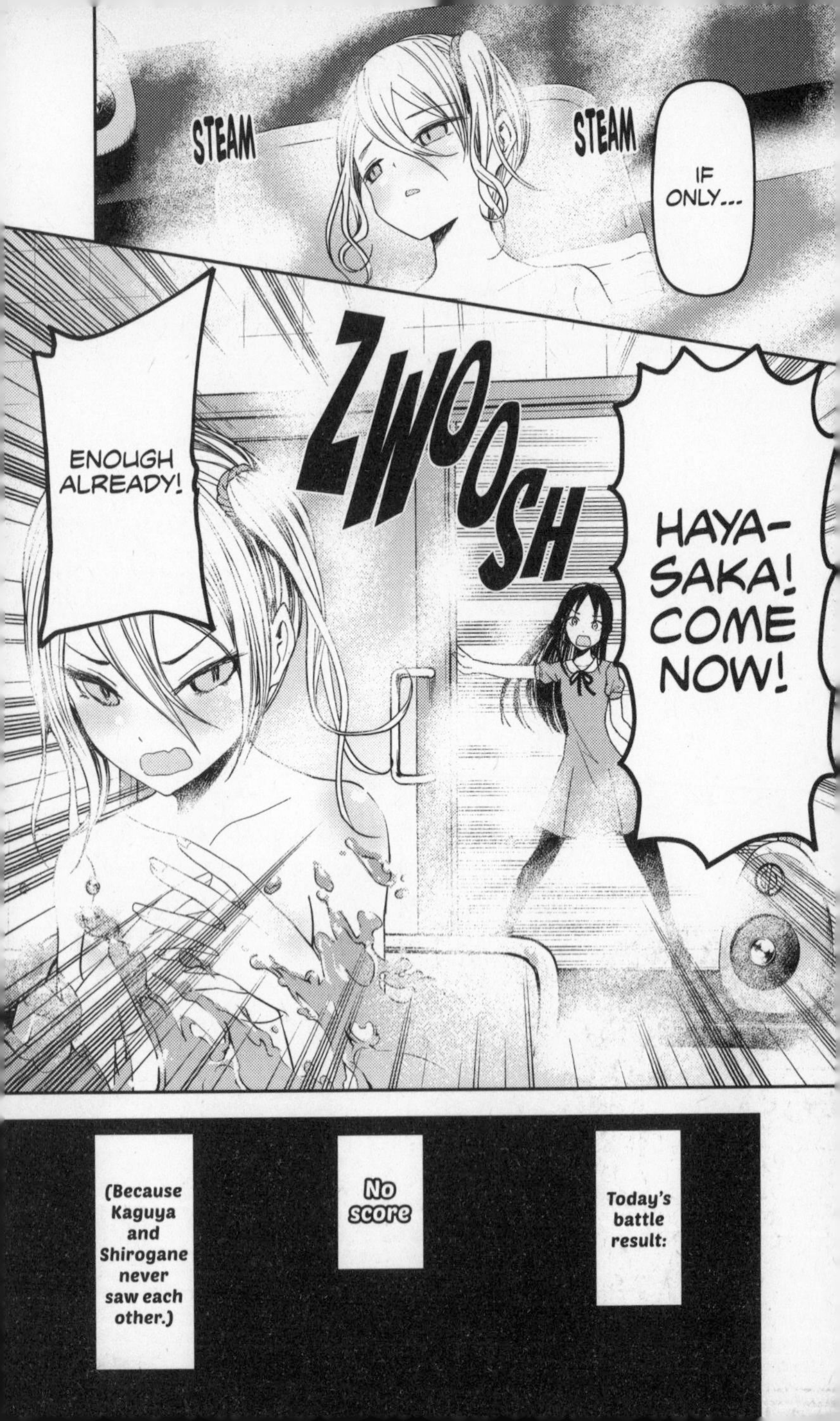
IF ONLY...
STEAM
STEAM
HAYA-SAKA! COME NOW!
ZWOOSH
ENOUGH ALREADY!
Today's battle result:
No score
(Because Kaguya and Shirogane never saw each other.)

SUPER-
FAST
TYPIST

TP TP TP TP TP TP

KAGUYA-SAMA
LOVE IS WAR

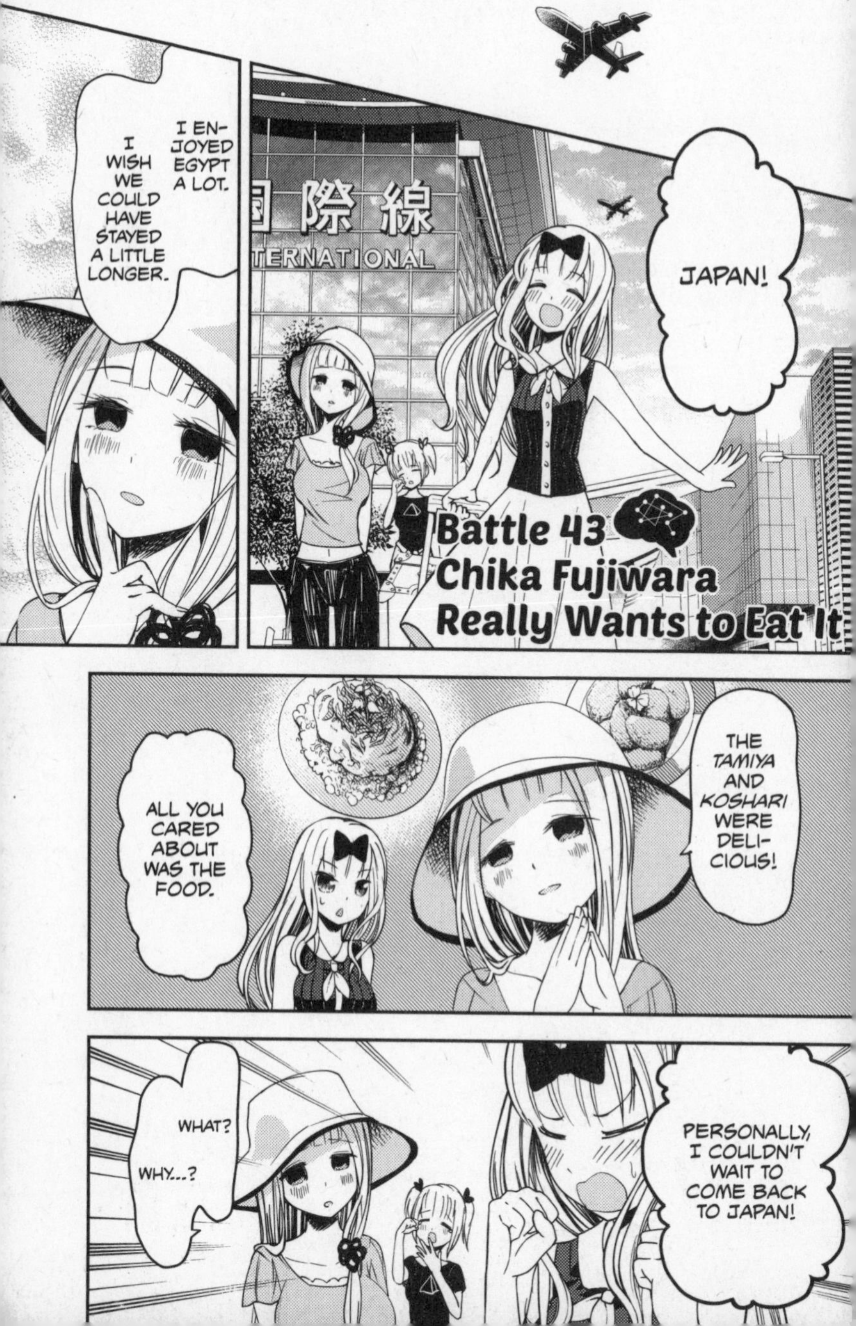
JAPAN!
Battle 43 Chika Fujiwara Really Wants to Eat It
I ENJOYED EGYPT A LOT.
I WISH WE COULD HAVE STAYED A LITTLE LONGER.
THE *TAMIYA* AND *KOSHARI* WERE DELICIOUS!
ALL YOU CARED ABOUT WAS THE FOOD.
PERSONALLY, I COULDN'T WAIT TO COME BACK TO JAPAN!
WHAT?
WHY...?

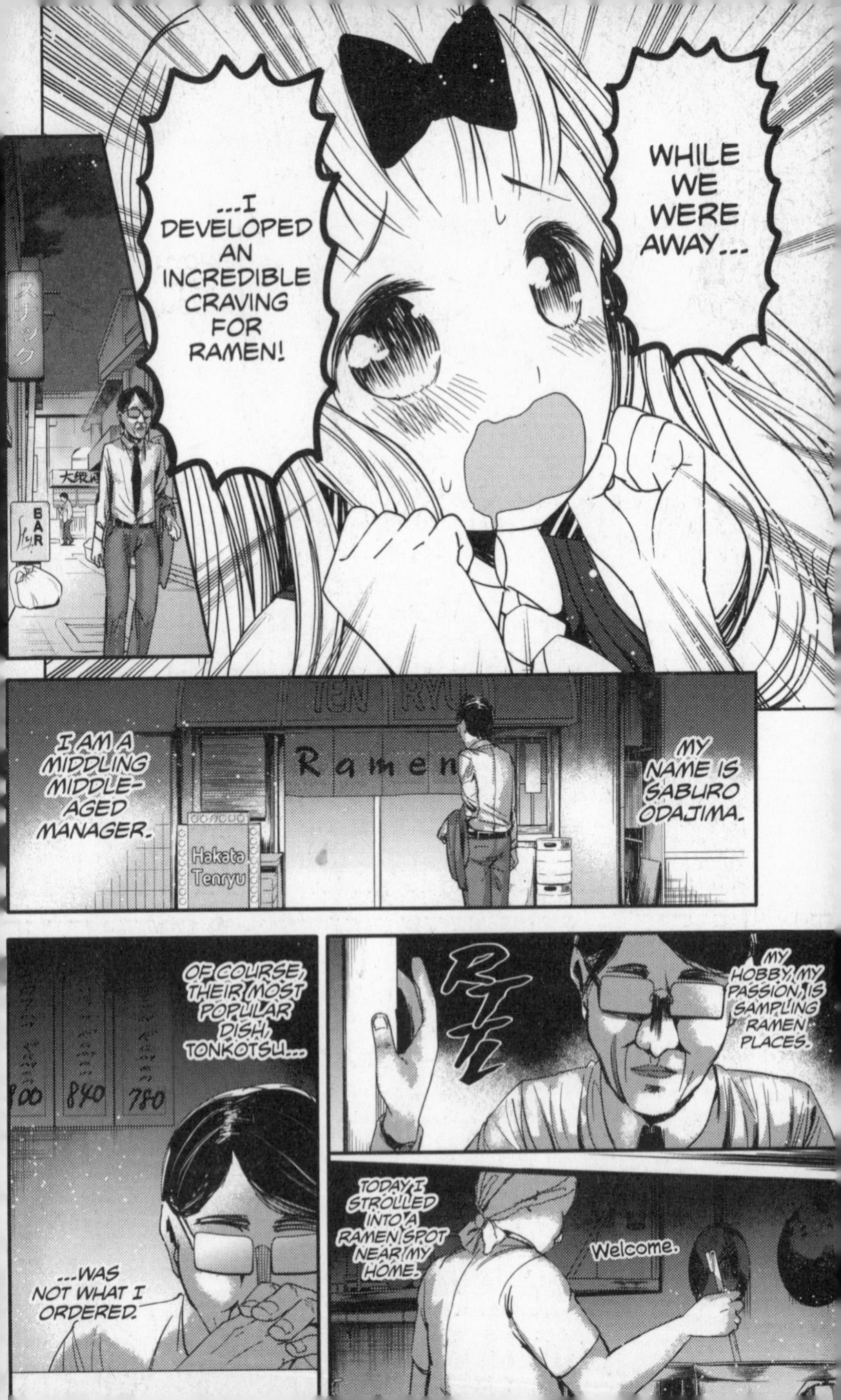

WHILE WE WERE AWAY...
...I DEVELOPED AN INCREDIBLE CRAVING FOR RAMEN!
BAR
MY NAME IS SABURO ODAJIMA.
I AM A MIDDLING MIDDLE-AGED MANAGER.
Ramen
Hakata Tenryu
MY HOBBY, MY PASSION, IS SAMPLING RAMEN PLACES.
TODAY I STROLLED INTO A RAMEN SPOT NEAR MY HOME.
Welcome.
OF COURSE, THEIR MOST POPULAR DISH, TONKOTSU...
840
780
...WAS NOT WHAT I ORDERED.

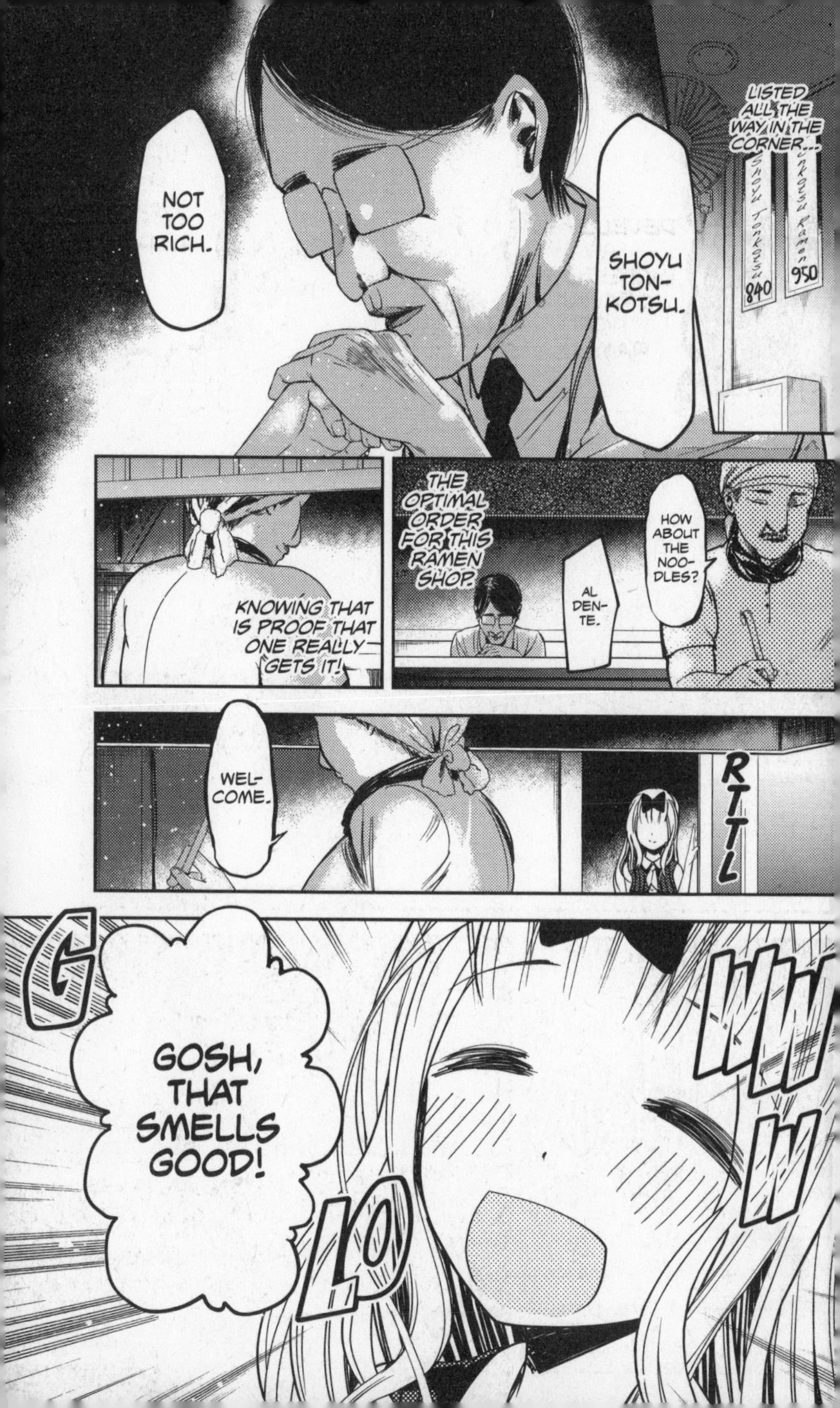
LISTED ALL THE WAY IN THE CORNER...
Shoyu Tonkotsu 840
950
SHOYU TON-KOTSU.
NOT TOO RICH.
HOW ABOUT THE NOO-DLES?
AL DEN-TE.
THE OPTIMAL ORDER FOR THIS RAMEN SHOP.
KNOWING THAT IS PROOF THAT ONE REALLY GETS IT!
RTTL
WEL-COME.
GOSH, THAT SMELLS GOOD!

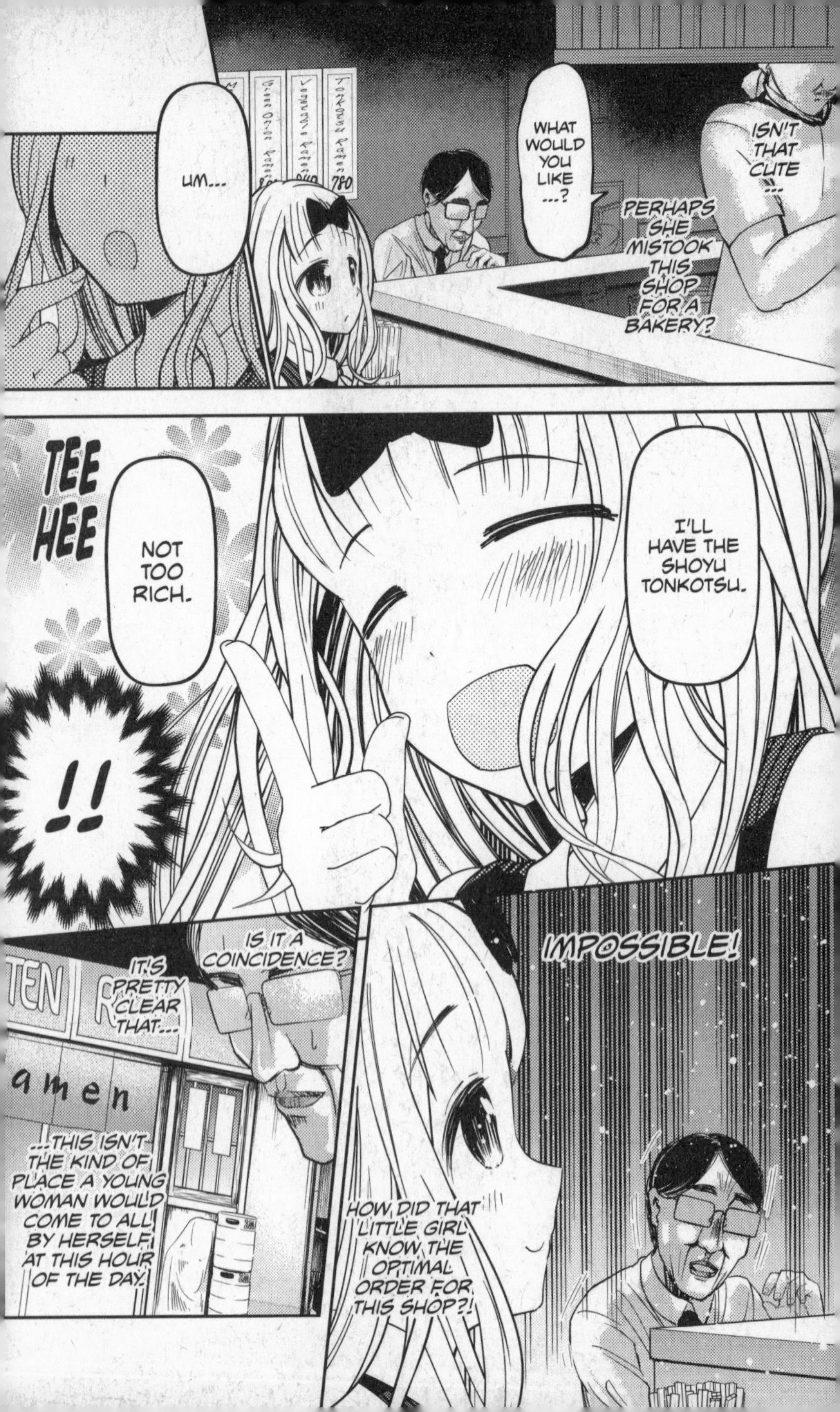
ISN'T THAT CUTE...
PERHAPS SHE MISTOOK THIS SHOP FOR A BAKERY?
WHAT WOULD YOU LIKE ...?
UM...
I'LL HAVE THE SHOYU TONKOTSU.
NOT TOO RICH.
TEE HEE
!!
IMPOSSIBLE!
HOW DID THAT LITTLE GIRL KNOW THE OPTIMAL ORDER FOR THIS SHOP?!
IS IT A COINCIDENCE?
IT'S PRETTY CLEAR THAT...
TEN
amen
...THIS ISN'T THE KIND OF PLACE A YOUNG WOMAN WOULD COME TO ALL BY HERSELF AT THIS HOUR OF THE DAY.

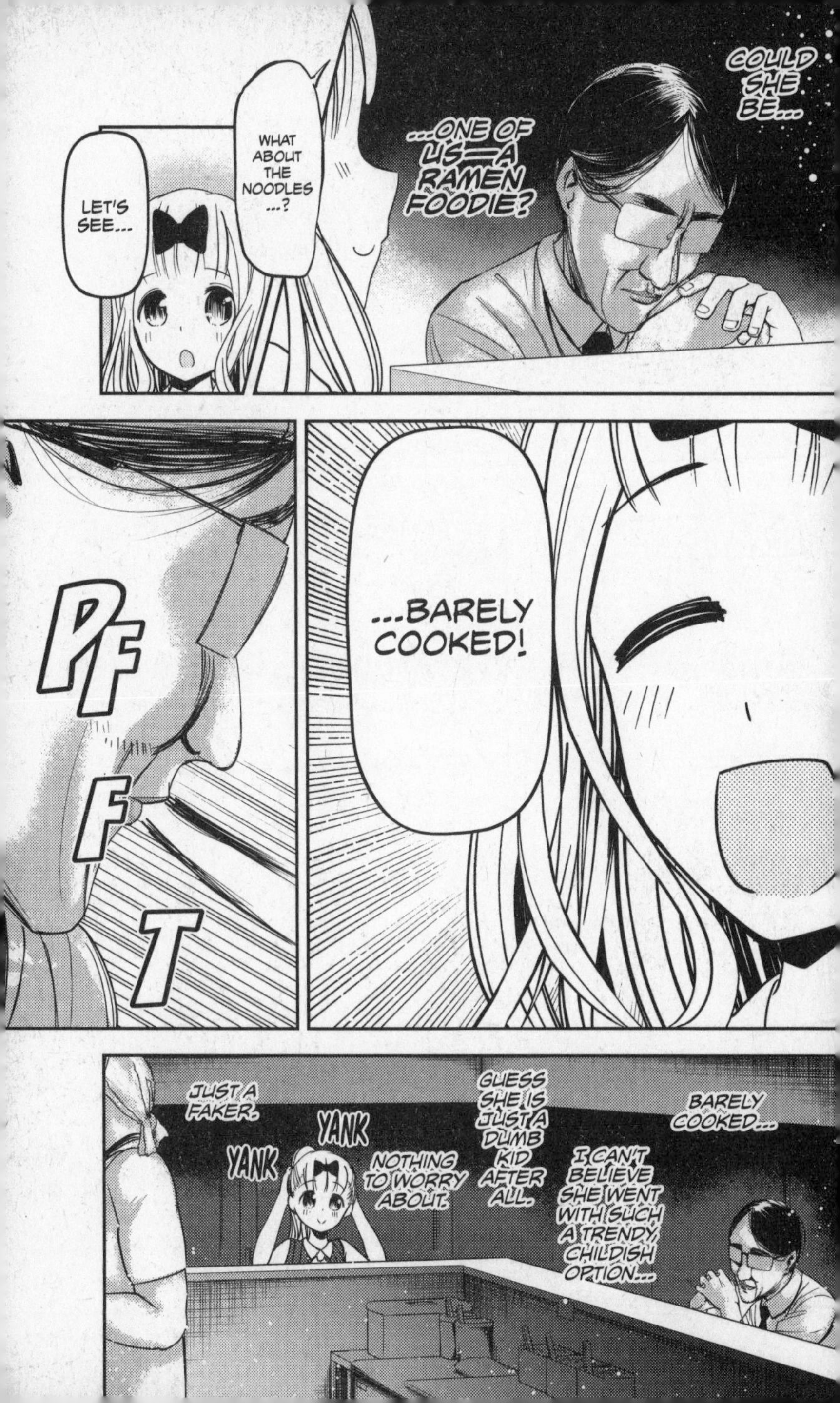
COULD SHE BE...
...ONE OF US—A RAMEN FOODIE?
WHAT ABOUT THE NOODLES...?
LET'S SEE...
...BARELY COOKED!
PFFT
BARELY COOKED...
I CAN'T BELIEVE SHE WENT WITH SUCH A TRENDY, CHILDISH OPTION...
GUESS SHE IS JUST A DUMB KID AFTER ALL.
NOTHING TO WORRY ABOUT.
YANK
JUST A FAKER.
YANK

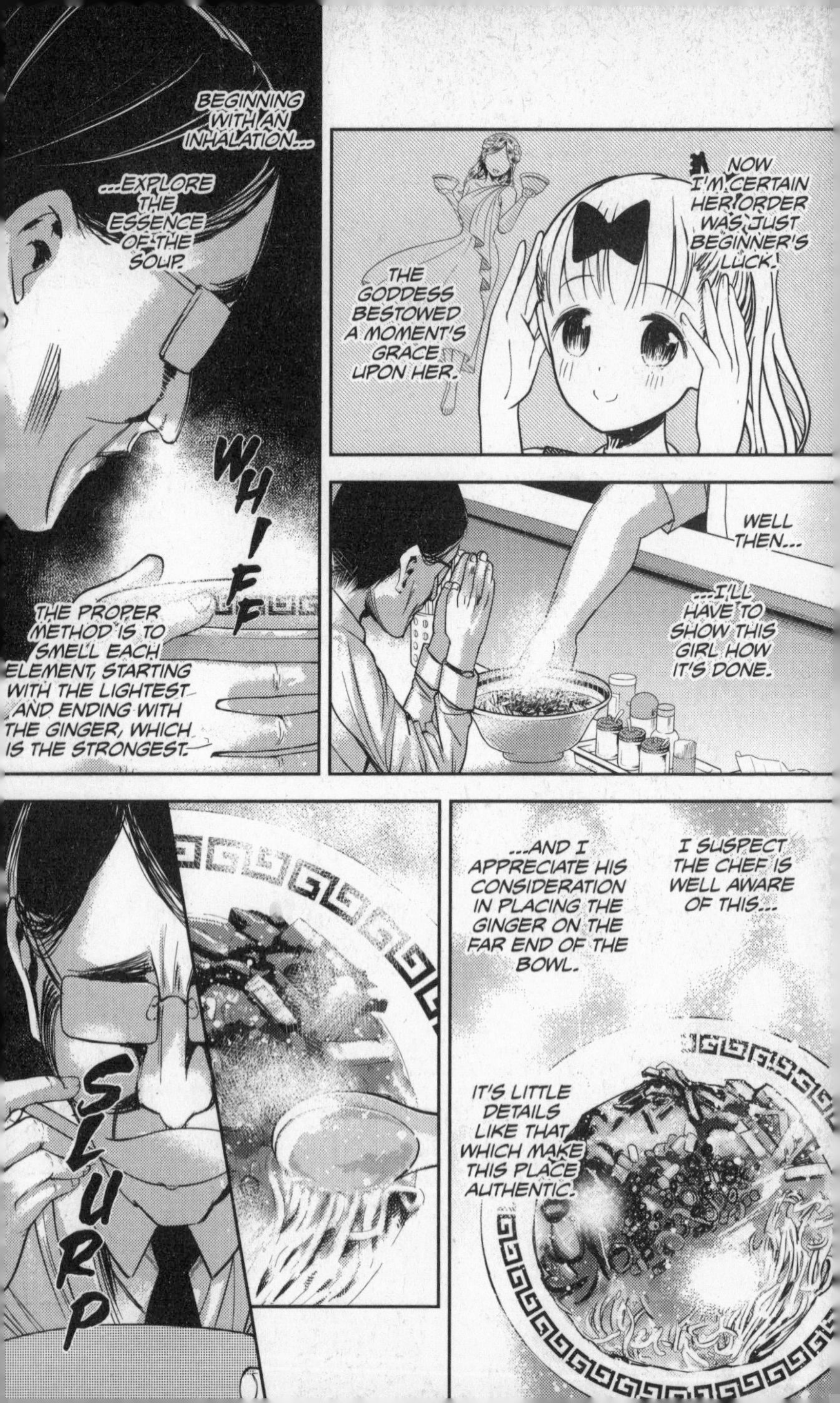
NOW I'M CERTAIN HER ORDER WAS JUST BEGINNER'S LUCK.
THE GODDESS BESTOWED A MOMENT'S GRACE UPON HER.
WELL THEN...
...I'LL HAVE TO SHOW THIS GIRL HOW IT'S DONE.
BEGINNING WITH AN INHALATION...
...EXPLORE THE ESSENCE OF THE SOUP.
WHIFF
THE PROPER METHOD IS TO SMELL EACH ELEMENT, STARTING WITH THE LIGHTEST AND ENDING WITH THE GINGER, WHICH IS THE STRONGEST.
I SUSPECT THE CHEF IS WELL AWARE OF THIS...
...AND I APPRECIATE HIS CONSIDERATION IN PLACING THE GINGER ON THE FAR END OF THE BOWL.
IT'S LITTLE DETAILS LIKE THAT WHICH MAKE THIS PLACE AUTHENTIC.
SLURP

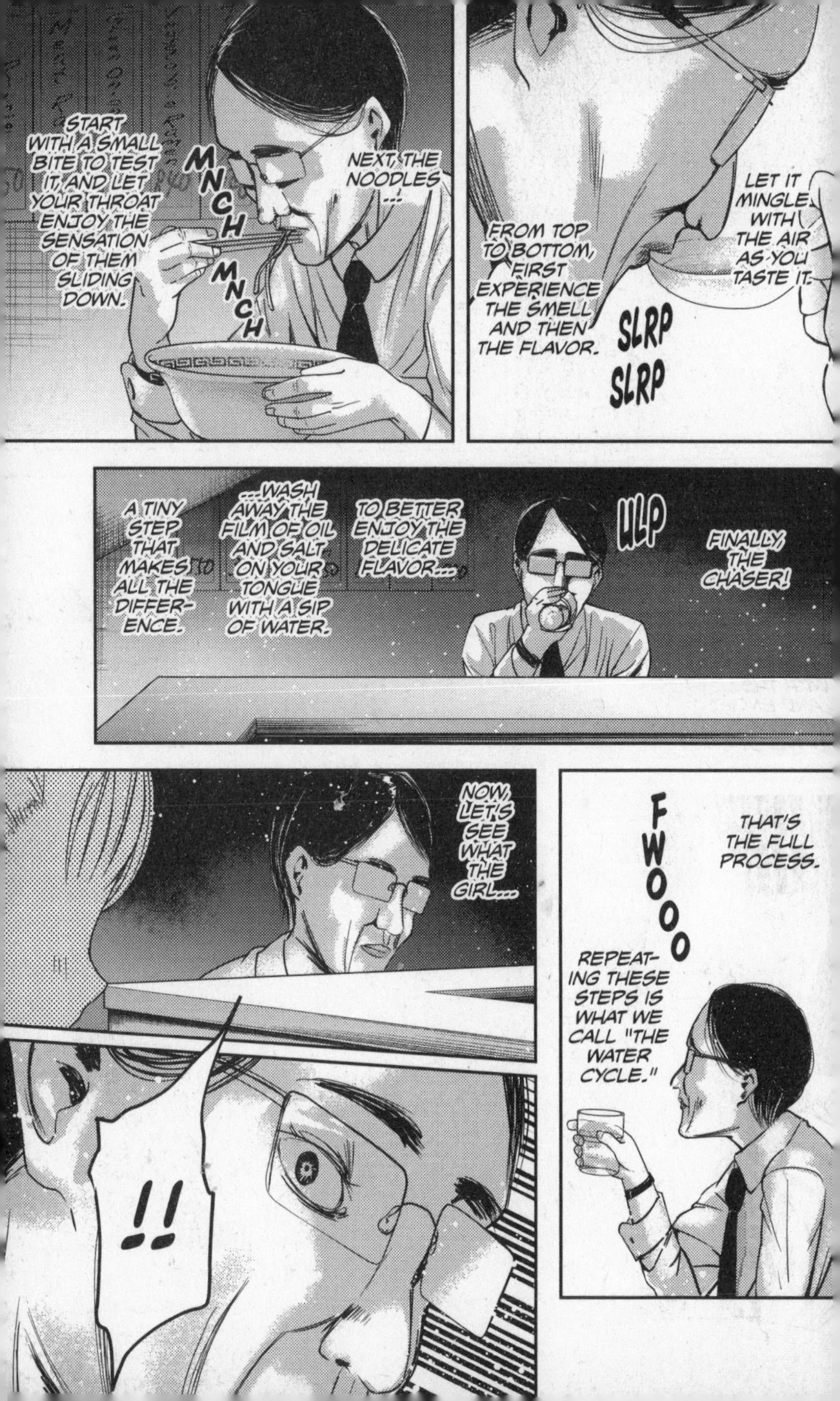
LET IT MINGLE WITH THE AIR AS YOU TASTE IT.
FROM TOP TO BOTTOM, FIRST EXPERIENCE THE SMELL AND THEN THE FLAVOR.
SLRP
SLRP
NEXT, THE NOODLES...
MNCH
MNCH
START WITH A SMALL BITE TO TEST IT, AND LET YOUR THROAT ENJOY THE SENSATION OF THEM SLIDING DOWN.
FINALLY, THE CHASER!
ULP
TO BETTER ENJOY THE DELICATE FLAVOR...
...WASH AWAY THE FILM OF OIL AND SALT ON YOUR TONGUE WITH A SIP OF WATER.
A TINY STEP THAT MAKES ALL THE DIFFERENCE.
THAT'S THE FULL PROCESS.
FWOOOO
REPEATING THESE STEPS IS WHAT WE CALL "THE WATER CYCLE."
NOW, LET'S SEE WHAT THE GIRL...
!!

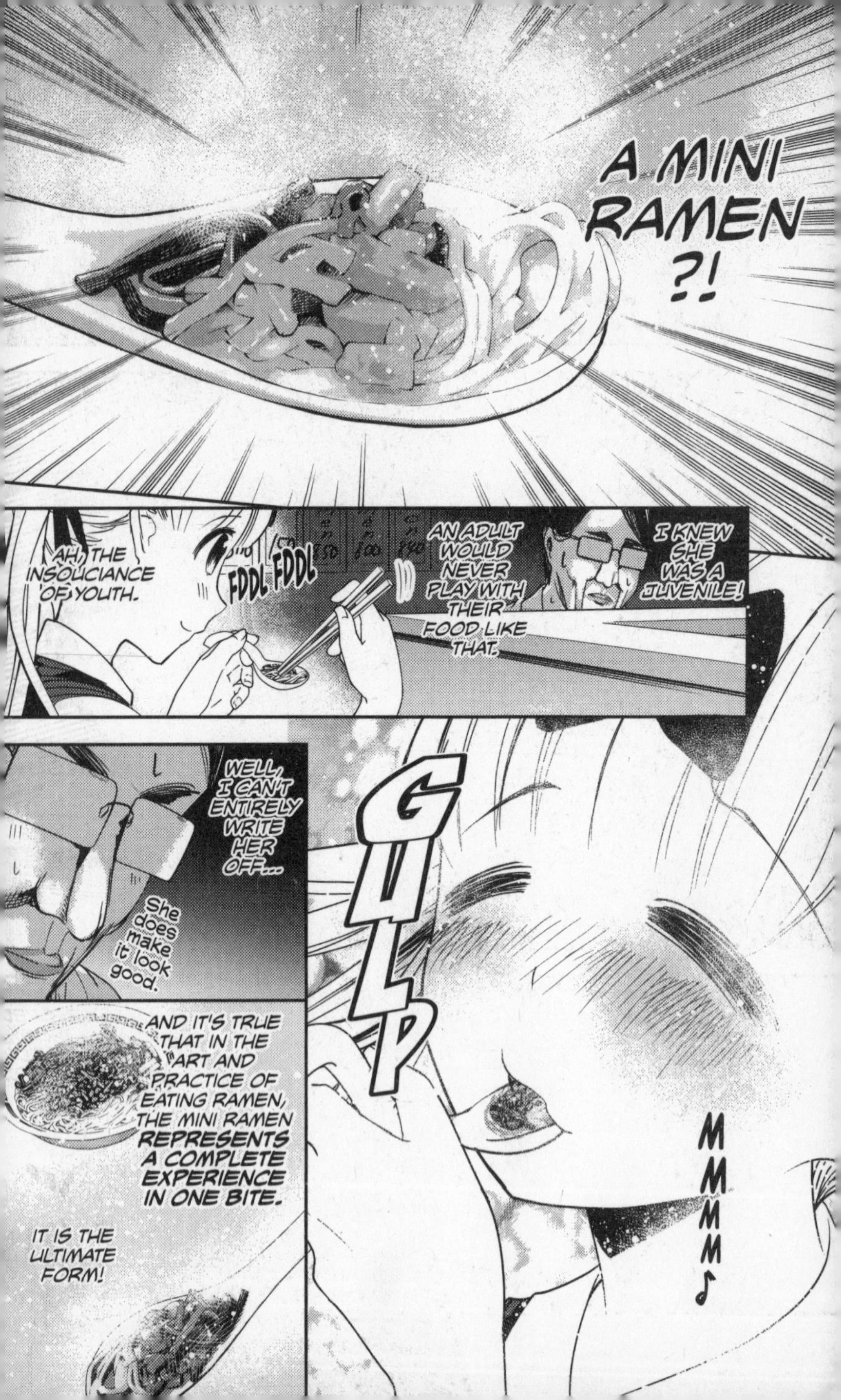
A MINI RAMEN ?!
I KNEW SHE WAS A JUVENILE!
AN ADULT WOULD NEVER PLAY WITH THEIR FOOD LIKE THAT.
FDDL FDDL
AH, THE INSOUCIANCE OF YOUTH.
GULP
WELL, I CAN'T ENTIRELY WRITE HER OFF...
She does make it look good.
MMMMM♪
AND IT'S TRUE THAT IN THE ART AND PRACTICE OF EATING RAMEN, THE MINI RAMEN REPRESENTS A COMPLETE EXPERIENCE IN ONE BITE.
IT IS THE ULTIMATE FORM!

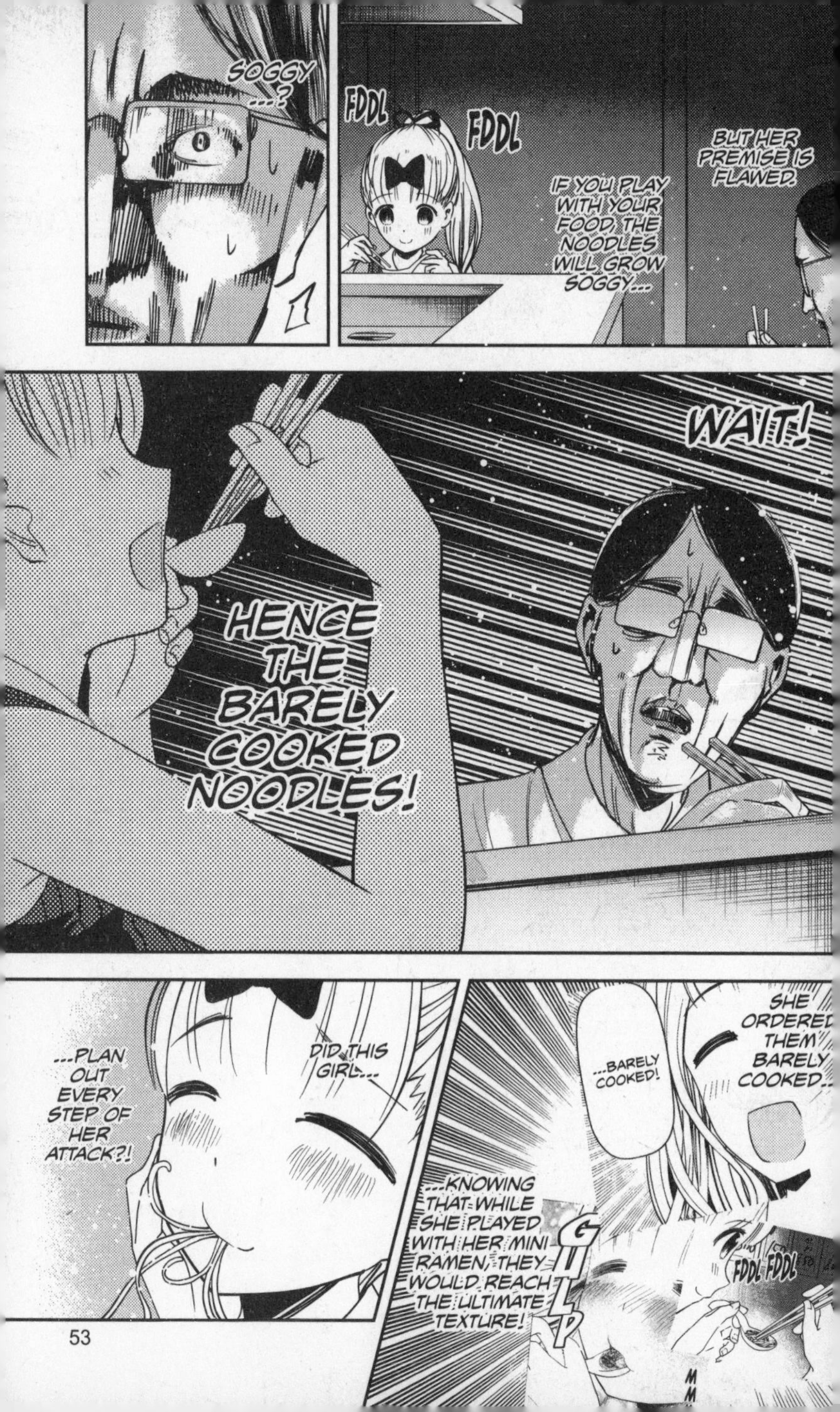
BUT HER PREMISE IS FLAWED.
IF YOU PLAY WITH YOUR FOOD THE NOODLES WILL GROW SOGGY...
FDDL
FDDL
SOGGY ...?
WAIT!
HENCE THE BARELY COOKED NOODLES!
SHE ORDERED THEM BARELY COOKED...
...BARELY COOKED!
FDDL FDDL
...KNOWING THAT WHILE SHE PLAYED WITH HER MINI RAMEN, THEY WOULD REACH THE ULTIMATE TEXTURE!
GULP
MM
DID THIS GIRL...
...PLAN OUT EVERY STEP OF HER ATTACK?!

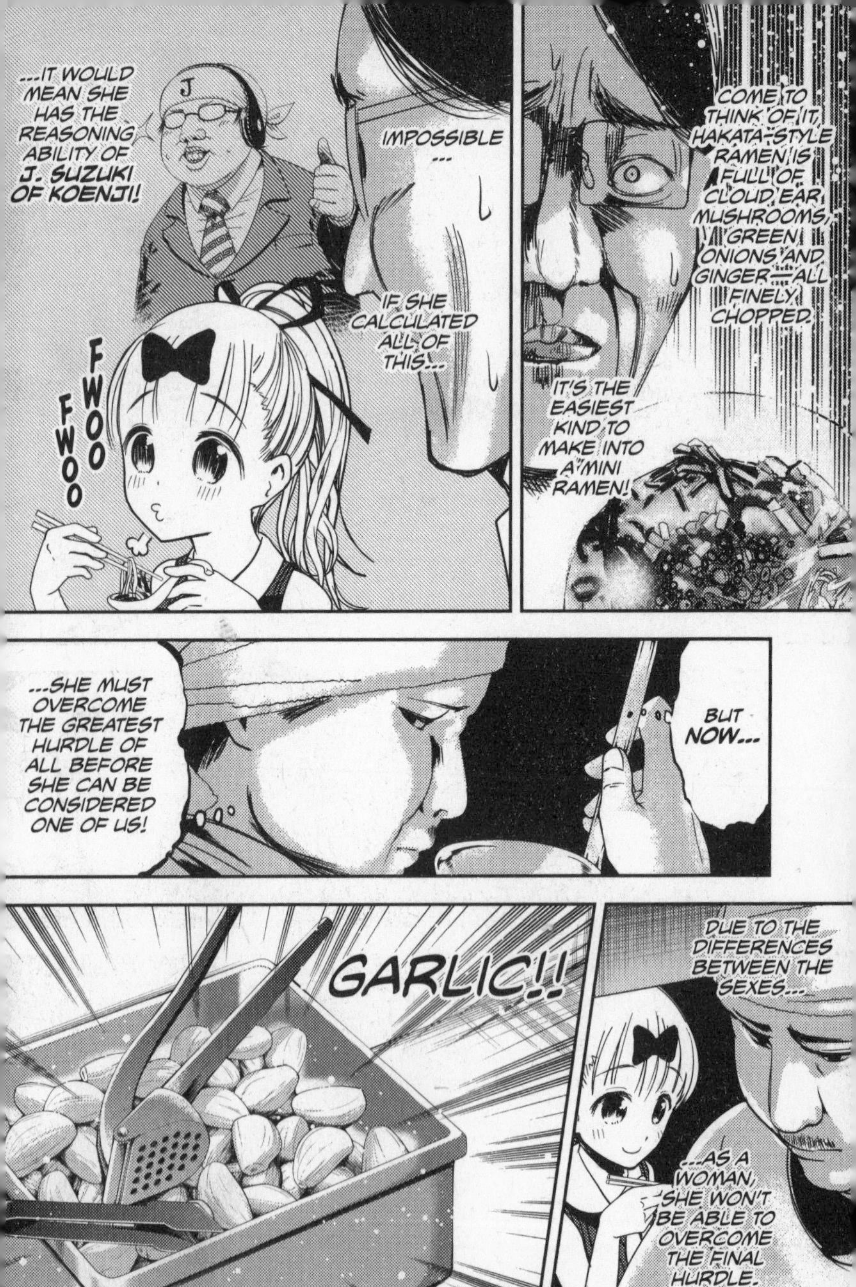
COME TO THINK OF IT, HAKATA-STYLE RAMEN IS FULL OF CLOUD EAR MUSHROOMS, GREEN ONIONS AND GINGER—ALL FINELY CHOPPED.
IT'S THE EASIEST KIND TO MAKE INTO A MINI RAMEN!
IMPOSSIBLE ...
IF SHE CALCULATED ALL OF THIS...
...IT WOULD MEAN SHE HAS THE REASONING ABILITY OF J. SUZUKI OF KOENJI!
FWOO FWOO FWOO
BUT NOW...
...SHE MUST OVERCOME THE GREATEST HURDLE OF ALL BEFORE SHE CAN BE CONSIDERED ONE OF US!
DUE TO THE DIFFERENCES BETWEEN THE SEXES...
...AS A WOMAN, SHE WON'T BE ABLE TO OVERCOME THE FINAL HURDLE.
GARLIC!!

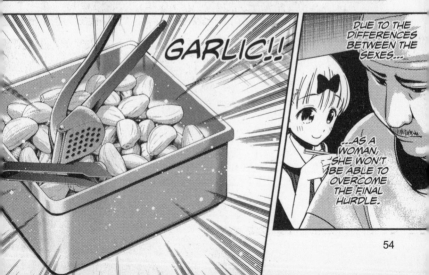

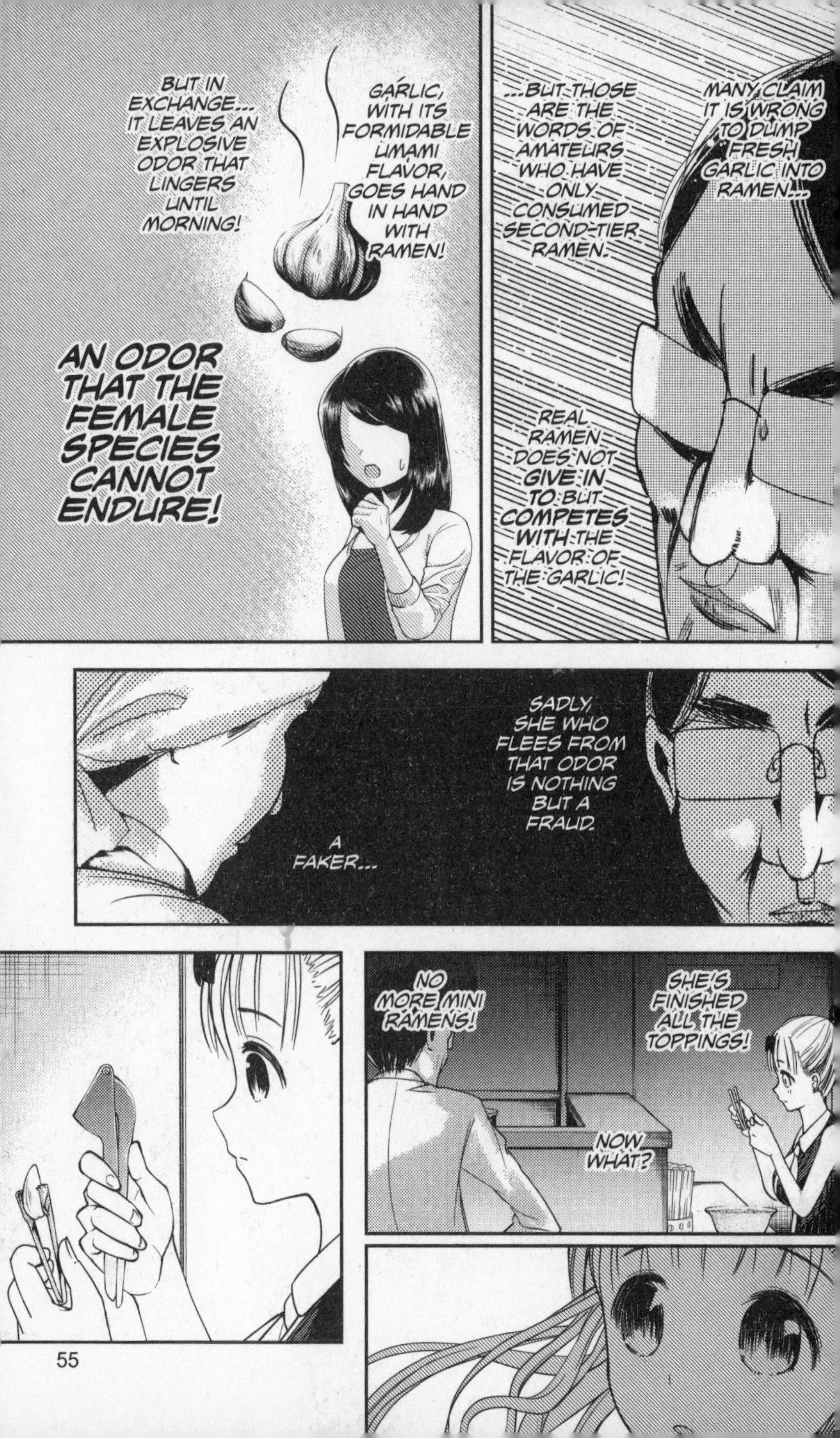

MANY CLAIM IT IS WRONG TO DUMP FRESH GARLIC INTO RAMEN...
...BUT THOSE ARE THE WORDS OF AMATEURS WHO HAVE ONLY CONSUMED SECOND-TIER RAMEN.
REAL RAMEN DOES NOT GIVE IN TO BUT COMPETES WITH THE FLAVOR OF THE GARLIC!
GARLIC, WITH ITS FORMIDABLE UMAMI FLAVOR, GOES HAND IN HAND WITH RAMEN!
BUT IN EXCHANGE... IT LEAVES AN EXPLOSIVE ODOR THAT LINGERS UNTIL MORNING!
AN ODOR THAT THE FEMALE SPECIES CANNOT ENDURE!
SADLY, SHE WHO FLEES FROM THAT ODOR IS NOTHING BUT A FRAUD.
A FAKER...
SHE'S FINISHED ALL THE TOPPINGS!
NO MORE MINI RAMENS!
NOW WHAT?

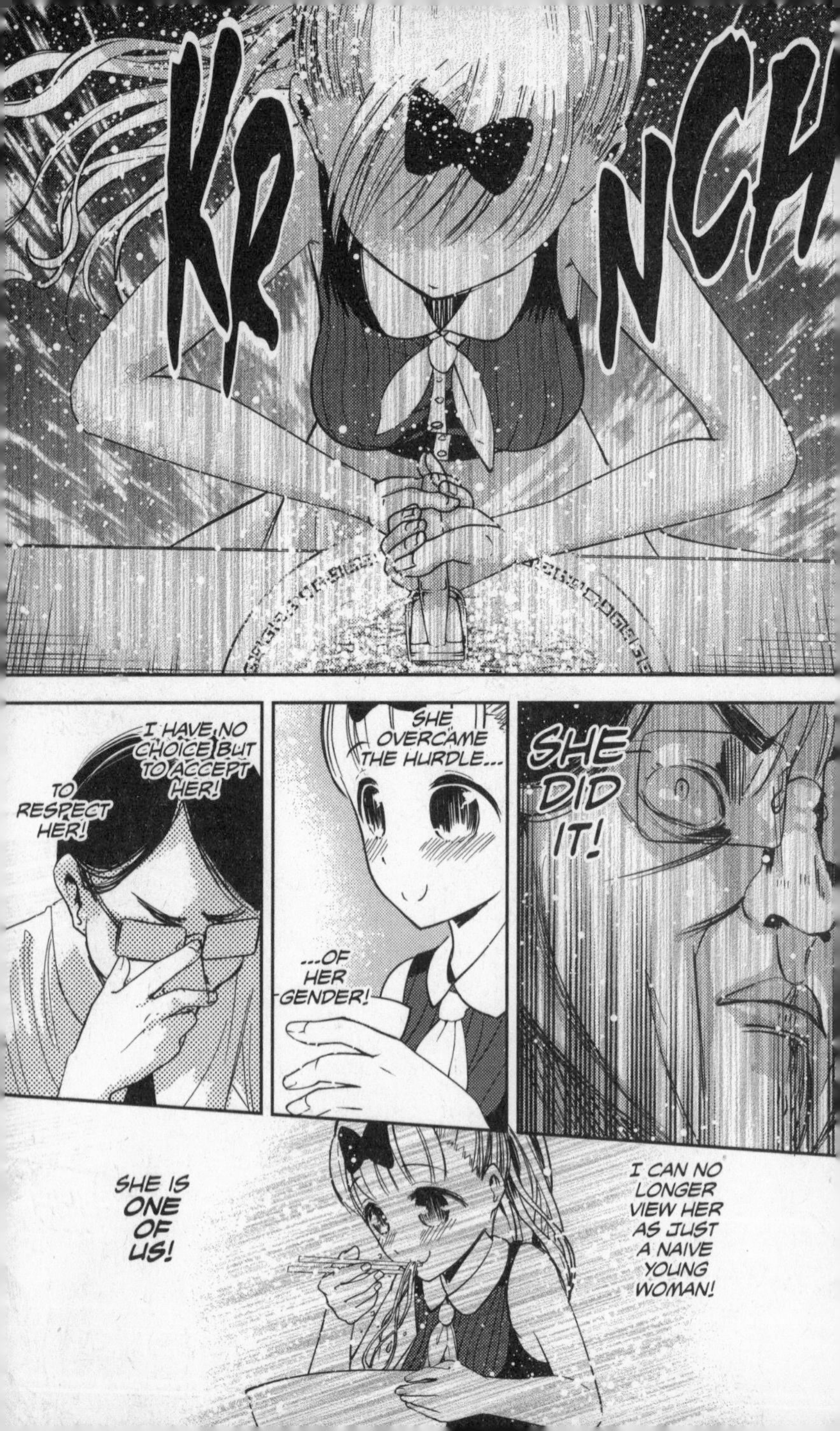
KR NCH
SHE DID IT!
SHE OVERCAME THE HURDLE...
...OF HER GENDER!
I HAVE NO CHOICE BUT TO ACCEPT HER!
TO RESPECT HER!
I CAN NO LONGER VIEW HER AS JUST A NAIVE YOUNG WOMAN!
SHE IS ONE OF US!

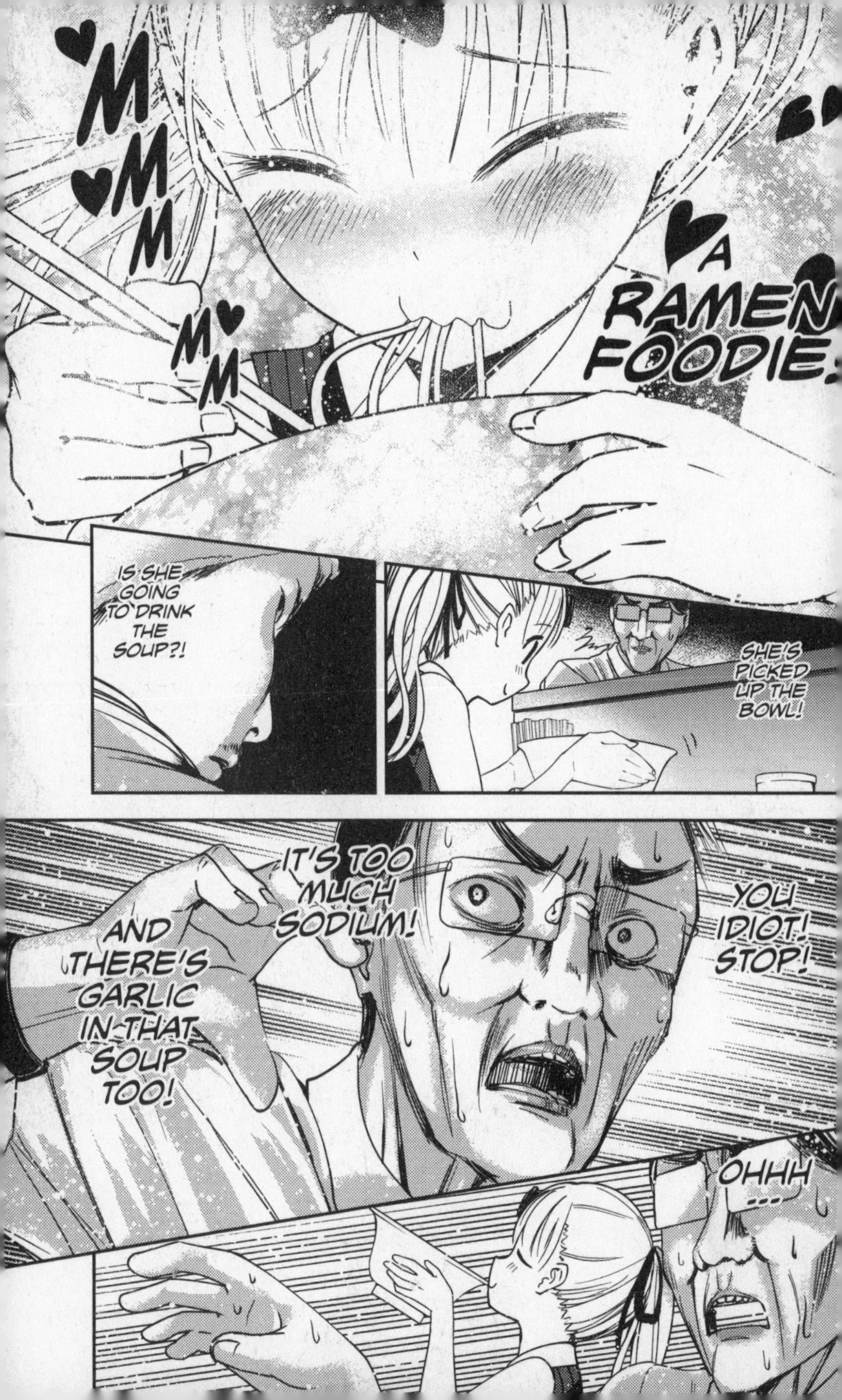

A RAMEN FOODIE!
MMMM MMM
SHE'S PICKED UP THE BOWL!
IS SHE GOING TO DRINK THE SOUP?!
YOU IDIOT! STOP!
IT'S TOO MUCH SODIUM!
AND THERE'S GARLIC IN THAT SOUP TOO!
OHHH...

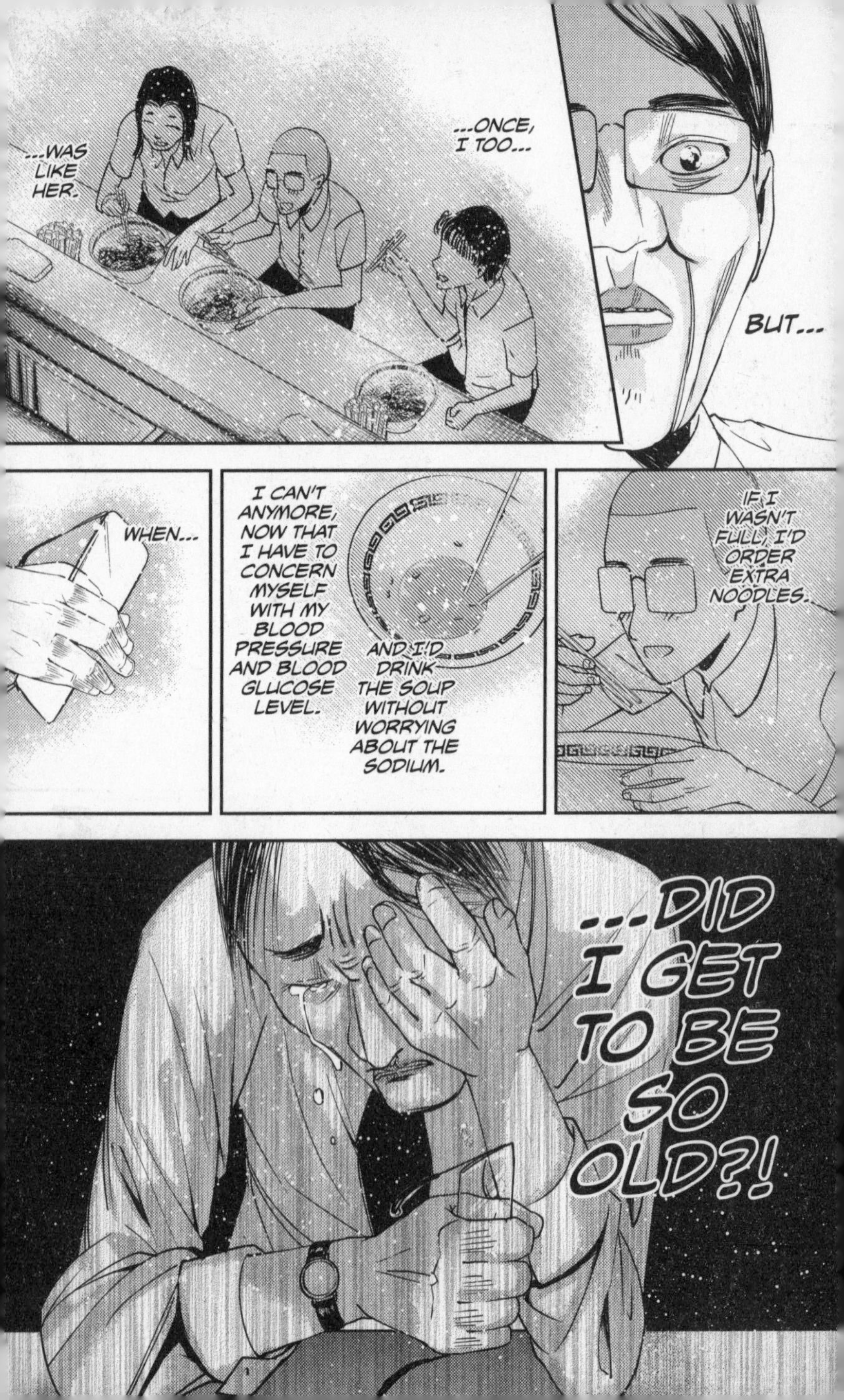

...ONCE, I TOO...
...WAS LIKE HER.
BUT...
IF I WASN'T FULL, I'D ORDER EXTRA NOODLES.
AND I'D DRINK THE SOUP WITHOUT WORRYING ABOUT THE SODIUM.
I CAN'T ANYMORE, NOW THAT I HAVE TO CONCERN MYSELF WITH MY BLOOD PRESSURE AND BLOOD GLUCOSE LEVEL.
WHEN...
...DID I GET TO BE SO OLD?!

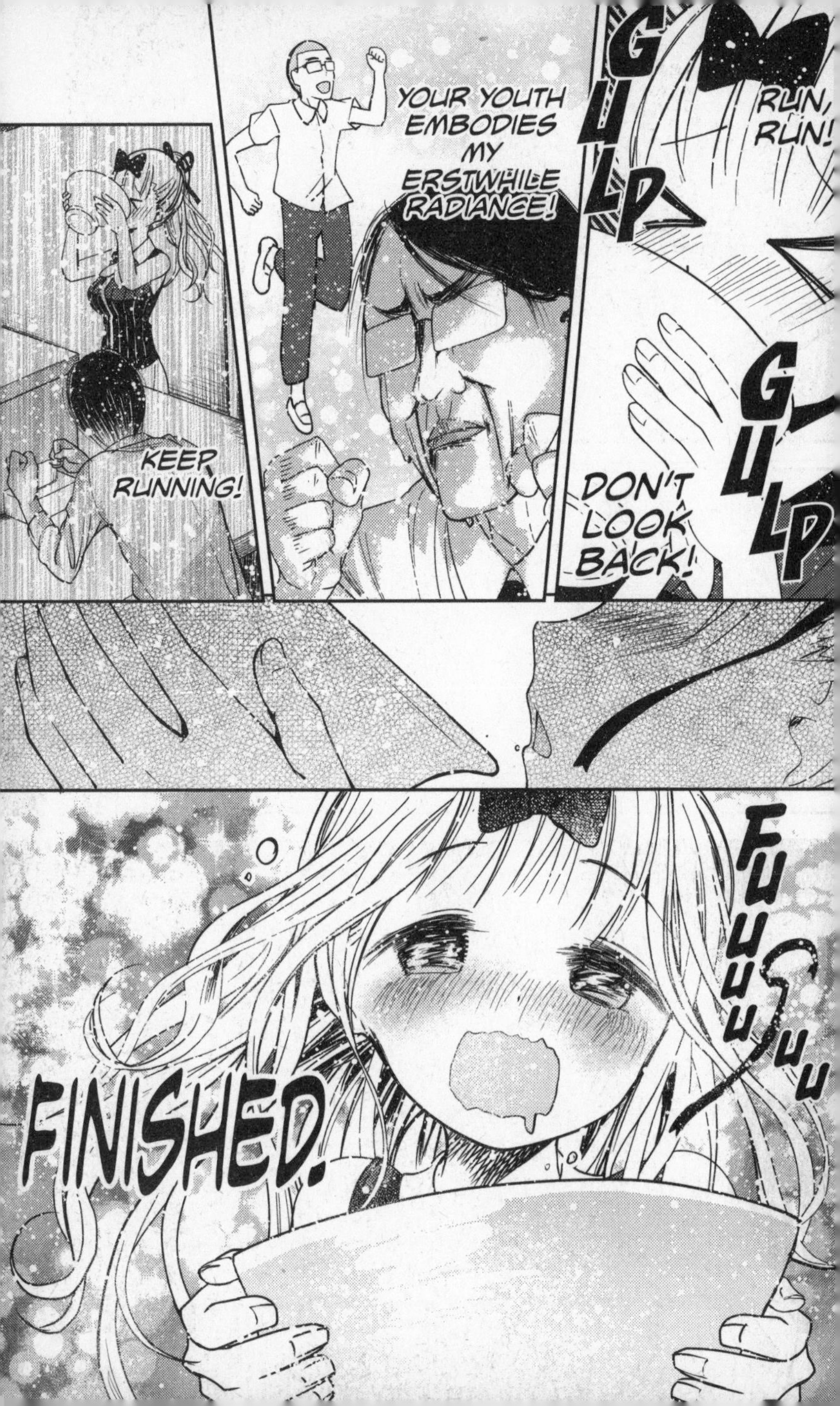
RUN, RUN!
GULP
GULP
DON'T LOOK BACK!
YOUR YOUTH EMBODIES MY ERSTWHILE RADIANCE!
KEEP RUNNING!
FUUUU
SUUU
FINISHED.

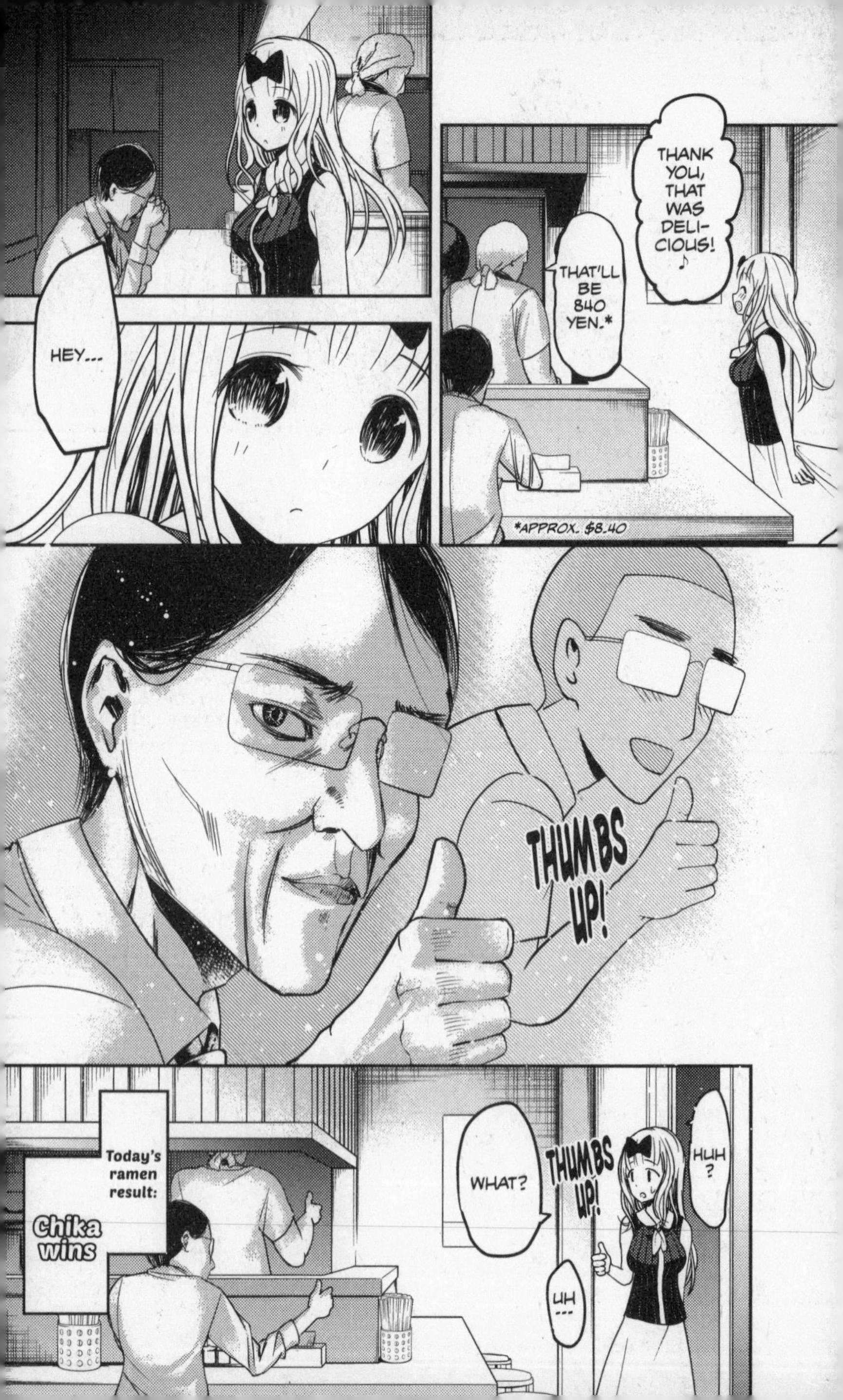
THANK YOU, THAT WAS DELICIOUS! ♪
THAT'LL BE 840 YEN.*
*APPROX. $8.40
HEY...
THUMBS UP!
HUH?
THUMBS UP!
WHAT?
UH...
Today's ramen result:
Chika wins

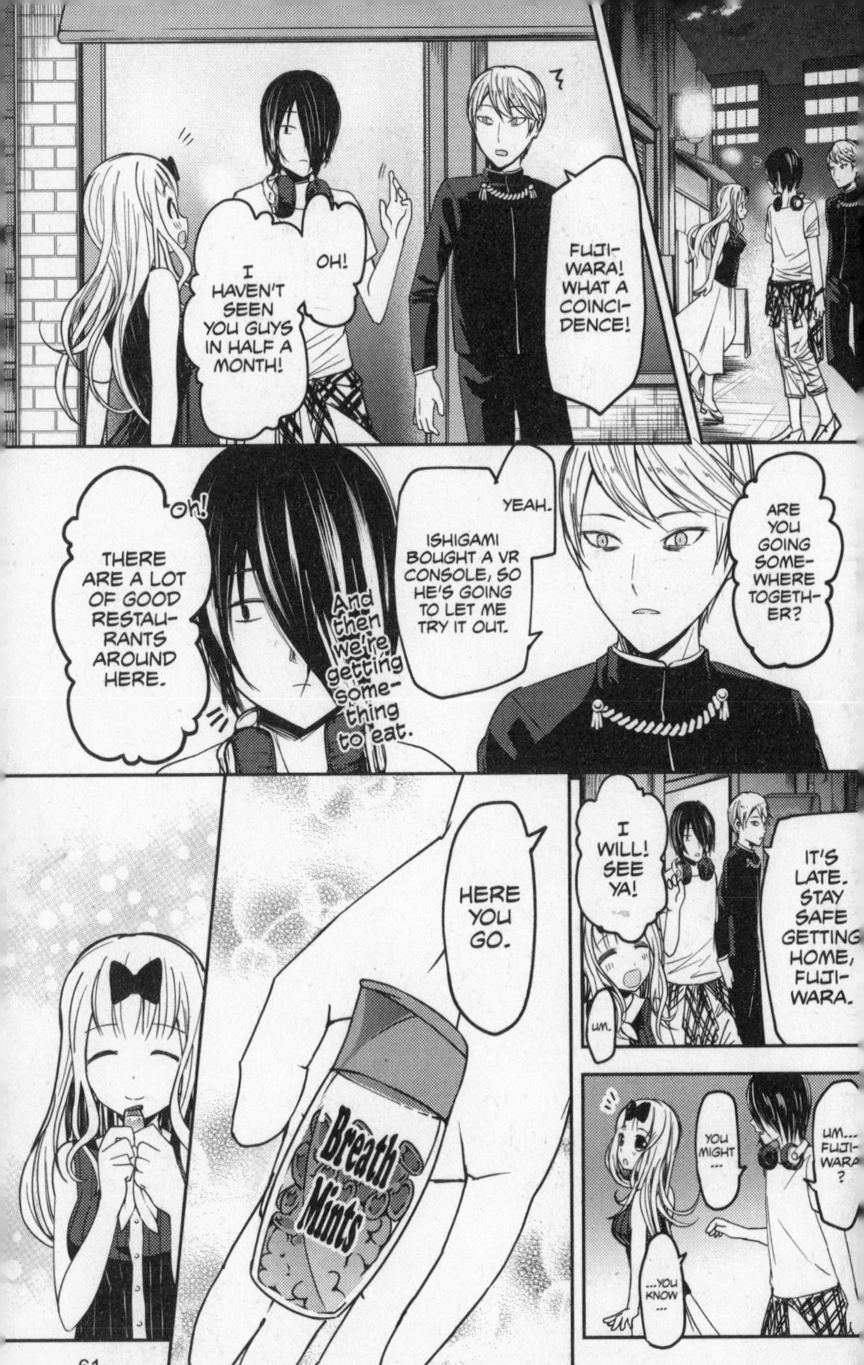
FUJI-WARA! WHAT A COINCI-DENCE!
OH!
I HAVEN'T SEEN YOU GUYS IN HALF A MONTH!
ARE YOU GOING SOME-WHERE TOGETH-ER?
YEAH.
ISHIGAMI BOUGHT A VR CONSOLE, SO HE'S GOING TO LET ME TRY IT OUT.
And then we're getting some-thing to eat.
Oh!
THERE ARE A LOT OF GOOD RESTAU-RANTS AROUND HERE.
IT'S LATE. STAY SAFE GETTING HOME, FUJI-WARA.
I WILL! SEE YA!
UM.
UM... FUJI-WARA?
YOU MIGHT...
...YOU KNOW...
HERE YOU GO.
Breath Mints

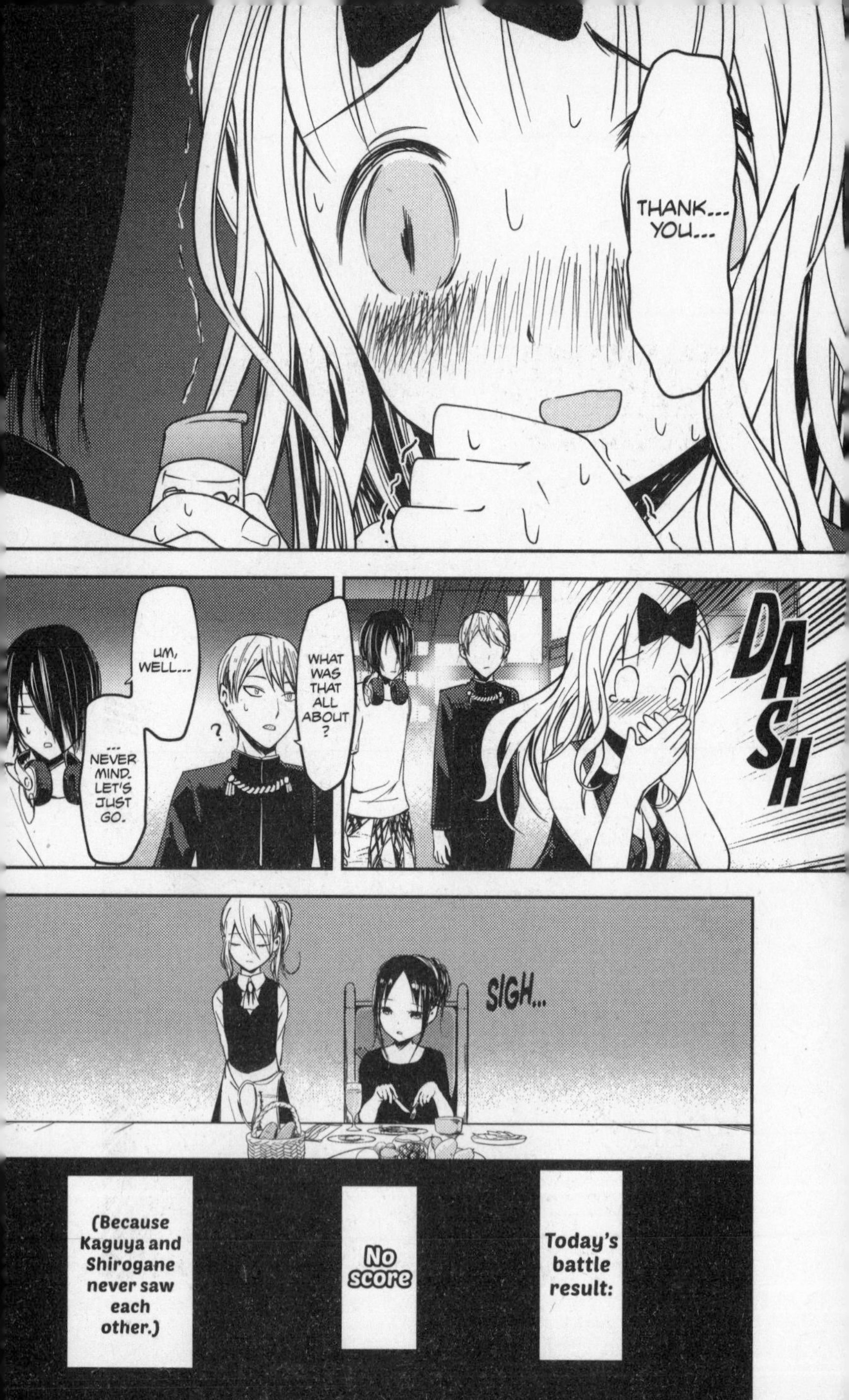
THANK... YOU...
DASH
WHAT WAS THAT ALL ABOUT?
UM, WELL...
...NEVER MIND. LET'S JUST GO.
SIGH...
Today's battle result:
No score
(Because Kaguya and Shirogane never saw each other.)

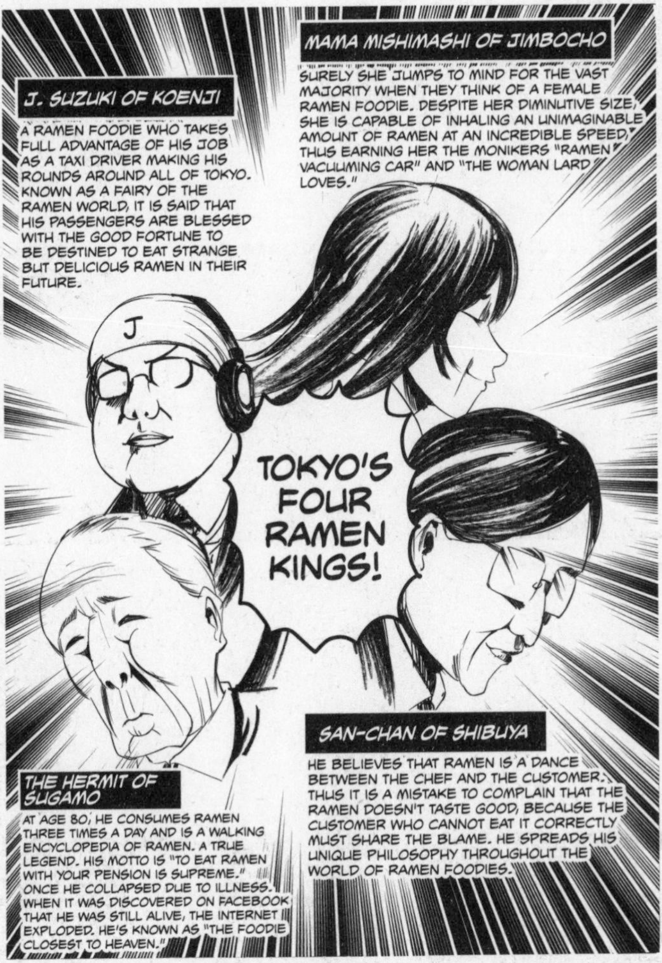
MAMA MISHIMASHI OF JIMBOCHO
SURELY SHE JUMPS TO MIND FOR THE VAST MAJORITY WHEN THEY THINK OF A FEMALE RAMEN FOODIE. DESPITE HER DIMINUTIVE SIZE, SHE IS CAPABLE OF INHALING AN UNIMAGINABLE AMOUNT OF RAMEN AT AN INCREDIBLE SPEED, THUS EARNING HER THE MONIKERS "RAMEN VACUUMING CAR" AND "THE WOMAN LARD LOVES."
J. SUZUKI OF KOENJI
A RAMEN FOODIE WHO TAKES FULL ADVANTAGE OF HIS JOB AS A TAXI DRIVER MAKING HIS ROUNDS AROUND ALL OF TOKYO. KNOWN AS A FAIRY OF THE RAMEN WORLD, IT IS SAID THAT HIS PASSENGERS ARE BLESSED WITH THE GOOD FORTUNE TO BE DESTINED TO EAT STRANGE BUT DELICIOUS RAMEN IN THEIR FUTURE.
J
TOKYO'S FOUR RAMEN KINGS!
SAN-CHAN OF SHIBUYA
HE BELIEVES THAT RAMEN IS A DANCE BETWEEN THE CHEF AND THE CUSTOMER. THUS IT IS A MISTAKE TO COMPLAIN THAT THE RAMEN DOESN'T TASTE GOOD, BECAUSE THE CUSTOMER WHO CANNOT EAT IT CORRECTLY MUST SHARE THE BLAME. HE SPREADS HIS UNIQUE PHILOSOPHY THROUGHOUT THE WORLD OF RAMEN FOODIES.
THE HERMIT OF SUGAMO
AT AGE 80, HE CONSUMES RAMEN THREE TIMES A DAY AND IS A WALKING ENCYCLOPEDIA OF RAMEN. A TRUE LEGEND. HIS MOTTO IS "TO EAT RAMEN WITH YOUR PENSION IS SUPREME." ONCE HE COLLAPSED DUE TO ILLNESS. WHEN IT WAS DISCOVERED ON FACEBOOK THAT HE WAS STILL ALIVE, THE INTERNET EXPLODED. HE'S KNOWN AS "THE FOODIE CLOSEST TO HEAVEN."

KAGUYA-SAMA

LOVE IS WAR

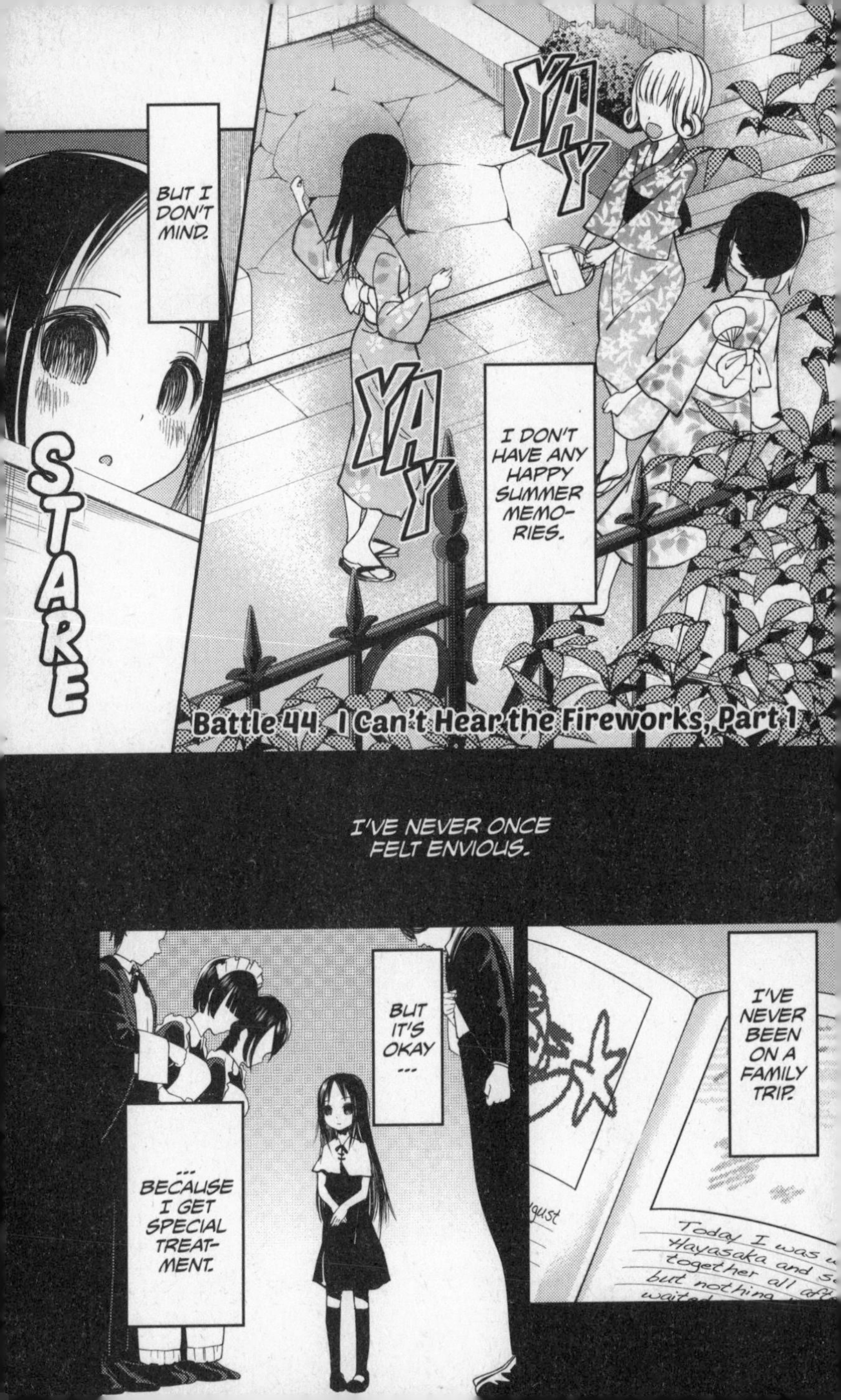
YAY
I DON'T HAVE ANY HAPPY SUMMER MEMORIES.
YAY
Battle 44 I Can't Hear the Fireworks, Part 1
BUT I DON'T MIND.
STARE
I'VE NEVER ONCE FELT ENVIOUS.
I'VE NEVER BEEN ON A FAMILY TRIP.
BUT IT'S OKAY...
...BECAUSE I GET SPECIAL TREATMENT.

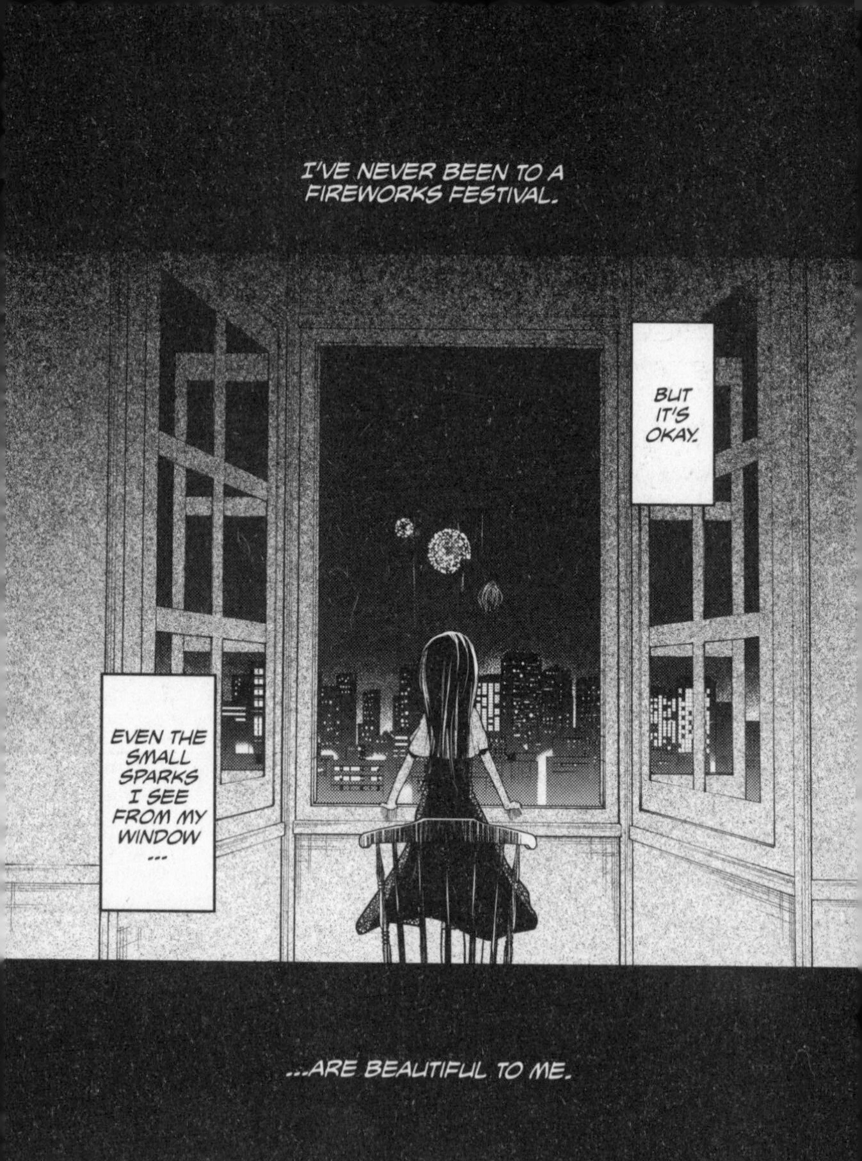
I'VE NEVER BEEN TO A FIREWORKS FESTIVAL.
BUT IT'S OKAY.
EVEN THE SMALL SPARKS I SEE FROM MY WINDOW ...
...ARE BEAUTIFUL TO ME.

Battle 44
I Can't Hear the Fireworks, Part 1

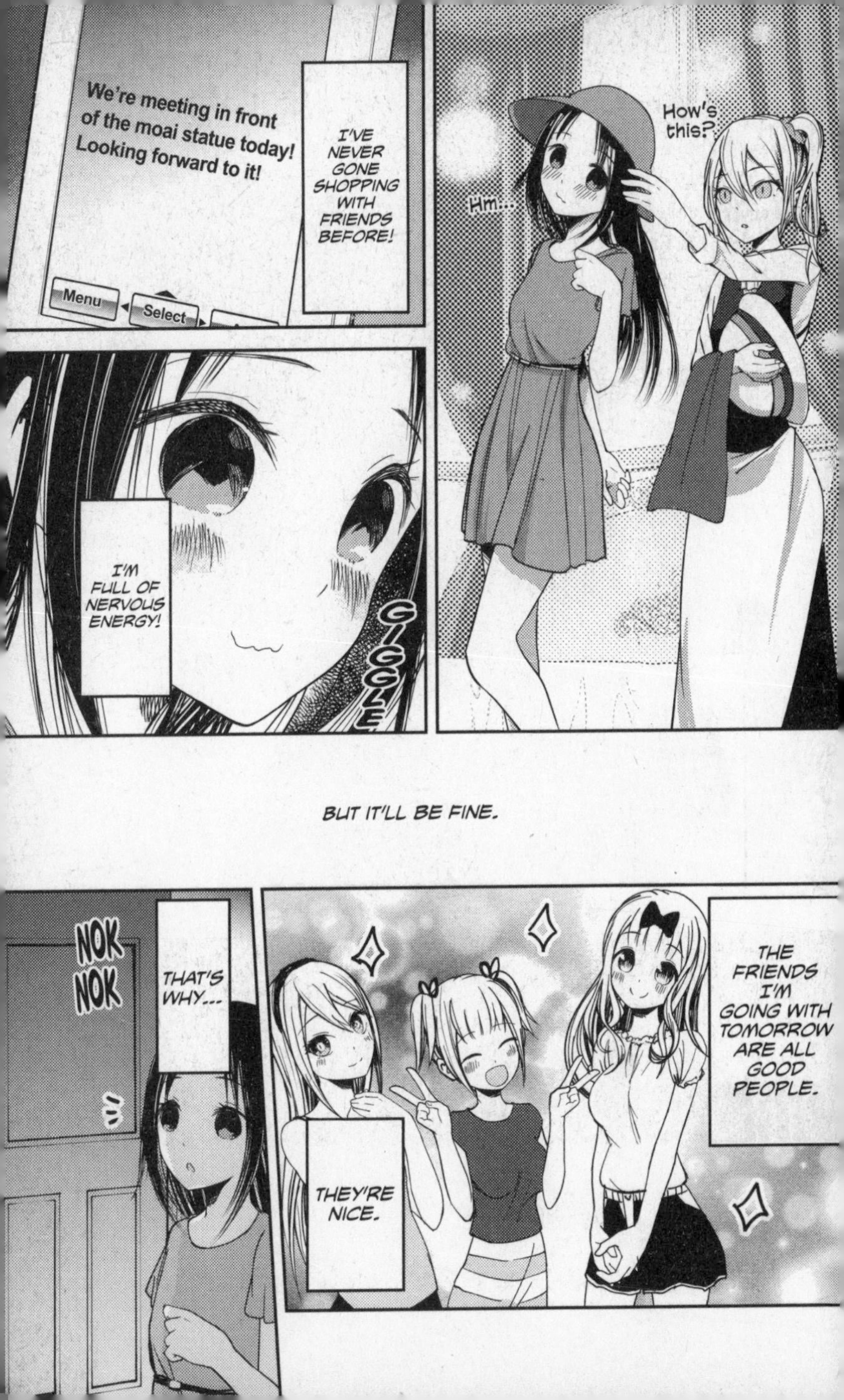
How's this?
Hm...
I'VE NEVER GONE SHOPPING WITH FRIENDS BEFORE!
We're meeting in front of the moai statue today! Looking forward to it!
Menu
Select
I'M FULL OF NERVOUS ENERGY!
GIGGLE
BUT IT'LL BE FINE.
THE FRIENDS I'M GOING WITH TOMORROW ARE ALL GOOD PEOPLE.
THEY'RE NICE.
THAT'S WHY...
NOK NOK

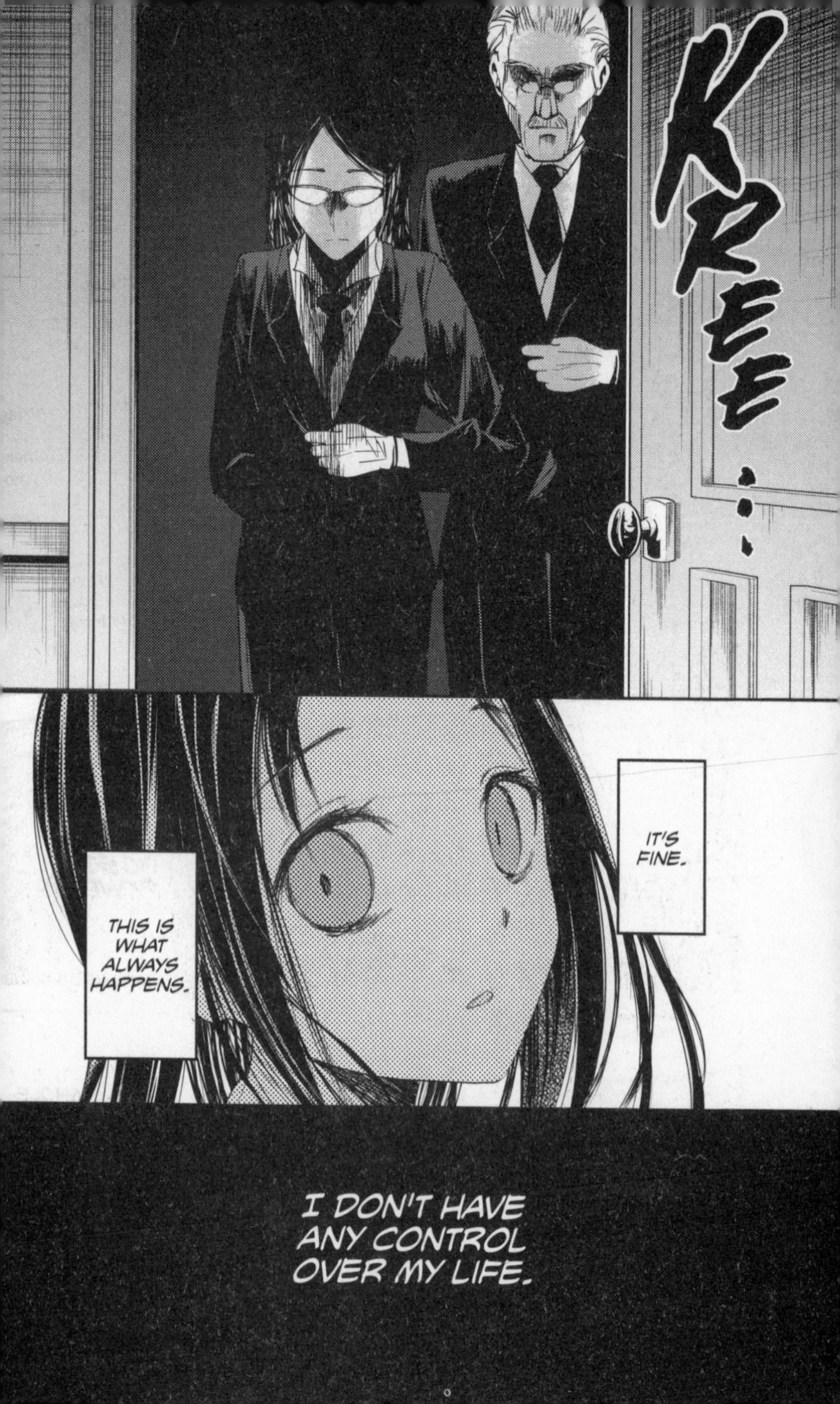
KREE...
IT'S FINE.
THIS IS WHAT ALWAYS HAPPENS.
I DON'T HAVE ANY CONTROL OVER MY LIFE.

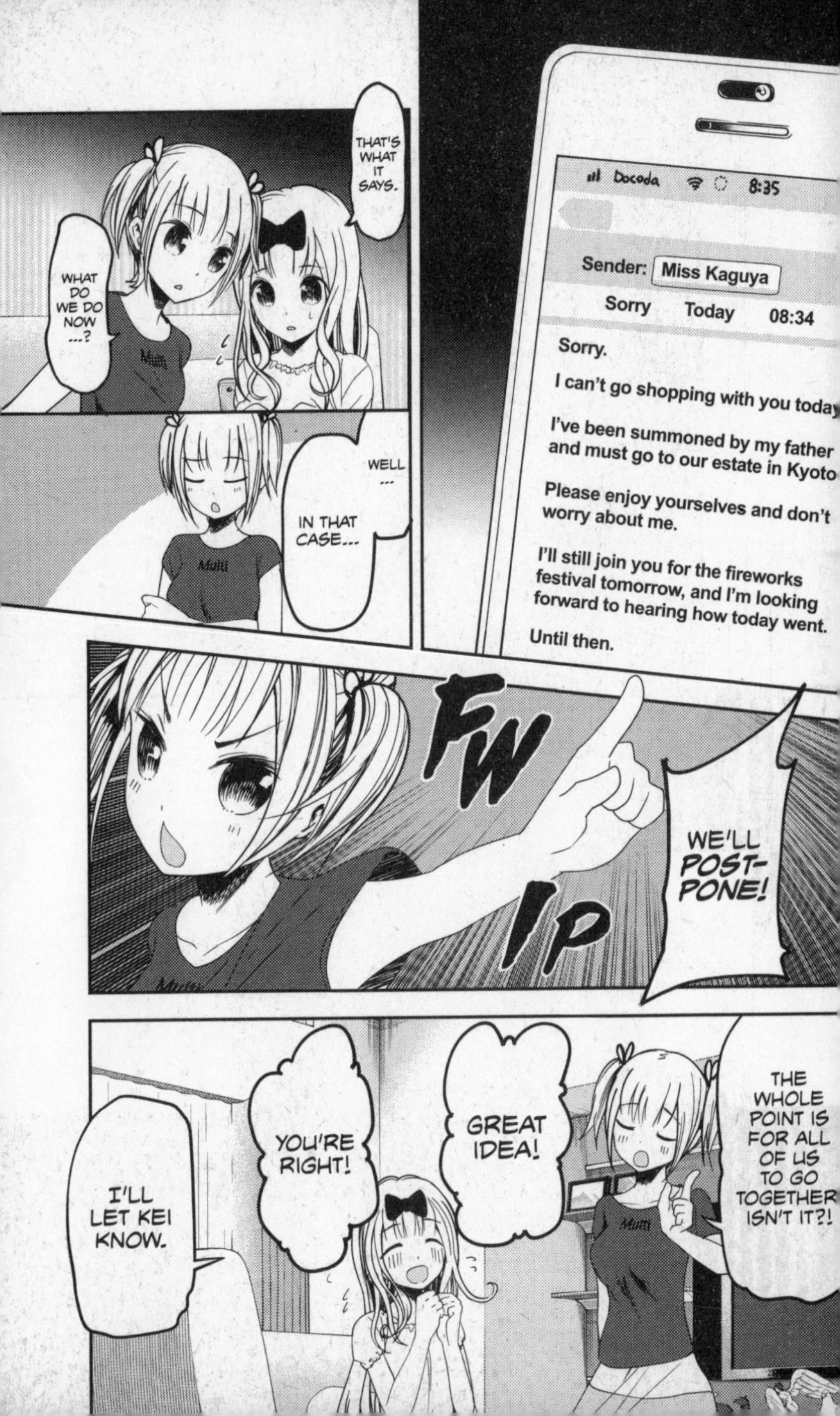
Docoda 8:35
Sender: Miss Kaguya
Sorry Today 08:34
Sorry.
I can't go shopping with you today
I've been summoned by my father and must go to our estate in Kyoto
Please enjoy yourselves and don't worry about me.
I'll still join you for the fireworks festival tomorrow, and I'm looking forward to hearing how today went.
Until then.
THAT'S WHAT IT SAYS.
WHAT DO WE DO NOW...?
WELL...
IN THAT CASE...
FWIP
WE'LL POSTPONE!
THE WHOLE POINT IS FOR ALL OF US TO GO TOGETHER ISN'T IT?!
GREAT IDEA!
YOU'RE RIGHT!
I'LL LET KEI KNOW.

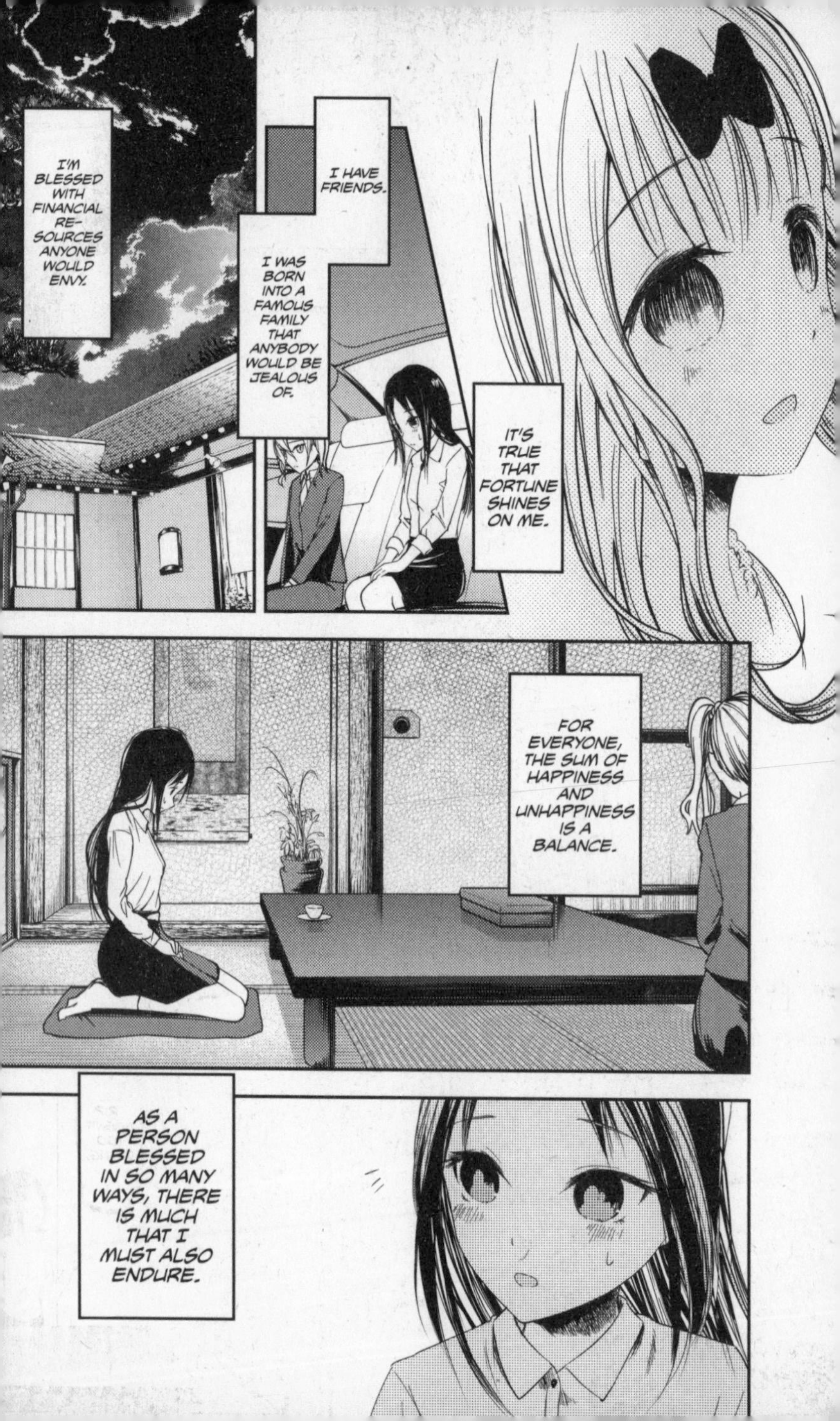
IT'S TRUE THAT FORTUNE SHINES ON ME.
I HAVE FRIENDS.
I WAS BORN INTO A FAMOUS FAMILY THAT ANYBODY WOULD BE JEALOUS OF.
I'M BLESSED WITH FINANCIAL RE-SOURCES ANYONE WOULD ENVY.
FOR EVERYONE, THE SUM OF HAPPINESS AND UNHAPPINESS IS A BALANCE.
AS A PERSON BLESSED IN SO MANY WAYS, THERE IS MUCH THAT I MUST ALSO ENDURE.

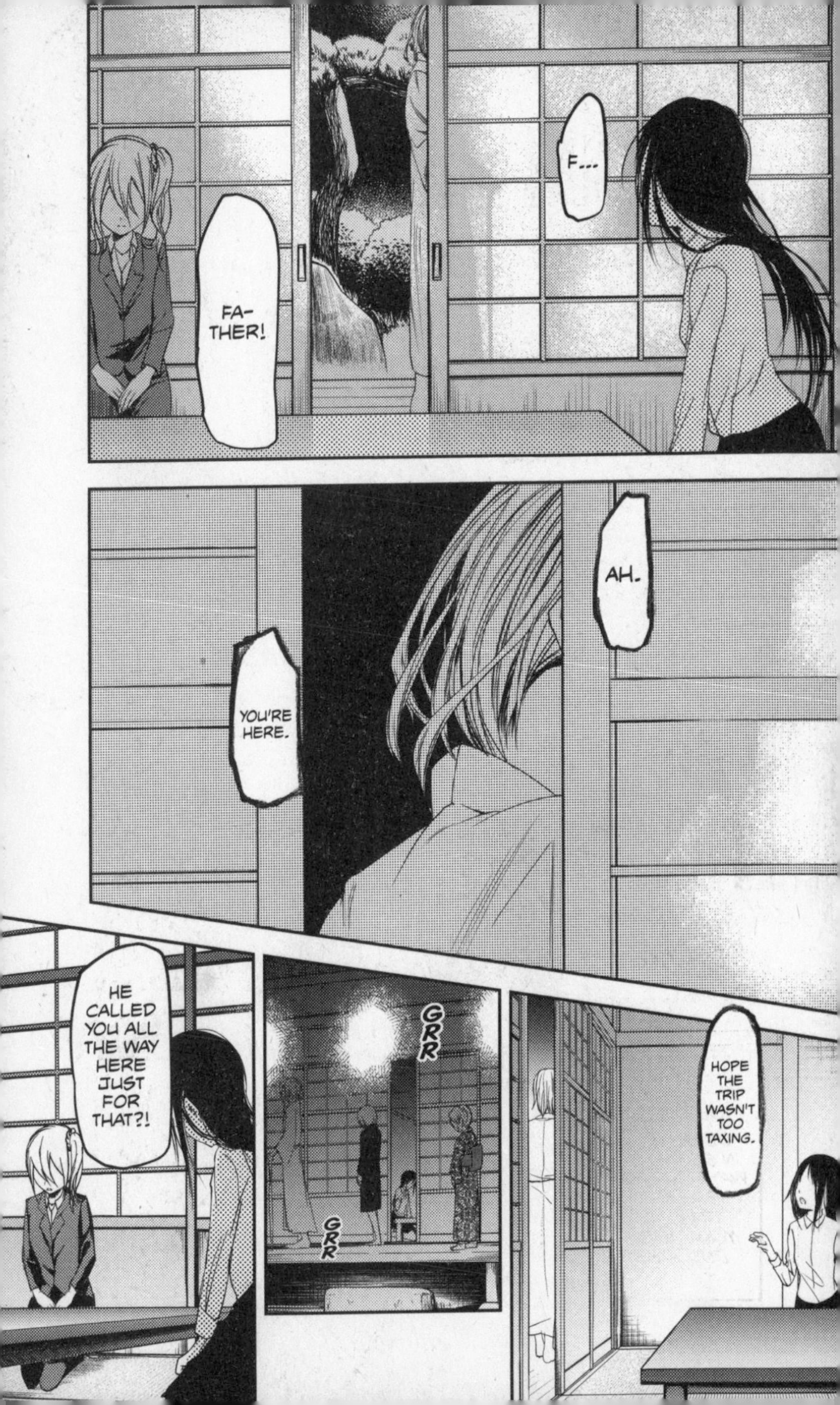

F...
FA-THER!
AH.
YOU'RE HERE.
HOPE THE TRIP WASN'T TOO TAXING.
GRR
GRR
HE CALLED YOU ALL THE WAY HERE JUST FOR THAT?!

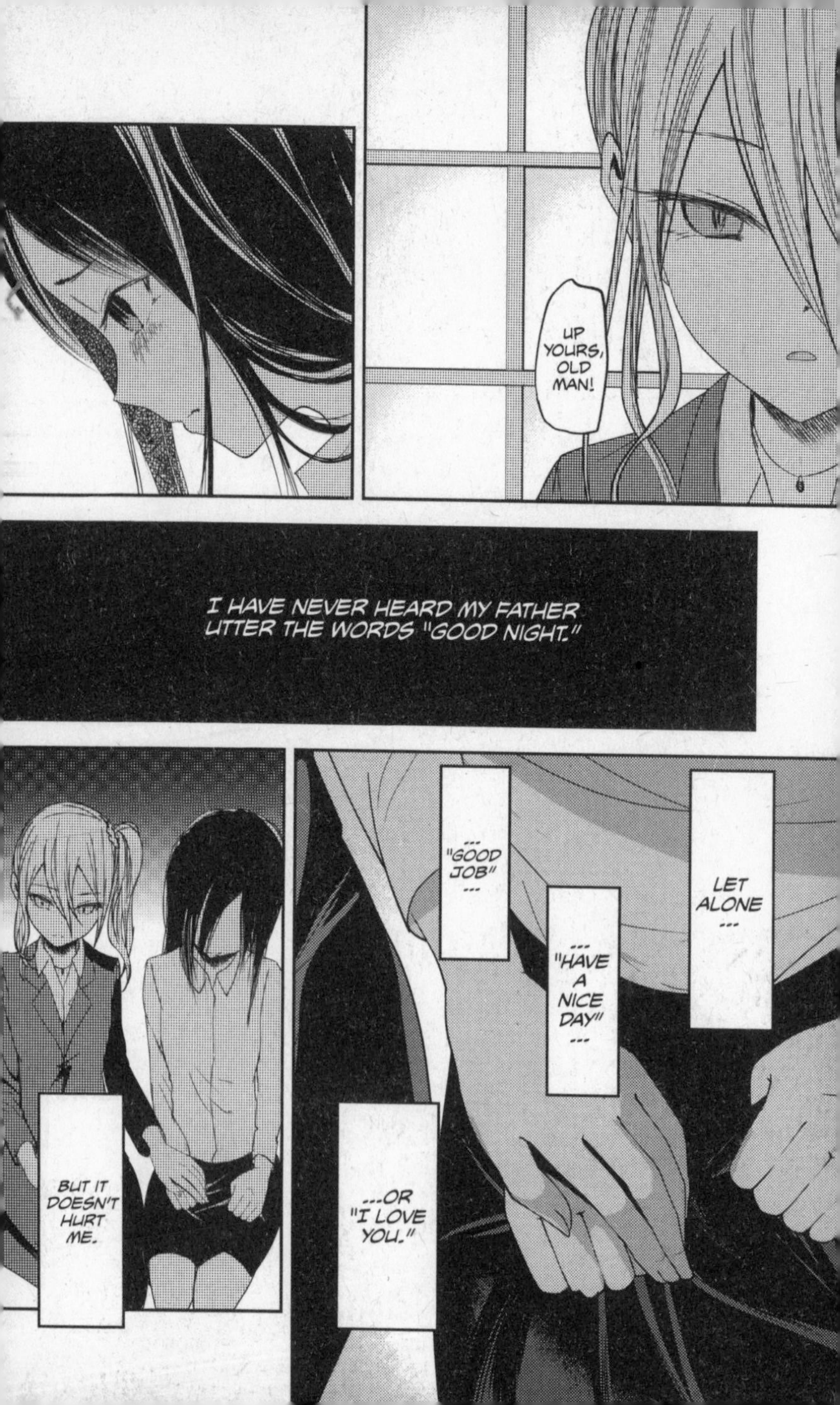
UP YOURS, OLD MAN!
I HAVE NEVER HEARD MY FATHER UTTER THE WORDS "GOOD NIGHT."
LET ALONE ---
--- "GOOD JOB" ---
--- "HAVE A NICE DAY" ---
---OR "I LOVE YOU."
BUT IT DOESN'T HURT ME.

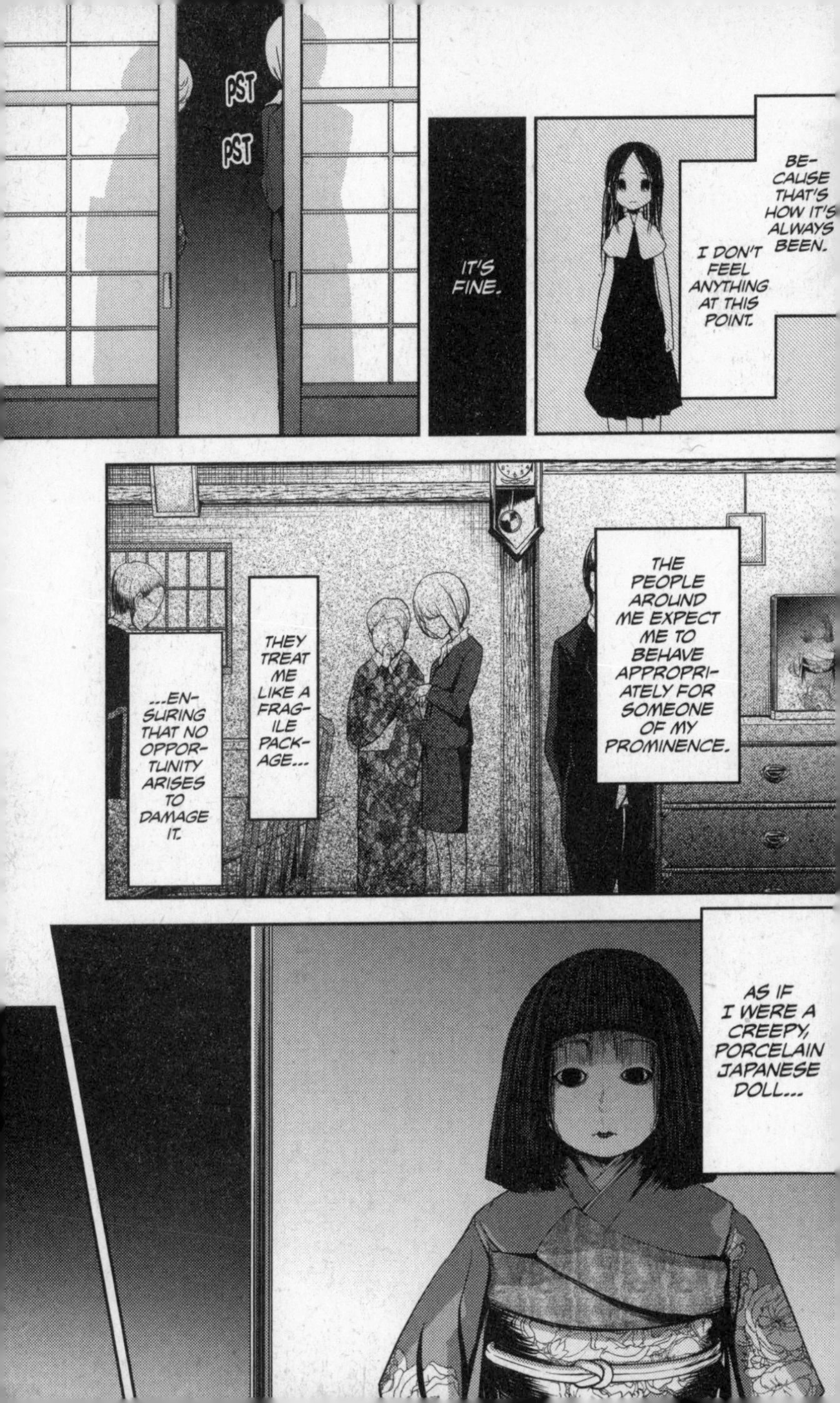
BE-CAUSE THAT'S HOW IT'S ALWAYS BEEN.
I DON'T FEEL ANYTHING AT THIS POINT.
IT'S FINE.
PST
PST
THE PEOPLE AROUND ME EXPECT ME TO BEHAVE APPROPRI-ATELY FOR SOMEONE OF MY PROMINENCE.
THEY TREAT ME LIKE A FRAG-ILE PACK-AGE...
...EN-SURING THAT NO OPPOR-TUNITY ARISES TO DAMAGE IT.
AS IF I WERE A CREEPY, PORCELAIN JAPANESE DOLL...

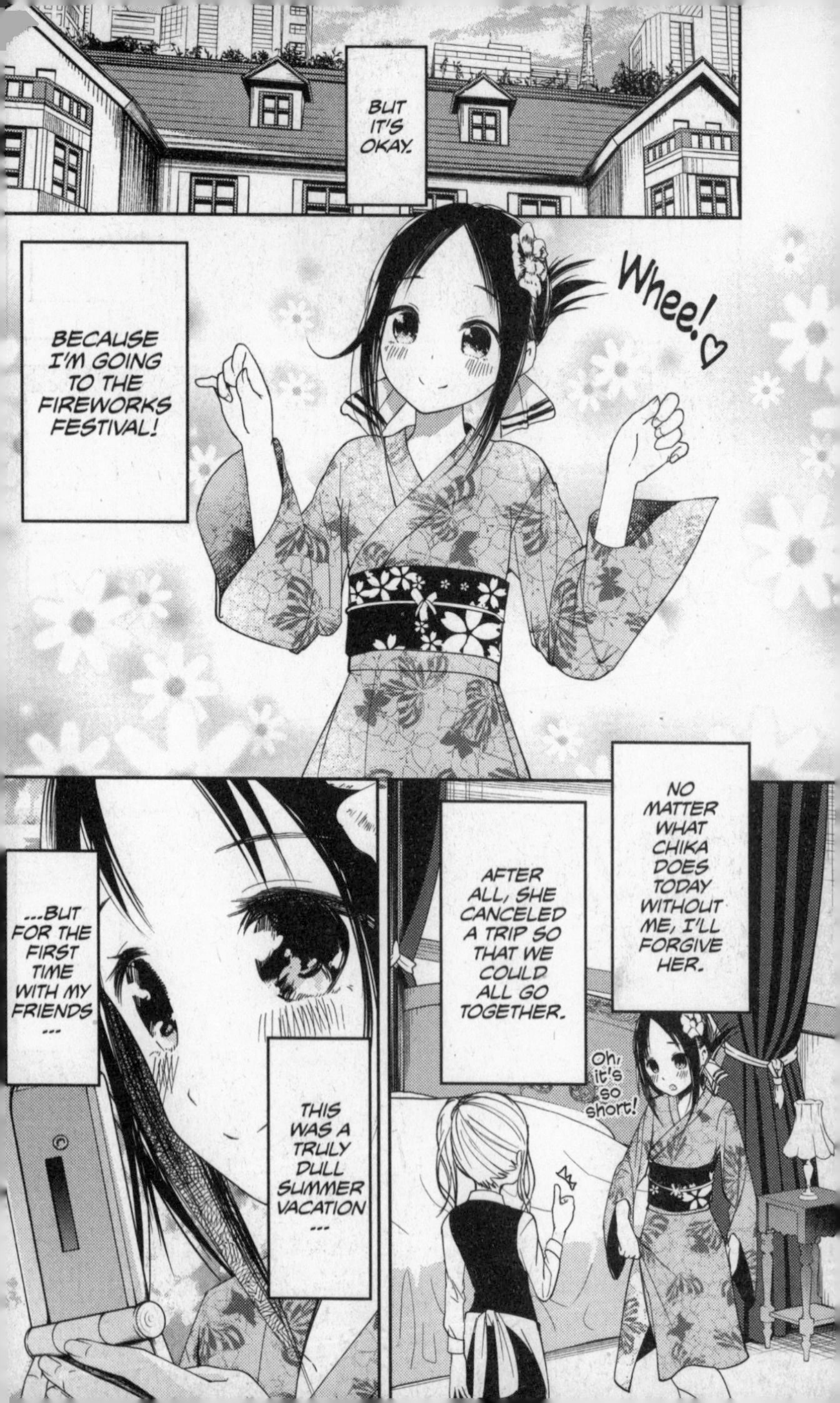
BUT IT'S OKAY.
BECAUSE I'M GOING TO THE FIREWORKS FESTIVAL!
Whee! ♡
NO MATTER WHAT CHIKA DOES TODAY WITHOUT ME, I'LL FORGIVE HER.
AFTER ALL, SHE CANCELED A TRIP SO THAT WE COULD ALL GO TOGETHER.
Oh, it's so short!
THIS WAS A TRULY DULL SUMMER VACATION...
...BUT FOR THE FIRST TIME WITH MY FRIENDS...

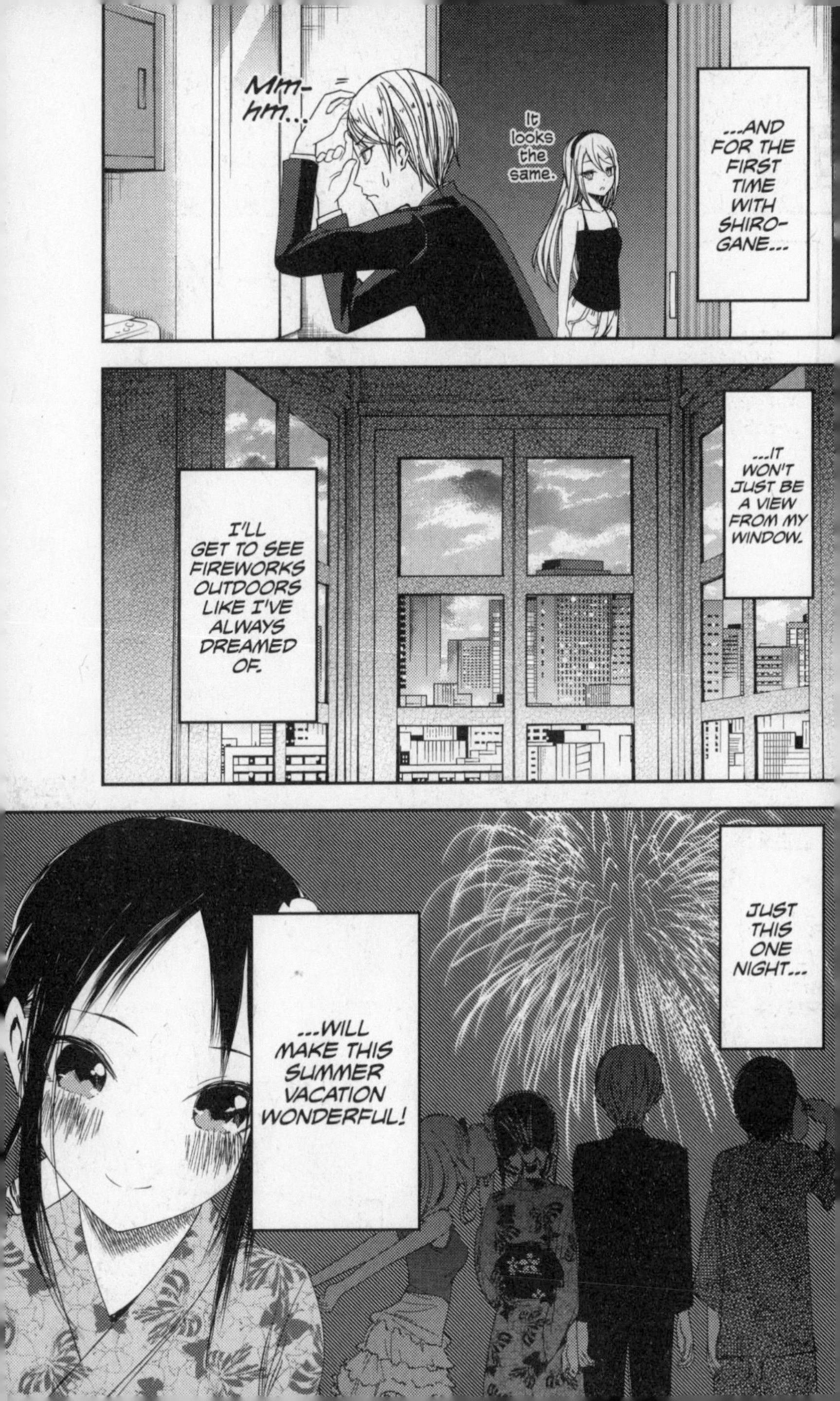
...AND FOR THE FIRST TIME WITH SHIROGANE...
It looks the same.
Mm-hm...
...IT WON'T JUST BE A VIEW FROM MY WINDOW.
I'LL GET TO SEE FIREWORKS OUTDOORS LIKE I'VE ALWAYS DREAMED OF.
JUST THIS ONE NIGHT...
...WILL MAKE THIS SUMMER VACATION WONDERFUL!

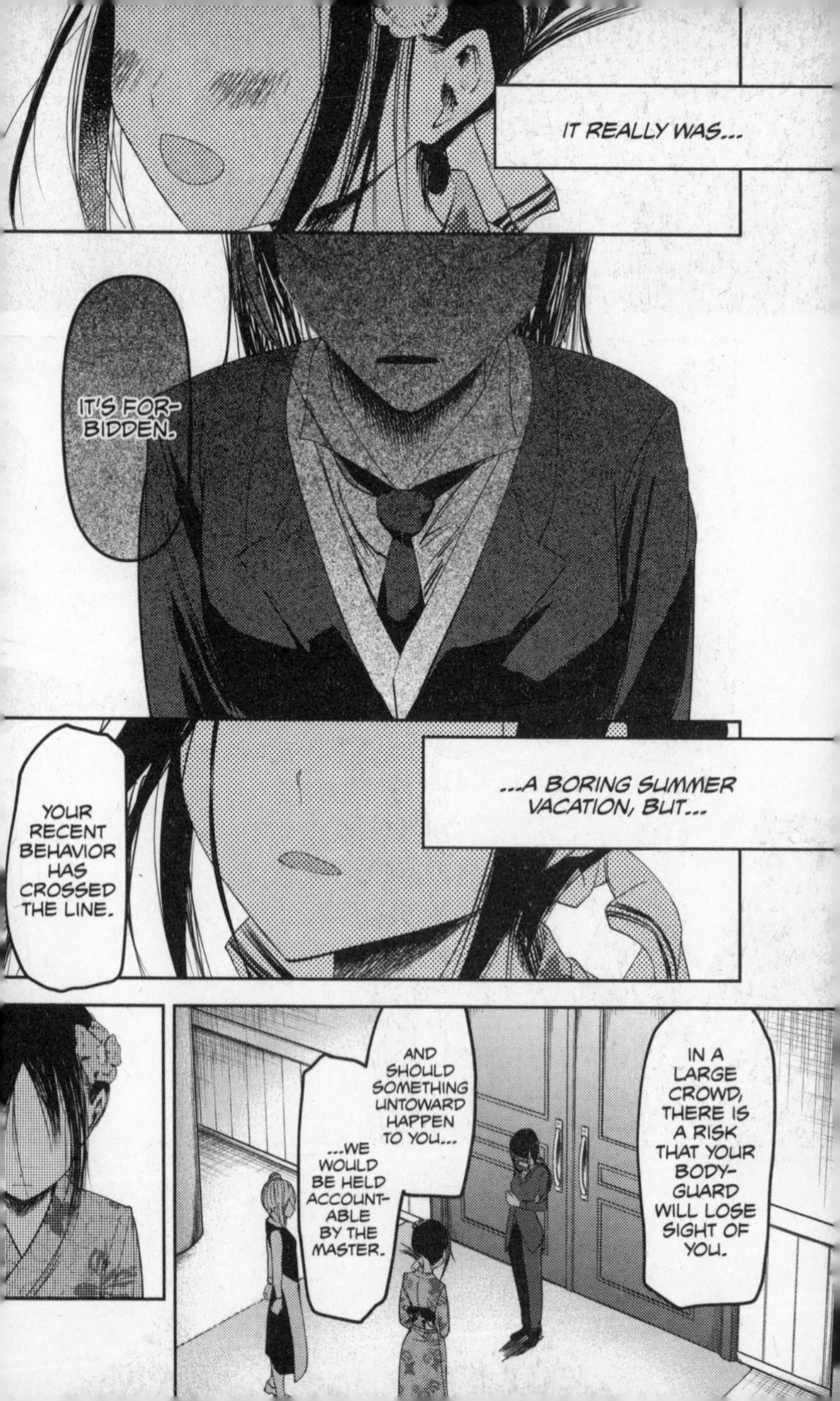
IT REALLY WAS...
IT'S FORBIDDEN.
...A BORING SUMMER VACATION, BUT...
YOUR RECENT BEHAVIOR HAS CROSSED THE LINE.
IN A LARGE CROWD, THERE IS A RISK THAT YOUR BODYGUARD WILL LOSE SIGHT OF YOU.
AND SHOULD SOMETHING UNTOWARD HAPPEN TO YOU...
...WE WOULD BE HELD ACCOUNTABLE BY THE MASTER.

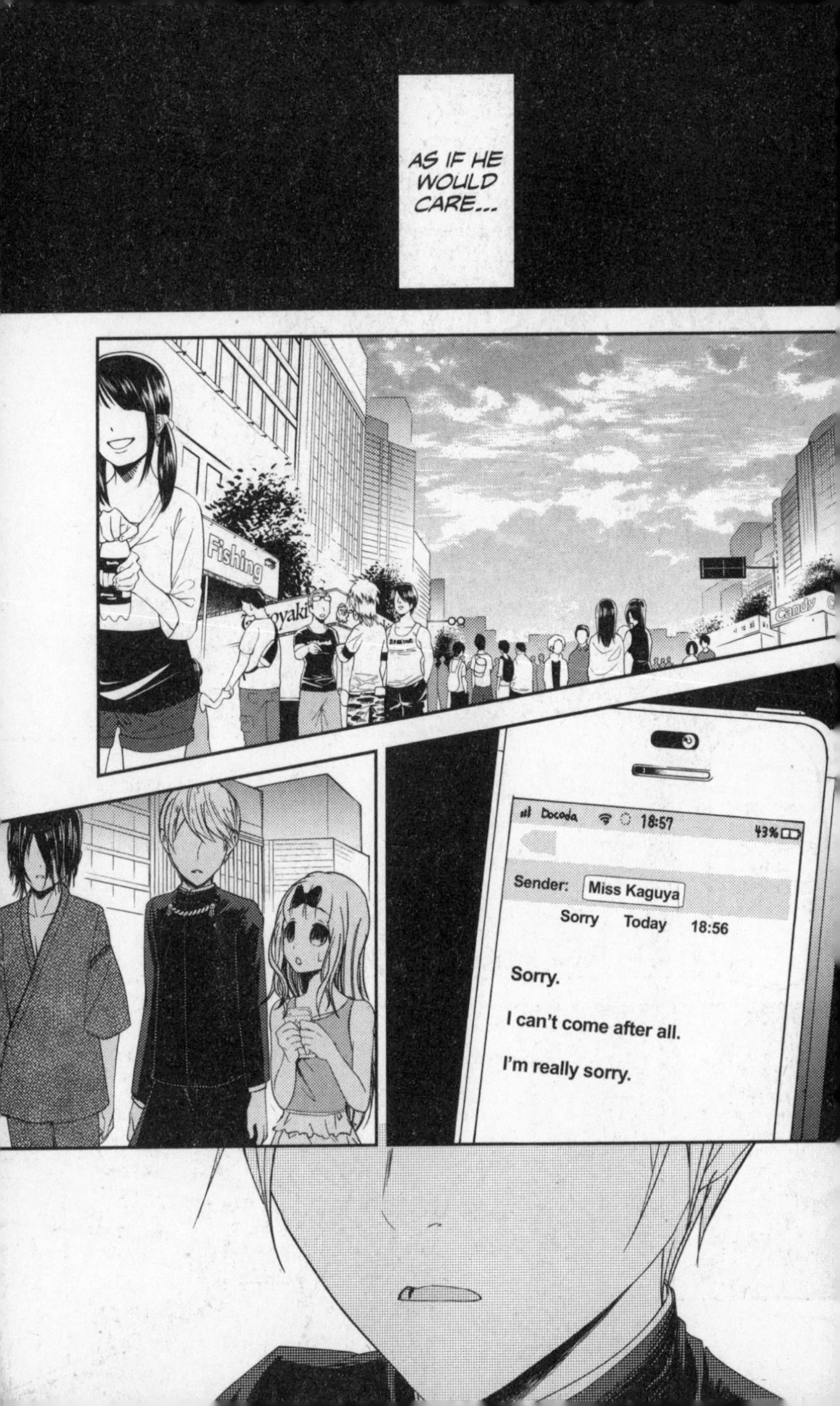
AS IF HE WOULD CARE...
Fishing
Candy
Docoda 18:57 43%
Sender: Miss Kaguya
Sorry Today 18:56
Sorry.
I can't come after all.
I'm really sorry.

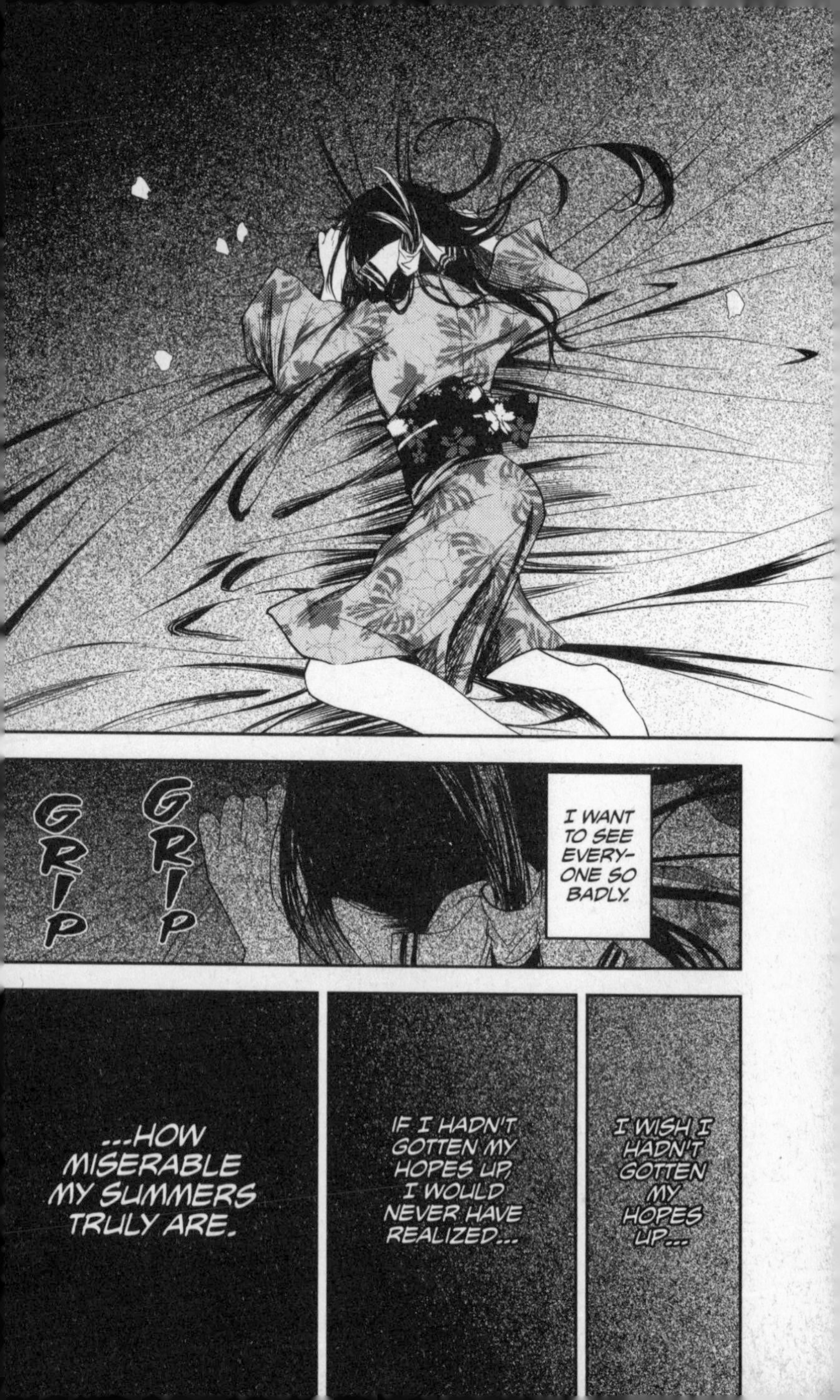
I WANT TO SEE EVERYONE SO BADLY.
GRIP
GRIP
I WISH I HADN'T GOTTEN MY HOPES UP...
IF I HADN'T GOTTEN MY HOPES UP, I WOULD NEVER HAVE REALIZED...
...HOW MISERABLE MY SUMMERS TRULY ARE.

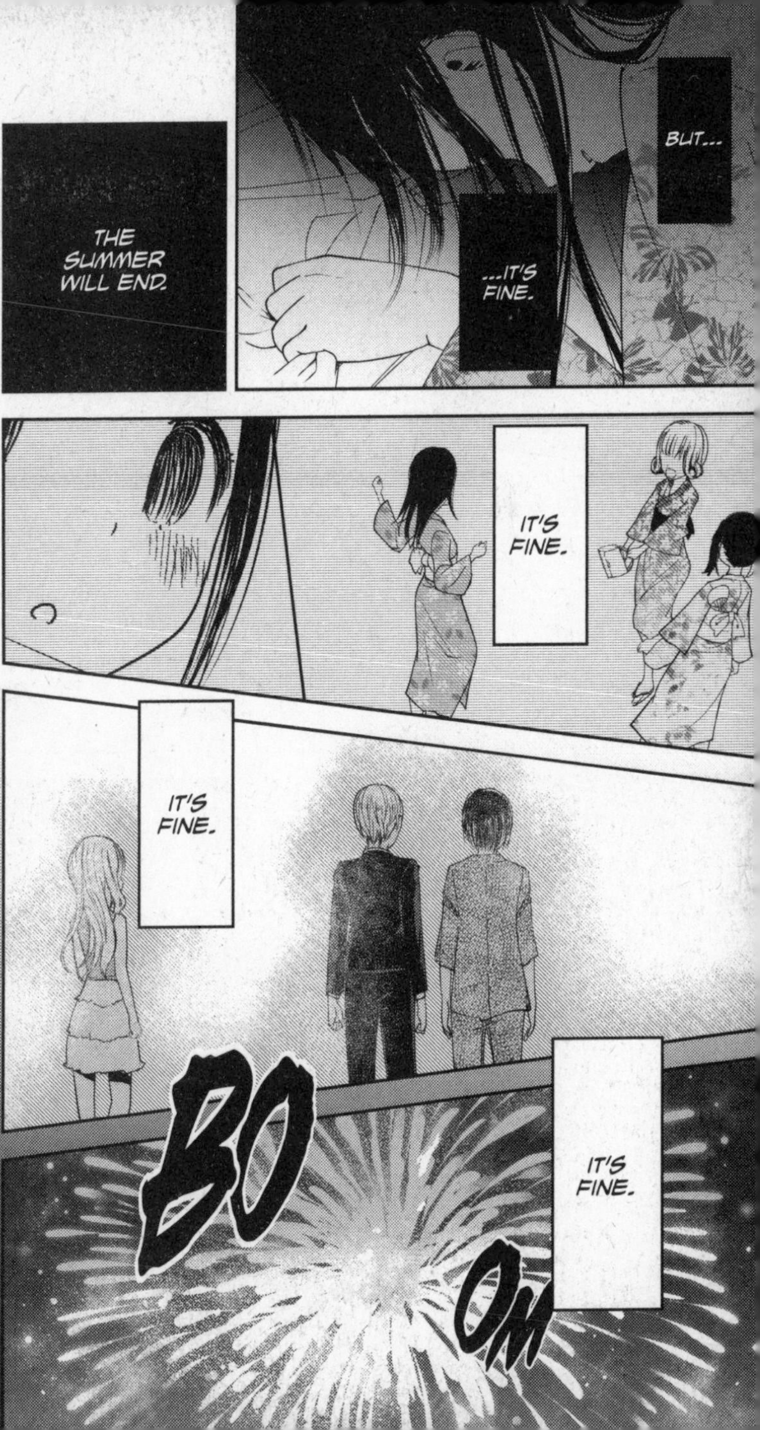
BUT...
...IT'S FINE.
THE SUMMER WILL END.
IT'S FINE.
IT'S FINE.
IT'S FINE.
BOOM

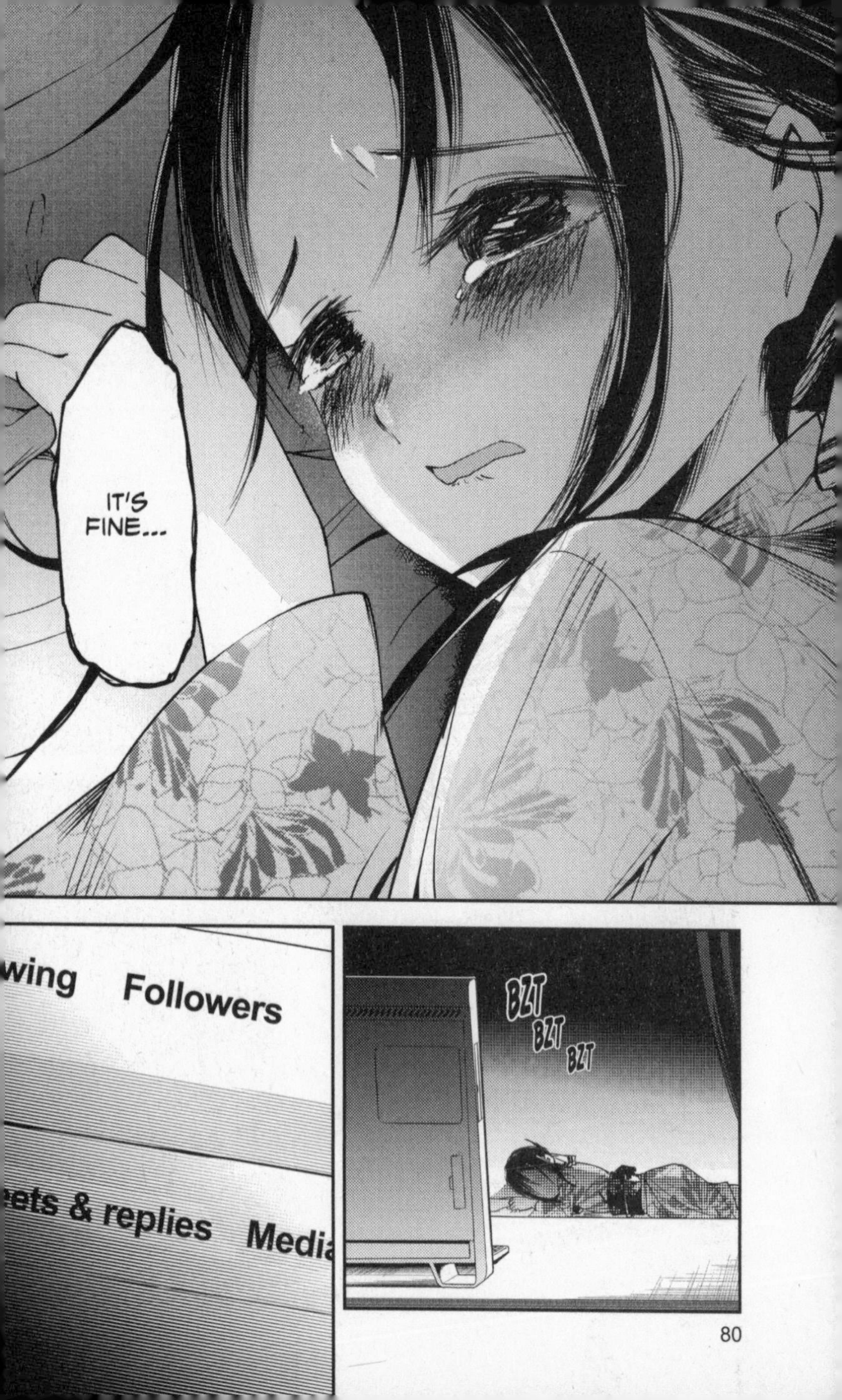
IT'S FINE...
BZT
BZT
BZT
wing Followers
eets & replies Media

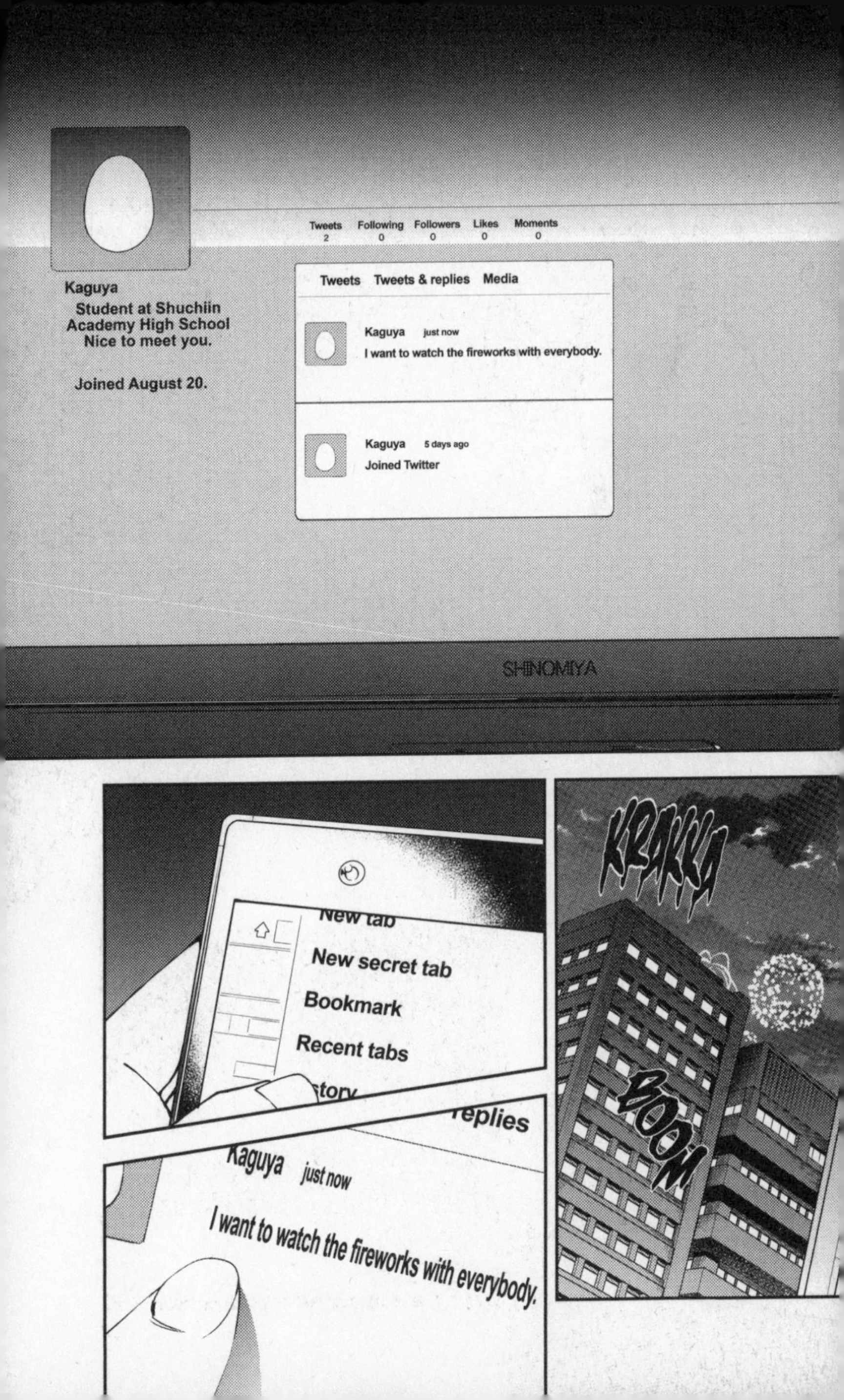
Tweets 2
Following 0
Followers 0
Likes 0
Moments 0
Kaguya
Student at Shuchiin Academy High School
Nice to meet you.
Joined August 20.
Tweets
Tweets & replies
Media
Kaguya just now
I want to watch the fireworks with everybody.
Kaguya 5 days ago
Joined Twitter
SHINOMIYA
KRAKKA
BOOM
New tab
New secret tab
Bookmark
Recent tabs
replies
Kaguya just now
I want to watch the fireworks with everybody.

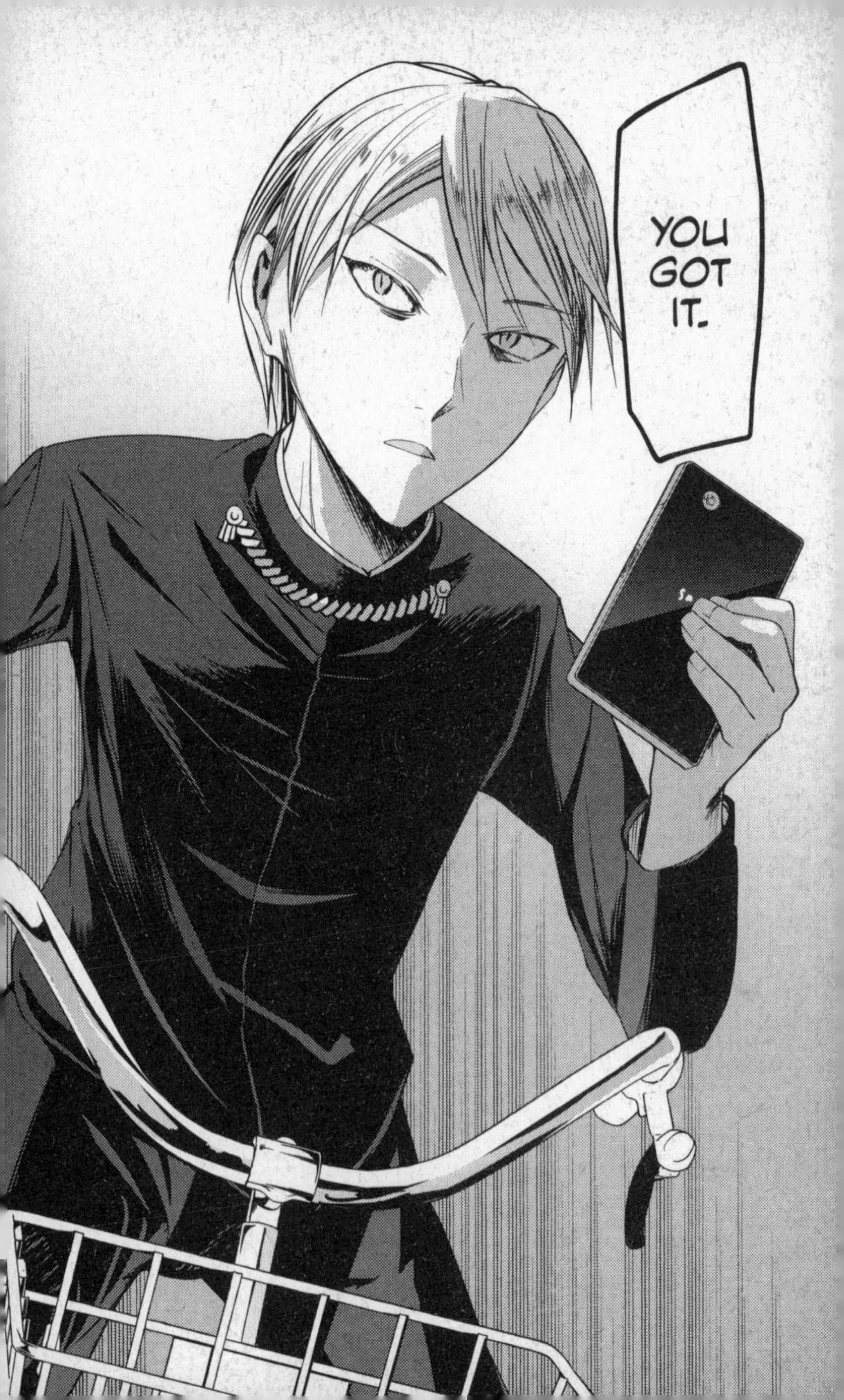
YOU GOT IT.

KAGUYA-SAMA
LOVE IS WAR

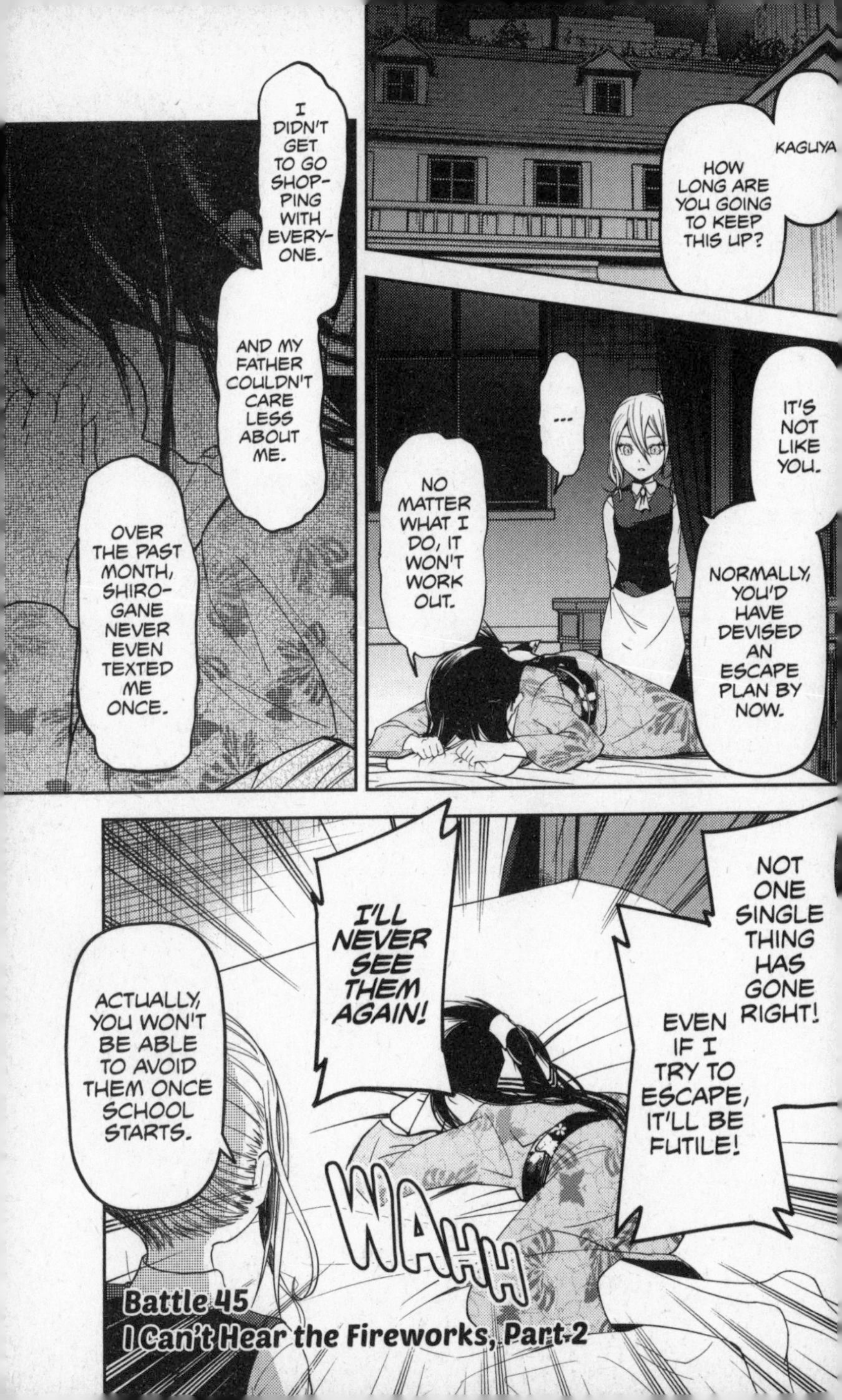
KAGUYA
HOW LONG ARE YOU GOING TO KEEP THIS UP?
IT'S NOT LIKE YOU.
NORMALLY, YOU'D HAVE DEVISED AN ESCAPE PLAN BY NOW.
...
NO MATTER WHAT I DO, IT WON'T WORK OUT.
I DIDN'T GET TO GO SHOP-PING WITH EVERY-ONE.
AND MY FATHER COULDN'T CARE LESS ABOUT ME.
OVER THE PAST MONTH, SHIRO-GANE NEVER EVEN TEXTED ME ONCE.
NOT ONE SINGLE THING HAS GONE RIGHT!
EVEN IF I TRY TO ESCAPE, IT'LL BE FUTILE!
I'LL NEVER SEE THEM AGAIN!
WAHHH
ACTUALLY, YOU WON'T BE ABLE TO AVOID THEM ONCE SCHOOL STARTS.
Battle 45
I Can't Hear the Fireworks, Part 2

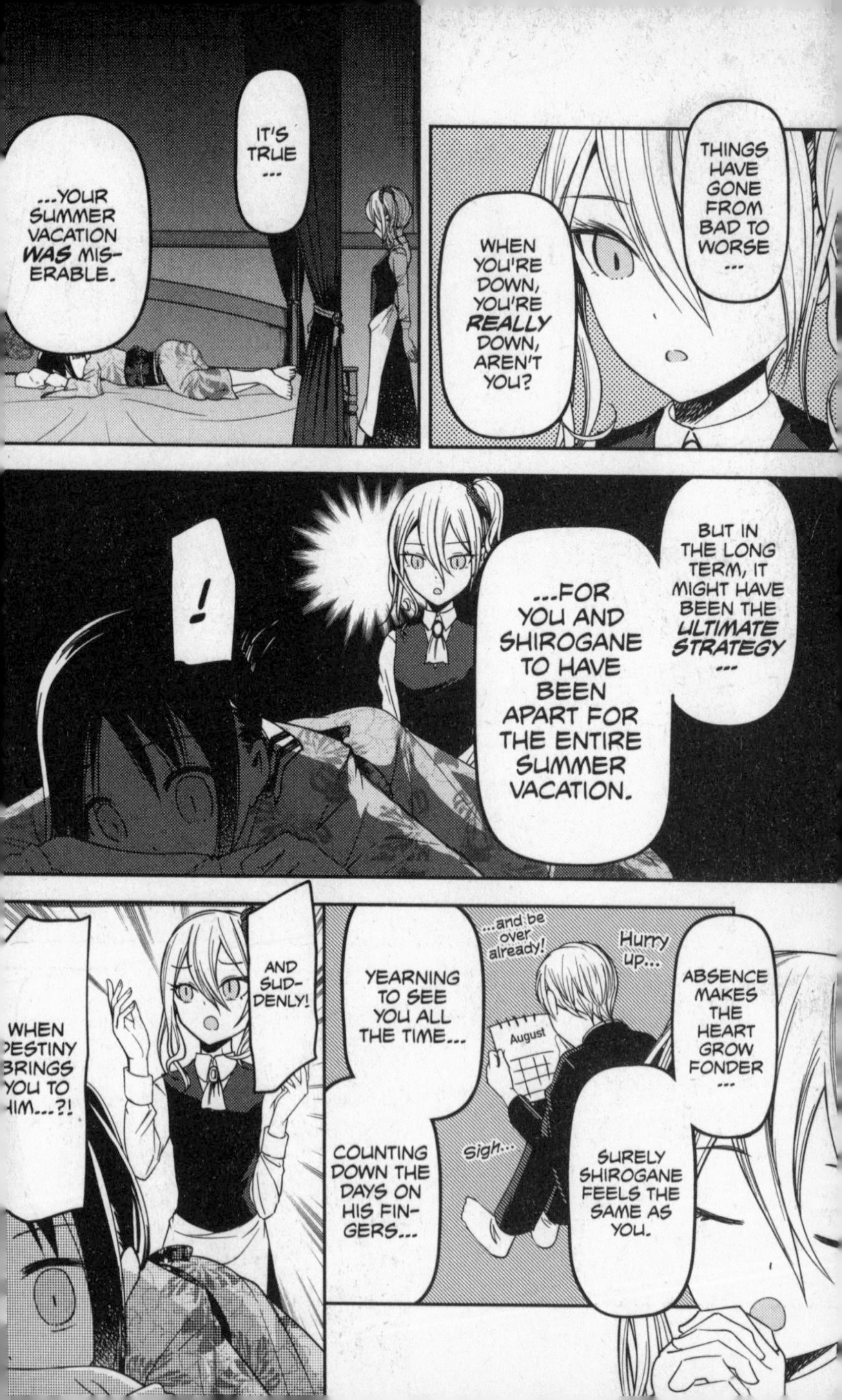
THINGS HAVE GONE FROM BAD TO WORSE ...
WHEN YOU'RE DOWN, YOU'RE REALLY DOWN, AREN'T YOU?
IT'S TRUE ...
...YOUR SUMMER VACATION WAS MISERABLE.
BUT IN THE LONG TERM, IT MIGHT HAVE BEEN THE ULTIMATE STRATEGY ...
...FOR YOU AND SHIROGANE TO HAVE BEEN APART FOR THE ENTIRE SUMMER VACATION.
!
ABSENCE MAKES THE HEART GROW FONDER ...
SURELY SHIROGANE FEELS THE SAME AS YOU.
Hurry up...
...and be over already!
August
Sigh...
YEARNING TO SEE YOU ALL THE TIME...
COUNTING DOWN THE DAYS ON HIS FINGERS...
AND SUDDENLY!
WHEN DESTINY BRINGS YOU TO HIM...?!

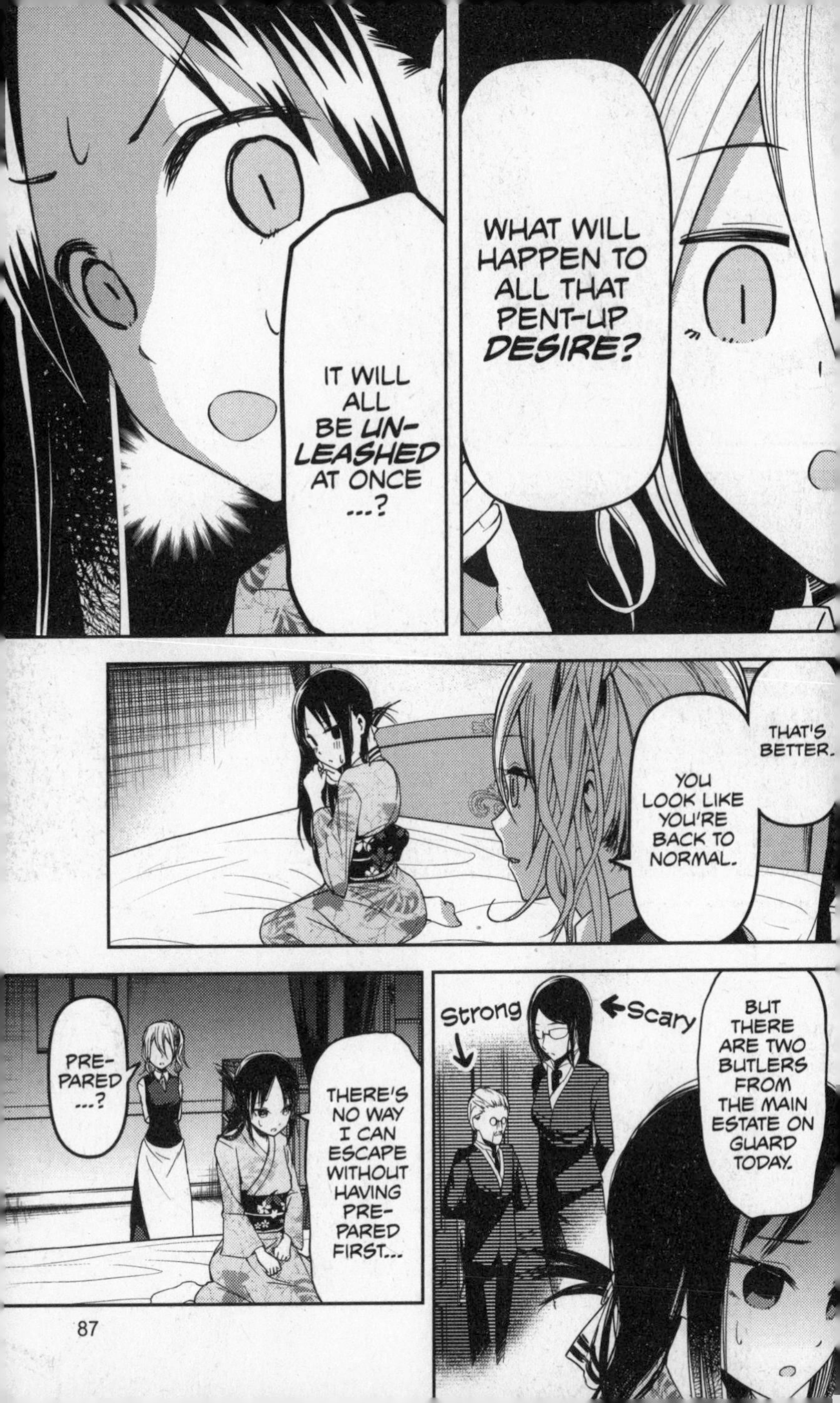
WHAT WILL HAPPEN TO ALL THAT PENT-UP *DESIRE?*
IT WILL ALL BE *UN-LEASHED* AT ONCE ...?
THAT'S BETTER.
YOU LOOK LIKE YOU'RE BACK TO NORMAL.
BUT THERE ARE TWO BUTLERS FROM THE MAIN ESTATE ON GUARD TODAY.
Scary
Strong
THERE'S NO WAY I CAN ESCAPE WITHOUT HAVING PRE-PARED FIRST...
PRE-PARED ...?

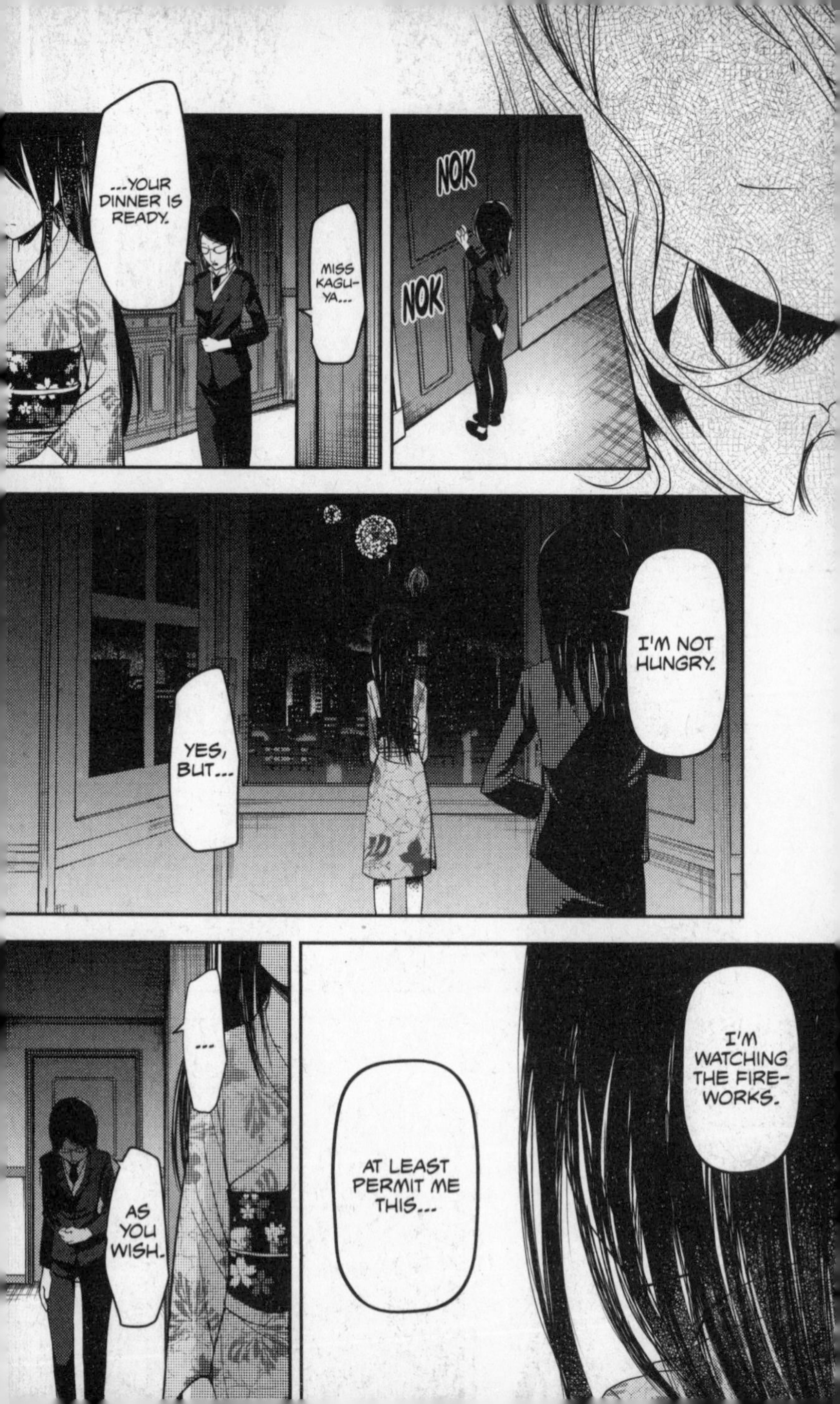
NOK
NOK
MISS KAGUYA...
...YOUR DINNER IS READY.
I'M NOT HUNGRY.
YES, BUT...
I'M WATCHING THE FIRE-WORKS.
AT LEAST PERMIT ME THIS...
...
AS YOU WISH.

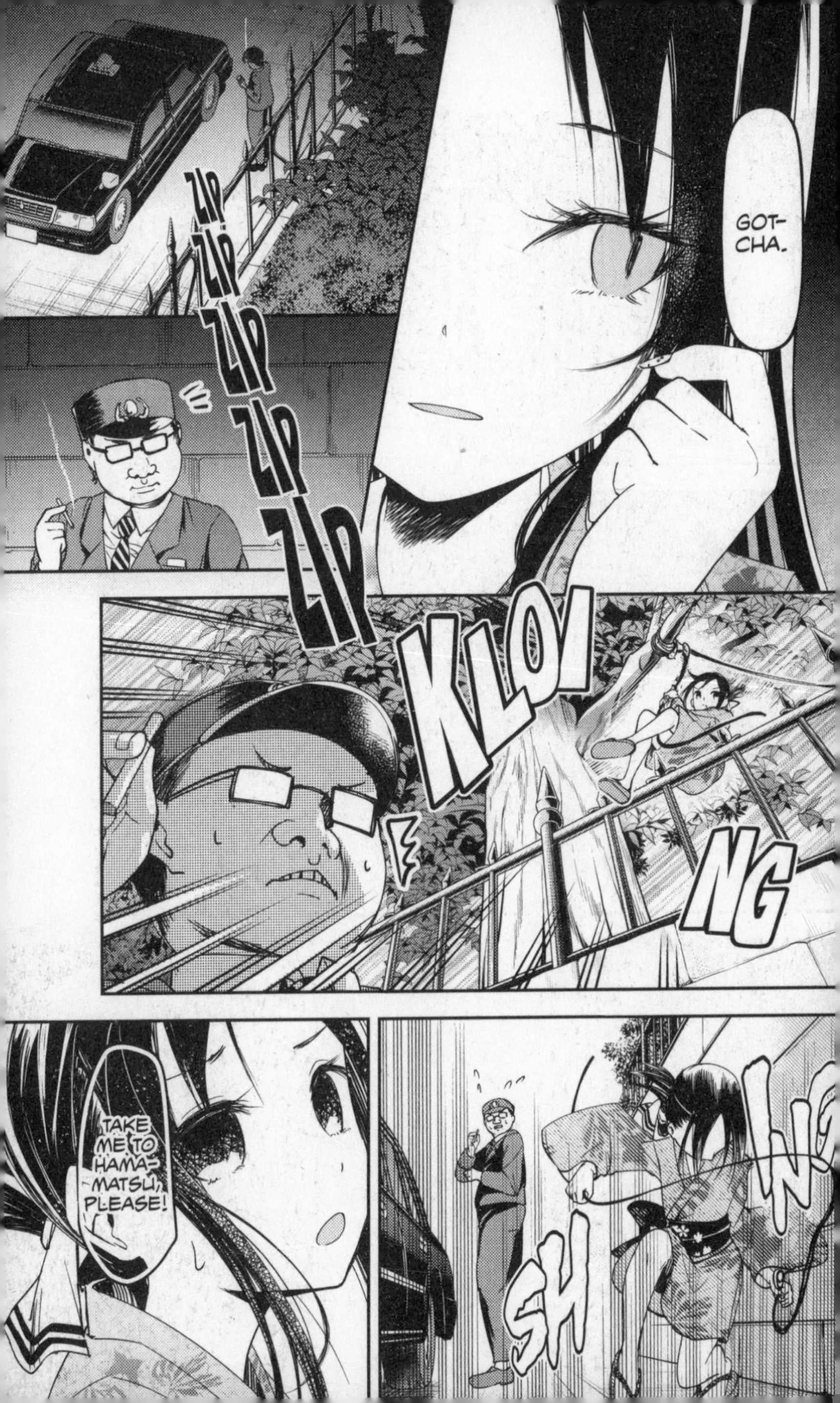
GOT-CHA.
ZIP ZIP ZIP ZIP ZIP ZIP
KLON
NG
SH
TAKE ME TO HAMA-MATSU, PLEASE!

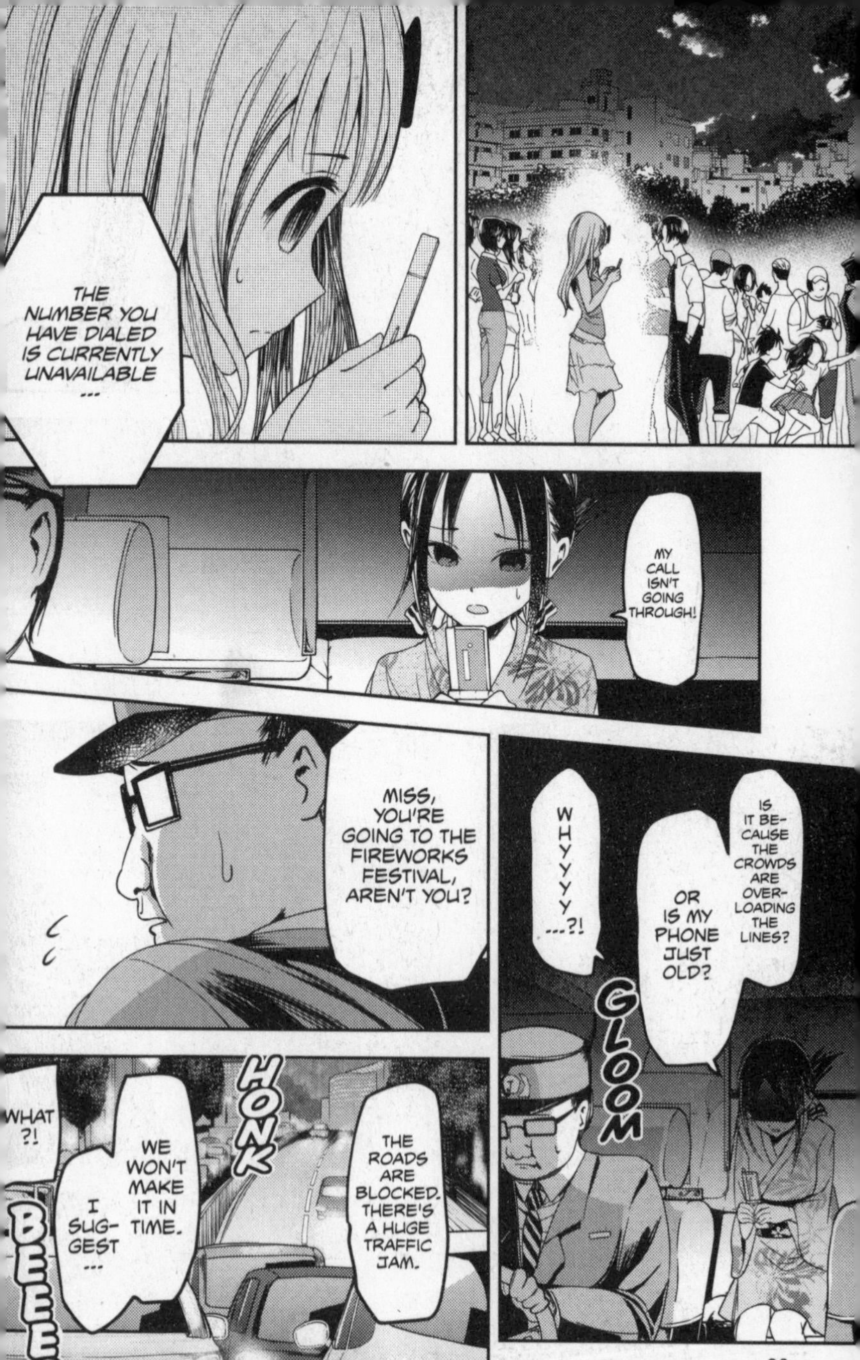
THE NUMBER YOU HAVE DIALED IS CURRENTLY UNAVAILABLE ...
MY CALL ISN'T GOING THROUGH!
IS IT BECAUSE THE CROWDS ARE OVER-LOADING THE LINES?
OR IS MY PHONE JUST OLD?
WHYYYY ...?!
GLOOM
MISS, YOU'RE GOING TO THE FIREWORKS FESTIVAL, AREN'T YOU?
THE ROADS ARE BLOCKED. THERE'S A HUGE TRAFFIC JAM.
HONK
WE WON'T MAKE IT IN TIME.
I SUG-GEST ...
WHAT ?!
BEEEP

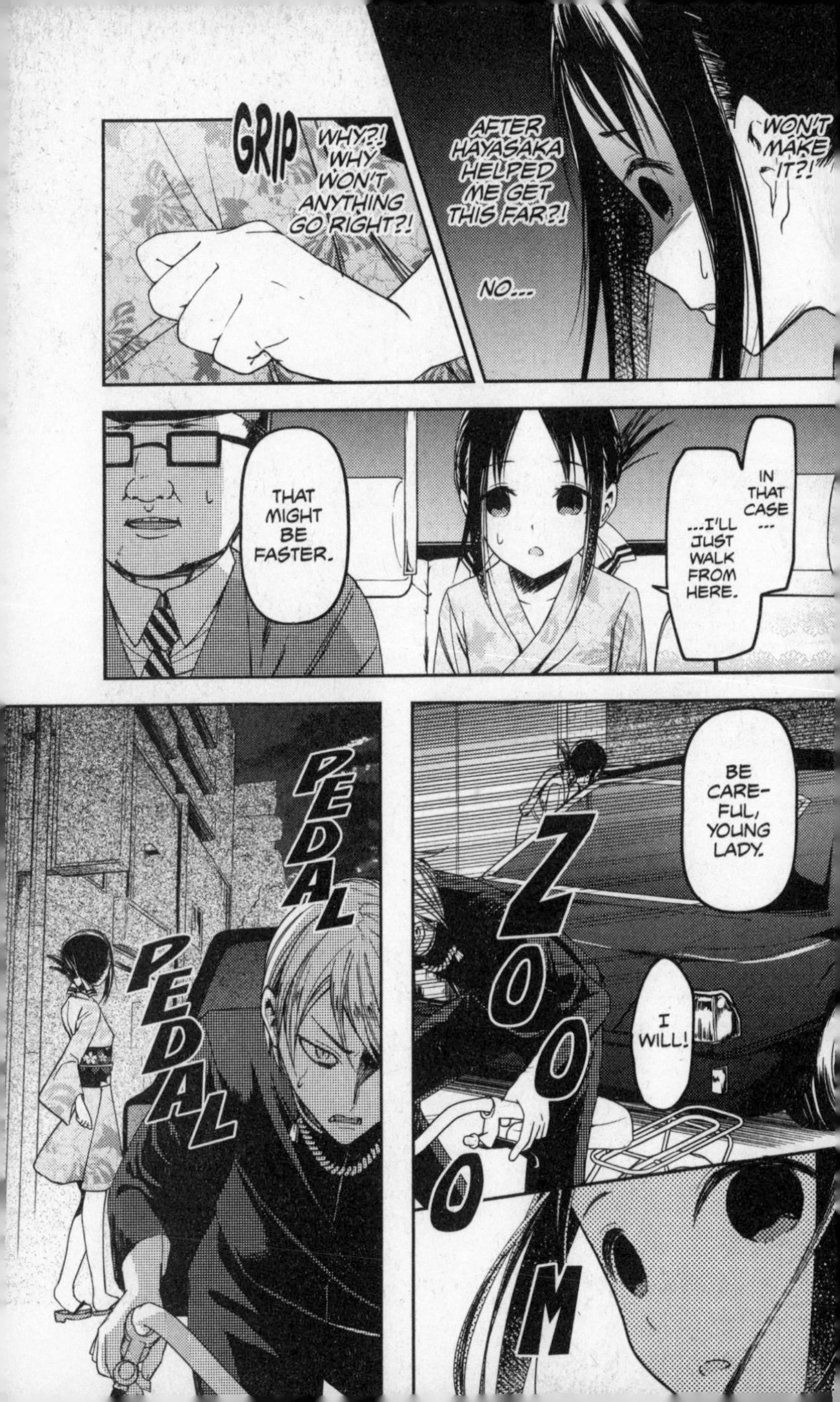
WON'T MAKE IT?!
AFTER HAYASAKA HELPED ME GET THIS FAR?!
NO...
WHY?! WHY WON'T ANYTHING GO RIGHT?!
GRIP
IN THAT CASE ---
...I'LL JUST WALK FROM HERE.
THAT MIGHT BE FASTER.
BE CARE-FUL, YOUNG LADY.
I WILL!
ZOOOOM
PEDAL
PEDAL

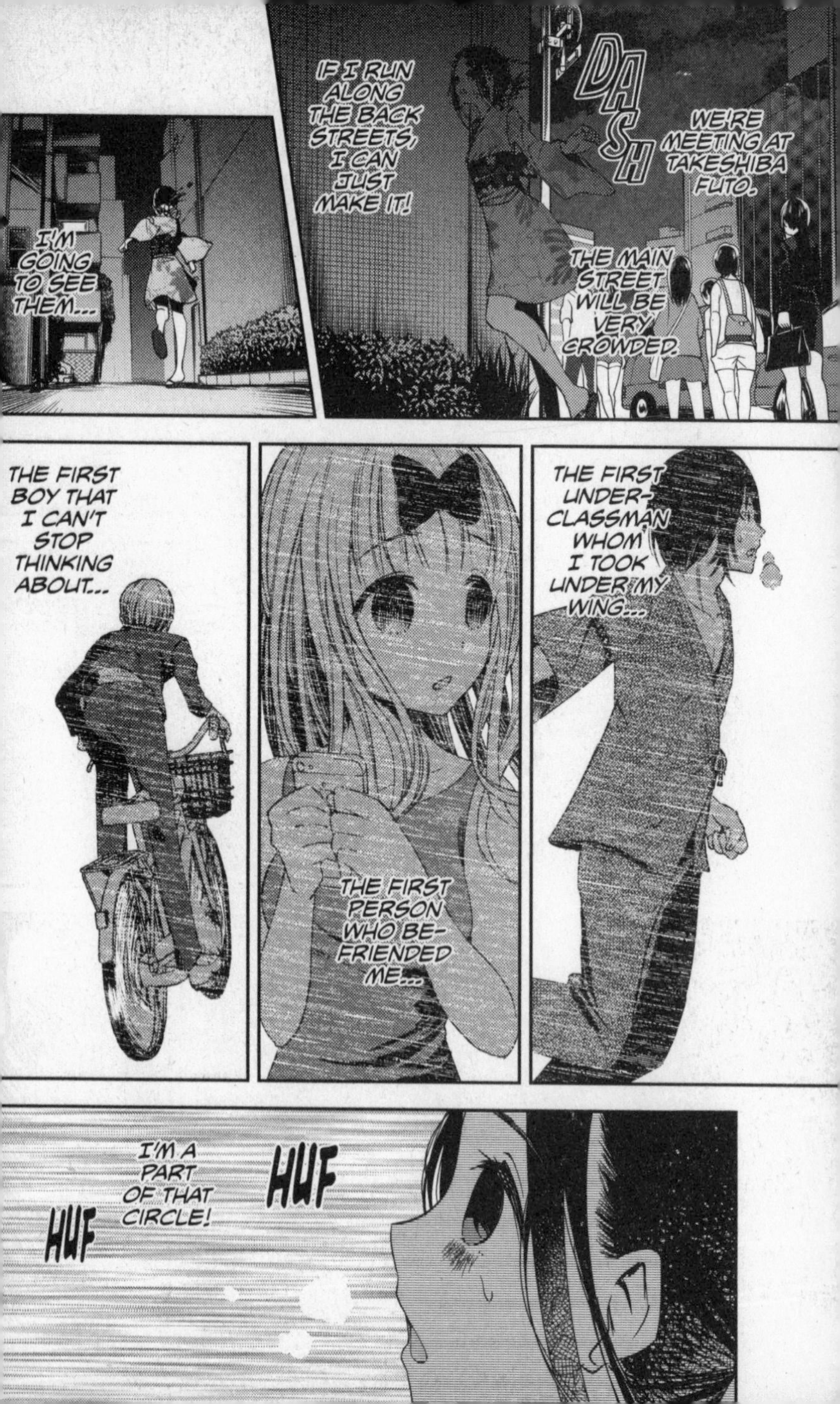
WE'RE MEETING AT TAKESHIBA FUTO.
DASH
IF I RUN ALONG THE BACK STREETS, I CAN JUST MAKE IT!
THE MAIN STREET WILL BE VERY CROWDED.
I'M GOING TO SEE THEM...
THE FIRST UNDER-CLASSMAN WHOM I TOOK UNDER MY WING...
THE FIRST PERSON WHO BE-FRIENDED ME...
THE FIRST BOY THAT I CAN'T STOP THINKING ABOUT...
HUF
I'M A PART OF THAT CIRCLE!
HUF

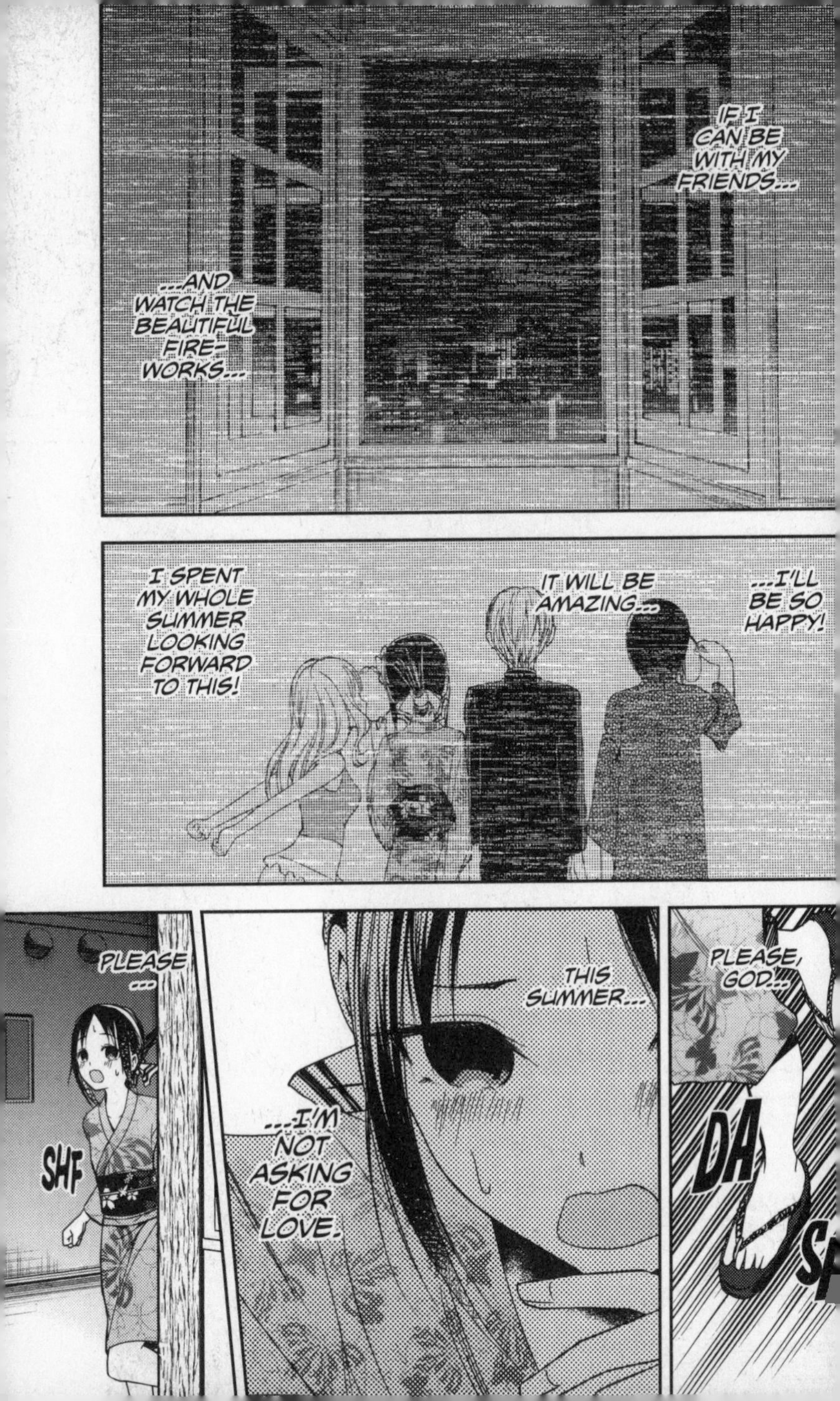
IF I CAN BE WITH MY FRIENDS...
...AND WATCH THE BEAUTIFUL FIRE-WORKS...
...I'LL BE SO HAPPY!
IT WILL BE AMAZING...
I SPENT MY WHOLE SUMMER LOOKING FORWARD TO THIS!
PLEASE, GOD...
DA
THIS SUMMER...
...I'M NOT ASKING FOR LOVE.
PLEASE ...
SHF

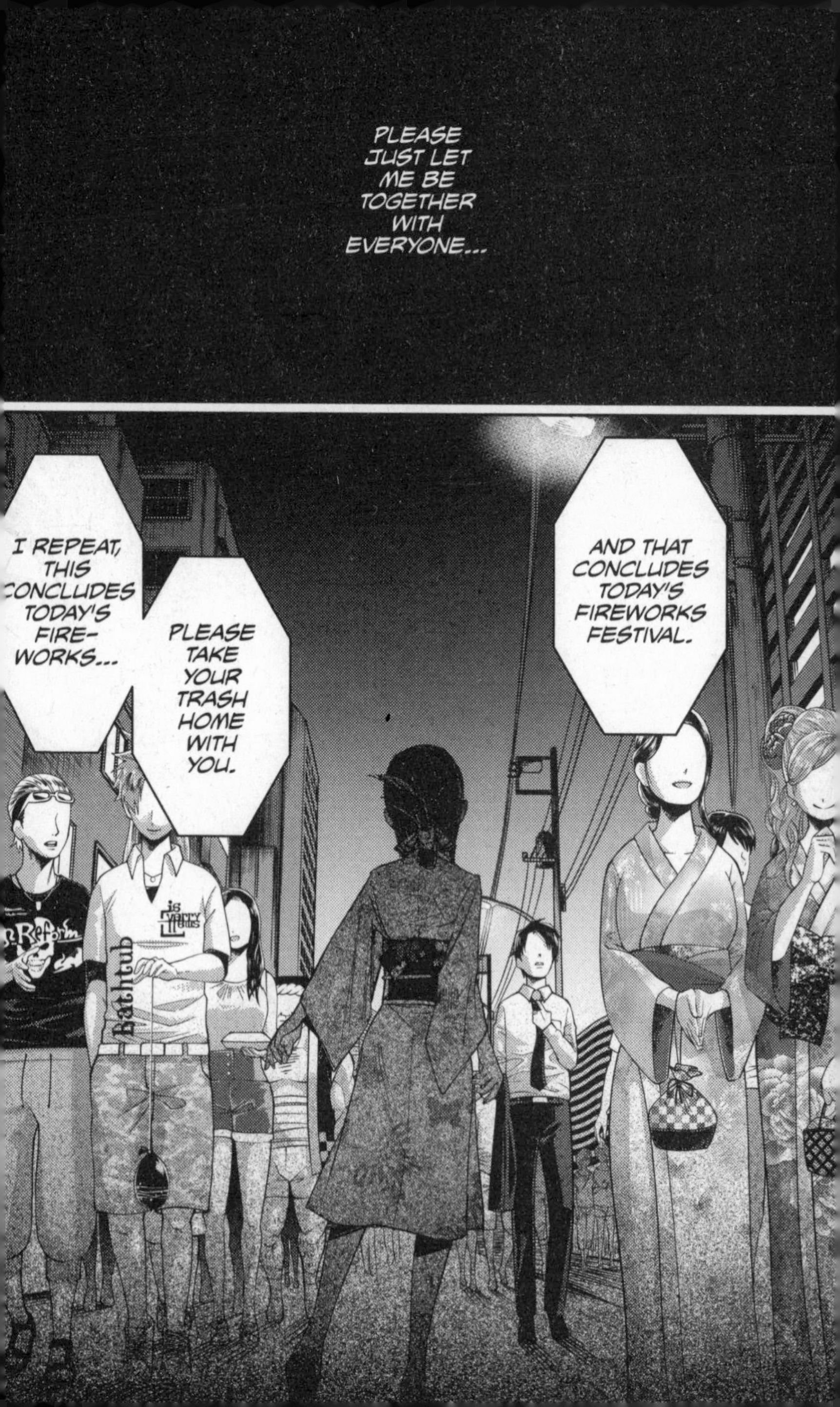
PLEASE JUST LET ME BE TOGETHER WITH EVERYONE...
AND THAT CONCLUDES TODAY'S FIREWORKS FESTIVAL.
I REPEAT, THIS CONCLUDES TODAY'S FIRE-WORKS...
PLEASE TAKE YOUR TRASH HOME WITH YOU.
Bathtub
is varry

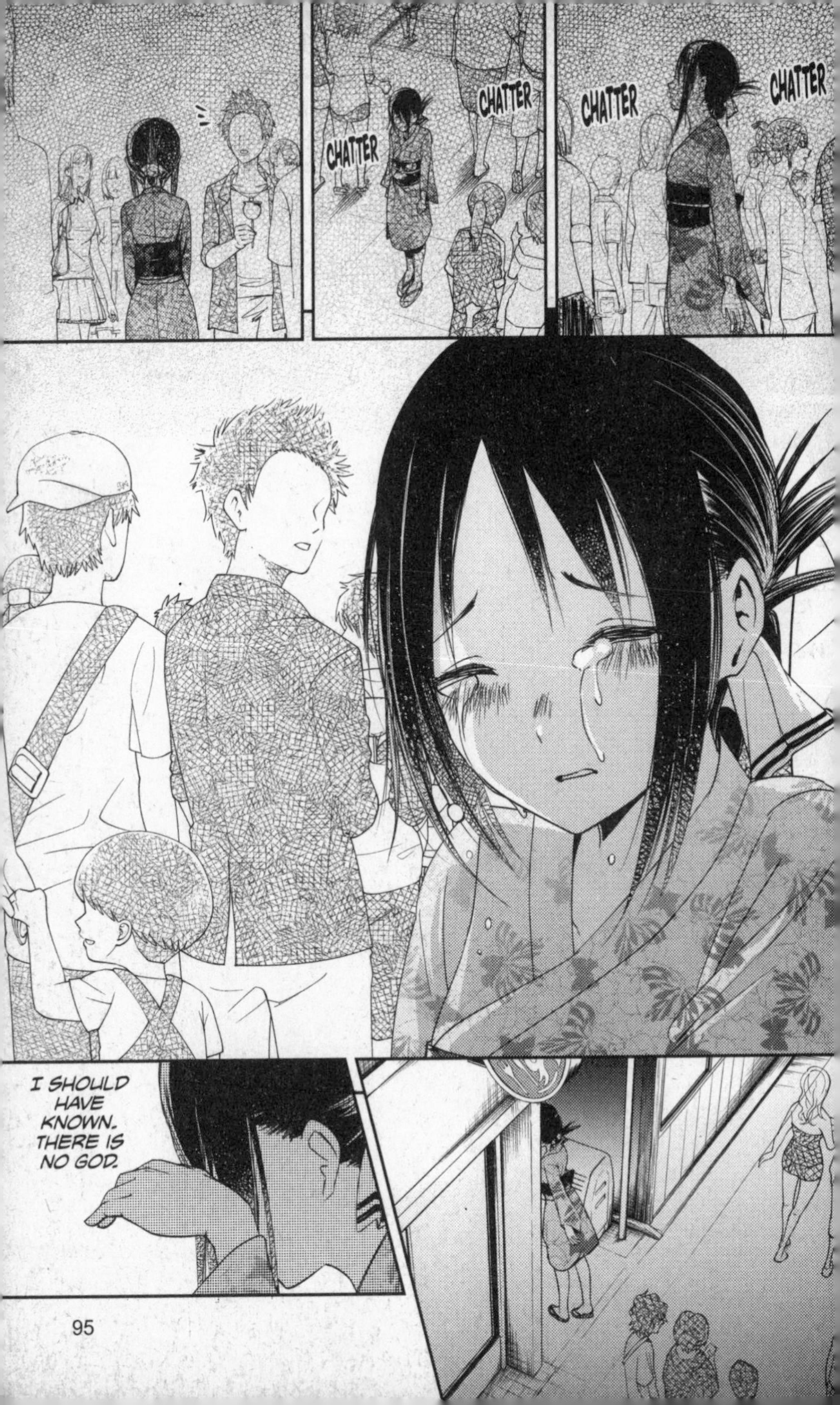
CHATTER
CHATTER
CHATTER
CHATTER
I SHOULD HAVE KNOWN. THERE IS NO GOD.

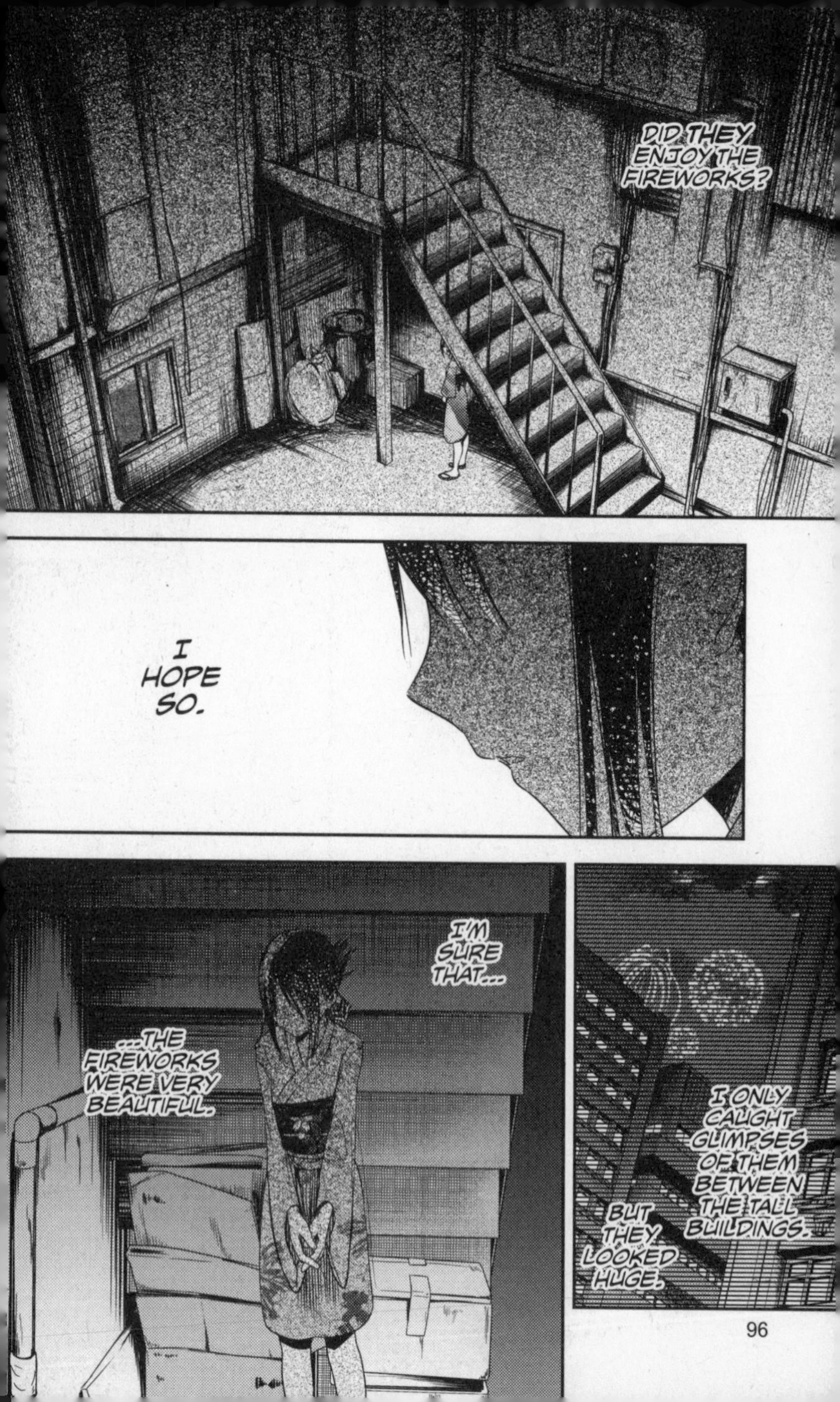
DID THEY ENJOY THE FIREWORKS?
I HOPE SO.
I ONLY CAUGHT GLIMPSES OF THEM BETWEEN THE TALL BUILDINGS.
BUT THEY LOOKED HUGE.
I'M SURE THAT...
...THE FIREWORKS WERE VERY BEAUTIFUL.

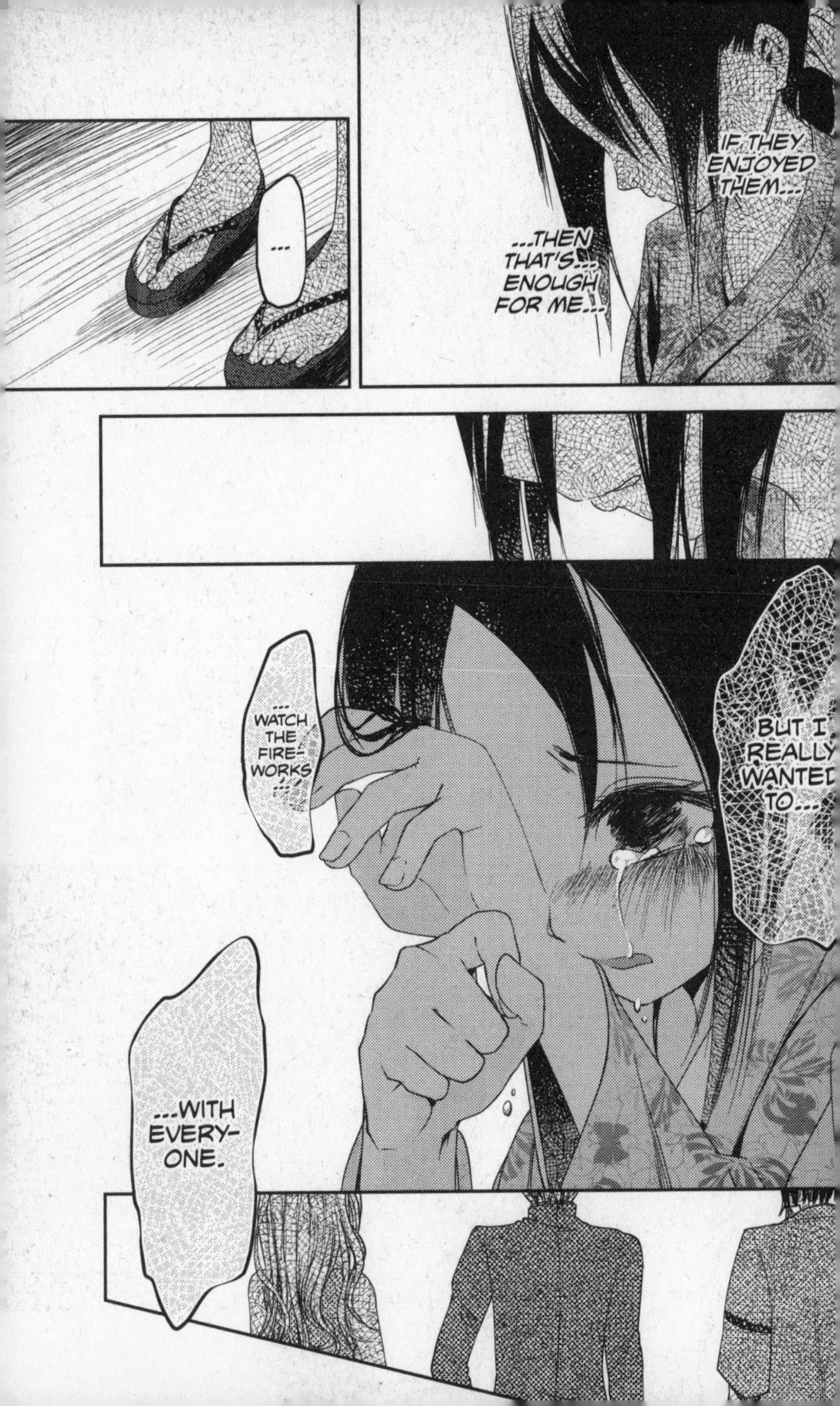
IF THEY ENJOYED THEM...
...THEN THAT'S... ENOUGH FOR ME...
...
BUT I REALLY WANTED TO...
...WATCH THE FIRE-WORKS...
...WITH EVERY-ONE.

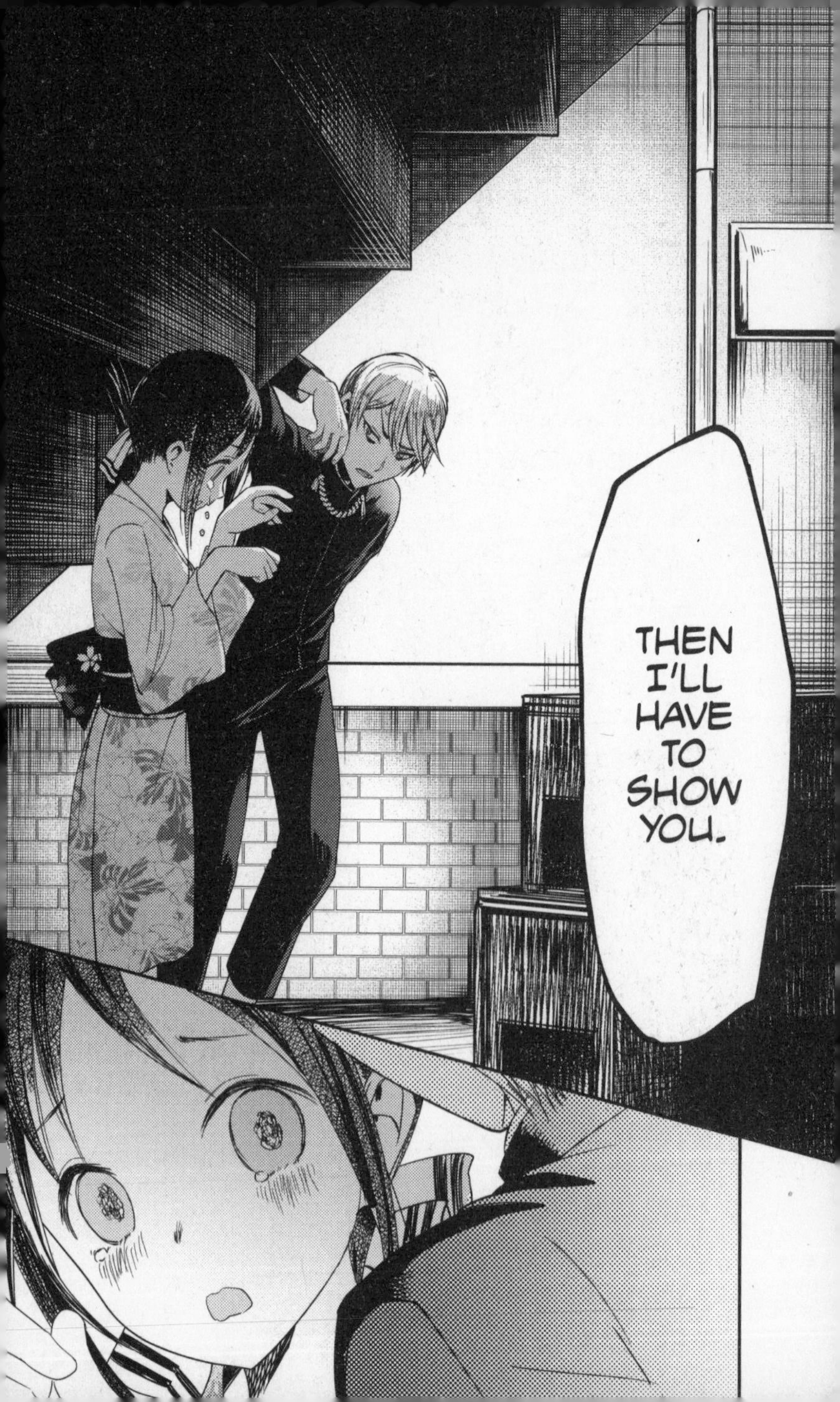
THEN I'LL HAVE TO SHOW YOU.

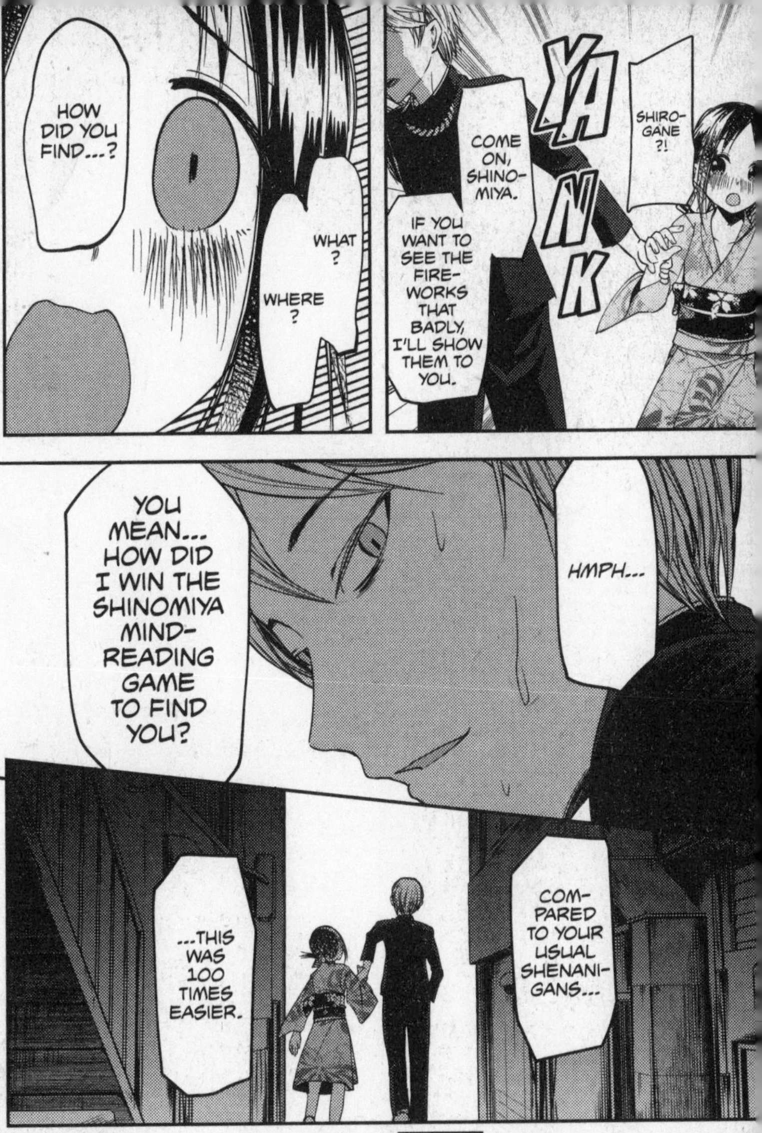
SHIRO-GANE ?!
YANK
COME ON, SHINO-MIYA.
IF YOU WANT TO SEE THE FIRE-WORKS THAT BADLY, I'LL SHOW THEM TO YOU.
WHAT ?
WHERE ?
HOW DID YOU FIND...?
HMPH...
YOU MEAN... HOW DID I WIN THE SHINOMIYA MIND-READING GAME TO FIND YOU?
COM-PARED TO YOUR USUAL SHENANI-GANS...
...THIS WAS 100 TIMES EASIER.

Today's battle result:

Shiro-gane wins

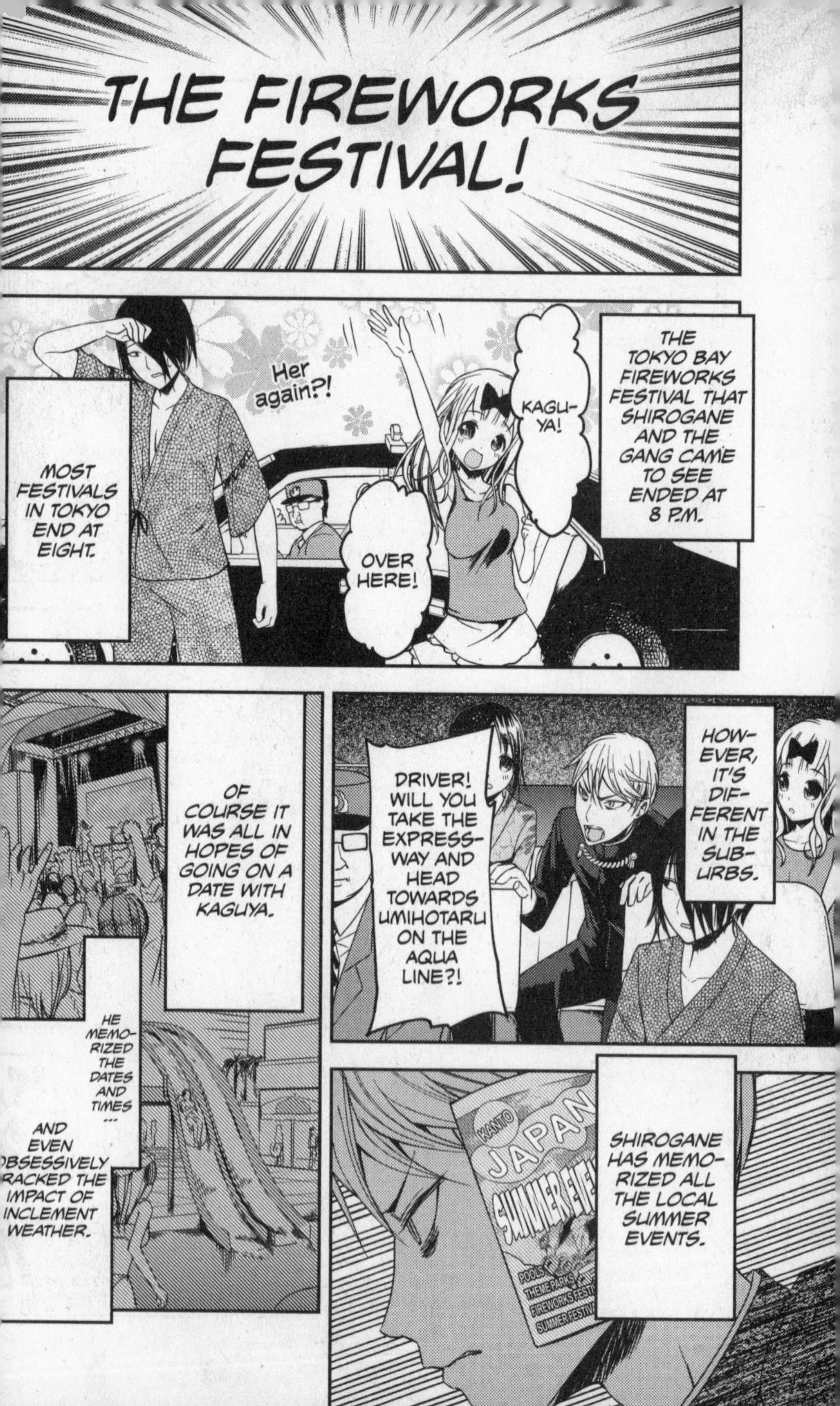
THE FIREWORKS FESTIVAL!
THE TOKYO BAY FIREWORKS FESTIVAL THAT SHIROGANE AND THE GANG CAME TO SEE ENDED AT 8 P.M.
KAGU-YA!
OVER HERE!
Her again?!
MOST FESTIVALS IN TOKYO END AT EIGHT.
HOW-EVER, IT'S DIF-FERENT IN THE SUB-URBS.
DRIVER! WILL YOU TAKE THE EXPRESS-WAY AND HEAD TOWARDS UMIHOTARU ON THE AQUA LINE?!
SHIROGANE HAS MEMO-RIZED ALL THE LOCAL SUMMER EVENTS.
KANTO
JAPAN
POOLS
THEME PARKS
OF COURSE IT WAS ALL IN HOPES OF GOING ON A DATE WITH KAGUYA.
HE MEMO-RIZED THE DATES AND TIMES...
AND EVEN OBSESSIVELY RACKED THE IMPACT OF INCLEMENT WEATHER.

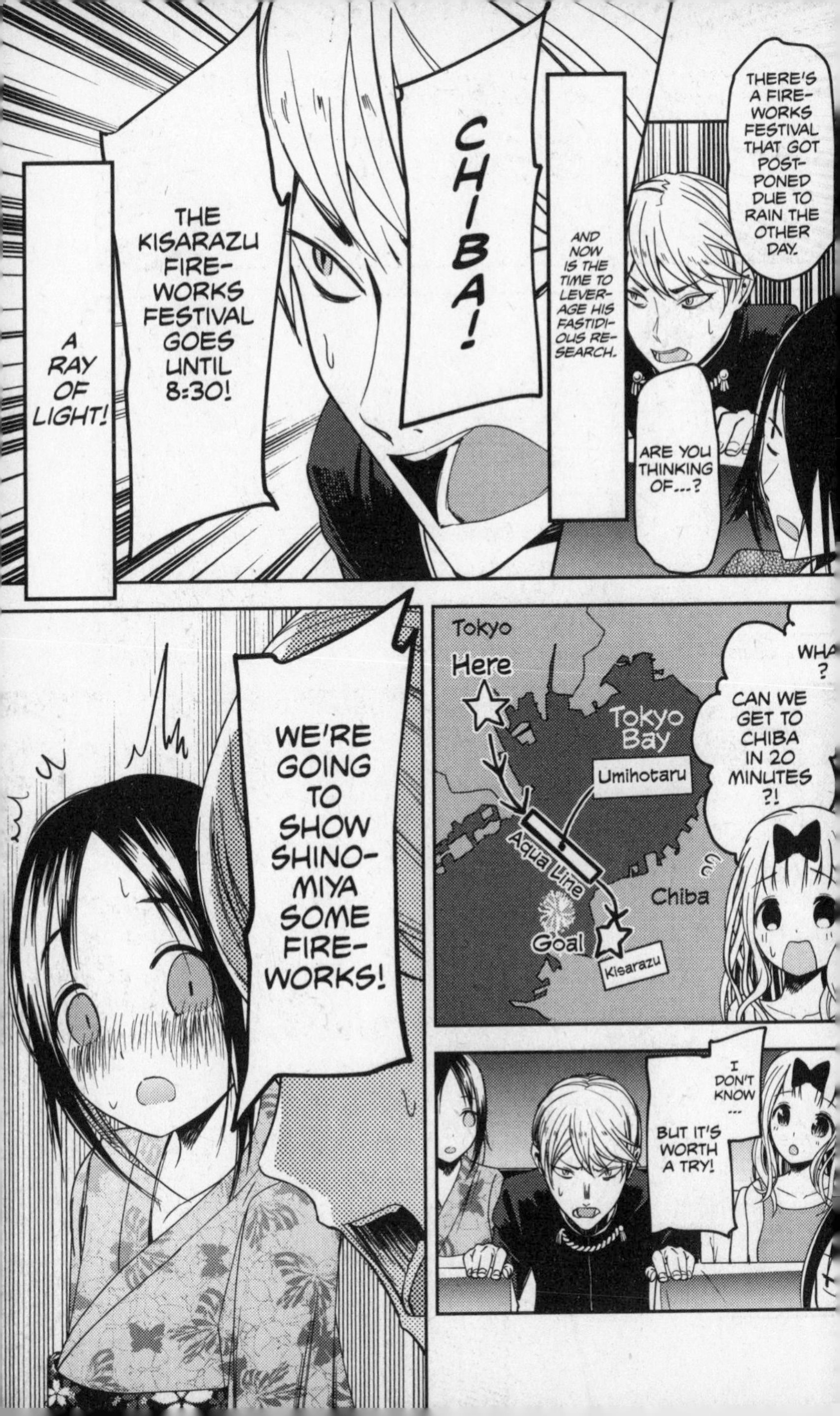
THERE'S A FIREWORKS FESTIVAL THAT GOT POSTPONED DUE TO RAIN THE OTHER DAY.
AND NOW IS THE TIME TO LEVERAGE HIS FASTIDIOUS RESEARCH.
ARE YOU THINKING OF...?
CHIBA!
THE KISARAZU FIREWORKS FESTIVAL GOES UNTIL 8:30!
A RAY OF LIGHT!
WHA?
CAN WE GET TO CHIBA IN 20 MINUTES?!
Tokyo
Here
Tokyo Bay
Umihotaru
Aqua Line
Chiba
Goal
Kisarazu
I DON'T KNOW...
BUT IT'S WORTH A TRY!
WE'RE GOING TO SHOW SHINOMIYA SOME FIREWORKS!

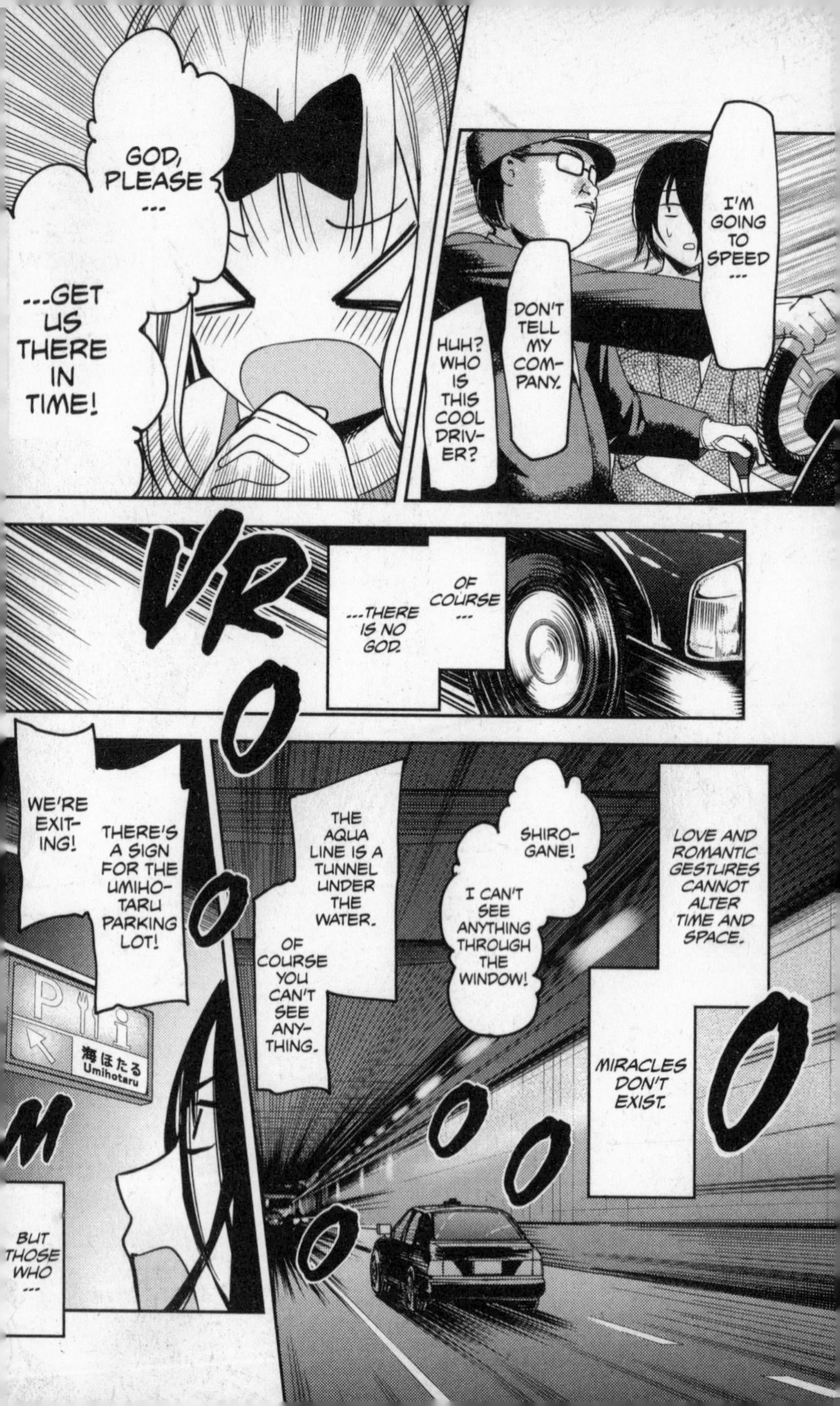
I'M GOING TO SPEED...
DON'T TELL MY COMPANY.
HUH? WHO IS THIS COOL DRIVER?
GOD, PLEASE...
...GET US THERE IN TIME!
VROOOOOOOM
OF COURSE...
...THERE IS NO GOD.
LOVE AND ROMANTIC GESTURES CANNOT ALTER TIME AND SPACE.
MIRACLES DON'T EXIST.
SHIRO-GANE!
I CAN'T SEE ANYTHING THROUGH THE WINDOW!
THE AQUA LINE IS A TUNNEL UNDER THE WATER.
OF COURSE YOU CAN'T SEE ANYTHING.
THERE'S A SIGN FOR THE UMIHO-TARU PARKING LOT!
WE'RE EXIT-ING!
海ほたる
Umihotaru
BUT THOSE WHO...

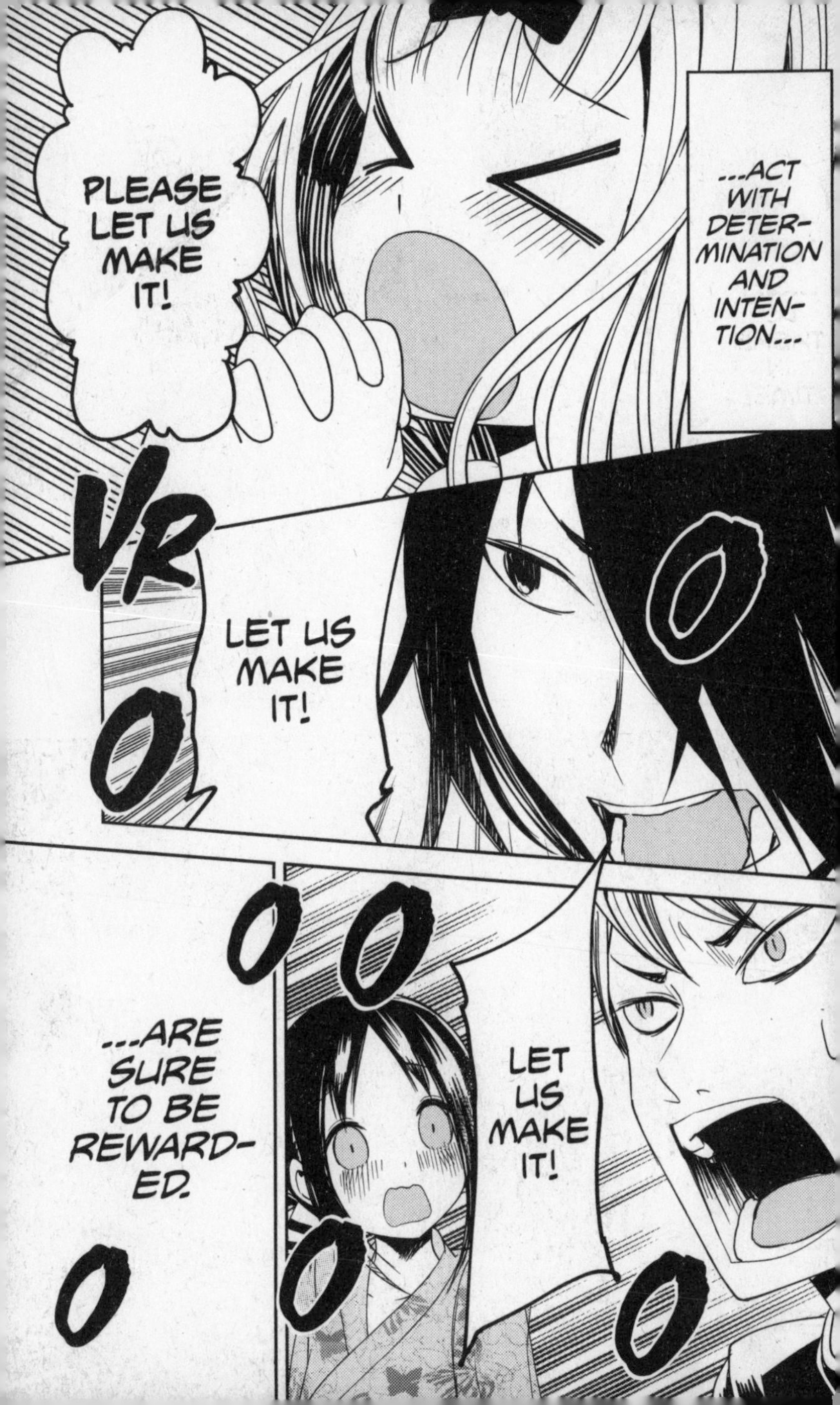
...ACT WITH DETER-MINATION AND INTEN-TION...
PLEASE LET US MAKE IT!
O
VR
LET US MAKE IT!
O
O
LET US MAKE IT!
O
O
...ARE SURE TO BE REWARD-ED.
O
O

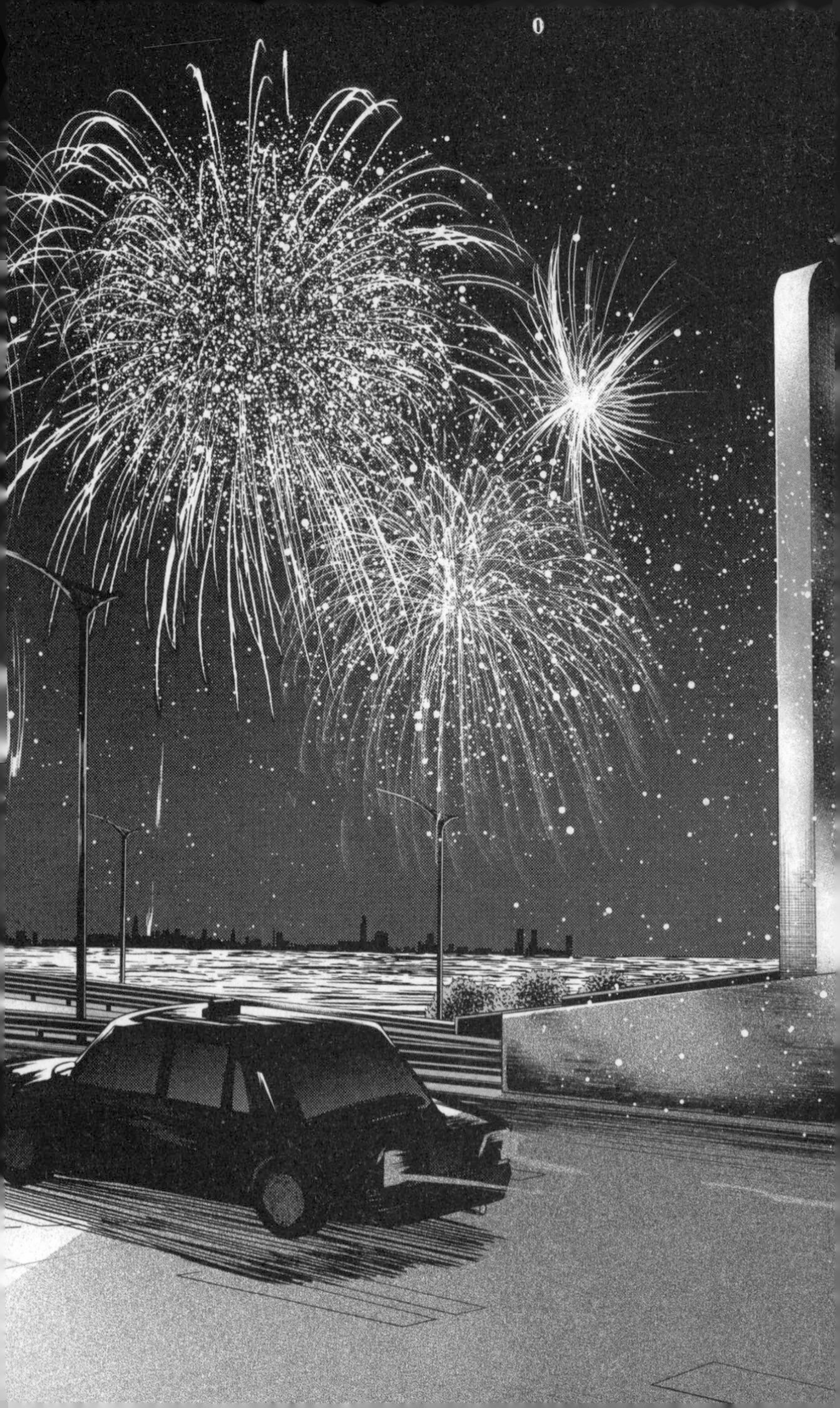

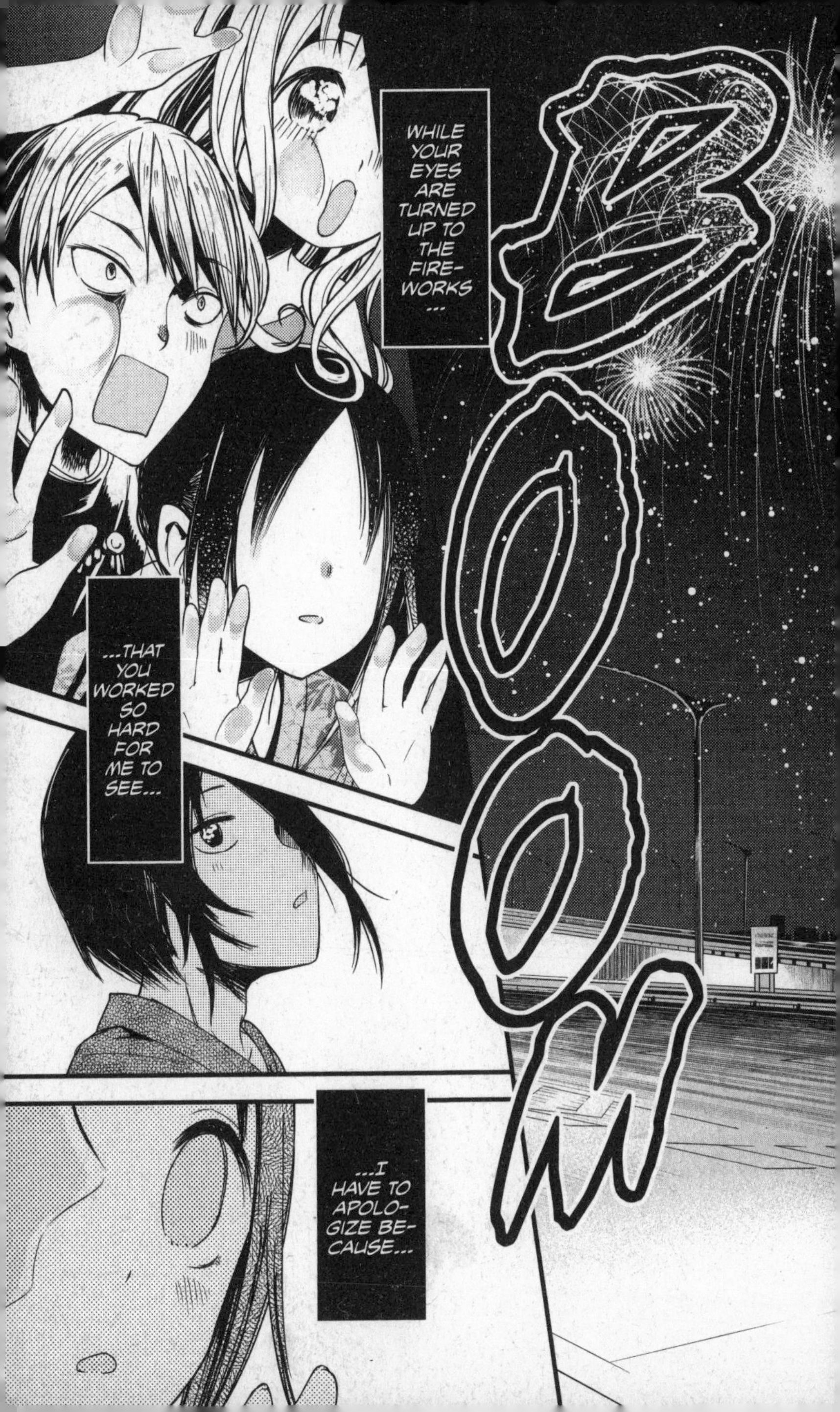
BOOOM
WHILE YOUR EYES ARE TURNED UP TO THE FIRE-WORKS...
...THAT YOU WORKED SO HARD FOR ME TO SEE...
...I HAVE TO APOLO-GIZE BE-CAUSE...

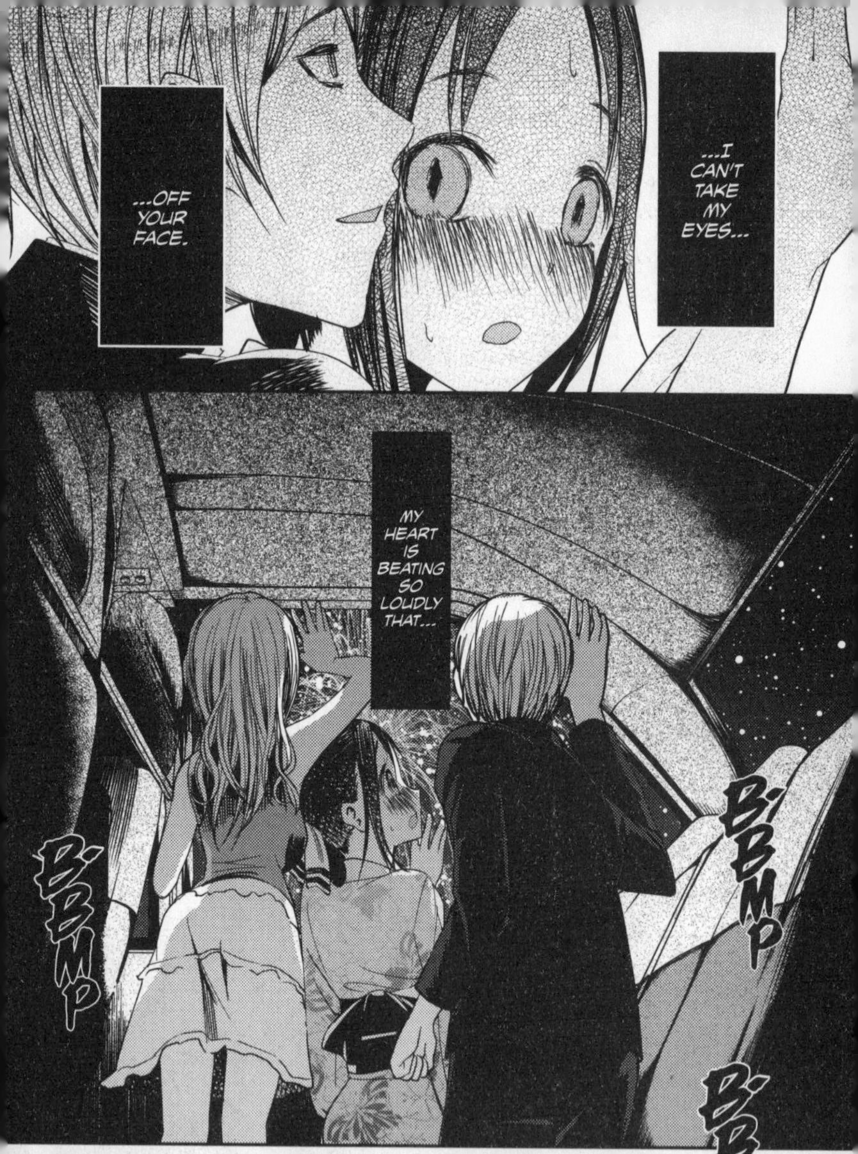
...I CAN'T TAKE MY EYES...
...OFF YOUR FACE.
MY HEART IS BEATING SO LOUDLY THAT...
B-BMP
B-BMP
B-BMP

Battle 45
I Can't Hear the Fireworks, Part 2

Record of Shirogane's Efforts

STAKED OUT A SPOT SIX HOURS IN ADVANCE

GOT THE TEXT THAT SHINOMIYA WASN'T COMING, DID SOME SEARCHES AND DISCOVERED HER TWEET

SPED ON HIS BIKE FROM HAMAMATSU TO THE SHINOMIYA ESTATE IN SENGAKUJI

SPOTTED KAGUYA'S BODY DOUBLE (HAYASAKA) THROUGH BINOCULARS AND RETREATED AT MACH SPEED

USING ALL HIS BRAIN POWER, CALCULATED THE DISTANCE AND ROUTE THAT SHINOMIYA WOULD TRAVEL IN ORDER TO DETERMINE HER LOCATION

WITH THE EVENT INFORMATION ALREADY INPUT INTO HIS BRAIN, HIRED A TAXI TO TAKE THEM ALL TO KISARAZU

PAID 17,320 YEN* FOR THE TAXI (PULLING FROM THE MONEY HE HAD BUDGETED TO SPEND ON DATES WITH SHINOMIYA OVER THE SUMMER)

*APPROX. $173

PANT

KAGUYA-SAMA
LOVE IS WAR

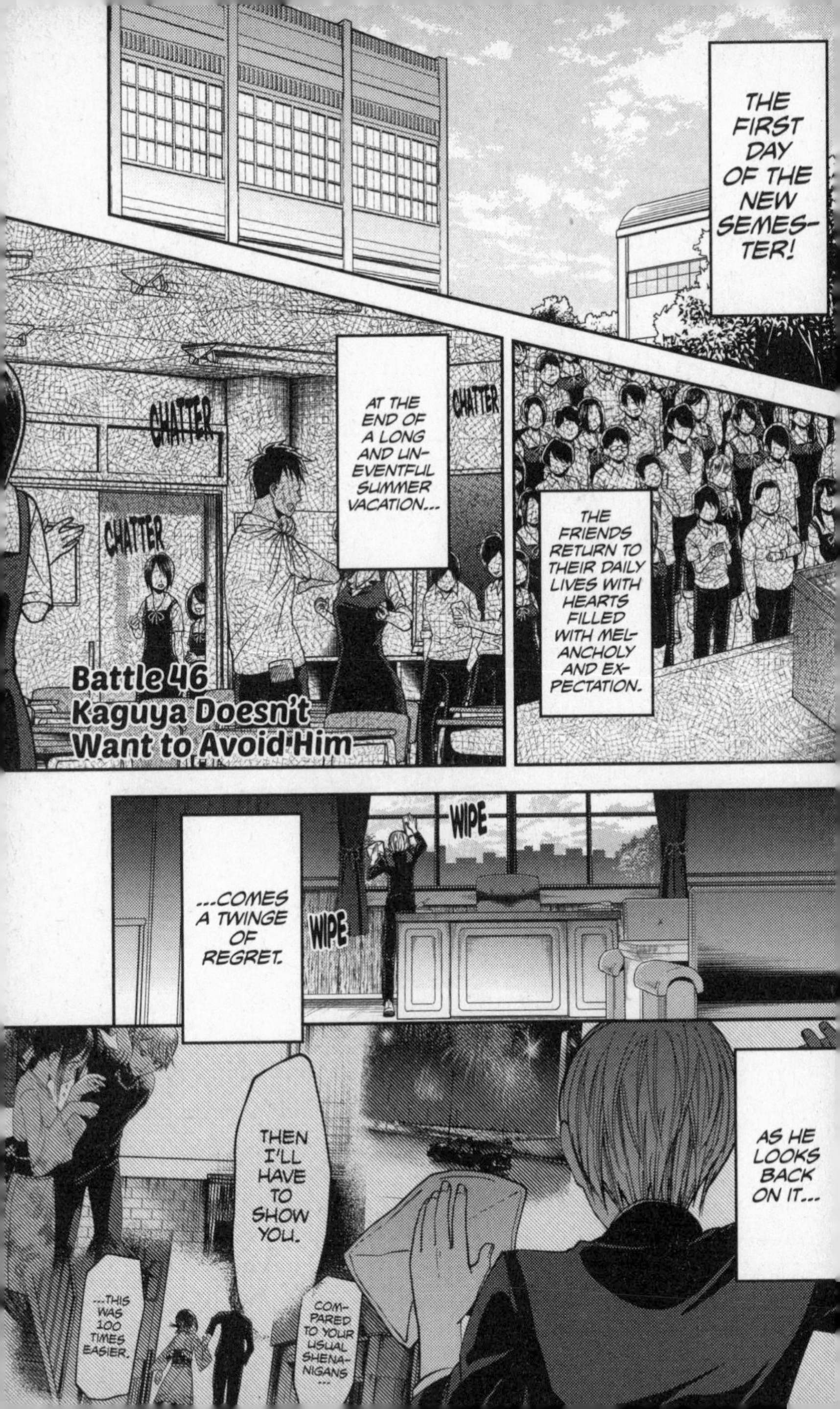
THE FIRST DAY OF THE NEW SEMESTER!
THE FRIENDS RETURN TO THEIR DAILY LIVES WITH HEARTS FILLED WITH MELANCHOLY AND EXPECTATION.
CHATTER
AT THE END OF A LONG AND UNEVENTFUL SUMMER VACATION...
CHATTER
CHATTER
Battle 46
Kaguya Doesn't Want to Avoid Him
WIPE
...COMES A TWINGE OF REGRET.
WIPE
AS HE LOOKS BACK ON IT...
THEN I'LL HAVE TO SHOW YOU.
COMPARED TO YOUR USUAL SHENANIGANS...
...THIS WAS 100 TIMES EASIER.

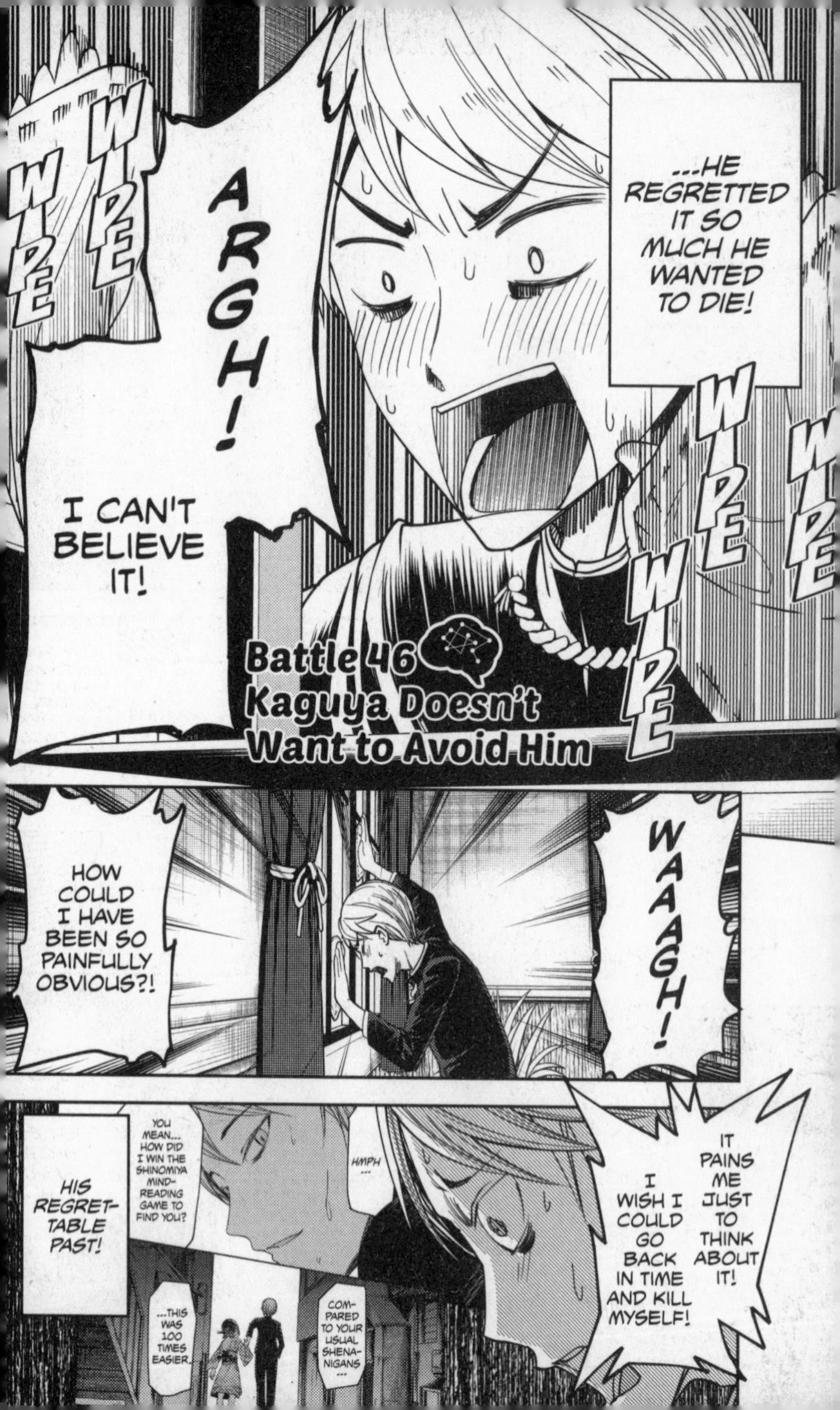

...HE REGRETTED IT SO MUCH HE WANTED TO DIE!
WIPE
WIPE
WIPE
ARGH!
WIPE
WIPE
I CAN'T BELIEVE IT!
Battle 46 Kaguya Doesn't Want to Avoid Him
WAAAGH!
HOW COULD I HAVE BEEN SO PAINFULLY OBVIOUS?!
IT PAINS ME JUST TO THINK ABOUT IT!
I WISH I COULD GO BACK IN TIME AND KILL MYSELF!
HMPH...
YOU MEAN... HOW DID I WIN THE SHINOMIYA MIND-READING GAME TO FIND YOU?
HIS REGRET-TABLE PAST!
COM-PARED TO YOUR USUAL SHENA-NIGANS...
...THIS WAS 100 TIMES EASIER.

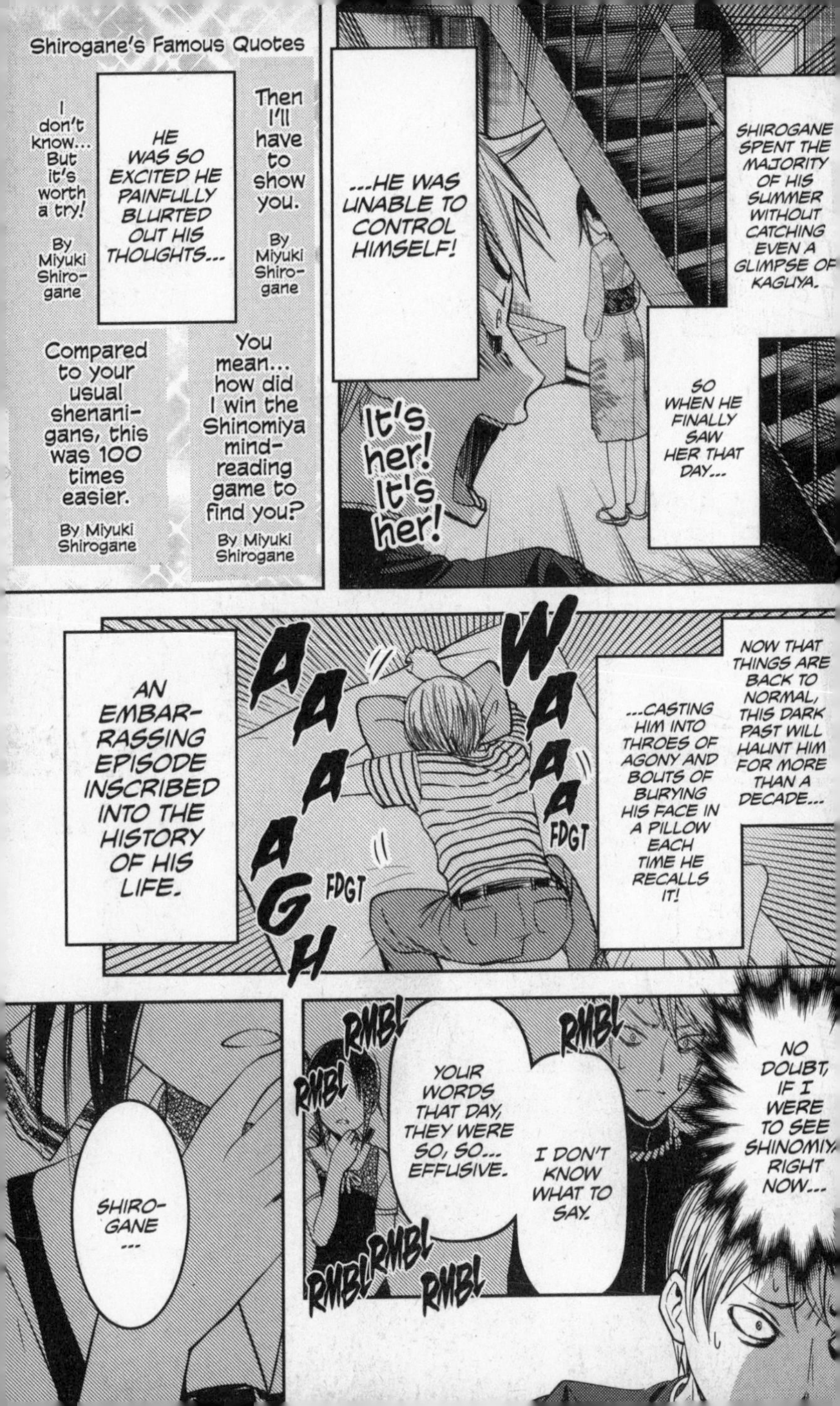
SHIROGANE SPENT THE MAJORITY OF HIS SUMMER WITHOUT CATCHING EVEN A GLIMPSE OF KAGUYA.
SO WHEN HE FINALLY SAW HER THAT DAY...
...HE WAS UNABLE TO CONTROL HIMSELF!
It's her! It's her!
Shirogane's Famous Quotes
Then I'll have to show you.
By Miyuki Shirogane
HE WAS SO EXCITED HE PAINFULLY BLURTED OUT HIS THOUGHTS...
I don't know... But it's worth a try!
By Miyuki Shirogane
You mean... how did I win the Shinomiya mind-reading game to find you?
By Miyuki Shirogane
Compared to your usual shenanigans, this was 100 times easier.
By Miyuki Shirogane
NOW THAT THINGS ARE BACK TO NORMAL, THIS DARK PAST WILL HAUNT HIM FOR MORE THAN A DECADE...
...CASTING HIM INTO THROES OF AGONY AND BOUTS OF BURYING HIS FACE IN A PILLOW EACH TIME HE RECALLS IT!
WAAAA
FDGT
AAAAAAGH
FDGT
AN EMBARRASSING EPISODE INSCRIBED INTO THE HISTORY OF HIS LIFE.
NO DOUBT, IF I WERE TO SEE SHINOMIYA RIGHT NOW...
RMBL
RMBL
RMBL
YOUR WORDS THAT DAY, THEY WERE SO, SO... EFFUSIVE.
I DON'T KNOW WHAT TO SAY.
RMBL
RMBL
RMBL
RMBL
SHIROGANE ...

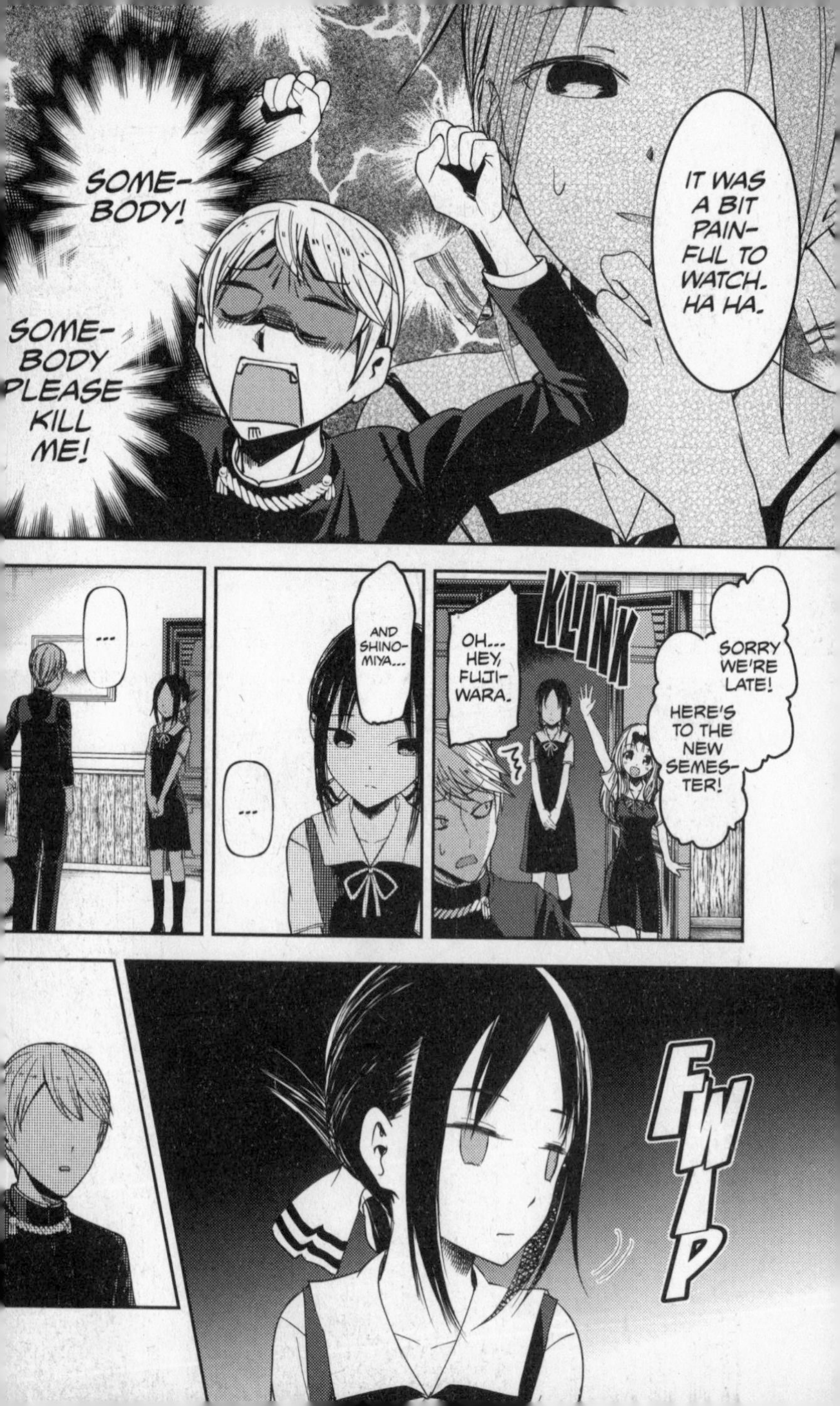
IT WAS A BIT PAINFUL TO WATCH. HA HA.
SOMEBODY!
SOMEBODY PLEASE KILL ME!
SORRY WE'RE LATE!
HERE'S TO THE NEW SEMESTER!
KLINK
OH... HEY, FUJIWARA.
AND SHINOMIYA...
...
...
FWIP

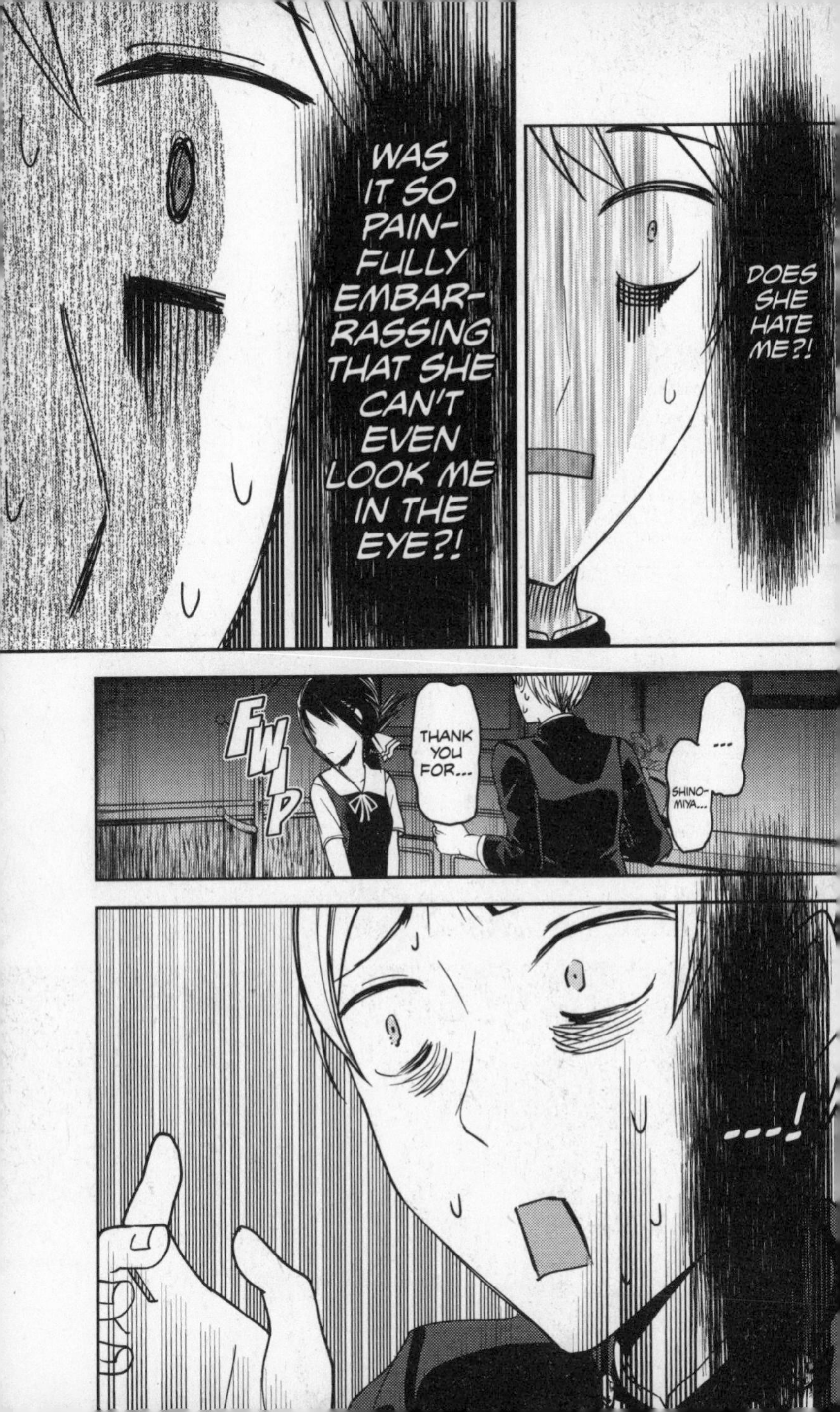
DOES SHE HATE ME?!
WAS IT SO PAIN-FULLY EMBAR-RASSING THAT SHE CAN'T EVEN LOOK ME IN THE EYE?!
...
SHINO-MIYA...
THANK YOU FOR...
FWIP
...!

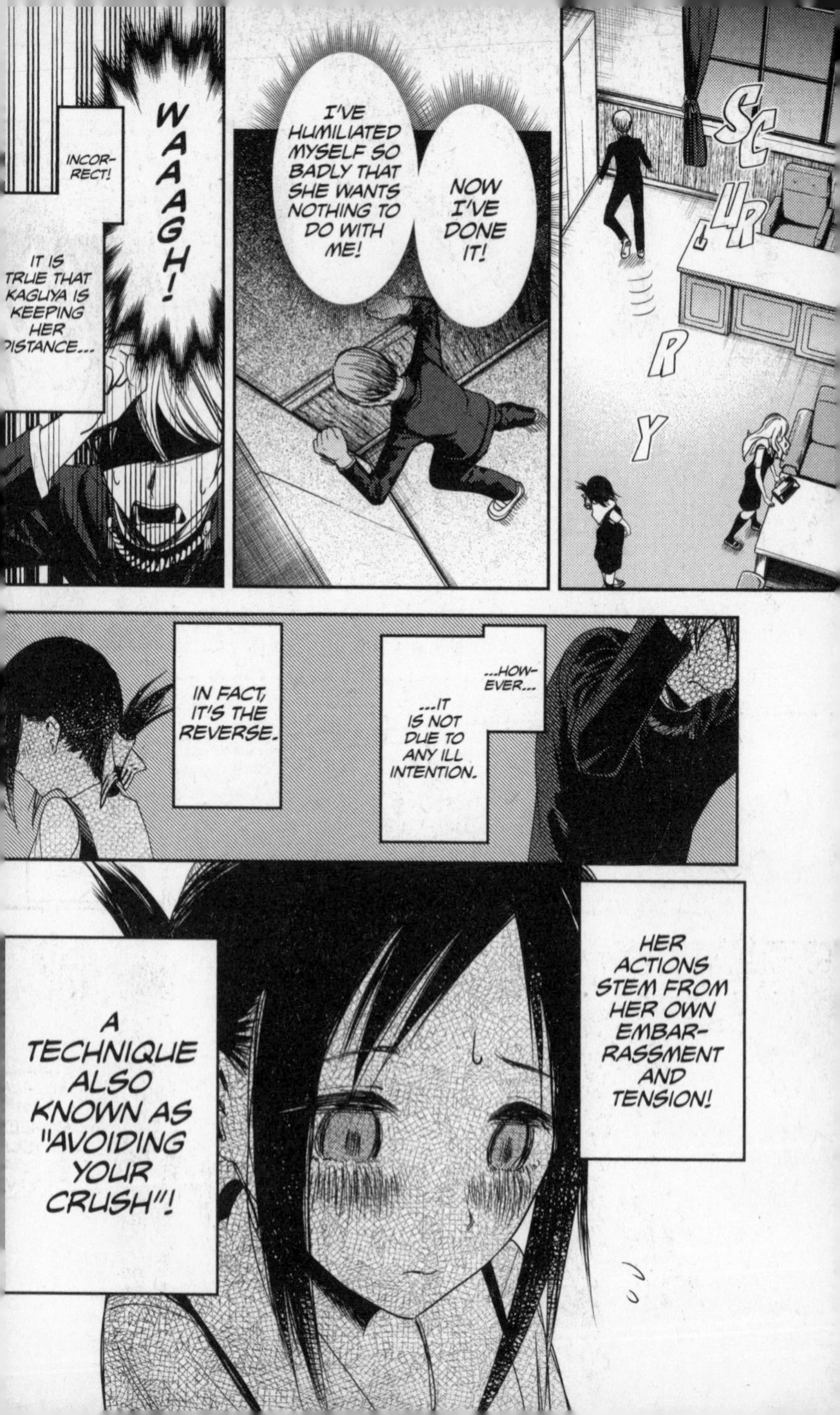

SCURRY
NOW I'VE DONE IT!
I'VE HUMILIATED MYSELF SO BADLY THAT SHE WANTS NOTHING TO DO WITH ME!
WAAAGH!
INCORRECT!
IT IS TRUE THAT KAGUYA IS KEEPING HER DISTANCE...
...HOWEVER...
...IT IS NOT DUE TO ANY ILL INTENTION.
IN FACT, IT'S THE REVERSE.
HER ACTIONS STEM FROM HER OWN EMBARRASSMENT AND TENSION!
A TECHNIQUE ALSO KNOWN AS "AVOIDING YOUR CRUSH"!

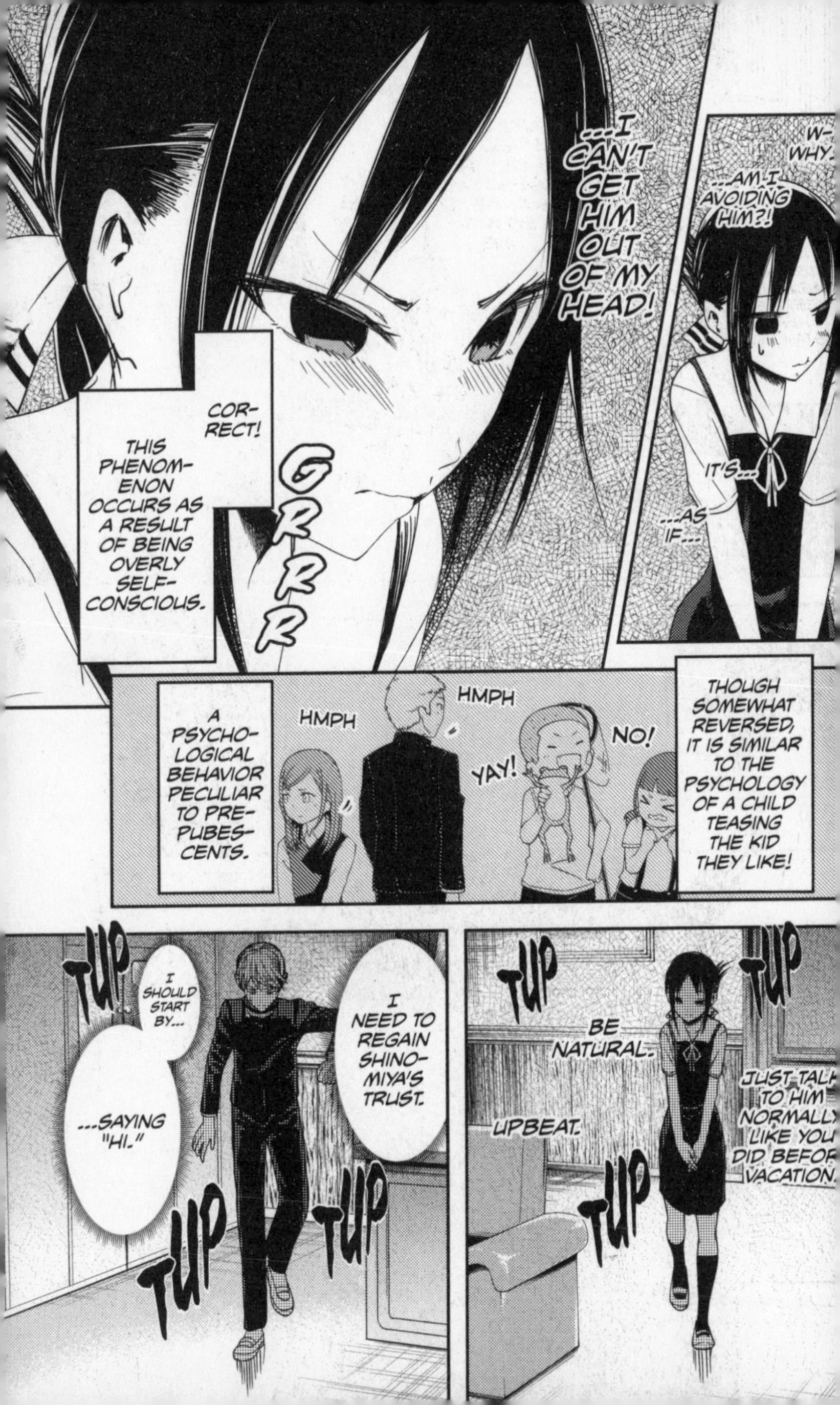
W-WHY...
...AM I AVOIDING HIM?!
IT'S...
...AS IF...
...I CAN'T GET HIM OUT OF MY HEAD!
CORRECT!
THIS PHENOMENON OCCURS AS A RESULT OF BEING OVERLY SELF-CONSCIOUS.
GRRR
THOUGH SOMEWHAT REVERSED, IT IS SIMILAR TO THE PSYCHOLOGY OF A CHILD TEASING THE KID THEY LIKE!
NO!
YAY!
HMPH
HMPH
A PSYCHOLOGICAL BEHAVIOR PECULIAR TO PREPUBESCENTS.
TUP
TUP
BE NATURAL.
JUST TALK TO HIM NORMALLY LIKE YOU DID BEFORE VACATION.
UPBEAT.
TUP
TUP
I NEED TO REGAIN SHINOMIYA'S TRUST.
I SHOULD START BY...
...SAYING "HI."
TUP
TUP

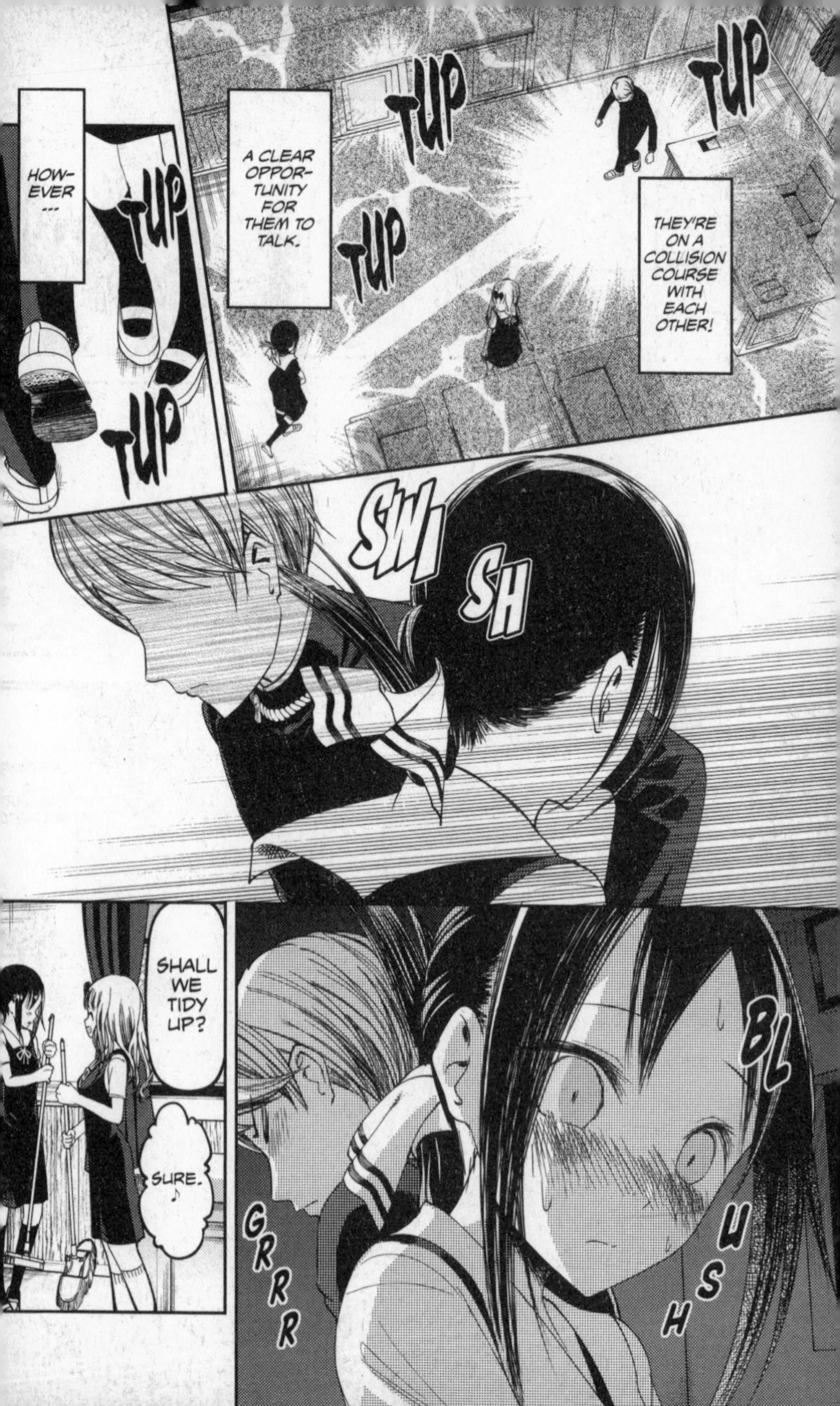
TUP
THEY'RE ON A COLLISION COURSE WITH EACH OTHER!
TUP
A CLEAR OPPORTUNITY FOR THEM TO TALK.
TUP
HOW-EVER ---
TUP
TUP
SWISH
BLUSH
GRRR
SHALL WE TIDY UP?
SURE. ♪

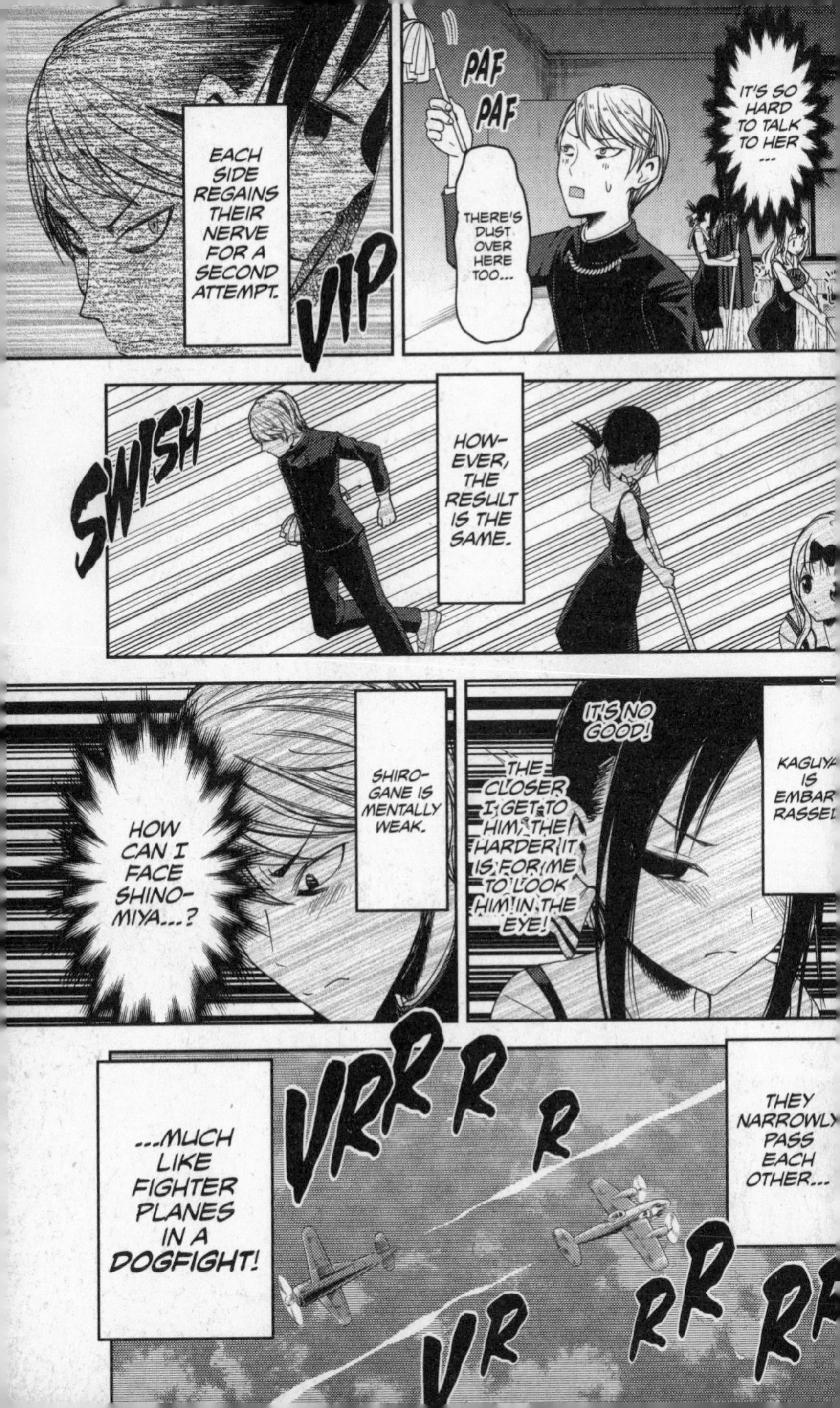
IT'S SO HARD TO TALK TO HER...
PAF PAF
THERE'S DUST OVER HERE TOO...
EACH SIDE REGAINS THEIR NERVE FOR A SECOND ATTEMPT.
VIP
HOW-EVER, THE RESULT IS THE SAME.
SWISH
KAGUYA IS EMBAR RASSE
IT'S NO GOOD!
THE CLOSER I GET TO HIM, THE HARDER IT IS FOR ME TO LOOK HIM IN THE EYE!
SHIRO-GANE IS MENTALLY WEAK.
HOW CAN I FACE SHINO-MIYA...?
THEY NARROWLY PASS EACH OTHER...
VRR R R
...MUCH LIKE FIGHTER PLANES IN A DOGFIGHT!
VR RR

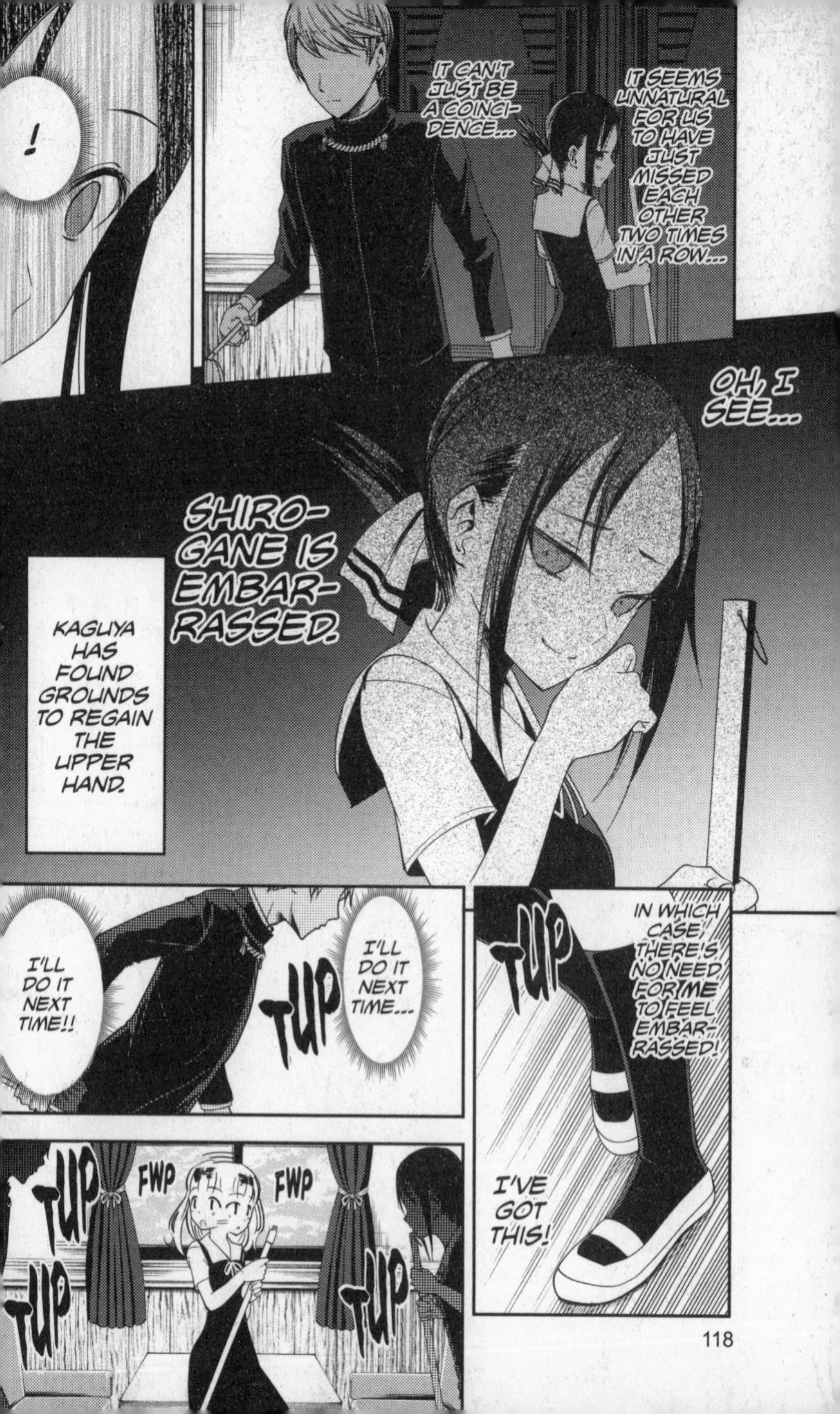
IT SEEMS UNNATURAL FOR US TO HAVE JUST MISSED EACH OTHER TWO TIMES IN A ROW...
IT CAN'T JUST BE A COINCIDENCE...
!
OH, I SEE...
SHIROGANE IS EMBARRASSED.
KAGUYA HAS FOUND GROUNDS TO REGAIN THE UPPER HAND.
TUP
IN WHICH CASE, THERE'S NO NEED FOR ME TO FEEL EMBARRASSED!
I'VE GOT THIS!
I'LL DO IT NEXT TIME...
TUP
I'LL DO IT NEXT TIME!!
TUP
FWP
FWP
TUP
TUP

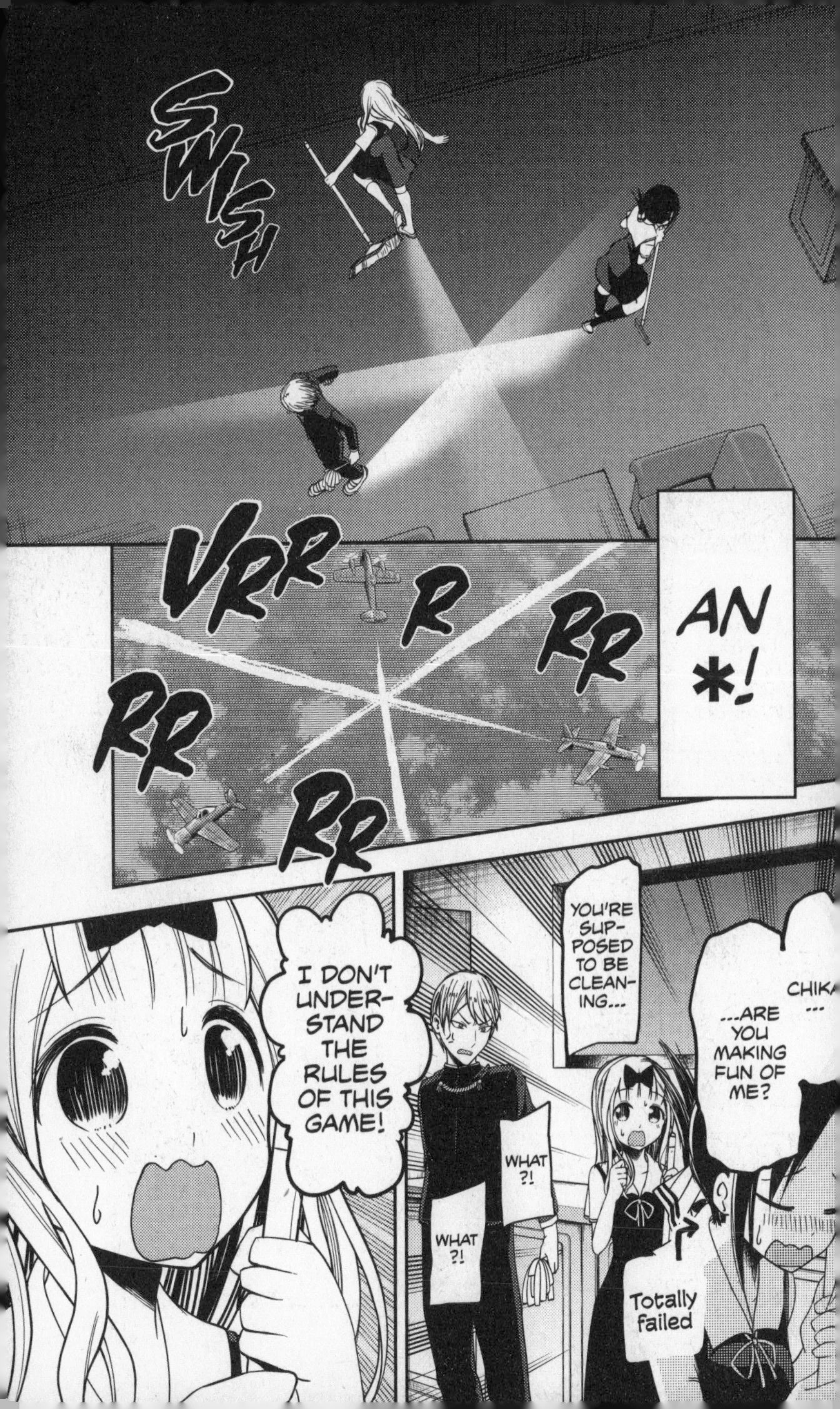
SWISH
AN *!
VRRRRRRRR
CHIKA---
...ARE YOU MAKING FUN OF ME?
YOU'RE SUP-POSED TO BE CLEAN-ING...
WHAT?!
WHAT?!
Totally failed
I DON'T UNDER-STAND THE RULES OF THIS GAME!

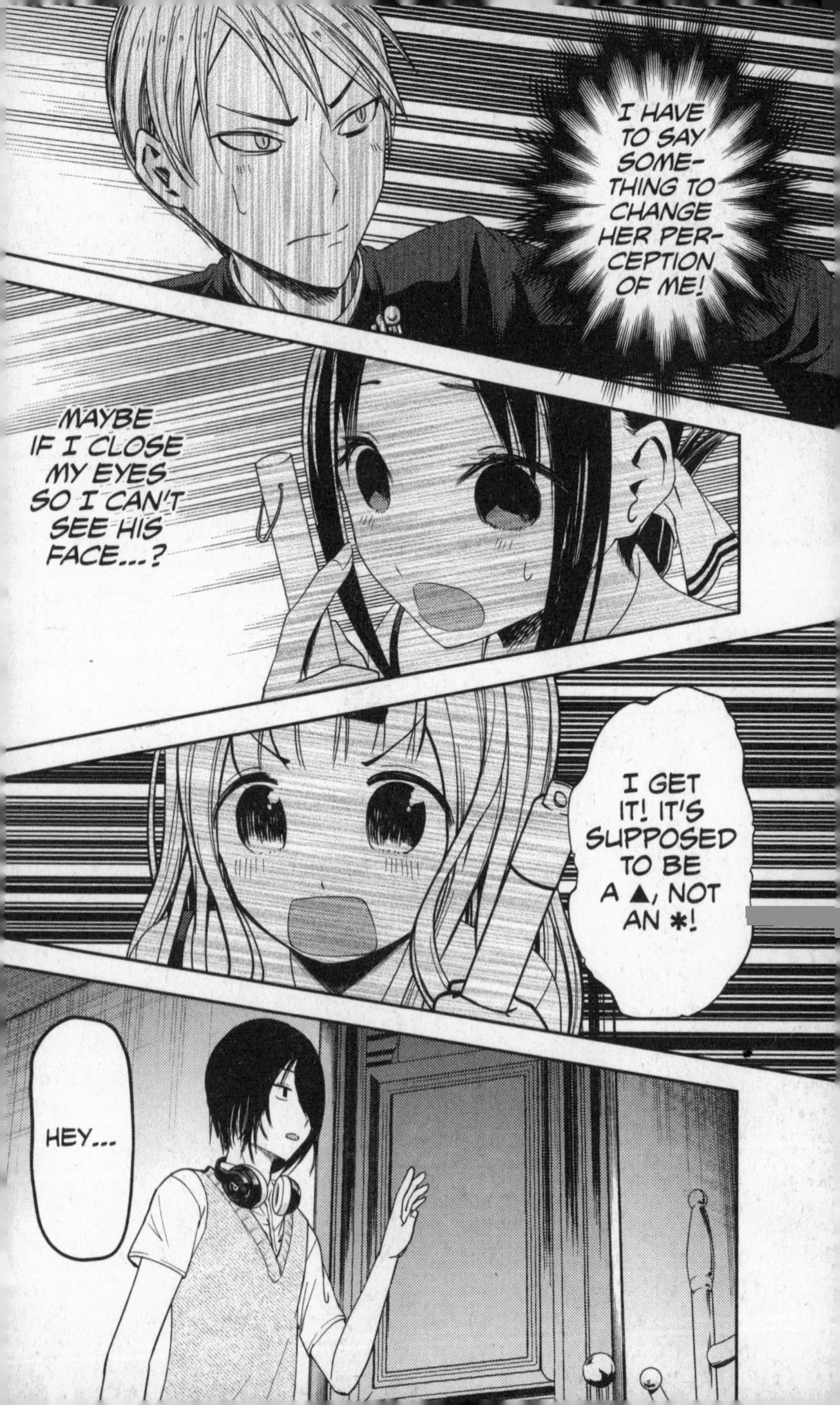
I HAVE TO SAY SOME-THING TO CHANGE HER PER-CEPTION OF ME!
MAYBE IF I CLOSE MY EYES SO I CAN'T SEE HIS FACE...?
I GET IT! IT'S SUPPOSED TO BE A ▲, NOT AN ✱!
HEY...

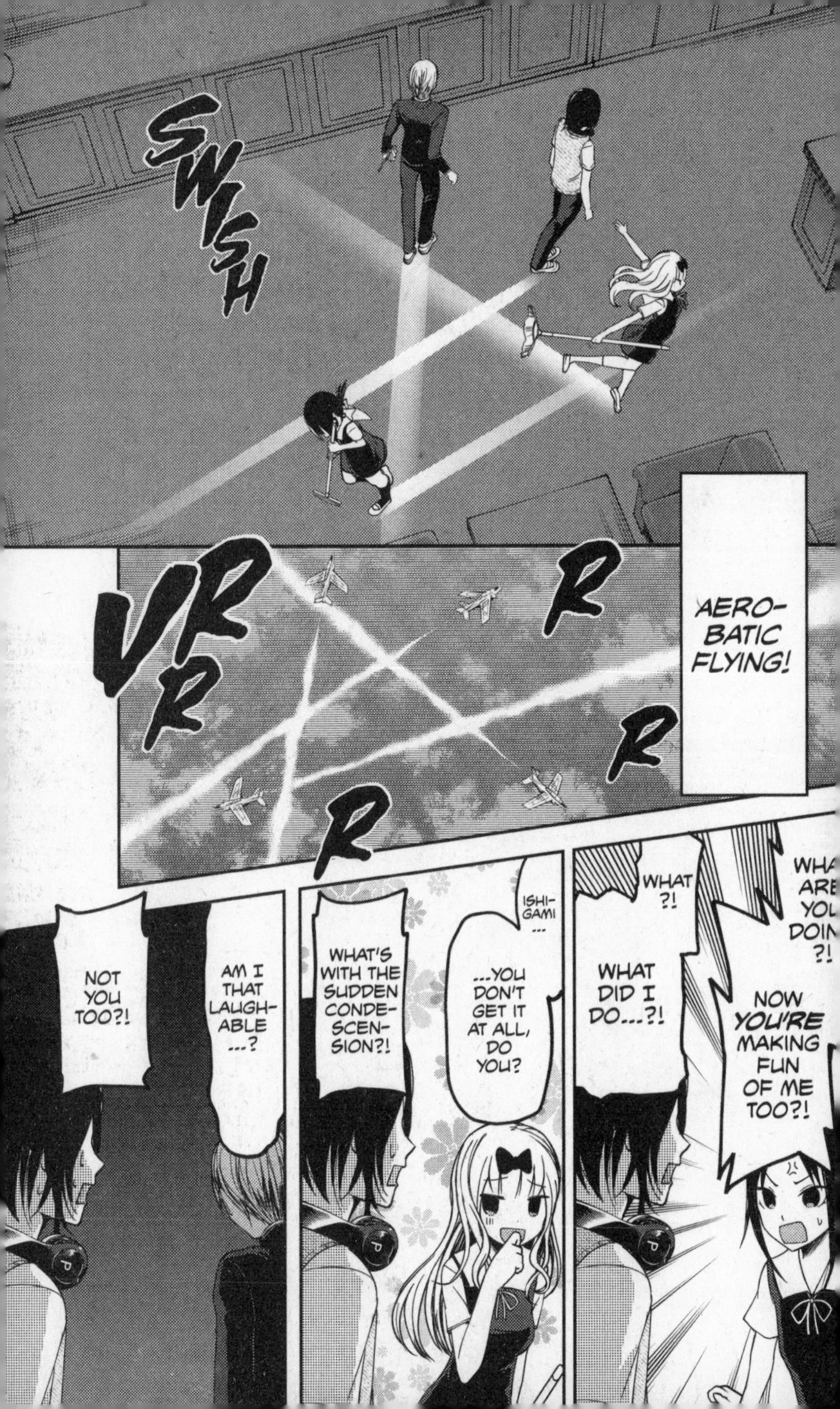
SWISH
AERO-BATIC FLYING!
VRRRRR
WHA ARE YOU DOIN ?!
NOW YOU'RE MAKING FUN OF ME TOO?!
WHAT?!
WHAT DID I DO...?!
ISHI-GAMI...
...YOU DON'T GET IT AT ALL, DO YOU?
WHAT'S WITH THE SUDDEN CONDE-SCEN-SION?!
AM I THAT LAUGH-ABLE...?
NOT YOU TOO?!

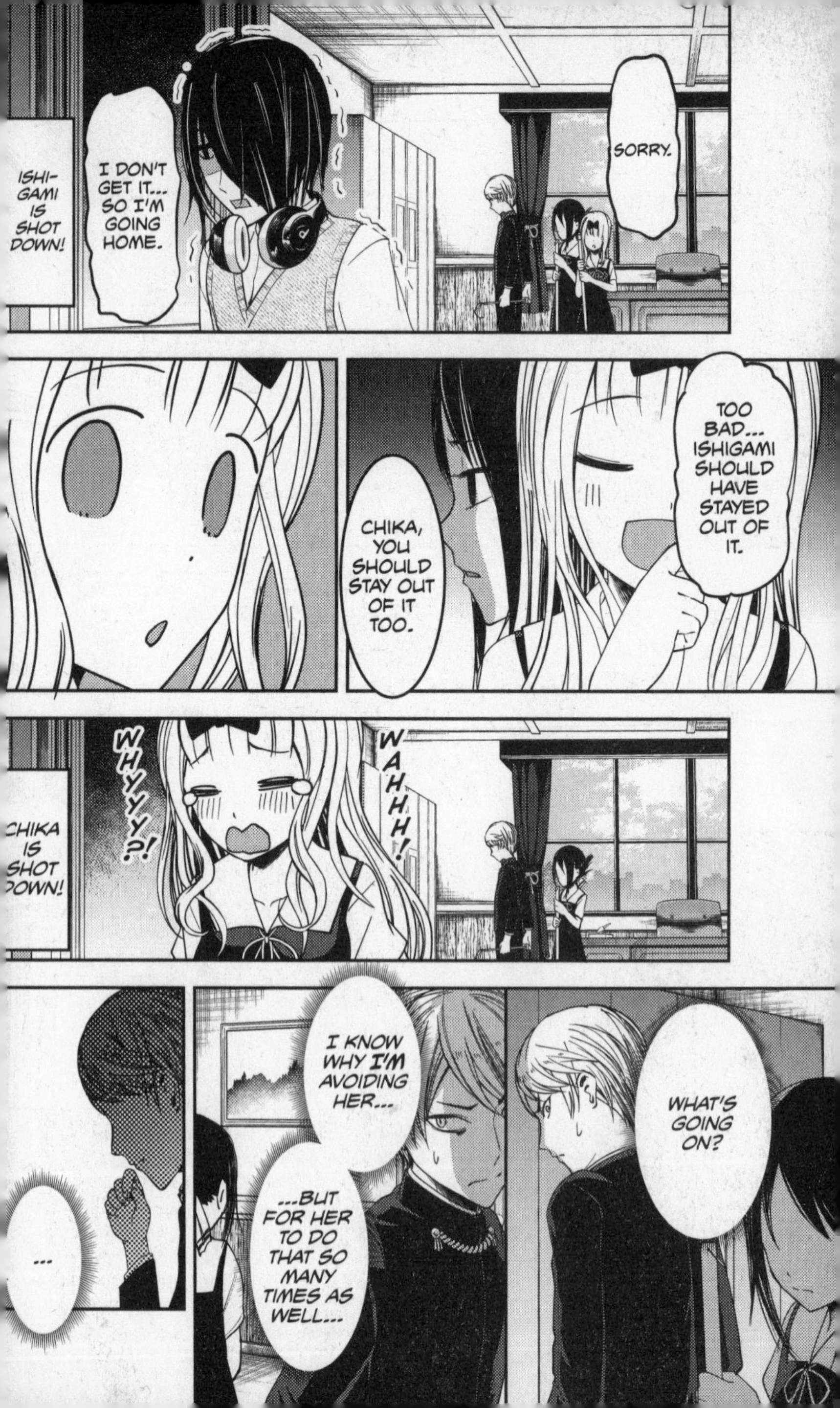
SORRY.
I DON'T GET IT... SO I'M GOING HOME.
ISHIGAMI IS SHOT DOWN!
TOO BAD... ISHIGAMI SHOULD HAVE STAYED OUT OF IT.
CHIKA, YOU SHOULD STAY OUT OF IT TOO.
WAHHH!
WHYYY?!
CHIKA IS SHOT DOWN!
WHAT'S GOING ON?
I KNOW WHY I'M AVOIDING HER...
...BUT FOR HER TO DO THAT SO MANY TIMES AS WELL...
...

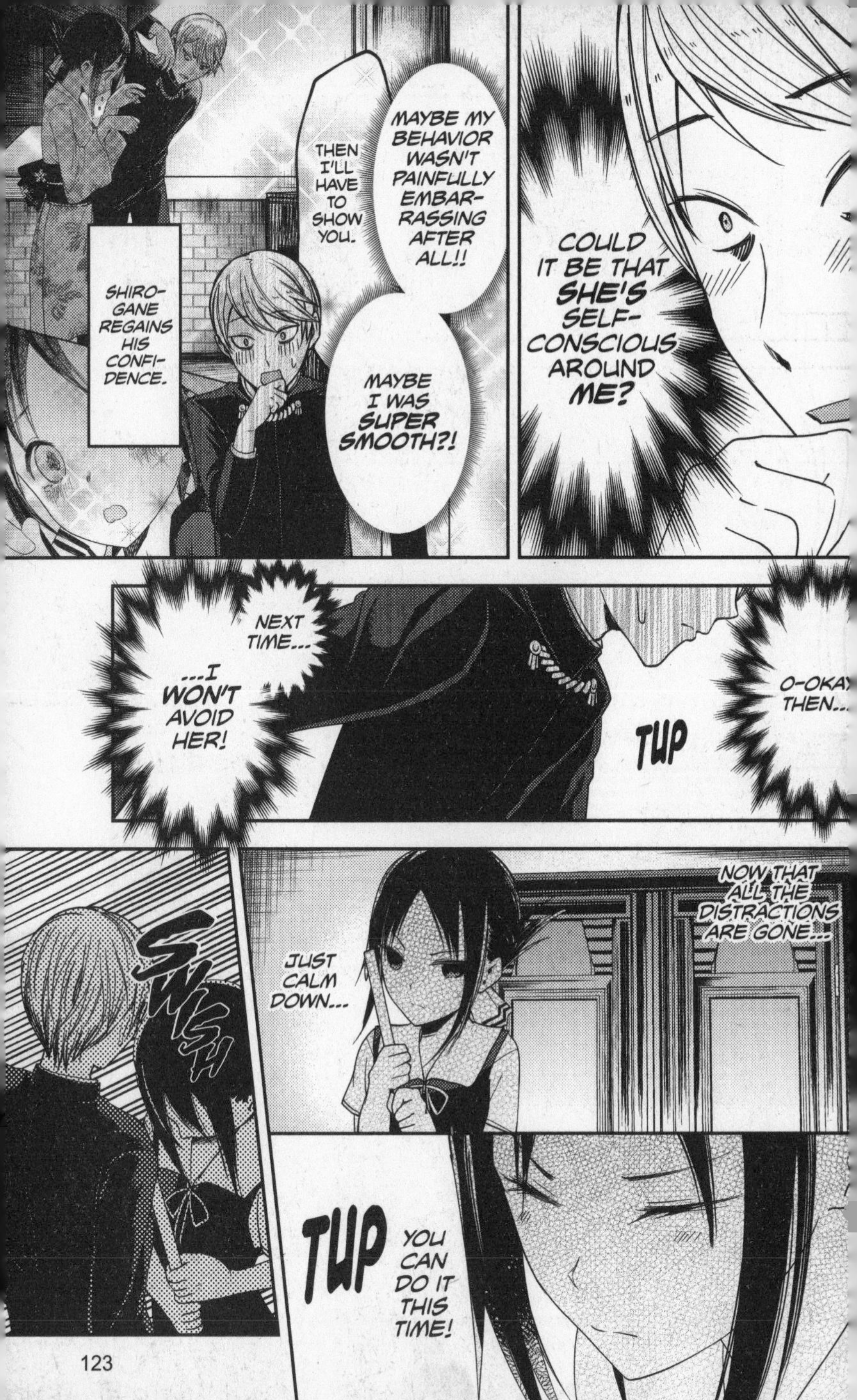

COULD IT BE THAT SHE'S SELF-CONSCIOUS AROUND ME?
MAYBE MY BEHAVIOR WASN'T PAINFULLY EMBARRASSING AFTER ALL!!
THEN I'LL HAVE TO SHOW YOU.
MAYBE I WAS SUPER SMOOTH?!
SHIRO-GANE REGAINS HIS CONFI-DENCE.
O-OKAY THEN...
TUP
NEXT TIME...
...I WON'T AVOID HER!
NOW THAT ALL THE DISTRACTIONS ARE GONE...
JUST CALM DOWN...
SWISH
YOU CAN DO IT THIS TIME!
TUP

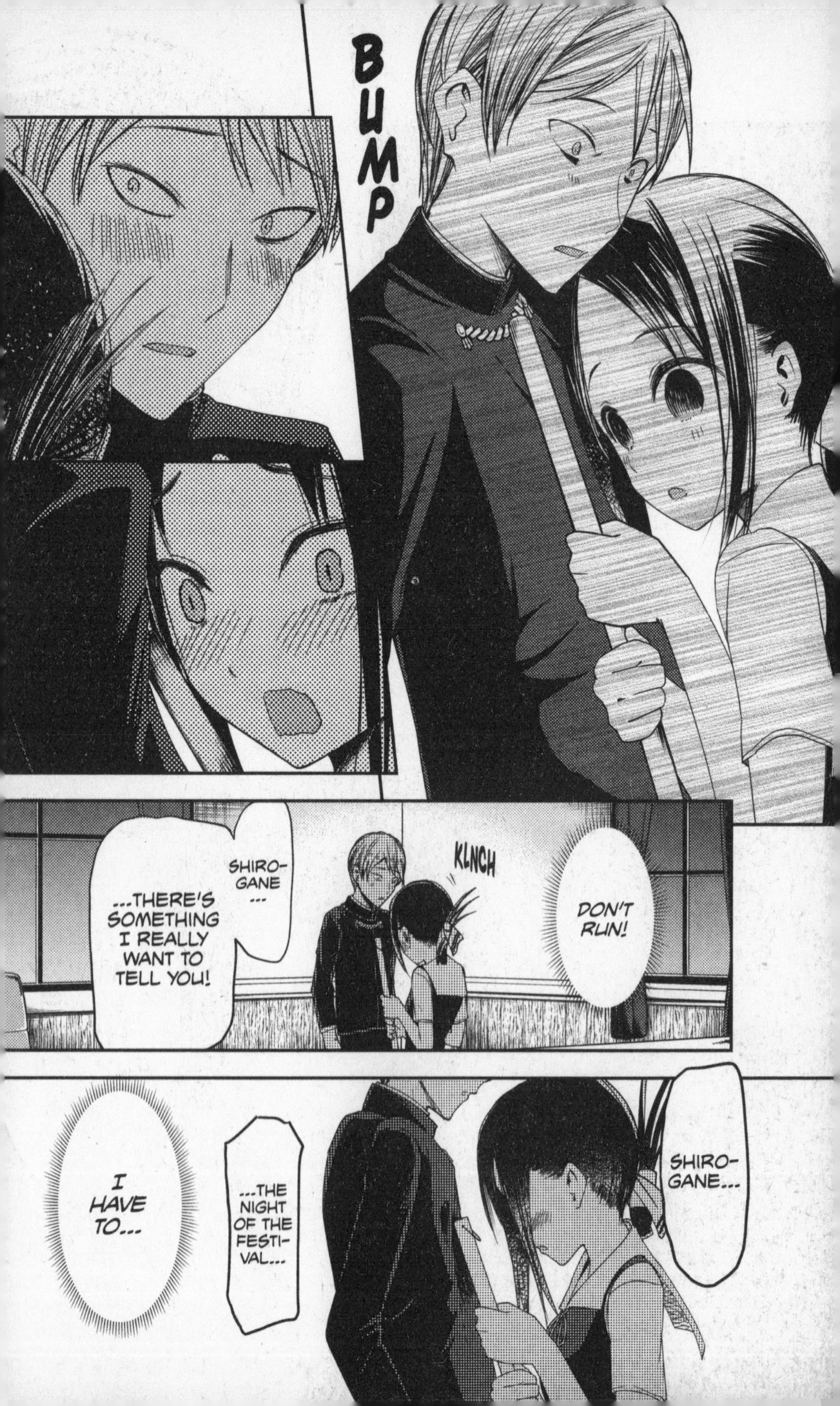
BUMP
DON'T RUN!
KLNCH
SHIRO-GANE...
...THERE'S SOMETHING I REALLY WANT TO TELL YOU!
SHIRO-GANE...
...THE NIGHT OF THE FESTI-VAL...
I HAVE TO...

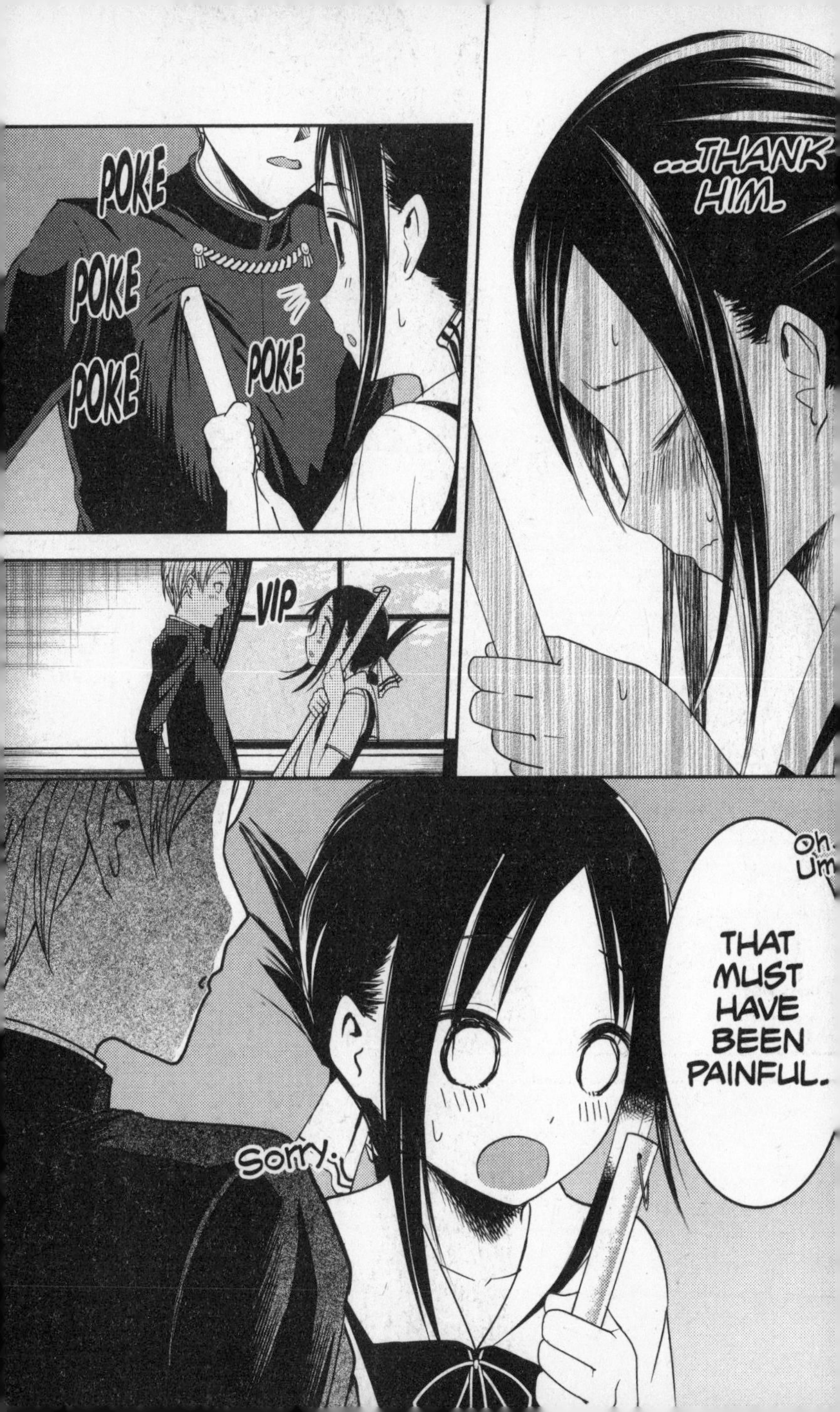
...THANK HIM.
POKE
POKE
POKE
POKE
VIP
Oh. Um
THAT MUST HAVE BEEN PAINFUL.
Sorry...

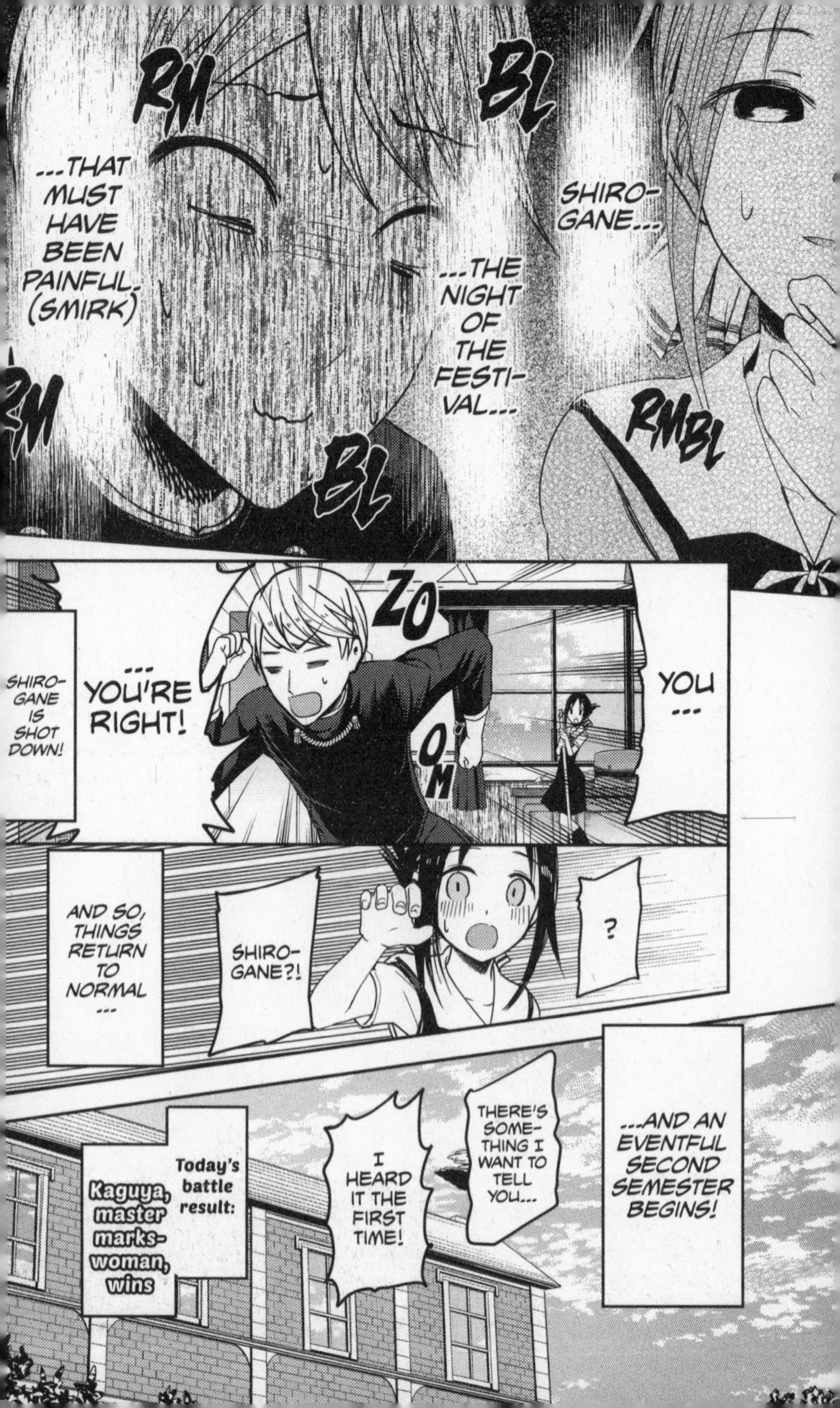
BL
SHIRO-GANE...
...THE NIGHT OF THE FESTI-VAL...
RM
...THAT MUST HAVE BEEN PAINFUL. (SMIRK)
RMBL
BL
RM
YOU...
ZO
OM
...YOU'RE RIGHT!
SHIRO-GANE IS SHOT DOWN!
?
SHIRO-GANE?!
AND SO, THINGS RETURN TO NORMAL...
...AND AN EVENTFUL SECOND SEMESTER BEGINS!
THERE'S SOME-THING I WANT TO TELL YOU...
I HEARD IT THE FIRST TIME!
Today's battle result:
Kaguya, master marks-woman, wins

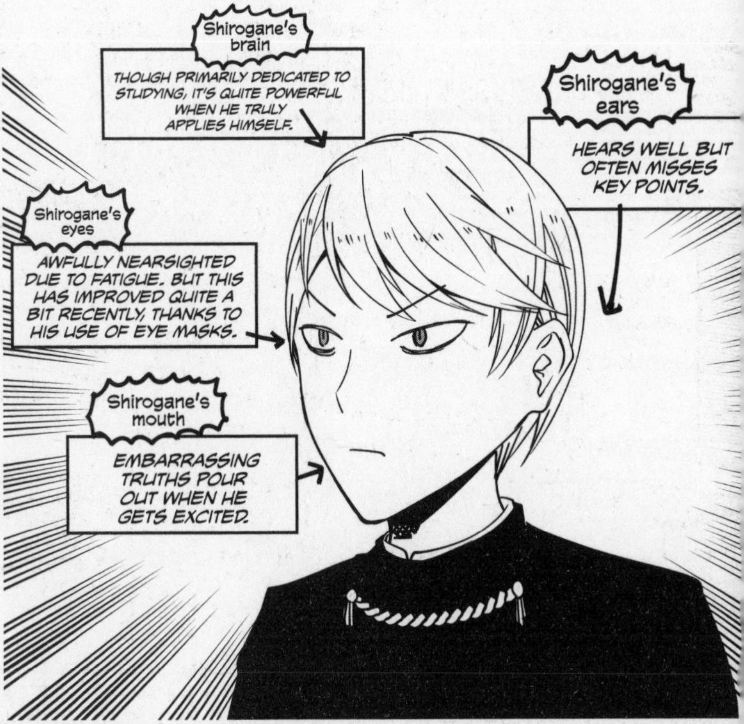

Shirogane's ears
HEARS WELL BUT OFTEN MISSES KEY POINTS.
Shirogane's brain
THOUGH PRIMARILY DEDICATED TO STUDYING, IT'S QUITE POWERFUL WHEN HE TRULY APPLIES HIMSELF.
Shirogane's eyes
AWFULLY NEARSIGHTED DUE TO FATIGUE. BUT THIS HAS IMPROVED QUITE A BIT RECENTLY, THANKS TO HIS USE OF EYE MASKS.
Shirogane's mouth
EMBARRASSING TRUTHS POUR OUT WHEN HE GETS EXCITED.

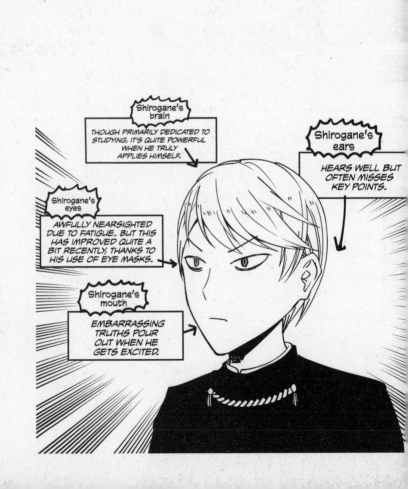

KAGUYA-SAMA
LOVE IS WAR

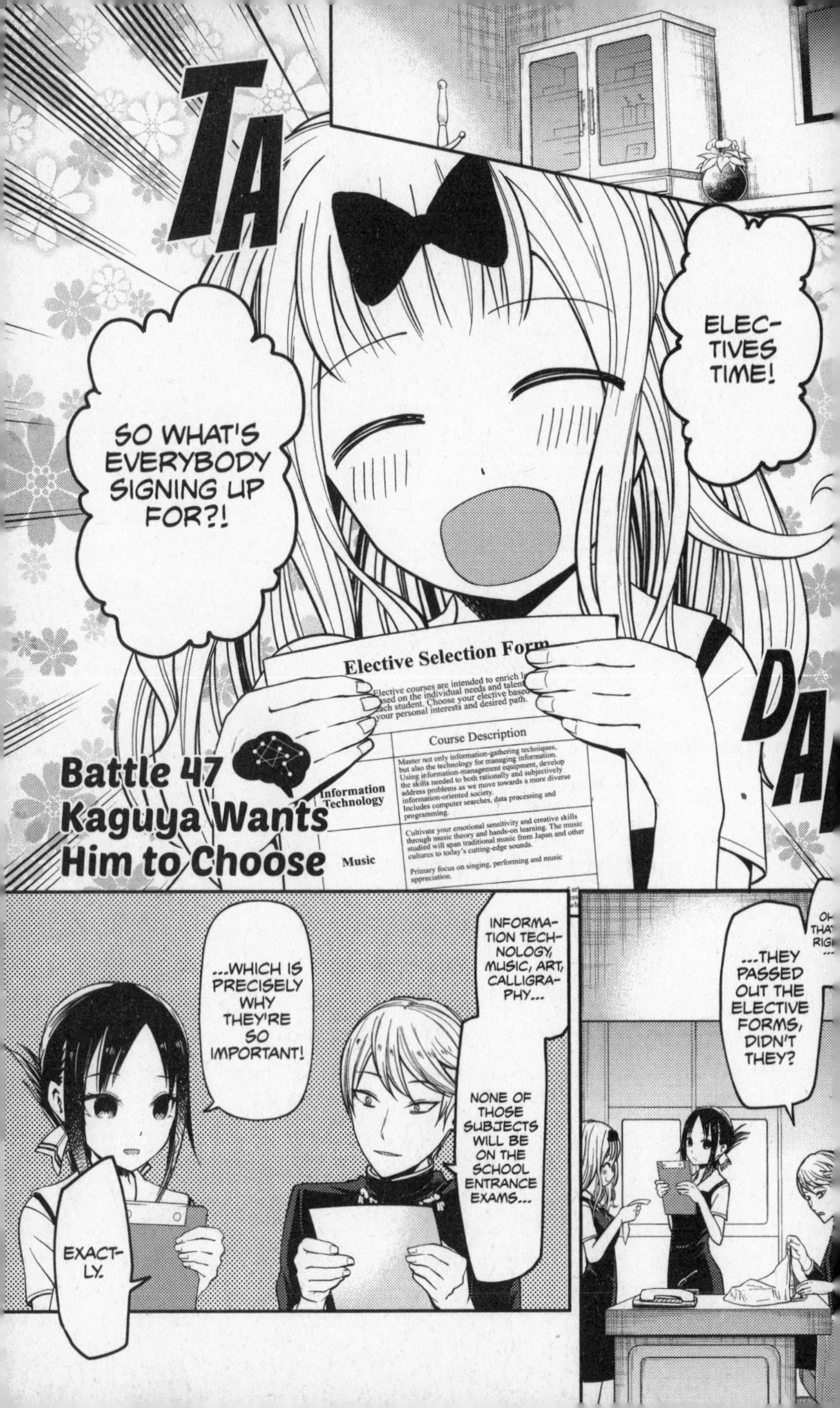
TA
ELECTIVES TIME!
SO WHAT'S EVERYBODY SIGNING UP FOR?!
DA
Battle 47 Kaguya Wants Him to Choose
Elective Selection Form
Course Description
Information Technology
Master not only information-gathering techniques, but also the technology for managing information. Using information-management equipment, develop the skills needed to both rationally and subjectively address problems as we move towards a more diverse information-oriented society. Includes computer searches, data processing and programming.
Music
Cultivate your emotional sensitivity and creative skills through music theory and hands-on learning. The music studied will span traditional music from Japan and other cultures to today's cutting-edge sounds.
Primary focus on singing, performing and music appreciation.
...THEY PASSED OUT THE ELECTIVE FORMS, DIDN'T THEY?
INFORMATION TECHNOLOGY, MUSIC, ART, CALLIGRAPHY...
NONE OF THOSE SUBJECTS WILL BE ON THE SCHOOL ENTRANCE EXAMS...
...WHICH IS PRECISELY WHY THEY'RE SO IMPORTANT!
EXACTLY.

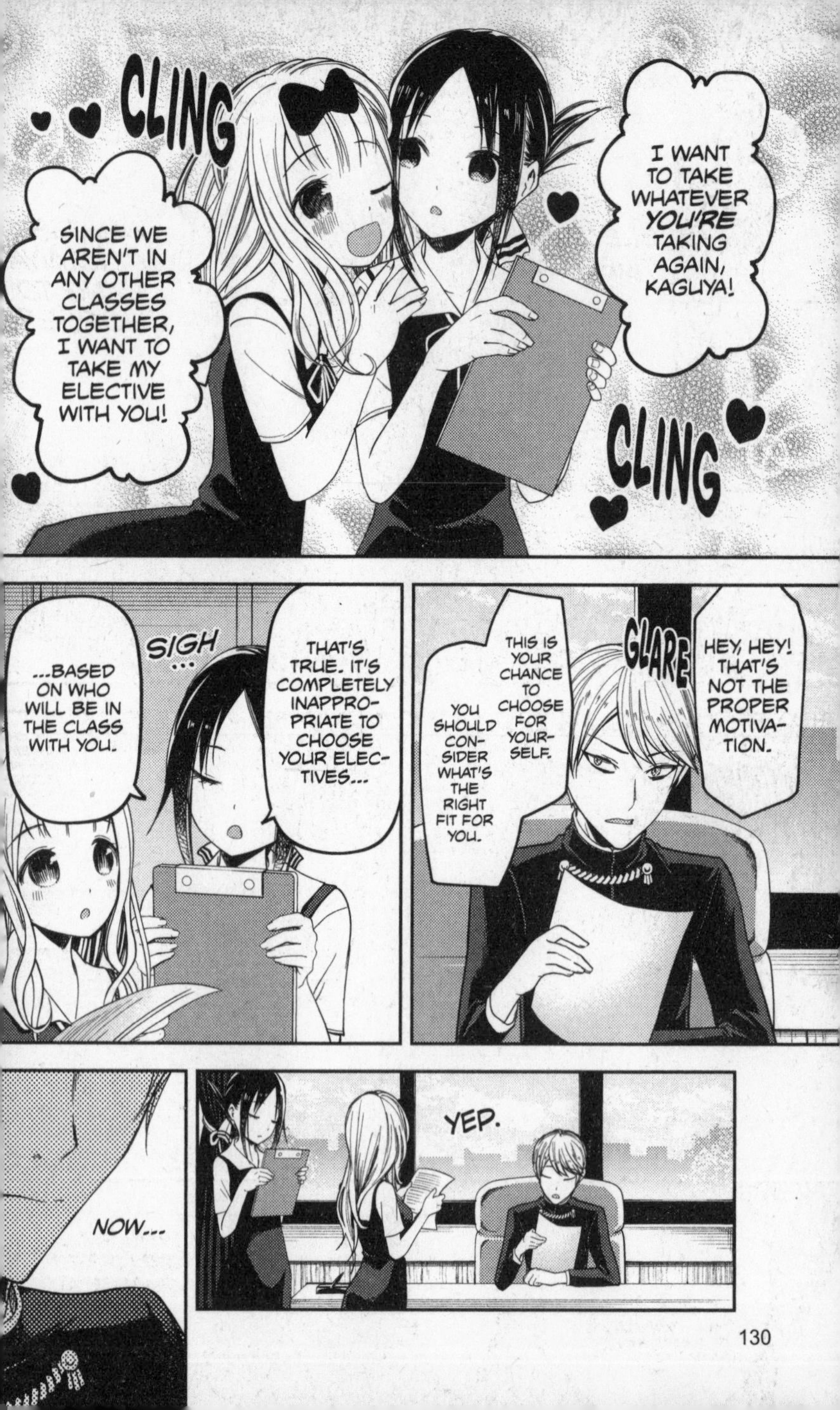
I WANT TO TAKE WHATEVER *YOU'RE* TAKING AGAIN, KAGUYA!
CLING
SINCE WE AREN'T IN ANY OTHER CLASSES TOGETHER, I WANT TO TAKE MY ELECTIVE WITH YOU!
CLING
HEY, HEY! THAT'S NOT THE PROPER MOTIVATION.
GLARE
THIS IS YOUR CHANCE TO CHOOSE FOR YOURSELF.
YOU SHOULD CONSIDER WHAT'S THE RIGHT FIT FOR YOU.
THAT'S TRUE. IT'S COMPLETELY INAPPROPRIATE TO CHOOSE YOUR ELECTIVES...
SIGH...
...BASED ON WHO WILL BE IN THE CLASS WITH YOU.
YEP.
NOW...

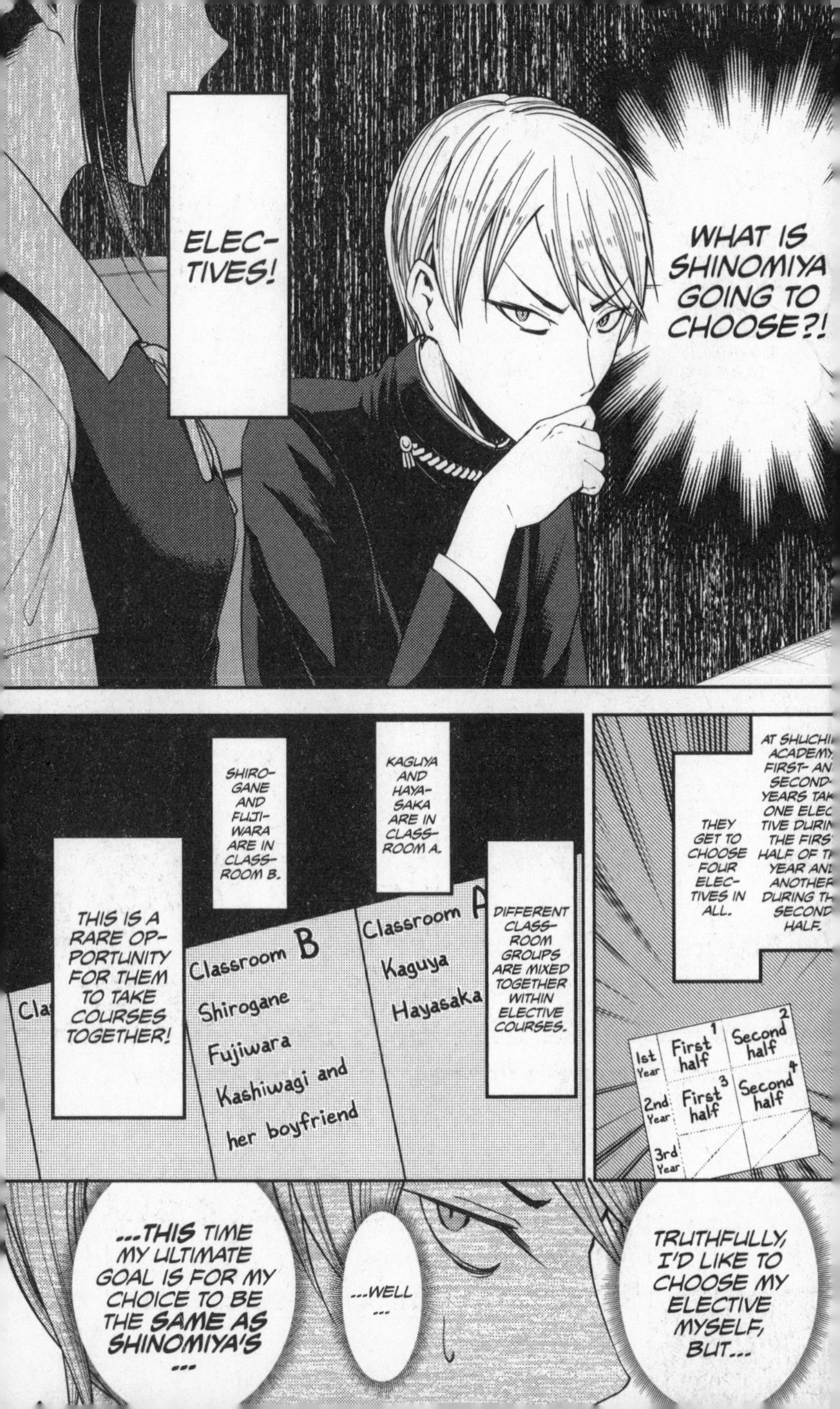
WHAT IS SHINOMIYA GOING TO CHOOSE?!
ELECTIVES!
AT SHUCHI ACADEMY, FIRST- AN SECOND-YEARS TAK ONE ELEC-TIVE DURIN THE FIRS HALF OF T YEAR AND ANOTHER DURING TH SECOND HALF.
THEY GET TO CHOOSE FOUR ELECTIVES IN ALL.
1st Year
First half 1
Second half 2
2nd Year
First half 3
Second half 4
3rd Year
KAGUYA AND HAYASAKA ARE IN CLASSROOM A.
SHIROGANE AND FUJIWARA ARE IN CLASSROOM B.
DIFFERENT CLASSROOM GROUPS ARE MIXED TOGETHER WITHIN ELECTIVE COURSES.
Classroom A
Kaguya
Hayasaka
Classroom B
Shirogane
Fujiwara
Kashiwagi and her boyfriend
THIS IS A RARE OPPORTUNITY FOR THEM TO TAKE COURSES TOGETHER!
TRUTHFULLY, I'D LIKE TO CHOOSE MY ELECTIVE MYSELF, BUT...
...WELL...
...THIS TIME MY ULTIMATE GOAL IS FOR MY CHOICE TO BE THE SAME AS SHINOMIYA'S...

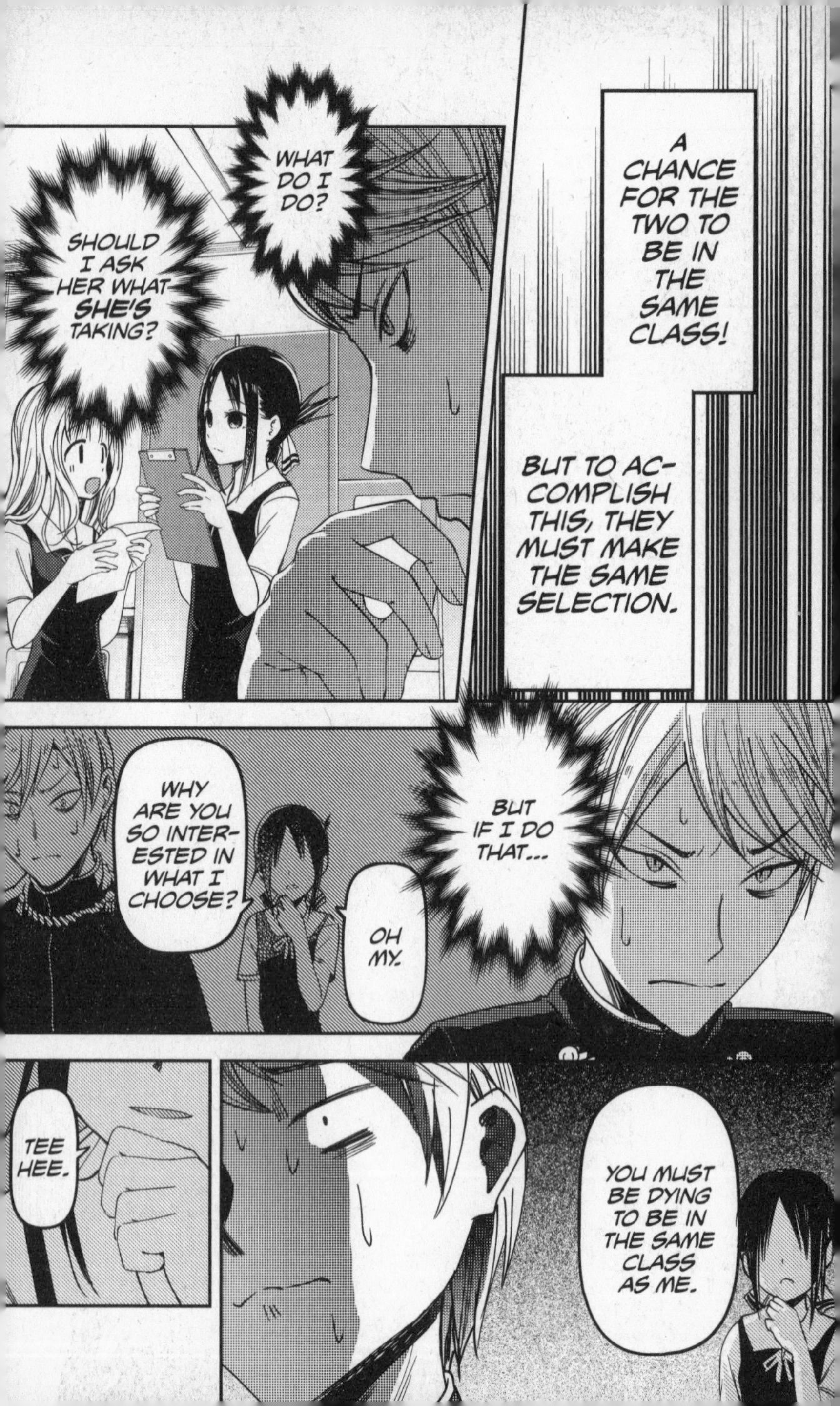
A CHANCE FOR THE TWO TO BE IN THE SAME CLASS!
BUT TO ACCOMPLISH THIS, THEY MUST MAKE THE SAME SELECTION.
WHAT DO I DO?
SHOULD I ASK HER WHAT SHE'S TAKING?
BUT IF I DO THAT...
OH MY.
WHY ARE YOU SO INTERESTED IN WHAT I CHOOSE?
YOU MUST BE DYING TO BE IN THE SAME CLASS AS ME.
TEE HEE.

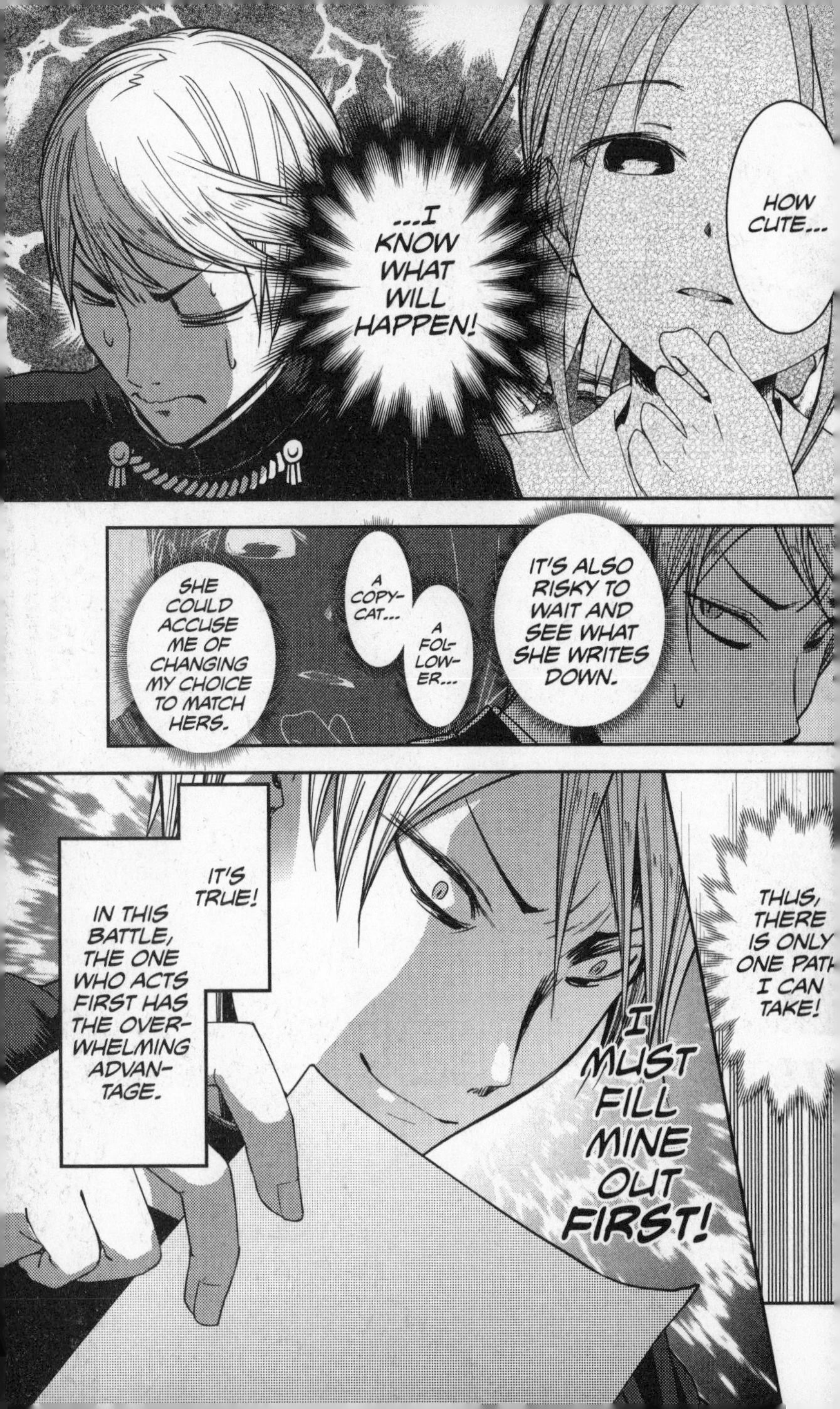
HOW CUTE...
...I KNOW WHAT WILL HAPPEN!
IT'S ALSO RISKY TO WAIT AND SEE WHAT SHE WRITES DOWN.
A COPY-CAT...
A FOL-LOW-ER...
SHE COULD ACCUSE ME OF CHANGING MY CHOICE TO MATCH HERS.
THUS, THERE IS ONLY ONE PATH I CAN TAKE!
I MUST FILL MINE OUT FIRST!
IT'S TRUE!
IN THIS BATTLE, THE ONE WHO ACTS FIRST HAS THE OVER-WHELMING ADVAN-TAGE.

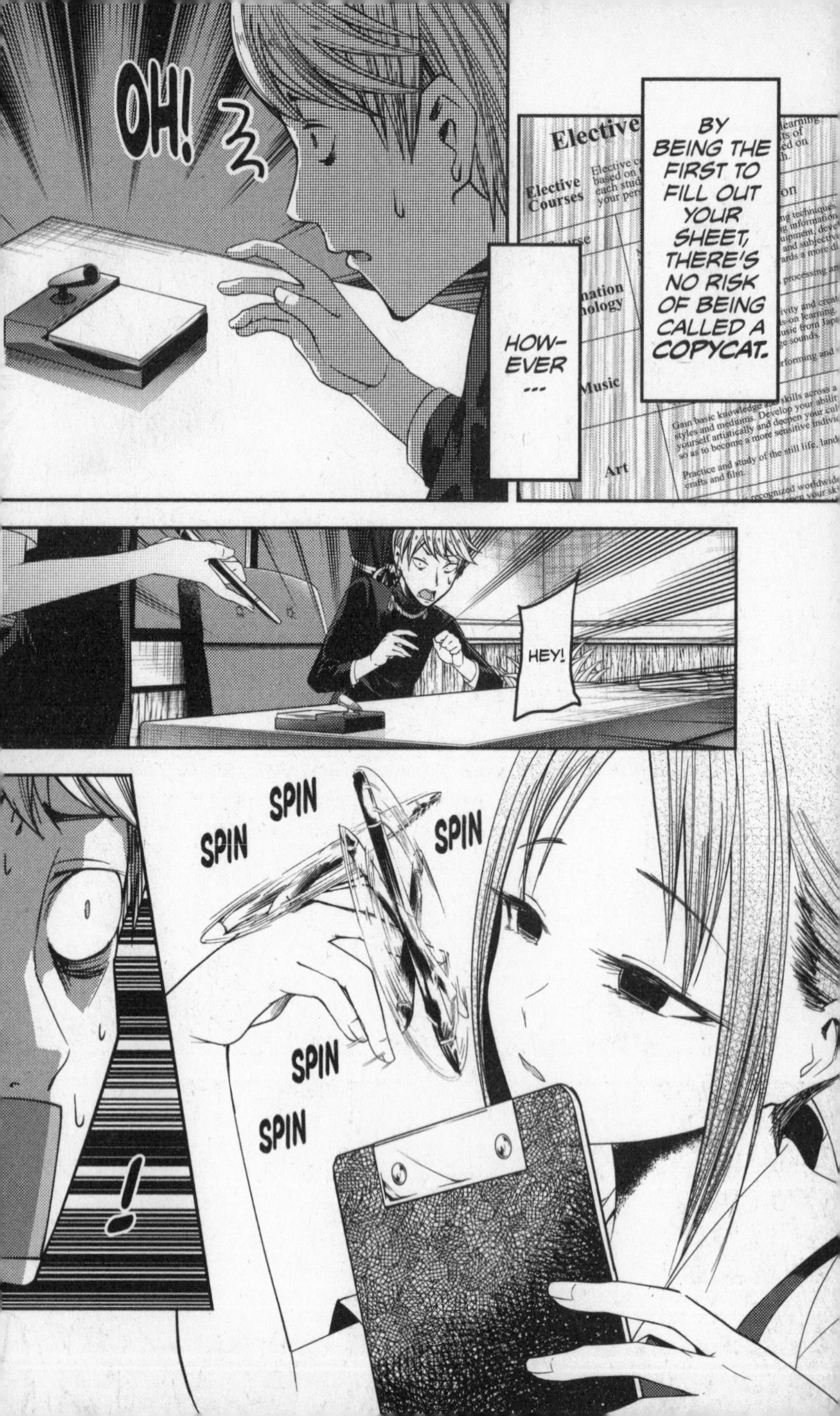

Elective
Elective Courses
Music
Art
BY BEING THE FIRST TO FILL OUT YOUR SHEET, THERE'S NO RISK OF BEING CALLED A COPYCAT.
HOW-EVER---
OH!
HEY!
SPIN
SPIN
SPIN
SPIN
SPIN
!

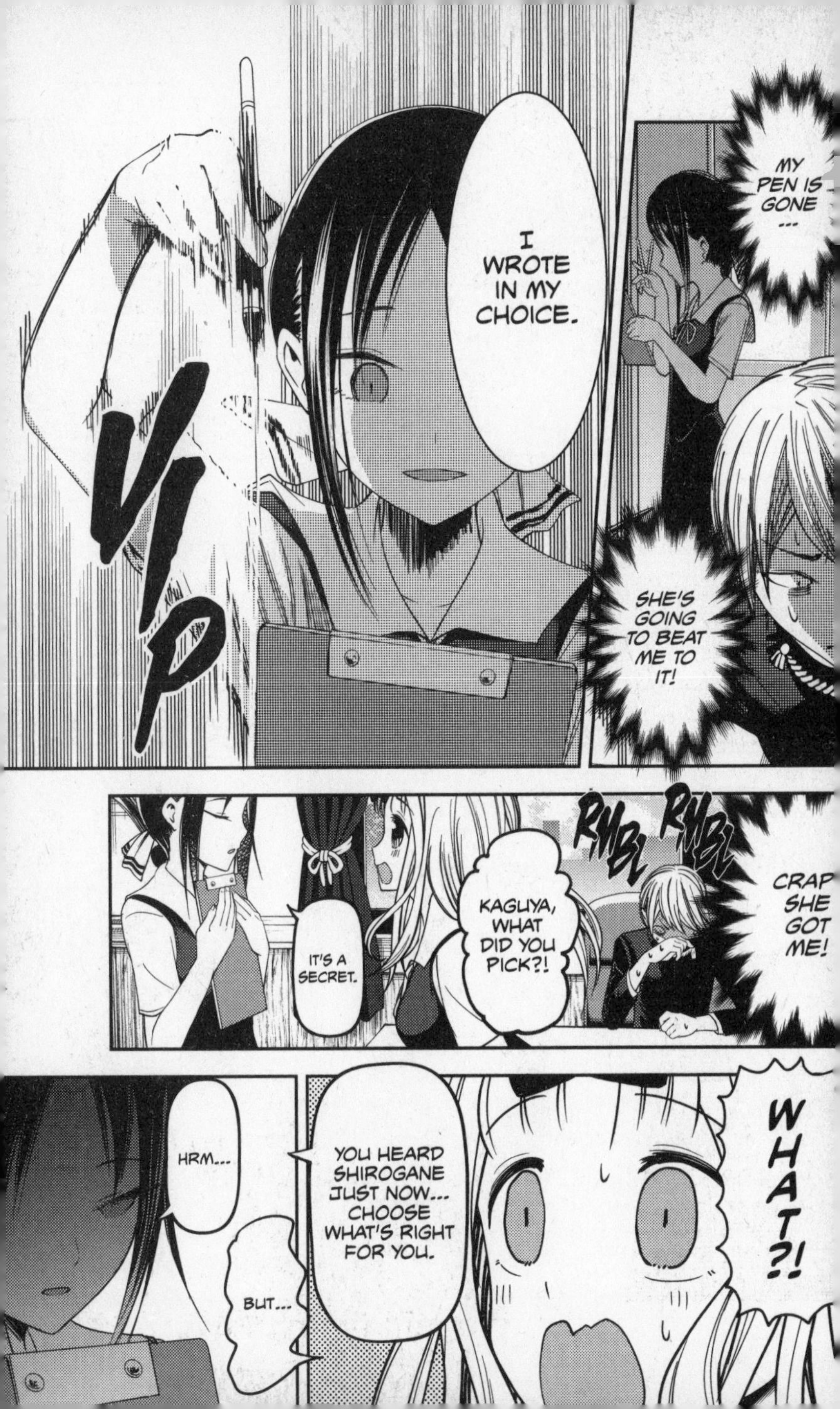
MY PEN IS GONE...
SHE'S GOING TO BEAT ME TO IT!
I WROTE IN MY CHOICE.
SLIP
CRAP SHE GOT ME!
RMBL RMBL
KAGUYA, WHAT DID YOU PICK?!
IT'S A SECRET.
WHAT?!
YOU HEARD SHIROGANE JUST NOW... CHOOSE WHAT'S RIGHT FOR YOU.
HRM...
BUT...

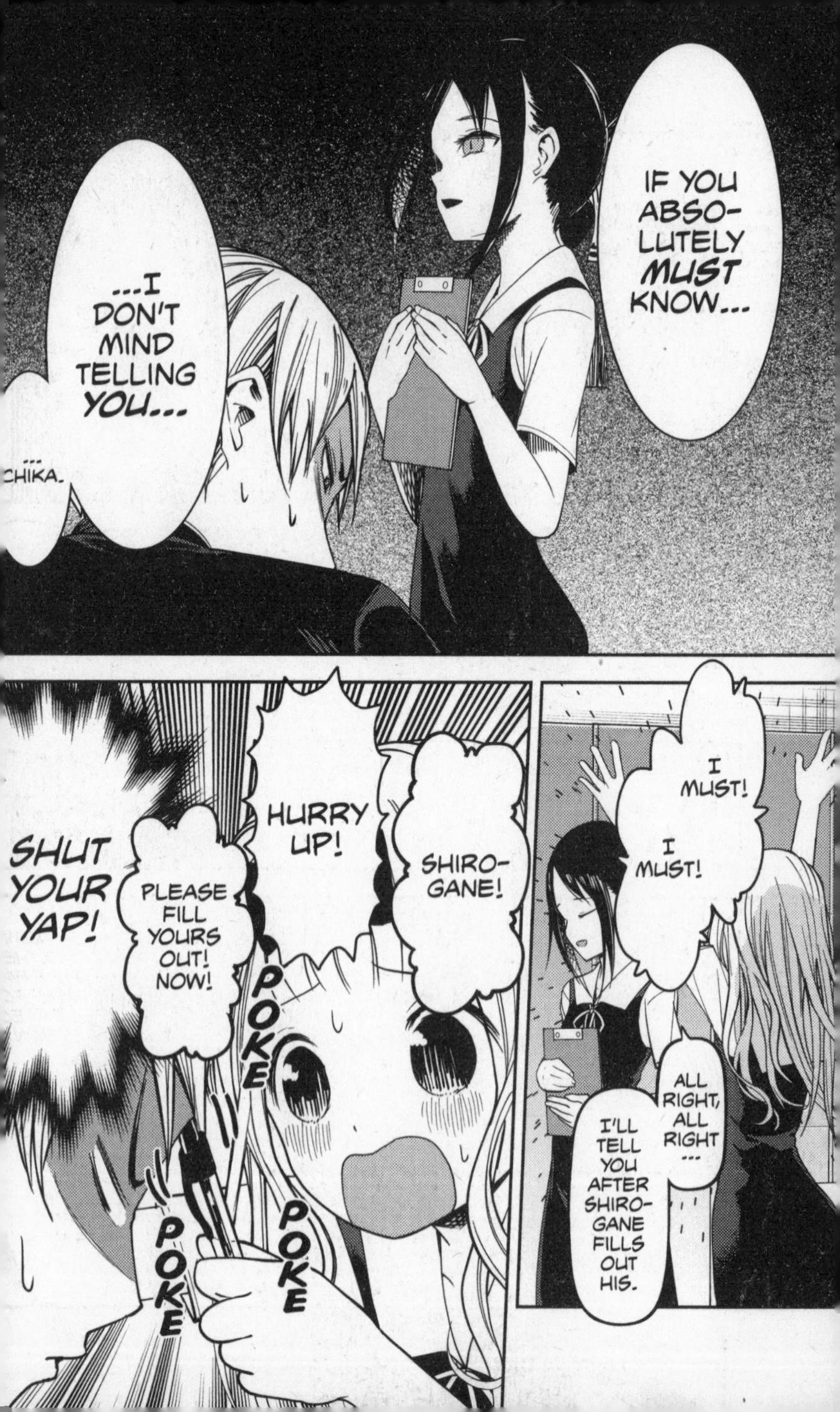
IF YOU ABSO-LUTELY MUST KNOW...
...I DON'T MIND TELLING YOU...
...CHIKA.
I MUST!
I MUST!
ALL RIGHT, ALL RIGHT...
I'LL TELL YOU AFTER SHIRO-GANE FILLS OUT HIS.
SHIRO-GANE!
HURRY UP!
PLEASE FILL YOURS OUT! NOW!
POKE
POKE
POKE
SHUT YOUR YAP!

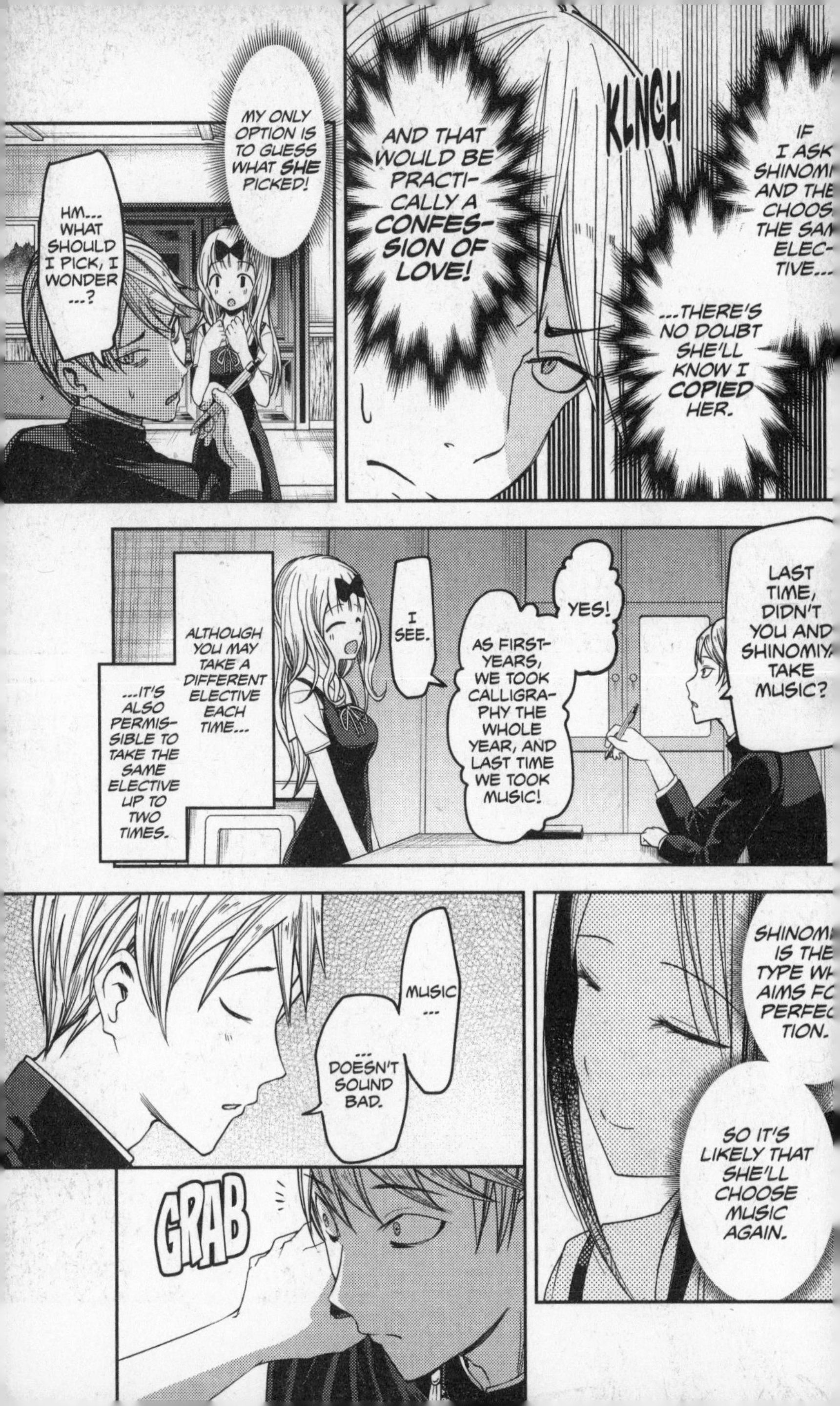
IF I ASK SHINOMI AND THE CHOOS THE SAM ELEC-TIVE...
KLNCH
...THERE'S NO DOUBT SHE'LL KNOW I COPIED HER.
AND THAT WOULD BE PRACTI-CALLY A CONFES-SION OF LOVE!
MY ONLY OPTION IS TO GUESS WHAT SHE PICKED!
HM... WHAT SHOULD I PICK, I WONDER...?
LAST TIME, DIDN'T YOU AND SHINOMIY TAKE MUSIC?
YES!
AS FIRST-YEARS, WE TOOK CALLIGRA-PHY THE WHOLE YEAR, AND LAST TIME WE TOOK MUSIC!
I SEE.
ALTHOUGH YOU MAY TAKE A DIFFERENT ELECTIVE EACH TIME...
...IT'S ALSO PERMIS-SIBLE TO TAKE THE SAME ELECTIVE UP TO TWO TIMES.
SHINOMI IS THE TYPE WH AIMS FO PERFEC TION.
SO IT'S LIKELY THAT SHE'LL CHOOSE MUSIC AGAIN.
MUSIC...
...DOESN'T SOUND BAD.
GRAB

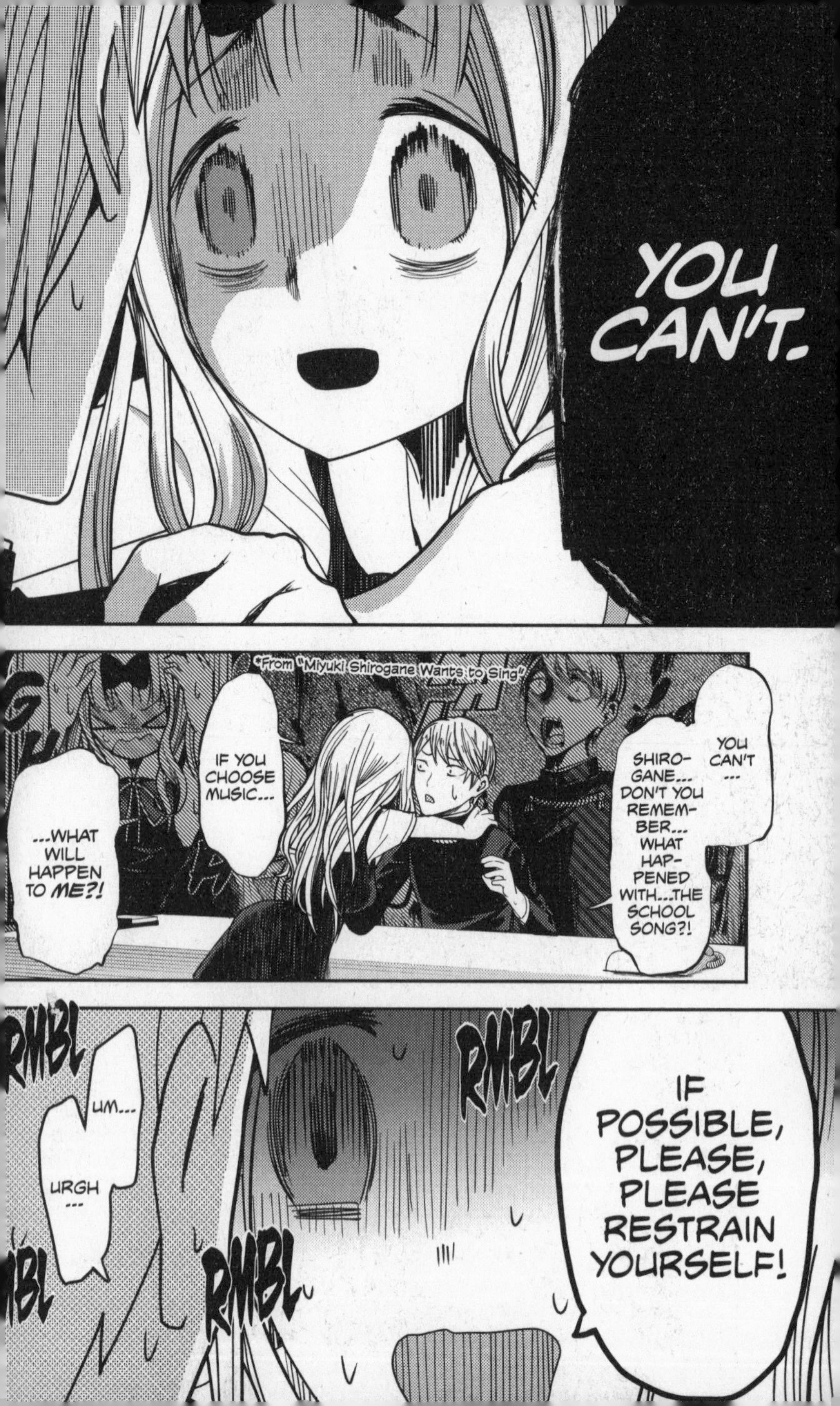
YOU CAN'T.
YOU CAN'T ...
SHIROGANE... DON'T YOU REMEMBER... WHAT HAPPENED WITH...THE SCHOOL SONG?!
*From "Miyuki Shirogane Wants to Sing"
IF YOU CHOOSE MUSIC...
...WHAT WILL HAPPEN TO ME?!
IF POSSIBLE, PLEASE, PLEASE RESTRAIN YOURSELF!
RMBL
RMBL
UM...
URGH ...
RMBL

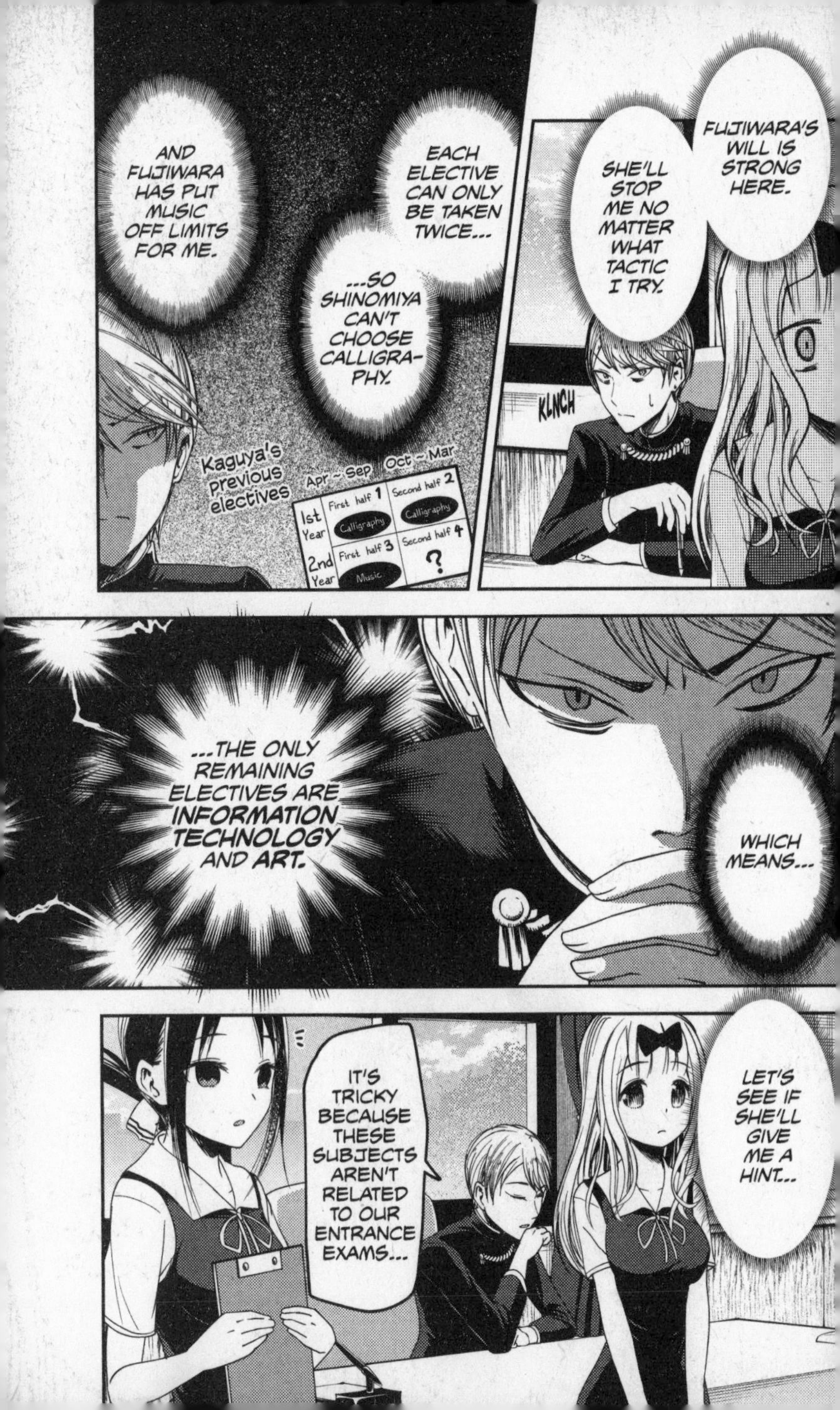

FUJIWARA'S WILL IS STRONG HERE.
SHE'LL STOP ME NO MATTER WHAT TACTIC I TRY.
KLNCH
EACH ELECTIVE CAN ONLY BE TAKEN TWICE...
...SO SHINOMIYA CAN'T CHOOSE CALLIGRA-PHY.
AND FUJIWARA HAS PUT MUSIC OFF LIMITS FOR ME.
Kaguya's previous electives
Apr ~ Sep
Oct ~ Mar
1st Year
First half 1
Calligraphy
Second half 2
Calligraphy
2nd Year
First half 3
Music
Second half 4
?
WHICH MEANS...
...THE ONLY REMAINING ELECTIVES ARE INFORMATION TECHNOLOGY AND ART.
LET'S SEE IF SHE'LL GIVE ME A HINT...
IT'S TRICKY BECAUSE THESE SUBJECTS AREN'T RELATED TO OUR ENTRANCE EXAMS...

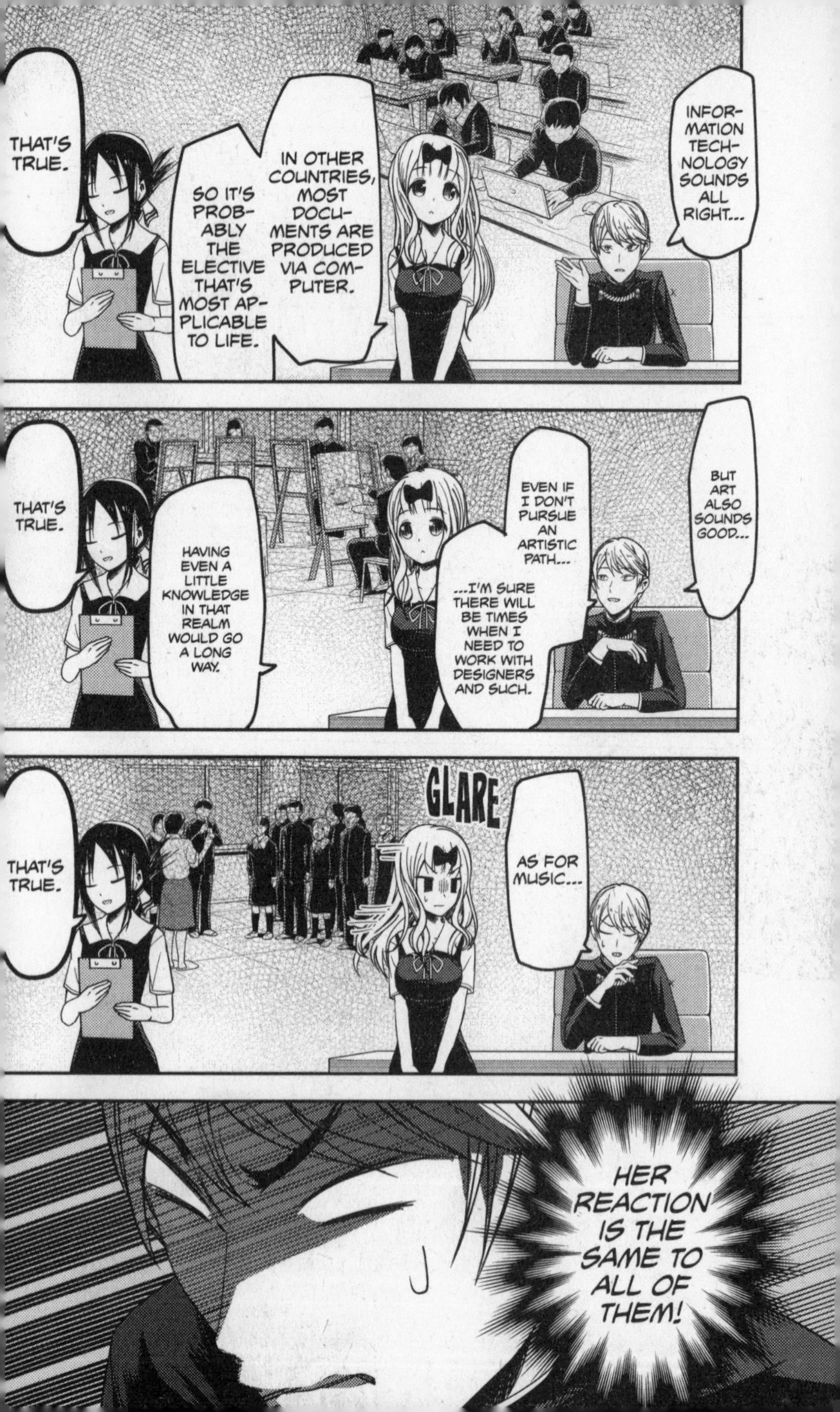
INFORMATION TECHNOLOGY SOUNDS ALL RIGHT...
IN OTHER COUNTRIES, MOST DOCUMENTS ARE PRODUCED VIA COMPUTER.
SO IT'S PROBABLY THE ELECTIVE THAT'S MOST APPLICABLE TO LIFE.
THAT'S TRUE.
BUT ART ALSO SOUNDS GOOD...
EVEN IF I DON'T PURSUE AN ARTISTIC PATH...
...I'M SURE THERE WILL BE TIMES WHEN I NEED TO WORK WITH DESIGNERS AND SUCH.
HAVING EVEN A LITTLE KNOWLEDGE IN THAT REALM WOULD GO A LONG WAY.
THAT'S TRUE.
AS FOR MUSIC...
GLARE
THAT'S TRUE.
HER REACTION IS THE SAME TO ALL OF THEM!

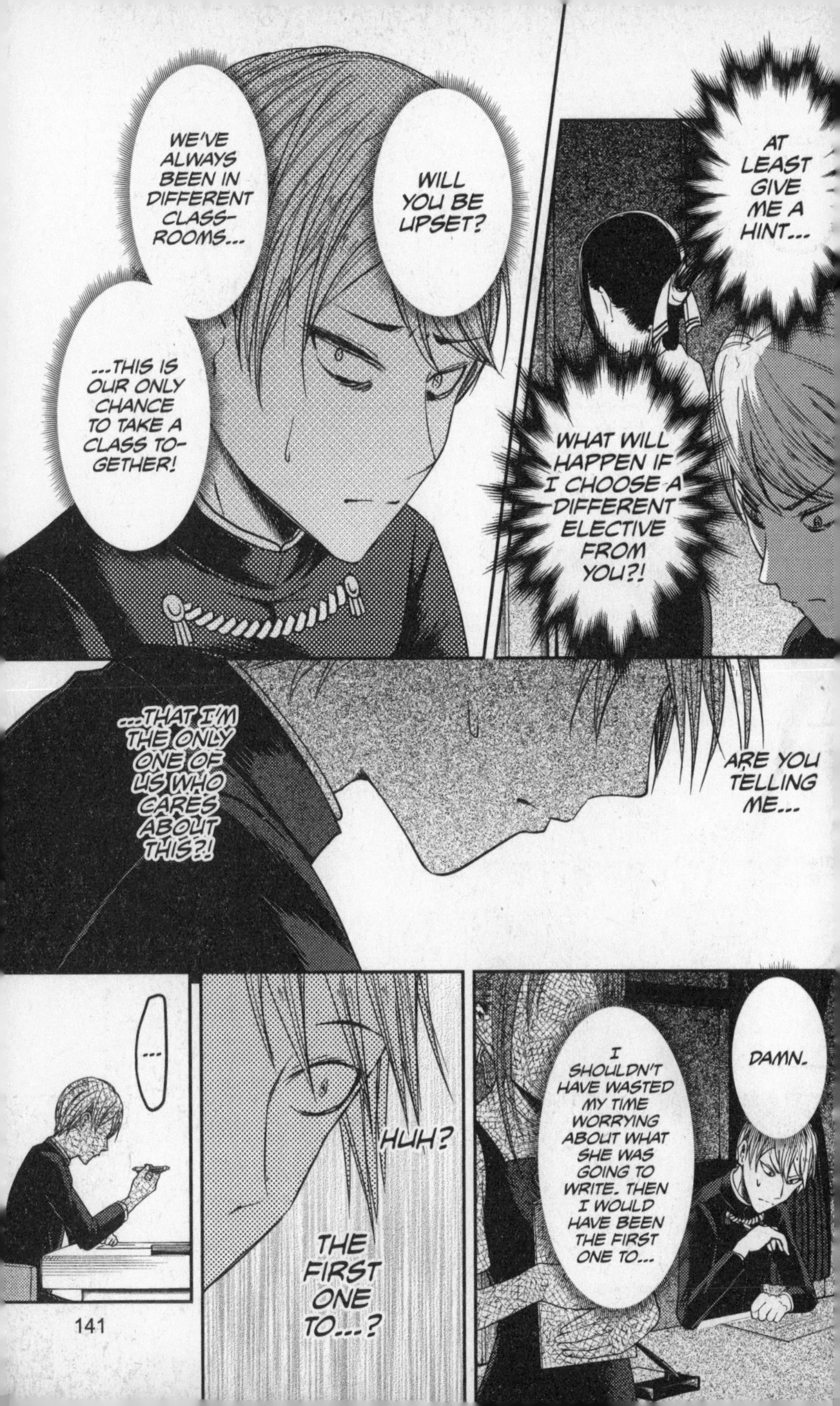
AT LEAST GIVE ME A HINT...
WHAT WILL HAPPEN IF I CHOOSE A DIFFERENT ELECTIVE FROM YOU?!
WILL YOU BE UPSET?
WE'VE ALWAYS BEEN IN DIFFERENT CLASS-ROOMS...
...THIS IS OUR ONLY CHANCE TO TAKE A CLASS TO-GETHER!
ARE YOU TELLING ME...
...THAT I'M THE ONLY ONE OF US WHO CARES ABOUT THIS?!
DAMN.
I SHOULDN'T HAVE WASTED MY TIME WORRYING ABOUT WHAT SHE WAS GOING TO WRITE. THEN I WOULD HAVE BEEN THE FIRST ONE TO...
HUH?
THE FIRST ONE TO...?
...

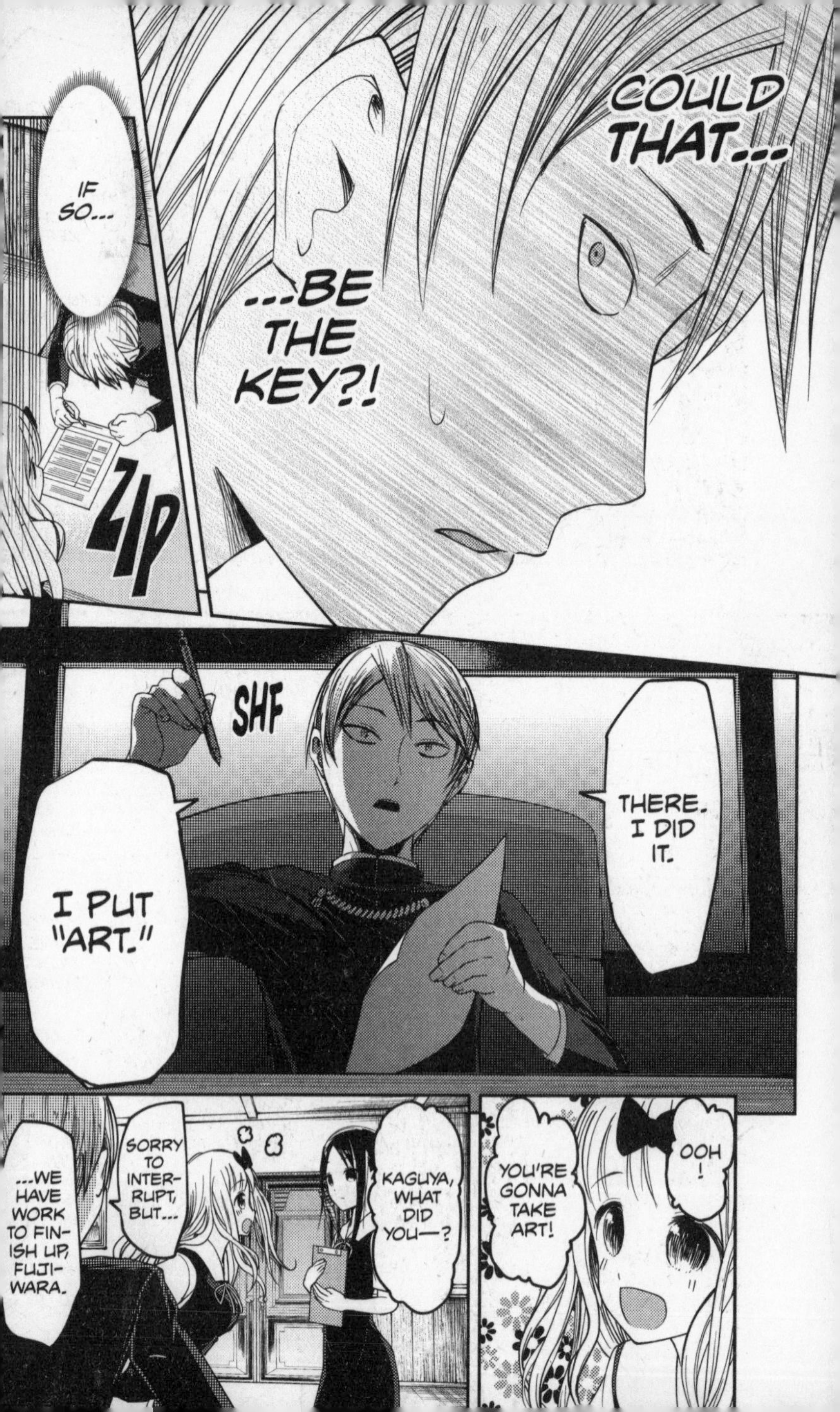
COULD THAT...
...BE THE KEY?!
IF SO...
ZIP
THERE. I DID IT.
SHF
I PUT "ART."
OOH!
YOU'RE GONNA TAKE ART!
KAGUYA, WHAT DID YOU—?
SORRY TO INTER-RUPT, BUT...
...WE HAVE WORK TO FIN-ISH UP, FUJI-WARA.

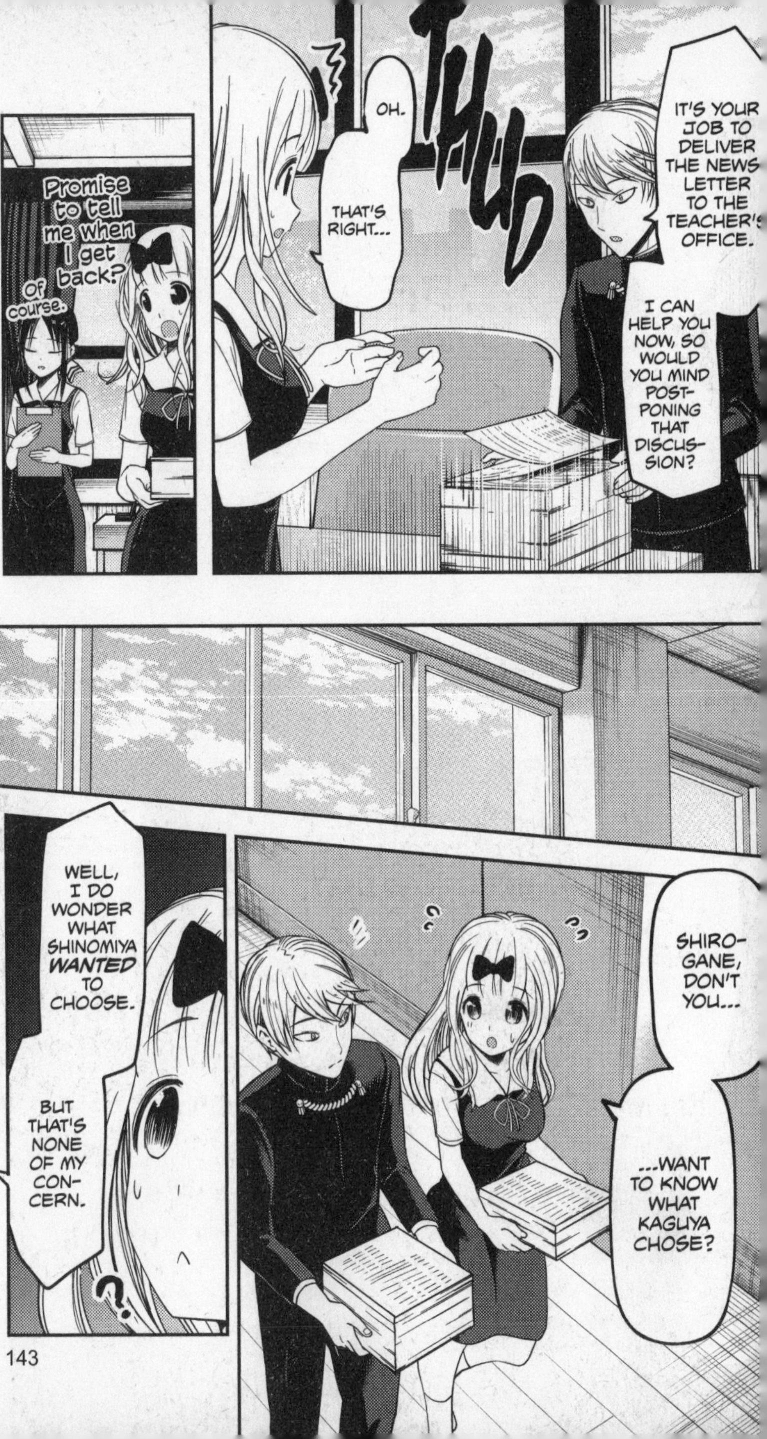
IT'S YOUR JOB TO DELIVER THE NEWSLETTER TO THE TEACHER'S OFFICE.
I CAN HELP YOU NOW, SO WOULD YOU MIND POSTPONING THAT DISCUSSION?
THUD
OH.
THAT'S RIGHT...
Promise to tell me when I get back?
Of course.
SHIROGANE, DON'T YOU...
...WANT TO KNOW WHAT KAGUYA CHOSE?
WELL, I DO WONDER WHAT SHINOMIYA *WANTED* TO CHOOSE.
BUT THAT'S NONE OF MY CONCERN.

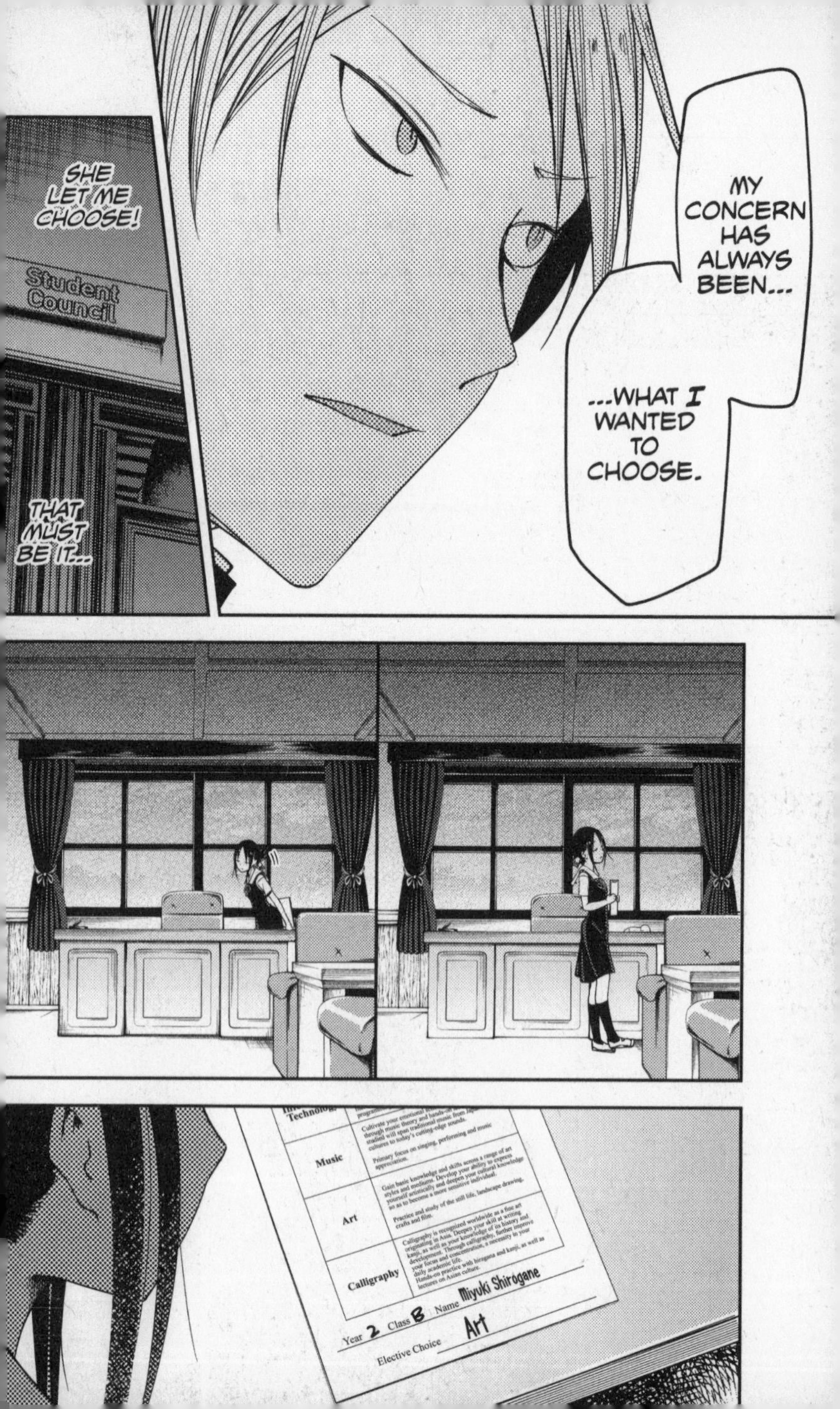
MY CONCERN HAS ALWAYS BEEN...
...WHAT I WANTED TO CHOOSE.
SHE LET ME CHOOSE!
Student Council
THAT MUST BE IT...
Technology
Music
Art
Calligraphy
Year 2 Class B Name Miyuki Shirogane
Elective Choice Art

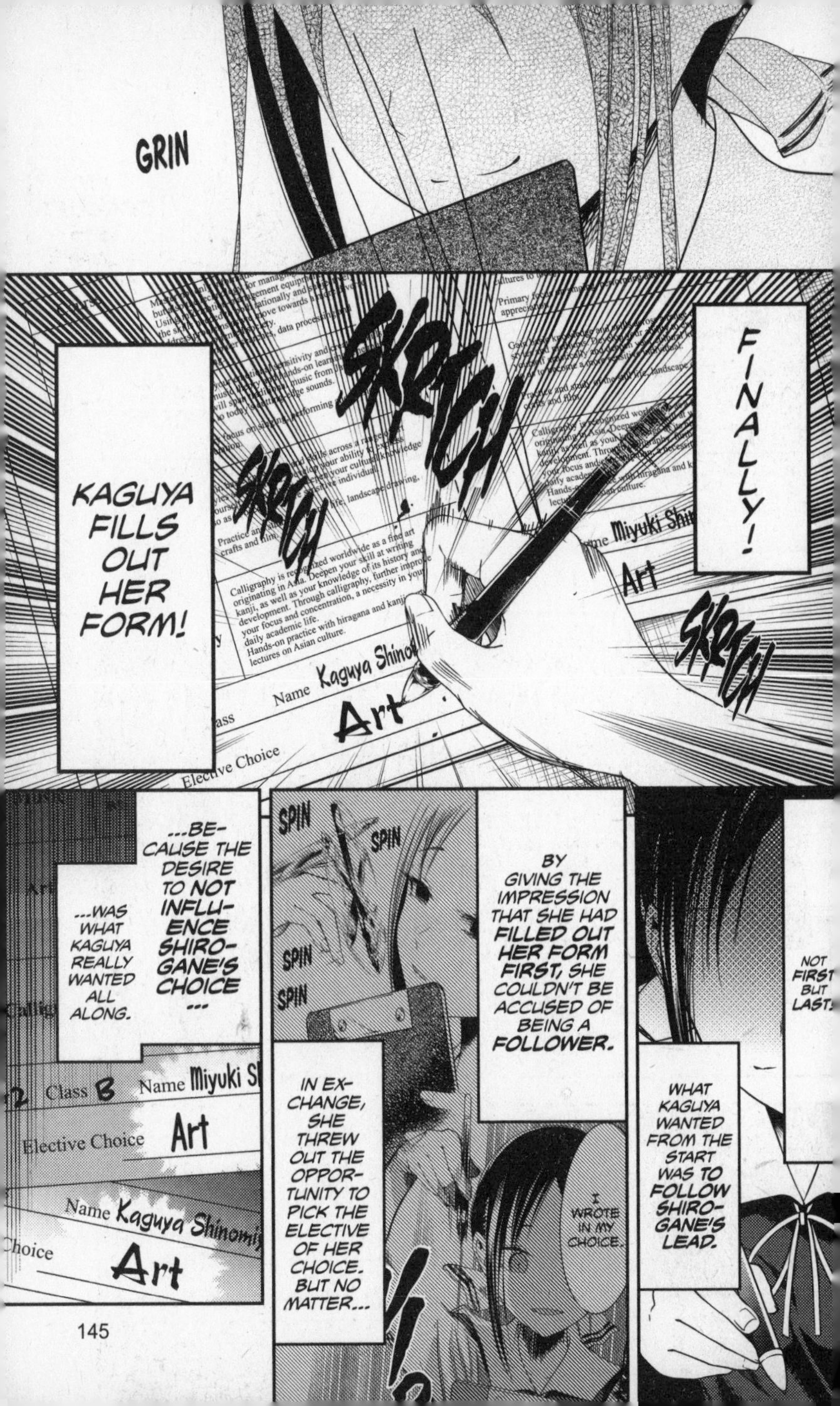
GRIN
FINALLY!
SKRITCH
SKRITCH
SKRITCH
KAGUYA FILLS OUT HER FORM!
Name Miyuki Shi
Art
Name Kaguya Shino
Art
Elective Choice
NOT FIRST BUT LAST.
WHAT KAGUYA WANTED FROM THE START WAS TO FOLLOW SHIROGANE'S LEAD.
BY GIVING THE IMPRESSION THAT SHE HAD FILLED OUT HER FORM FIRST, SHE COULDN'T BE ACCUSED OF BEING A FOLLOWER.
SPIN
SPIN
SPIN
SPIN
IN EXCHANGE, SHE THREW OUT THE OPPORTUNITY TO PICK THE ELECTIVE OF HER CHOICE. BUT NO MATTER...
I WROTE IN MY CHOICE.
...BECAUSE THE DESIRE TO NOT INFLUENCE SHIROGANE'S CHOICE...
...WAS WHAT KAGUYA REALLY WANTED ALL ALONG.
Class B Name Miyuki Sh
Elective Choice Art
Name Kaguya Shinomiy
Choice Art

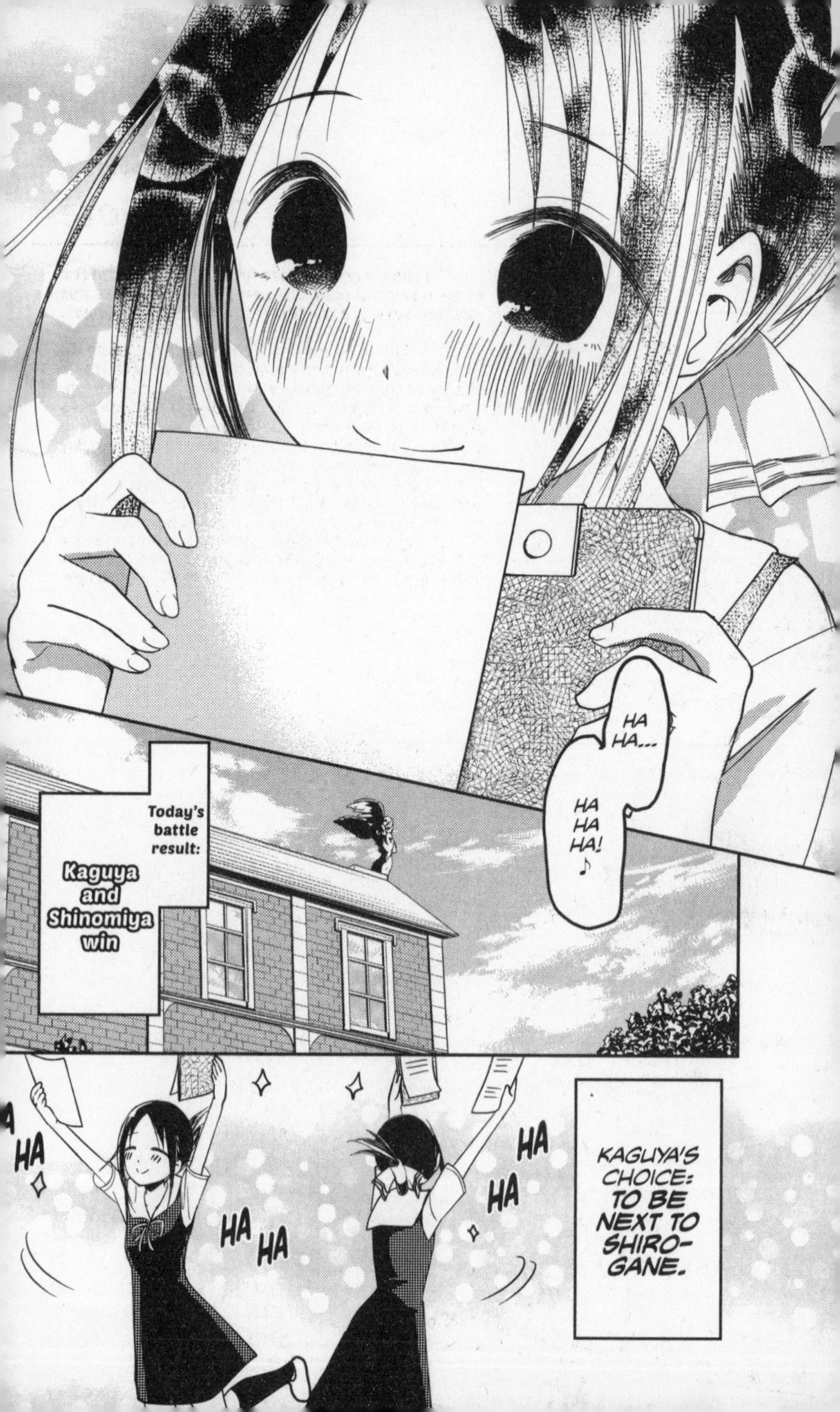
HA HA...
HA HA HA! ♪
Today's battle result:
Kaguya and Shinomiya win
KAGUYA'S CHOICE: TO BE NEXT TO SHIRO-GANE.
HA
HA
HA
HA
HA

Shuchiin Class Note

Students change classes once a year, and for first-years and second-years, classrooms are not divided between the liberal arts and the sciences.

Third-years are divided up depending on whether students plan to study at an outside university or continue within the Shuchiin institution. The understanding is that an outside school indicates a path in the sciences, and to continue at Shuchiin indicates a path in the liberal arts. The next step for Shuchiin students is typically Shuchiin University or Teikoku University. Based on scores alone, Teikoku University ranks higher, but Shuchiin gains value from its ample research budget and future opportunities tied to its academic societies. Ultimately, the choice of which school to attend is determined by each student's vision for their future.

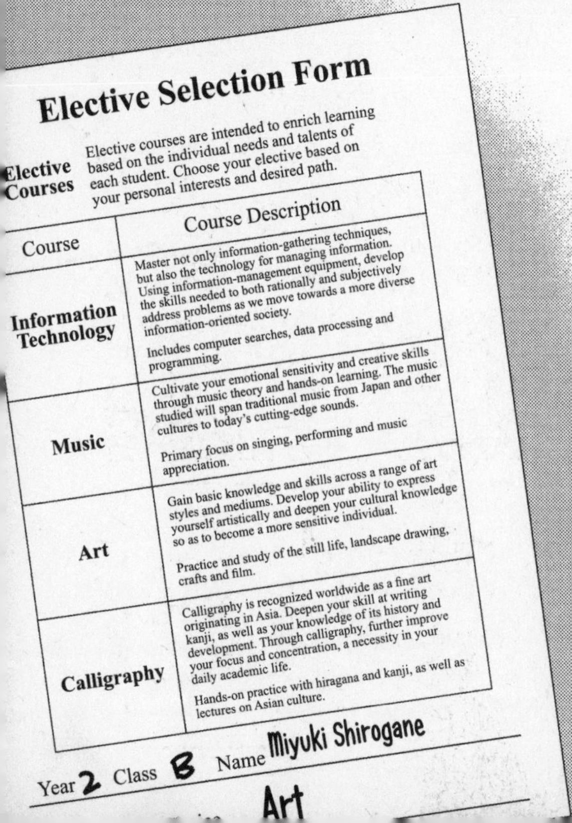

Elective Selection Form

Elective Courses Elective courses are intended to enrich learning based on the individual needs and talents of each student. Choose your elective based on your personal interests and desired path.

Course	Course Description
Information Technology	Master not only information-gathering techniques, but also the technology for managing information. Using information-management equipment, develop the skills needed to both rationally and subjectively address problems as we move towards a more diverse information-oriented society. Includes computer searches, data processing and programming.
Music	Cultivate your emotional sensitivity and creative skills through music theory and hands-on learning. The music studied will span traditional music from Japan and other cultures to today's cutting-edge sounds. Primary focus on singing, performing and music appreciation.
Art	Gain basic knowledge and skills across a range of art styles and mediums. Develop your ability to express yourself artistically and deepen your cultural knowledge so as to become a more sensitive individual. Practice and study of the still life, landscape drawing, crafts and film.
Calligraphy	Calligraphy is recognized worldwide as a fine art originating in Asia. Deepen your skill at writing kanji, as well as your knowledge of its history and development. Through calligraphy, further improve your focus and concentration, a necessity in your daily academic life. Hands-on practice with hiragana and kanji, as well as lectures on Asian culture.

Year 2 Class B Name Miyuki Shirogane

Art

KAGUYA-SAMA
LOVE IS WAR

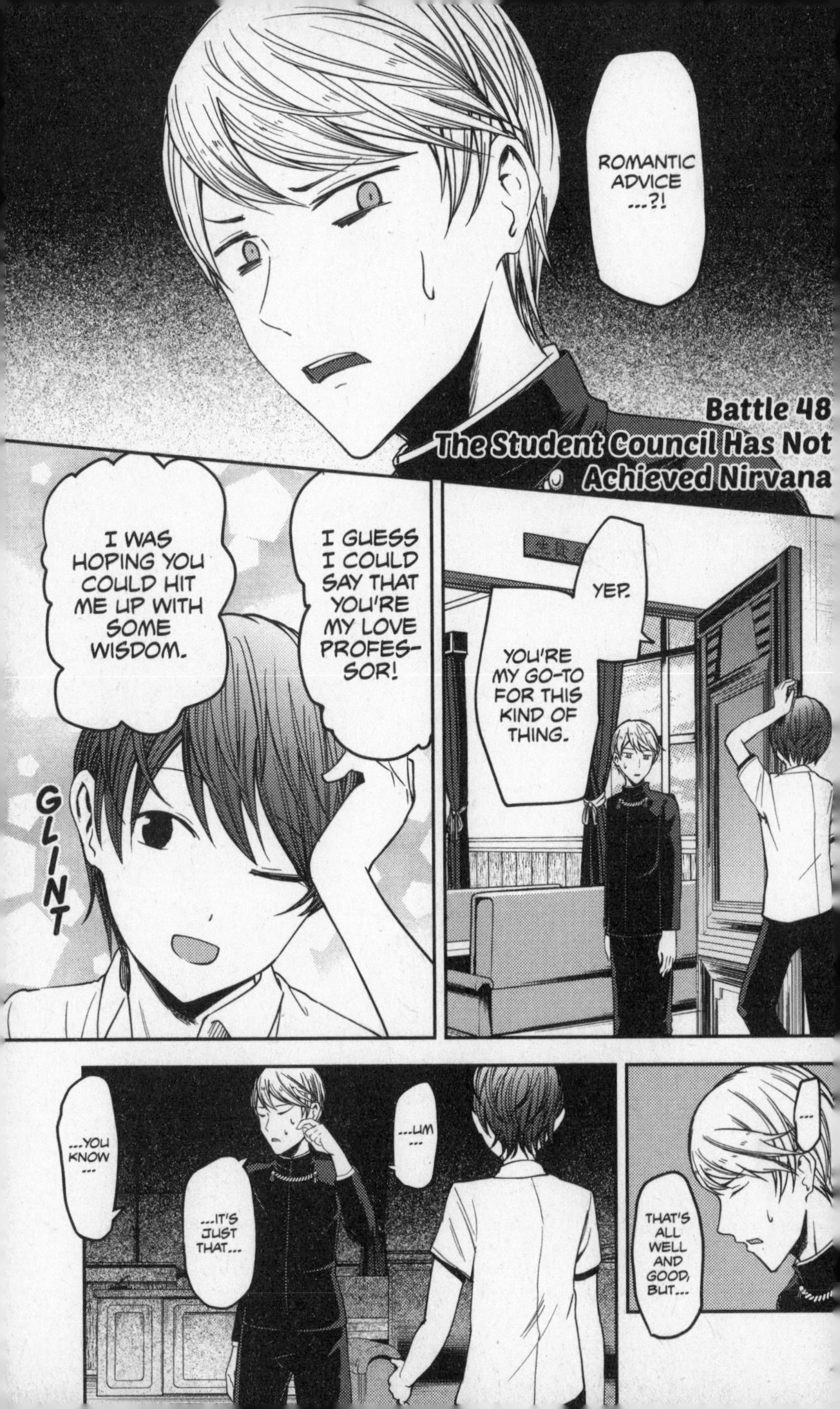
ROMANTIC ADVICE ...?!
Battle 48
The Student Council Has Not Achieved Nirvana
YEP.
YOU'RE MY GO-TO FOR THIS KIND OF THING.
I GUESS I COULD SAY THAT YOU'RE MY LOVE PROFES-SOR!
I WAS HOPING YOU COULD HIT ME UP WITH SOME WISDOM.
GLINT
...
THAT'S ALL WELL AND GOOD, BUT...
...UM...
...YOU KNOW...
...IT'S JUST THAT...

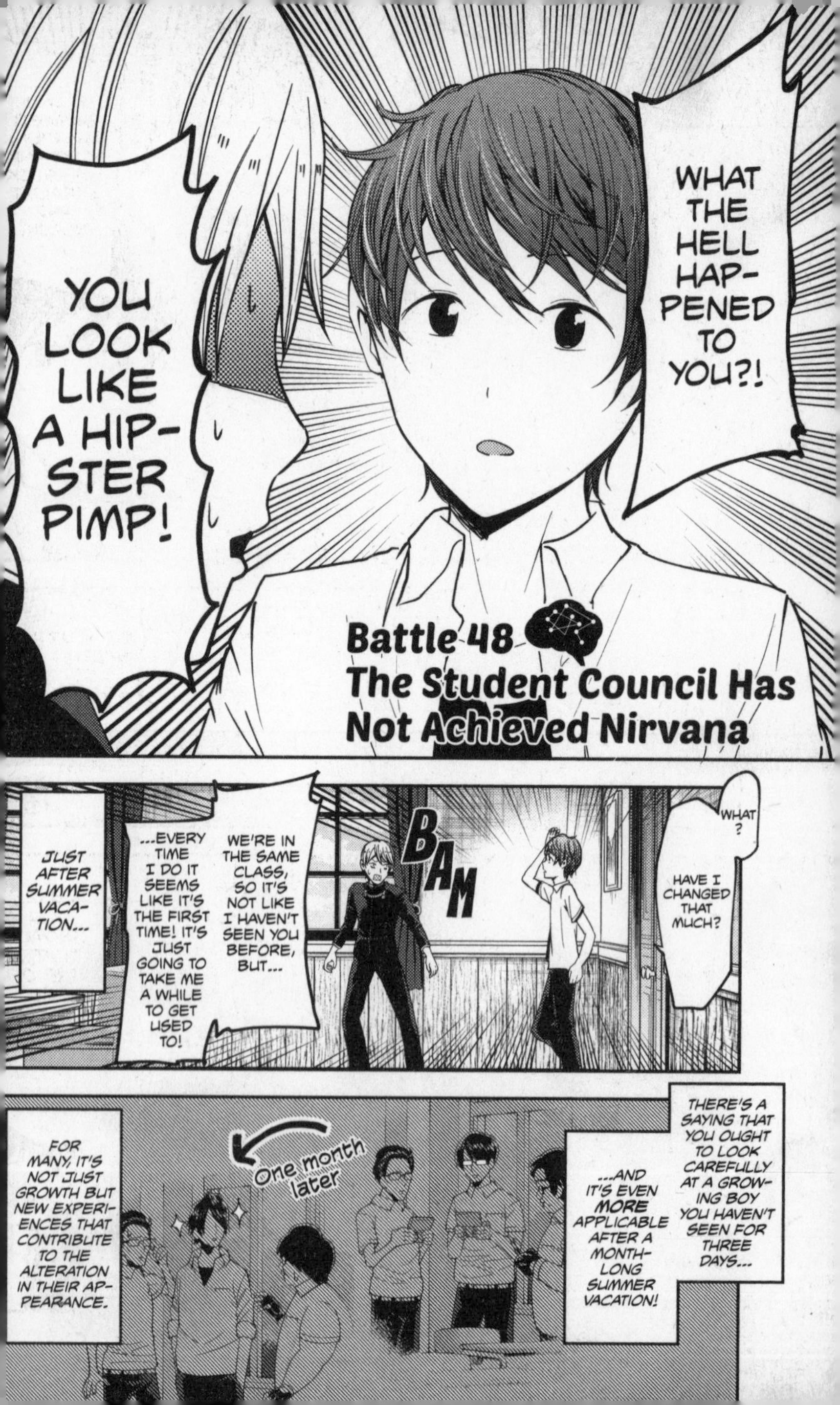
WHAT THE HELL HAPPENED TO YOU?!
YOU LOOK LIKE A HIPSTER PIMP!
Battle 48
The Student Council Has Not Achieved Nirvana
WHAT?
HAVE I CHANGED THAT MUCH?
BAM
WE'RE IN THE SAME CLASS, SO IT'S NOT LIKE I HAVEN'T SEEN YOU BEFORE, BUT...
...EVERY TIME I DO IT SEEMS LIKE IT'S THE FIRST TIME! IT'S JUST GOING TO TAKE ME A WHILE TO GET USED TO!
JUST AFTER SUMMER VACATION...
THERE'S A SAYING THAT YOU OUGHT TO LOOK CAREFULLY AT A GROWING BOY YOU HAVEN'T SEEN FOR THREE DAYS...
...AND IT'S EVEN MORE APPLICABLE AFTER A MONTH-LONG SUMMER VACATION!
One month later
FOR MANY, IT'S NOT JUST GROWTH BUT NEW EXPERIENCES THAT CONTRIBUTE TO THE ALTERATION IN THEIR APPEARANCE.

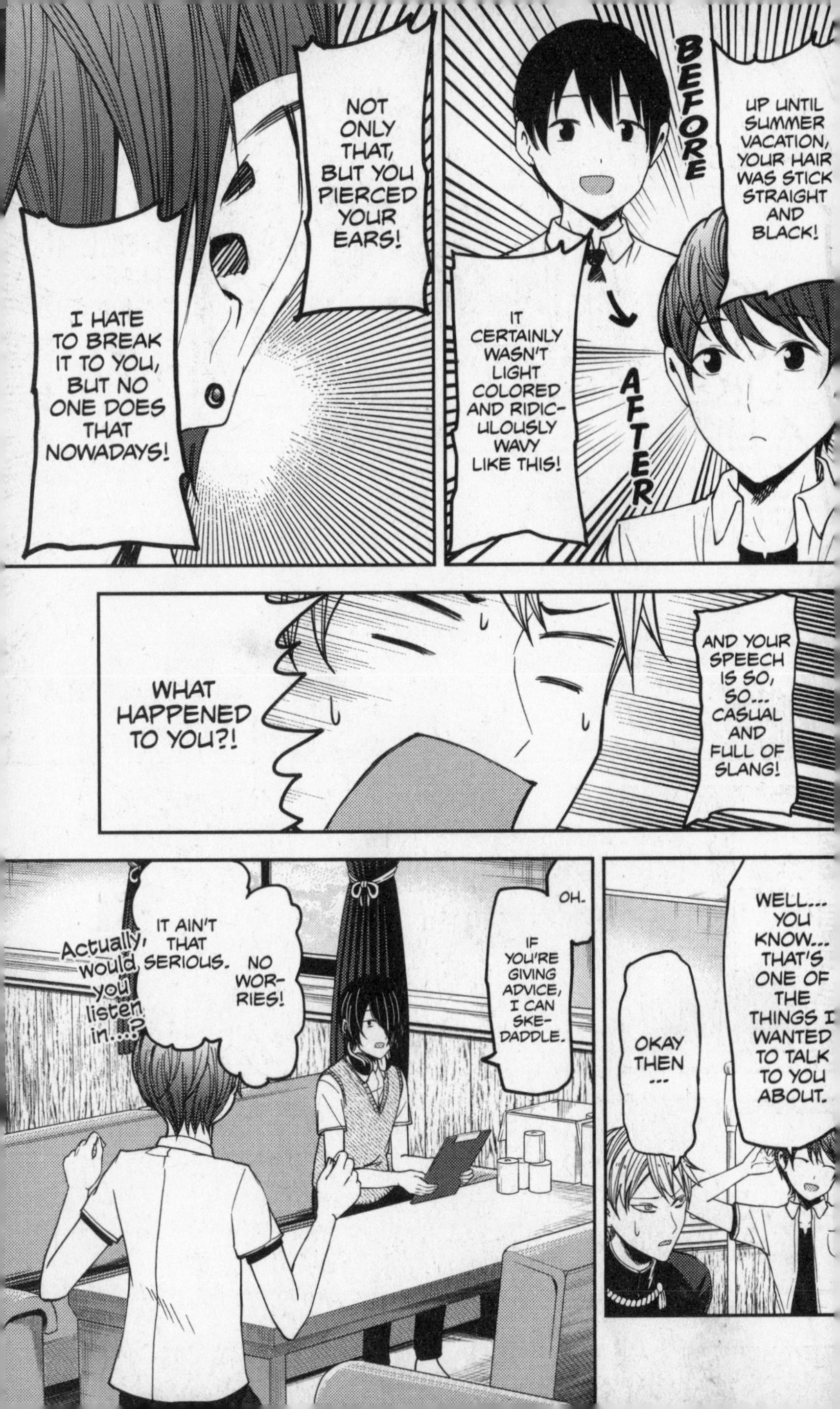
UP UNTIL SUMMER VACATION, YOUR HAIR WAS STICK STRAIGHT AND BLACK!
BEFORE
AFTER
IT CERTAINLY WASN'T LIGHT COLORED AND RIDICULOUSLY WAVY LIKE THIS!
NOT ONLY THAT, BUT YOU PIERCED YOUR EARS!
I HATE TO BREAK IT TO YOU, BUT NO ONE DOES THAT NOWADAYS!
AND YOUR SPEECH IS SO, SO... CASUAL AND FULL OF SLANG!
WHAT HAPPENED TO YOU?!
WELL... YOU KNOW... THAT'S ONE OF THE THINGS I WANTED TO TALK TO YOU ABOUT.
OKAY THEN ...
OH.
IF YOU'RE GIVING ADVICE, I CAN SKEDADDLE.
IT AIN'T THAT SERIOUS.
NO WORRIES!
Actually, would you listen in...?

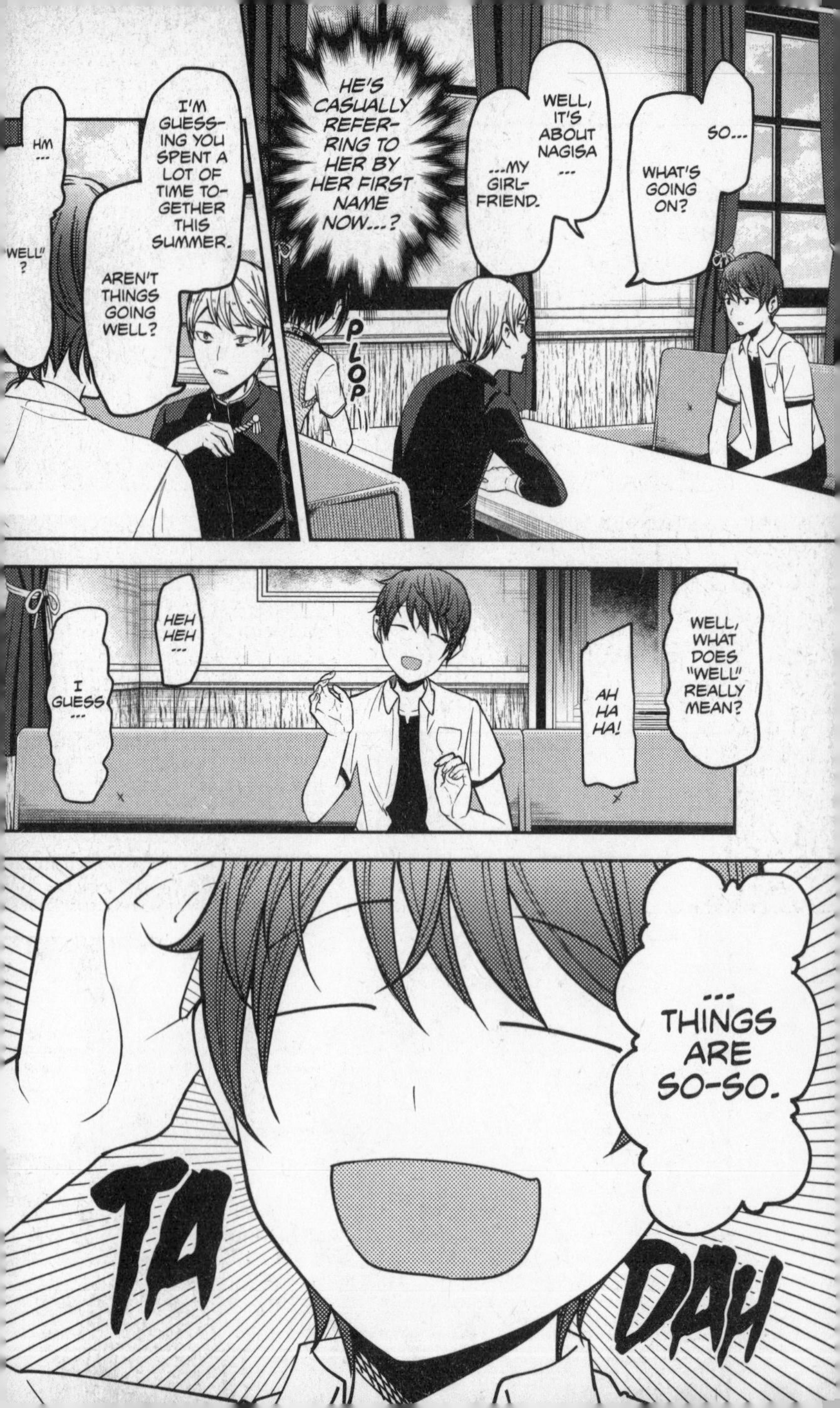
SO...
WHAT'S GOING ON?
WELL, IT'S ABOUT NAGISA...
...MY GIRLFRIEND.
HE'S CASUALLY REFERRING TO HER BY HER FIRST NAME NOW...?
PLOP
I'M GUESSING YOU SPENT A LOT OF TIME TOGETHER THIS SUMMER.
AREN'T THINGS GOING WELL?
HM...
"WELL"?
WELL, WHAT DOES "WELL" REALLY MEAN?
AH HA HA!
HEH HEH...
I GUESS...
...THINGS ARE SO-SO.
TA
DAH

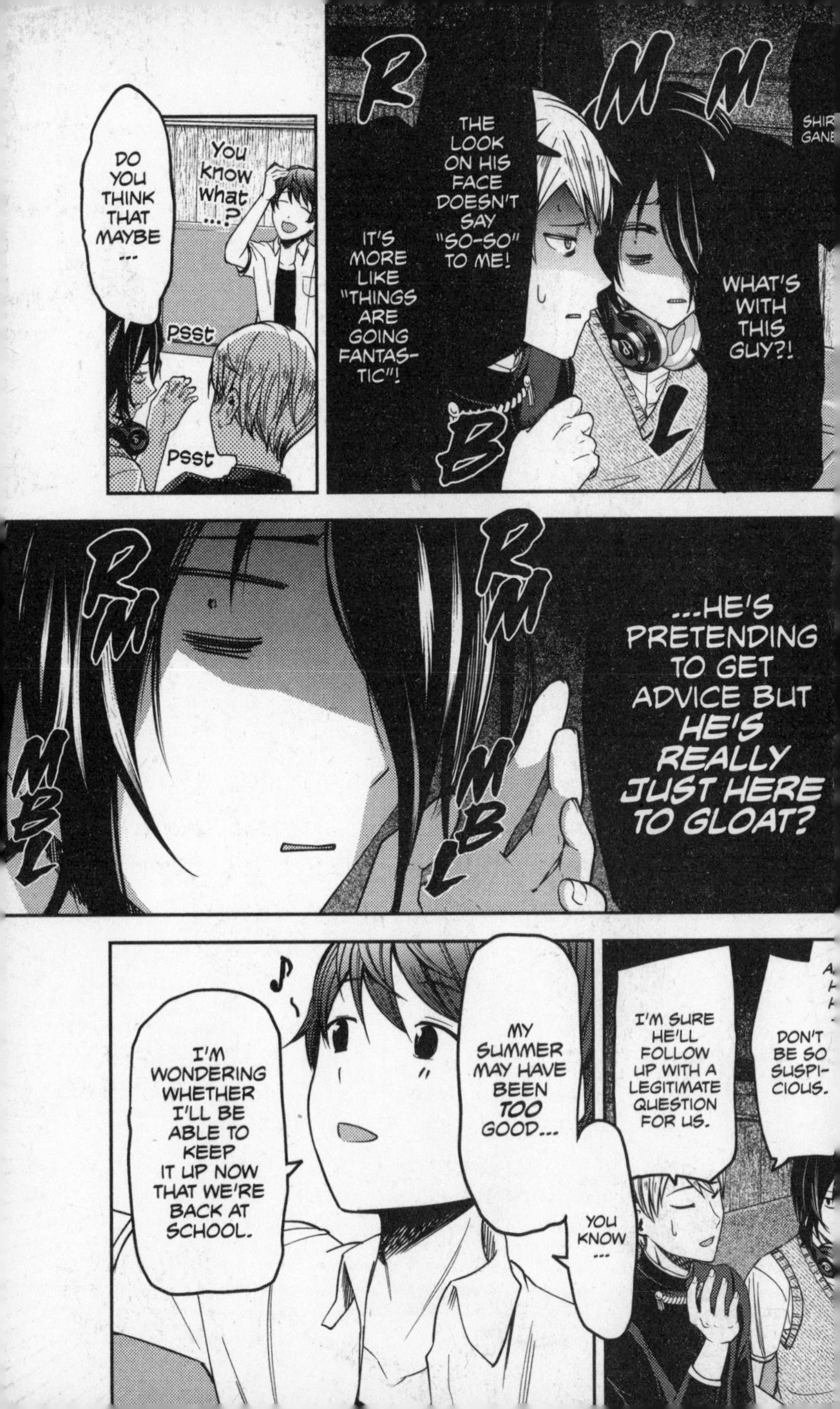
R M M
WHAT'S WITH THIS GUY?!
THE LOOK ON HIS FACE DOESN'T SAY "SO-SO" TO ME!
IT'S MORE LIKE "THINGS ARE GOING FANTAS-TIC"!
B L
You know what ...?
DO YOU THINK THAT MAYBE ...
Psst
Psst
...HE'S PRETENDING TO GET ADVICE BUT HE'S REALLY JUST HERE TO GLOAT?
RMMBL
RMMBL
DON'T BE SO SUSPI-CIOUS.
I'M SURE HE'LL FOLLOW UP WITH A LEGITIMATE QUESTION FOR US.
YOU KNOW ...
MY SUMMER MAY HAVE BEEN TOO GOOD...
I'M WONDERING WHETHER I'LL BE ABLE TO KEEP IT UP NOW THAT WE'RE BACK AT SCHOOL.

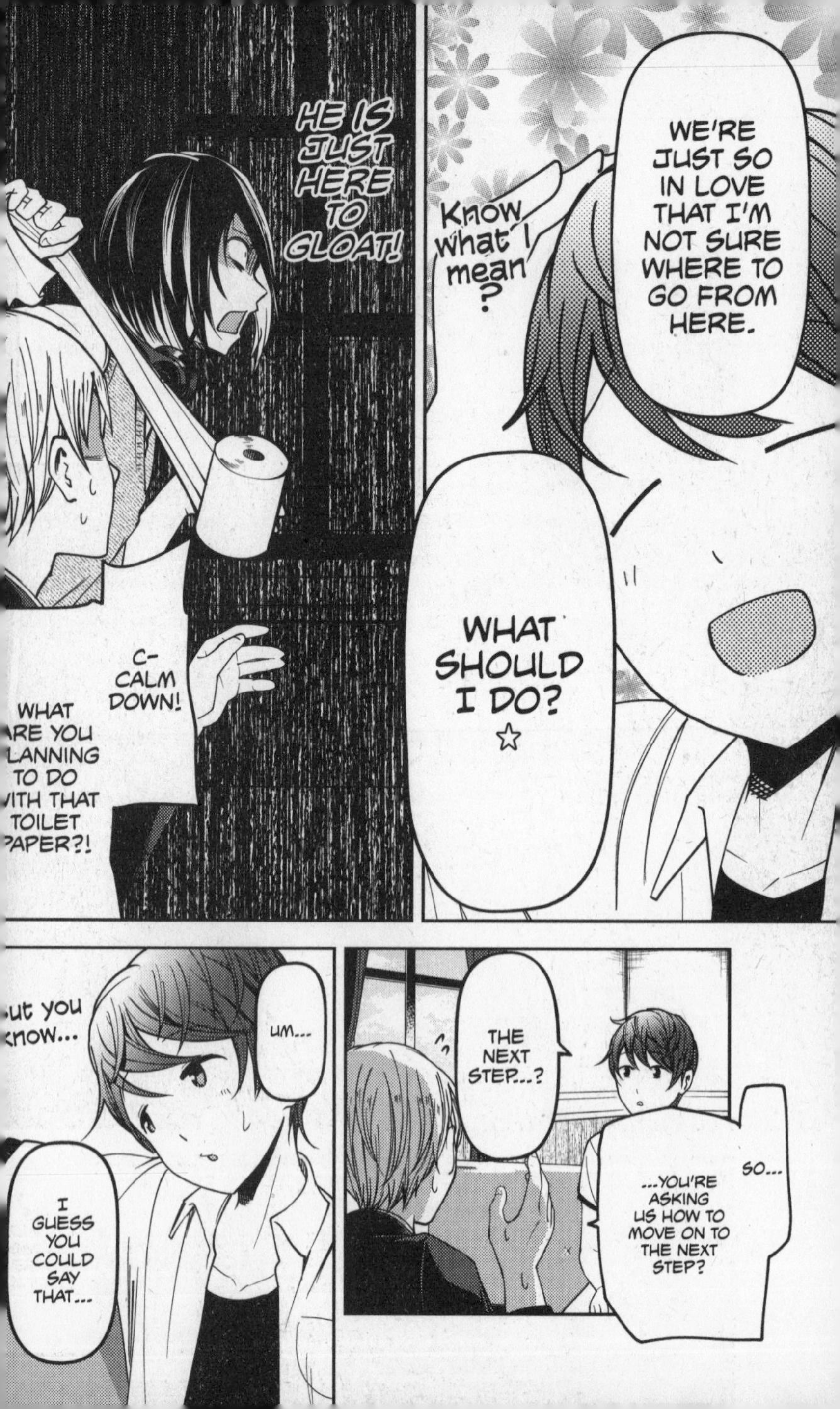
WE'RE JUST SO IN LOVE THAT I'M NOT SURE WHERE TO GO FROM HERE.
Know what I mean?
WHAT SHOULD I DO? ☆
HE IS JUST HERE TO GLOAT!
C-CALM DOWN!
WHAT ARE YOU PLANNING TO DO WITH THAT TOILET PAPER?!
THE NEXT STEP...?
SO...
...YOU'RE ASKING US HOW TO MOVE ON TO THE NEXT STEP?
But you know...
UM...
I GUESS YOU COULD SAY THAT...

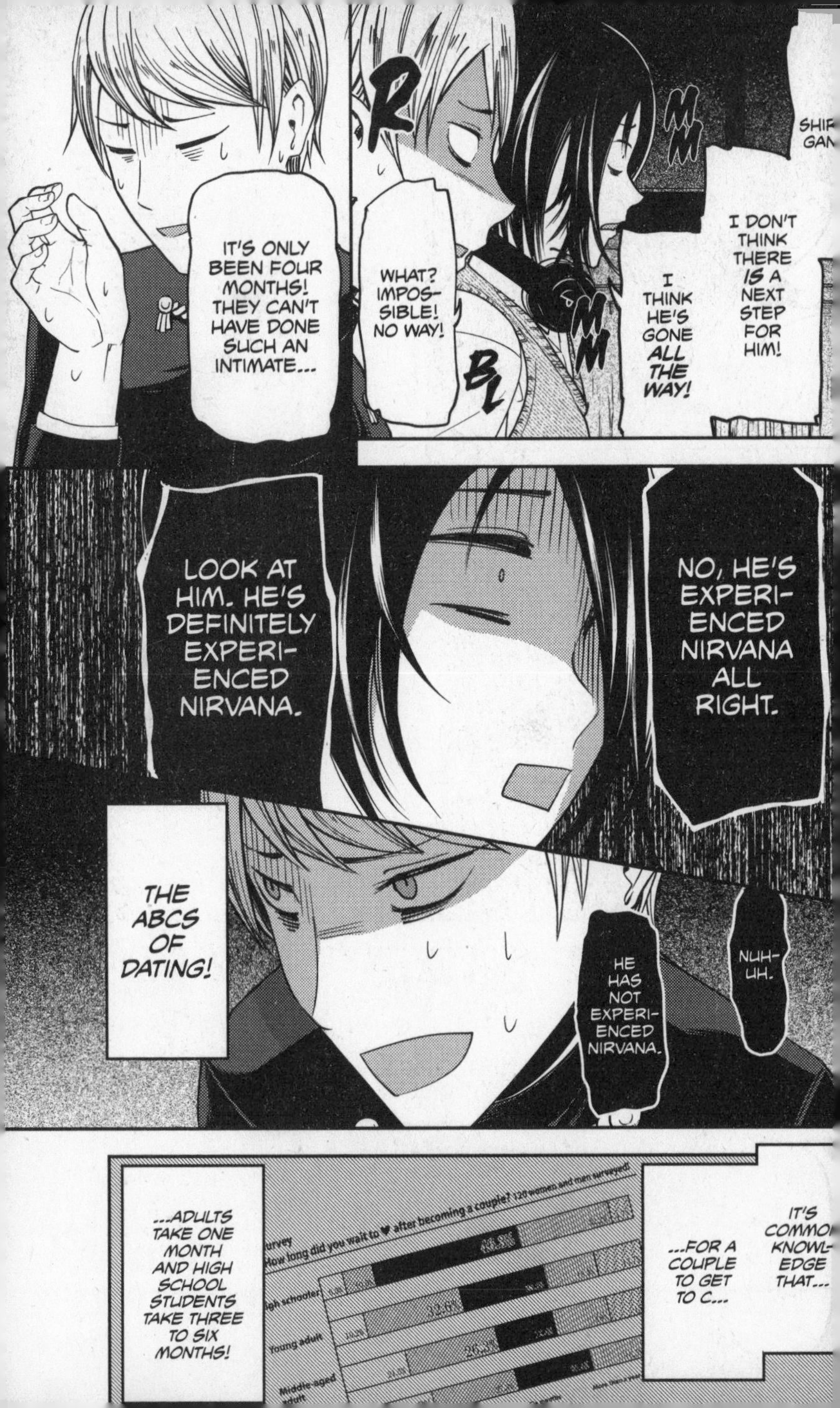
SHIR GAN
I DON'T THINK THERE IS A NEXT STEP FOR HIM!
I THINK HE'S GONE ALL THE WAY!
MM
R
MMM
BL
WHAT? IMPOSSIBLE! NO WAY!
IT'S ONLY BEEN FOUR MONTHS! THEY CAN'T HAVE DONE SUCH AN INTIMATE...
NO, HE'S EXPERIENCED NIRVANA ALL RIGHT.
LOOK AT HIM. HE'S DEFINITELY EXPERIENCED NIRVANA.
NUH-UH.
HE HAS NOT EXPERIENCED NIRVANA.
THE ABCS OF DATING!
IT'S COMMO KNOWL-EDGE THAT...
...FOR A COUPLE TO GET TO C...
Survey
How long did you wait to ♥ after becoming a couple? 120 women and men surveyed!
High schooler
Young adult
Middle-aged adult
46.9%
32.6%
26.3%
...ADULTS TAKE ONE MONTH AND HIGH SCHOOL STUDENTS TAKE THREE TO SIX MONTHS!

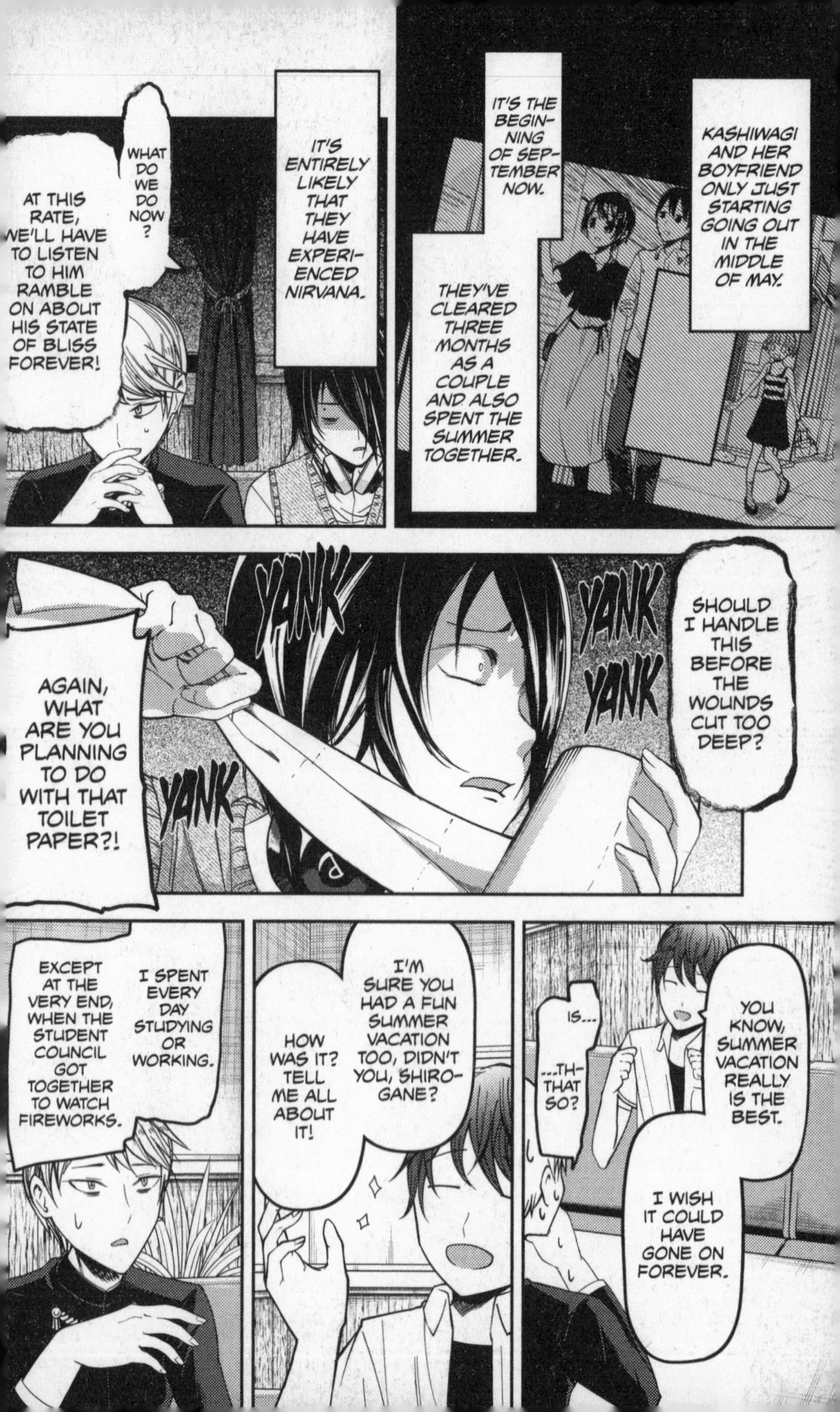
KASHIWAGI AND HER BOYFRIEND ONLY JUST STARTING GOING OUT IN THE MIDDLE OF MAY.
IT'S THE BEGINNING OF SEPTEMBER NOW.
THEY'VE CLEARED THREE MONTHS AS A COUPLE AND ALSO SPENT THE SUMMER TOGETHER.
IT'S ENTIRELY LIKELY THAT THEY HAVE EXPERIENCED NIRVANA.
WHAT DO WE DO NOW?
AT THIS RATE, WE'LL HAVE TO LISTEN TO HIM RAMBLE ON ABOUT HIS STATE OF BLISS FOREVER!
SHOULD I HANDLE THIS BEFORE THE WOUNDS CUT TOO DEEP?
YANK
YANK
YANK
YANK
AGAIN, WHAT ARE YOU PLANNING TO DO WITH THAT TOILET PAPER?!
YOU KNOW, SUMMER VACATION REALLY IS THE BEST.
I WISH IT COULD HAVE GONE ON FOREVER.
IS...
...TH-THAT SO?
I'M SURE YOU HAD A FUN SUMMER VACATION TOO, DIDN'T YOU, SHIROGANE?
HOW WAS IT? TELL ME ALL ABOUT IT!
I SPENT EVERY DAY STUDYING OR WORKING.
EXCEPT AT THE VERY END, WHEN THE STUDENT COUNCIL GOT TOGETHER TO WATCH FIREWORKS.

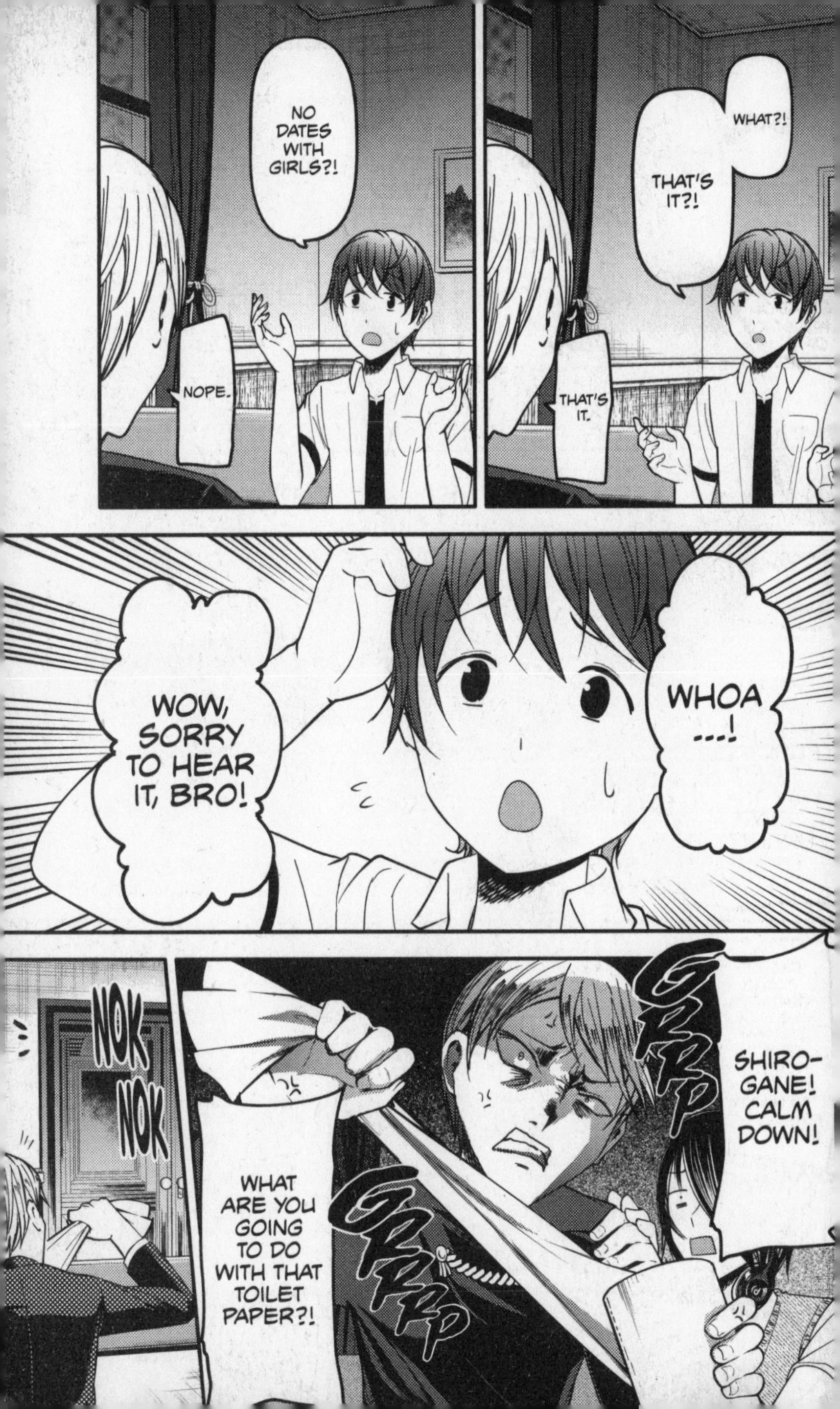
WHAT?!
THAT'S IT?!
THAT'S IT.
NO DATES WITH GIRLS?!
NOPE.
WHOA ...!
WOW, SORRY TO HEAR IT, BRO!
GRRP
SHIRO-GANE! CALM DOWN!
WHAT ARE YOU GOING TO DO WITH THAT TOILET PAPER?!
GRRRP
NOK NOK

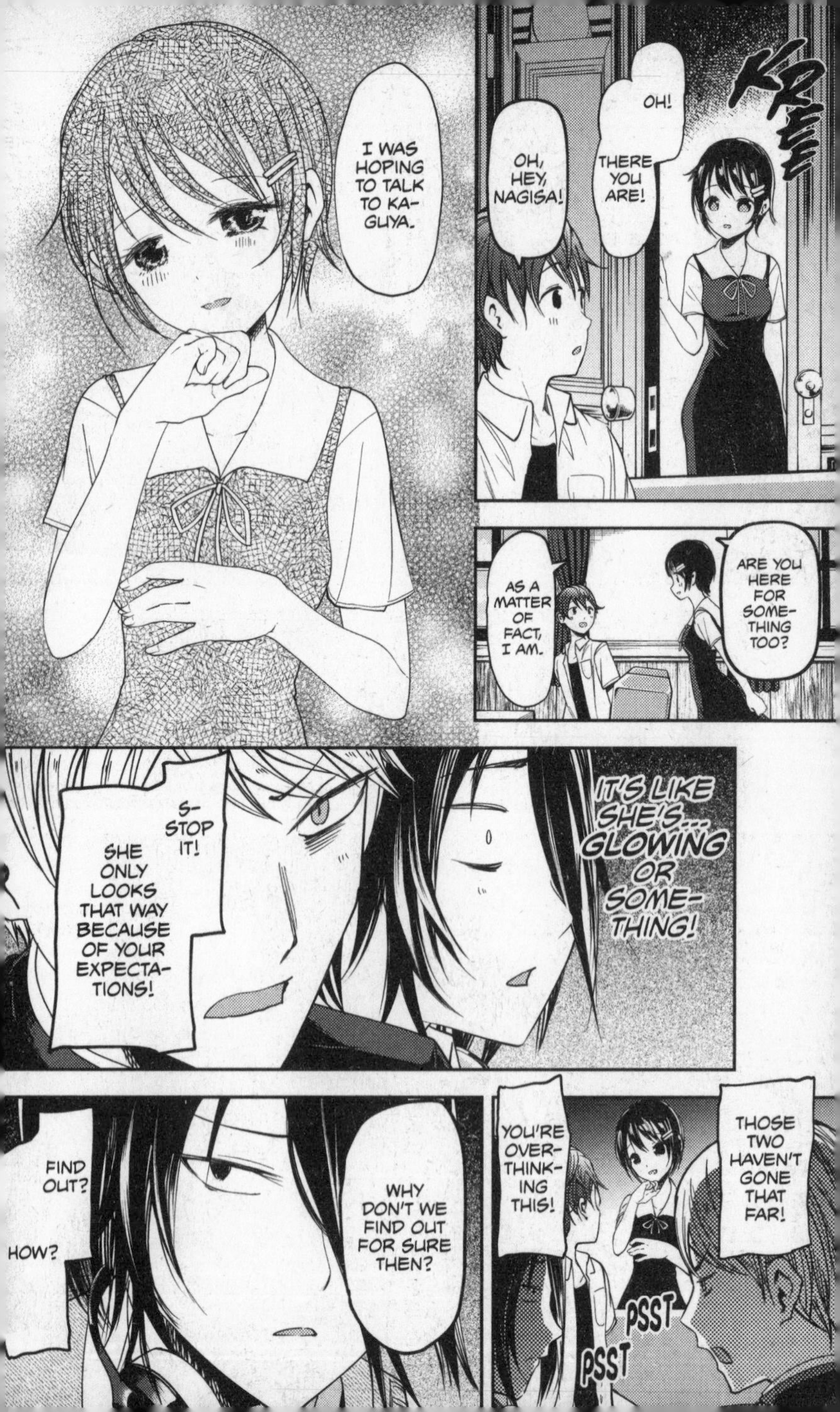
KREEE
OH!
THERE YOU ARE!
OH, HEY, NAGISA!
ARE YOU HERE FOR SOME-THING TOO?
AS A MATTER OF FACT, I AM.
I WAS HOPING TO TALK TO KA-GUYA.
IT'S LIKE SHE'S... GLOWING OR SOME-THING!
S-STOP IT!
SHE ONLY LOOKS THAT WAY BECAUSE OF YOUR EXPECTA-TIONS!
THOSE TWO HAVEN'T GONE THAT FAR!
YOU'RE OVER-THINK-ING THIS!
PSST
PSST
WHY DON'T WE FIND OUT FOR SURE THEN?
FIND OUT?
HOW?

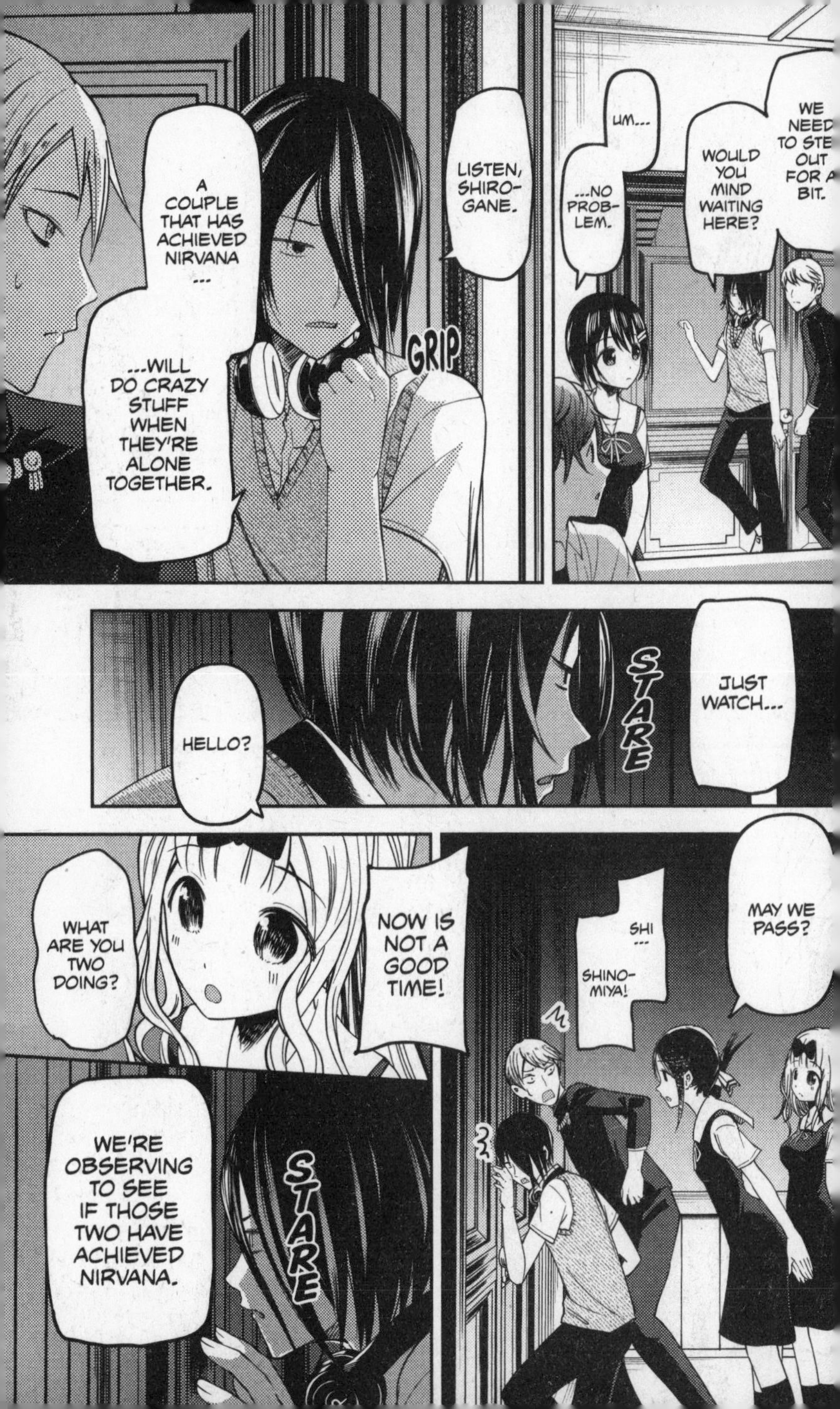
WE NEED TO STE OUT FOR A BIT.
WOULD YOU MIND WAITING HERE?
UM...
...NO PROB-LEM.
LISTEN, SHIRO-GANE.
GRIP
A COUPLE THAT HAS ACHIEVED NIRVANA...
...WILL DO CRAZY STUFF WHEN THEY'RE ALONE TOGETHER.
JUST WATCH...
STARE
HELLO?
MAY WE PASS?
SHI... SHINO-MIYA!
NOW IS NOT A GOOD TIME!
WHAT ARE YOU TWO DOING?
STARE
WE'RE OBSERVING TO SEE IF THOSE TWO HAVE ACHIEVED NIRVANA.

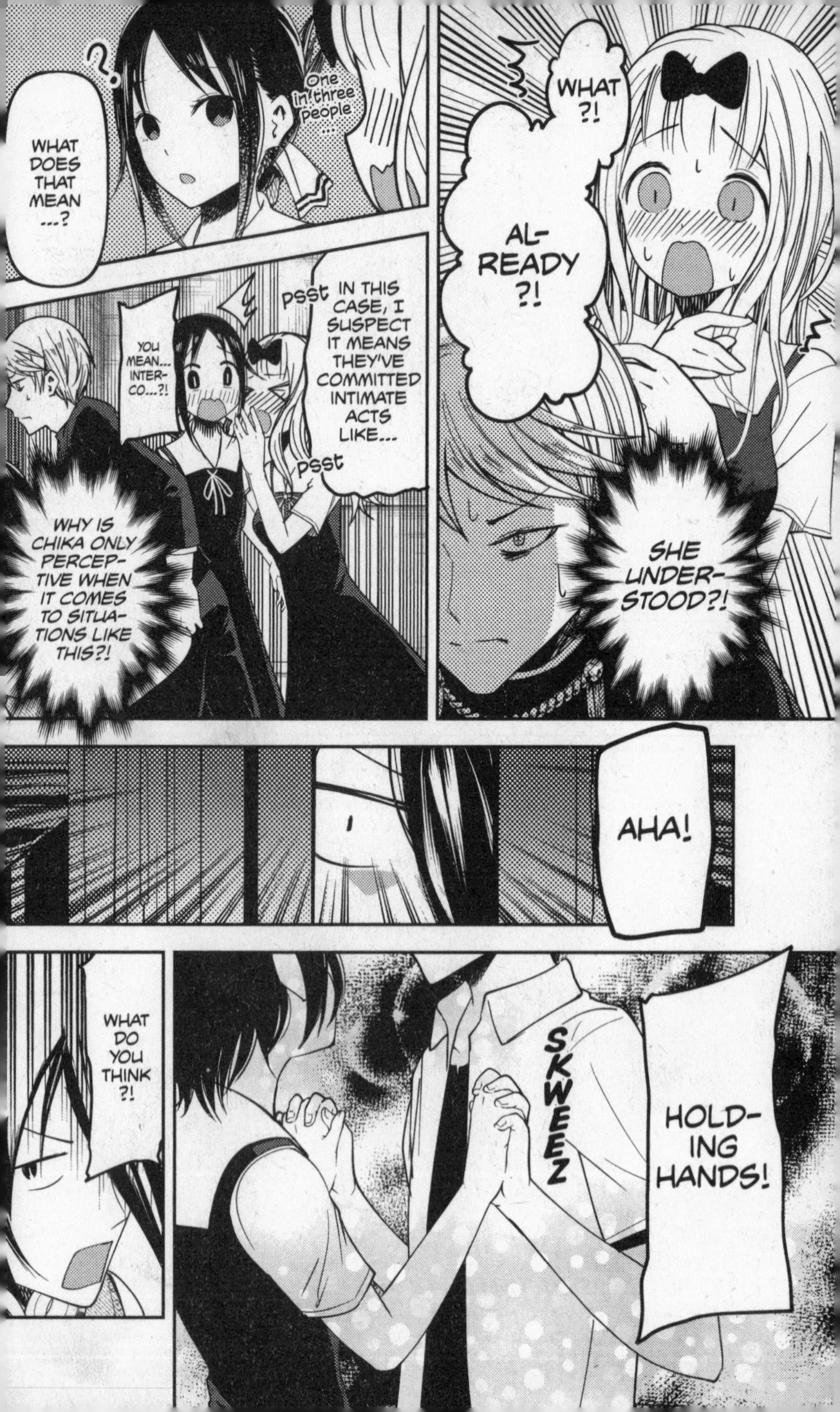
WHAT ?!
AL-READY ?!
SHE UNDER-STOOD?!
One in three people ...
WHAT DOES THAT MEAN ...?
psst IN THIS CASE, I SUSPECT IT MEANS THEY'VE COMMITTED INTIMATE ACTS LIKE... psst
YOU MEAN... INTER-CO...?!
WHY IS CHIKA ONLY PERCEP-TIVE WHEN IT COMES TO SITUA-TIONS LIKE THIS?!
AHA!
HOLD-ING HANDS!
SKWEEZ
WHAT DO YOU THINK ?!

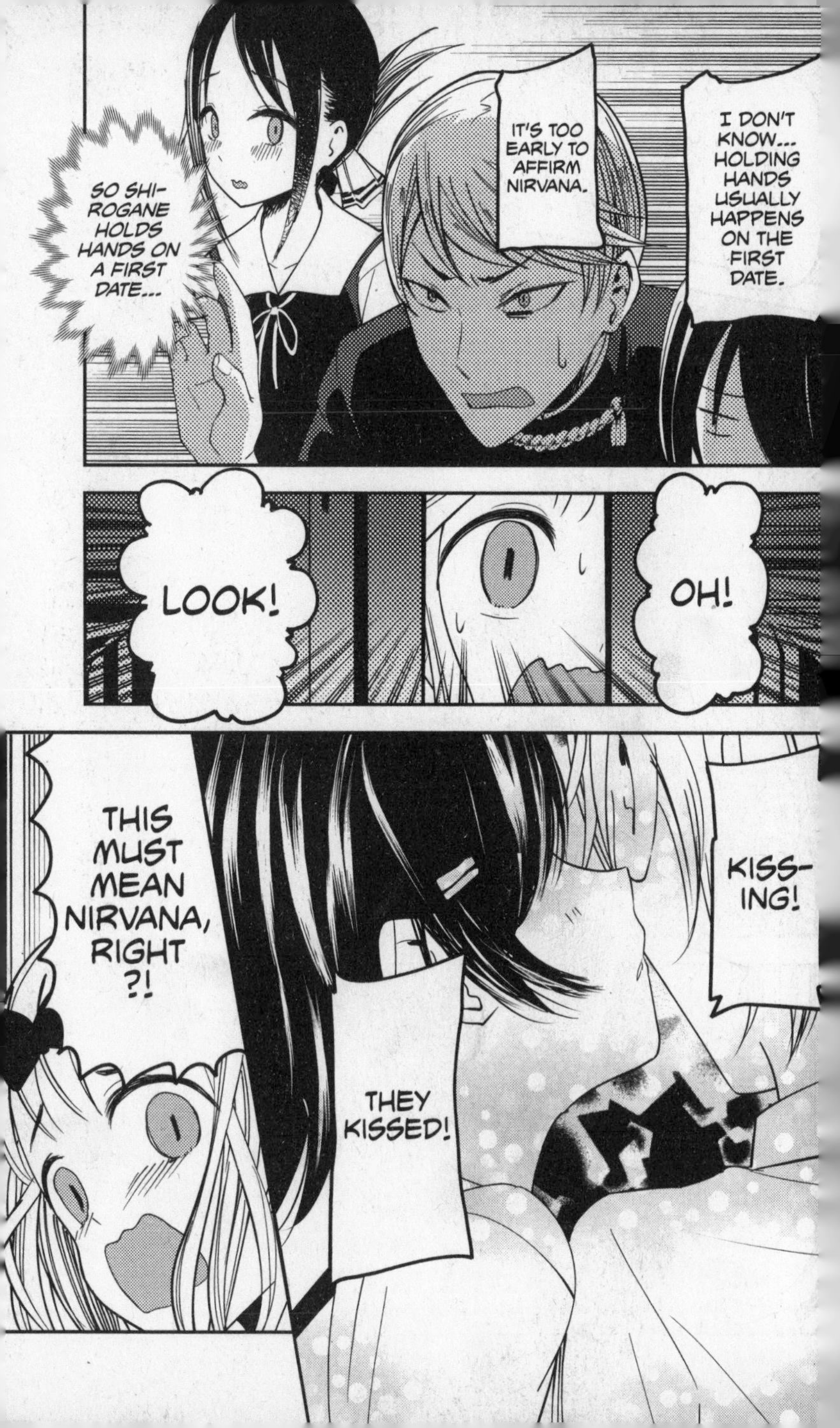
I DON'T KNOW... HOLDING HANDS USUALLY HAPPENS ON THE FIRST DATE.
IT'S TOO EARLY TO AFFIRM NIRVANA.
SO SHIROGANE HOLDS HANDS ON A FIRST DATE...
OH!
LOOK!
KISSING!
THIS MUST MEAN NIRVANA, RIGHT?!
THEY KISSED!

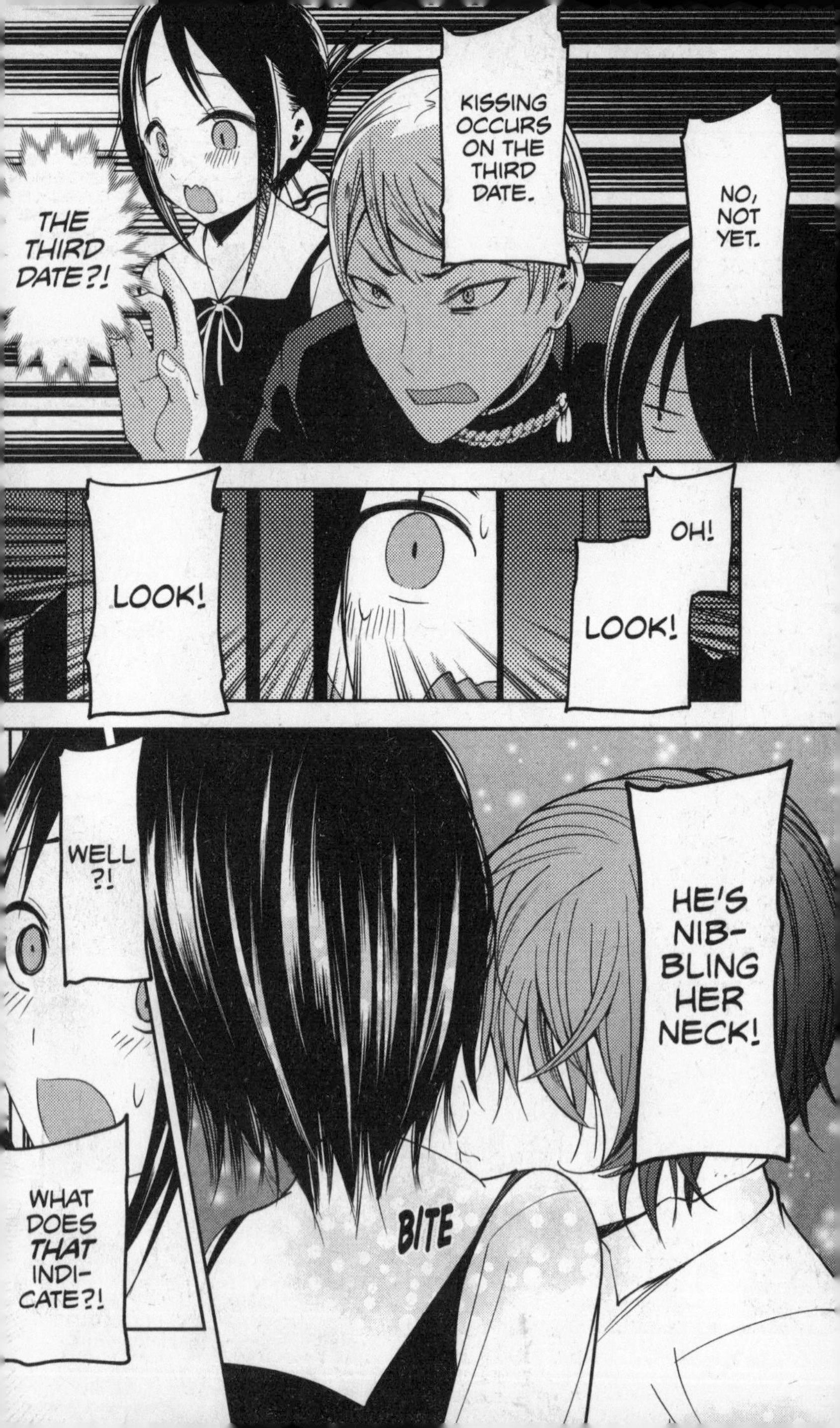
NO, NOT YET.
KISSING OCCURS ON THE THIRD DATE.
THE THIRD DATE?!
OH!
LOOK!
LOOK!
HE'S NIBBLING HER NECK!
WELL?!
BITE
WHAT DOES THAT INDICATE?!

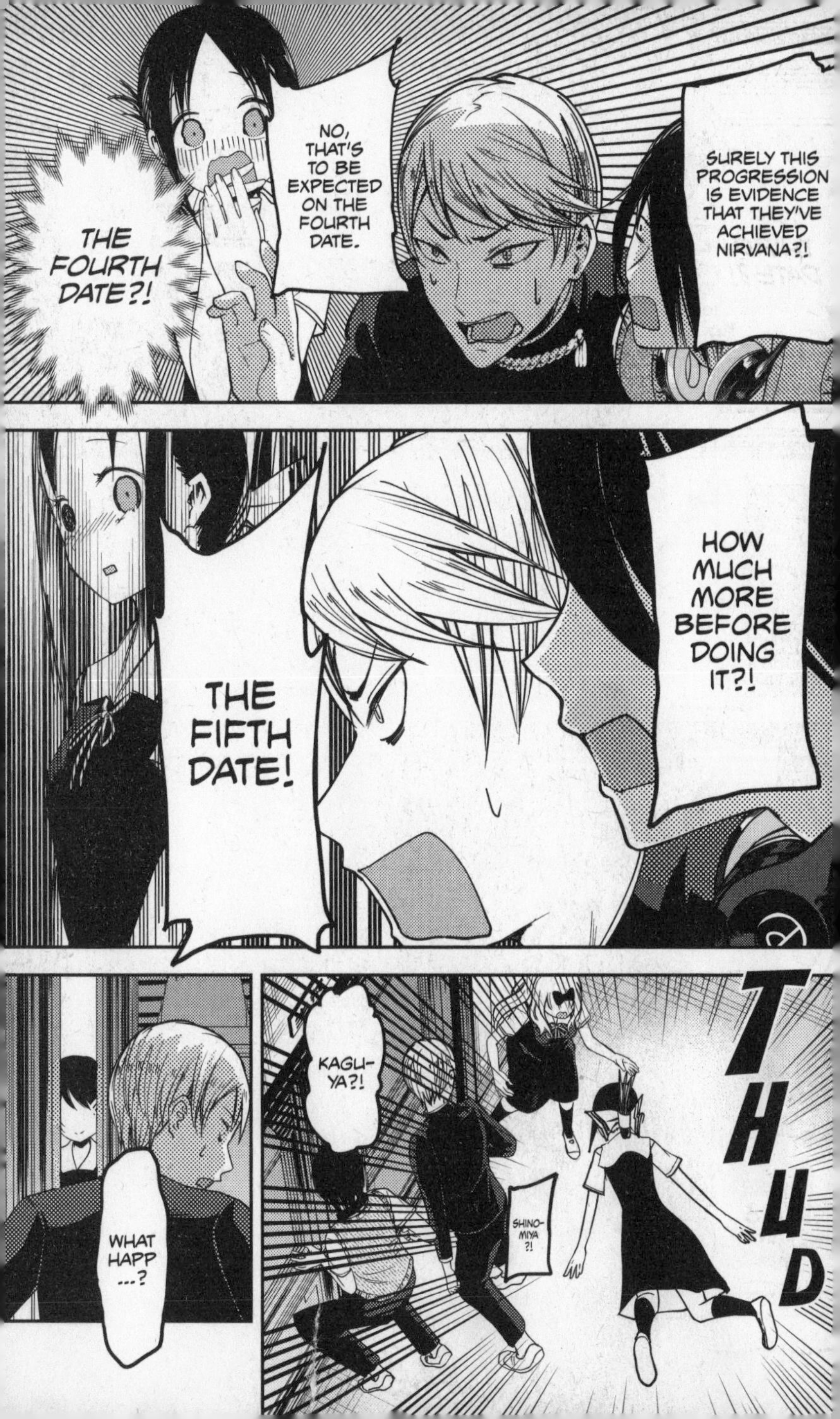
SURELY THIS PROGRESSION IS EVIDENCE THAT THEY'VE ACHIEVED NIRVANA?!
NO, THAT'S TO BE EXPECTED ON THE FOURTH DATE.
THE FOURTH DATE?!
HOW MUCH MORE BEFORE DOING IT?!
THE FIFTH DATE!
THUD
KAGU-YA?!
SHINO-MIYA?!
WHAT HAPP ---?

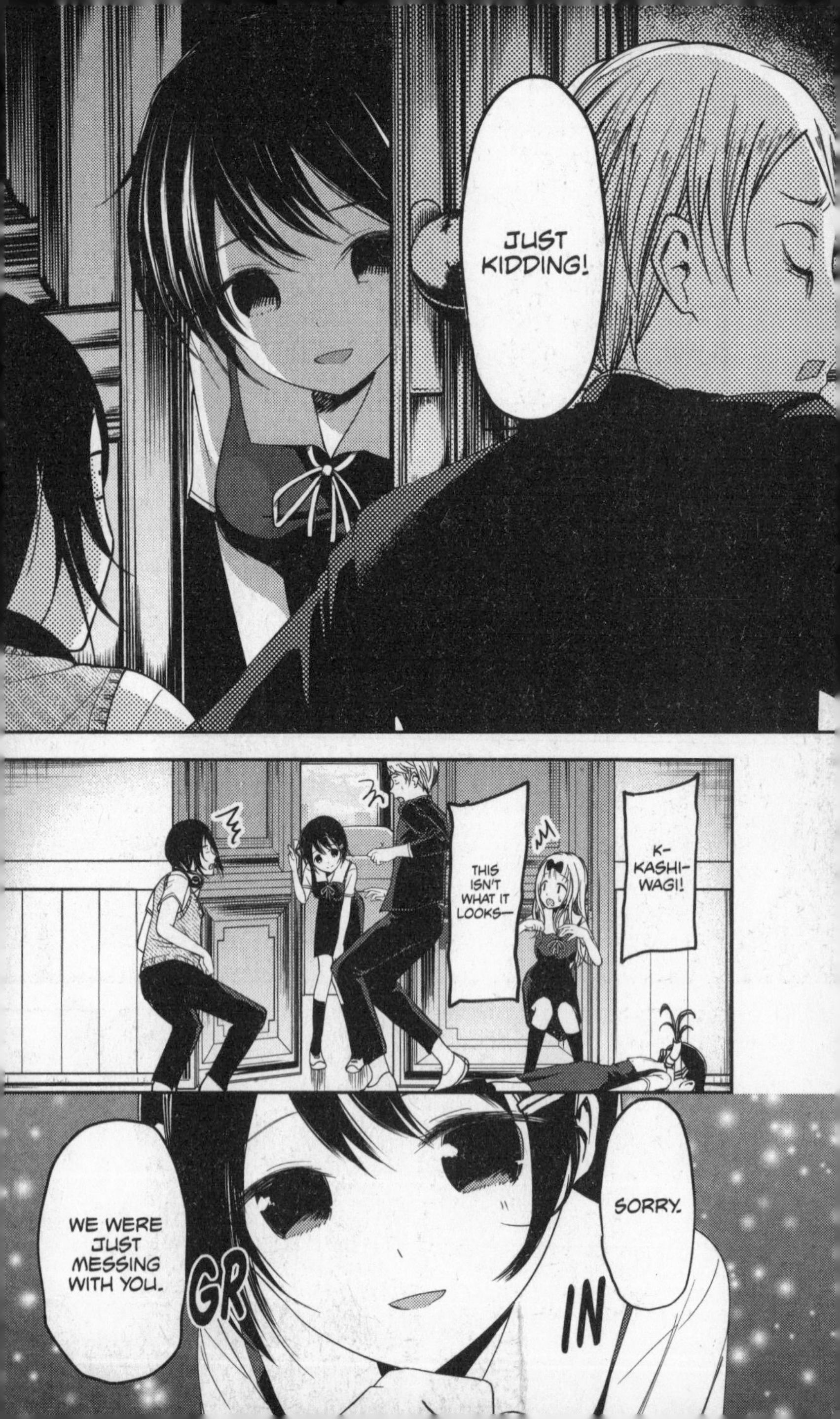
JUST KIDDING!
K-KASHIWAGI!
THIS ISN'T WHAT IT LOOKS—
SORRY.
IN
GR
WE WERE JUST MESSING WITH YOU.

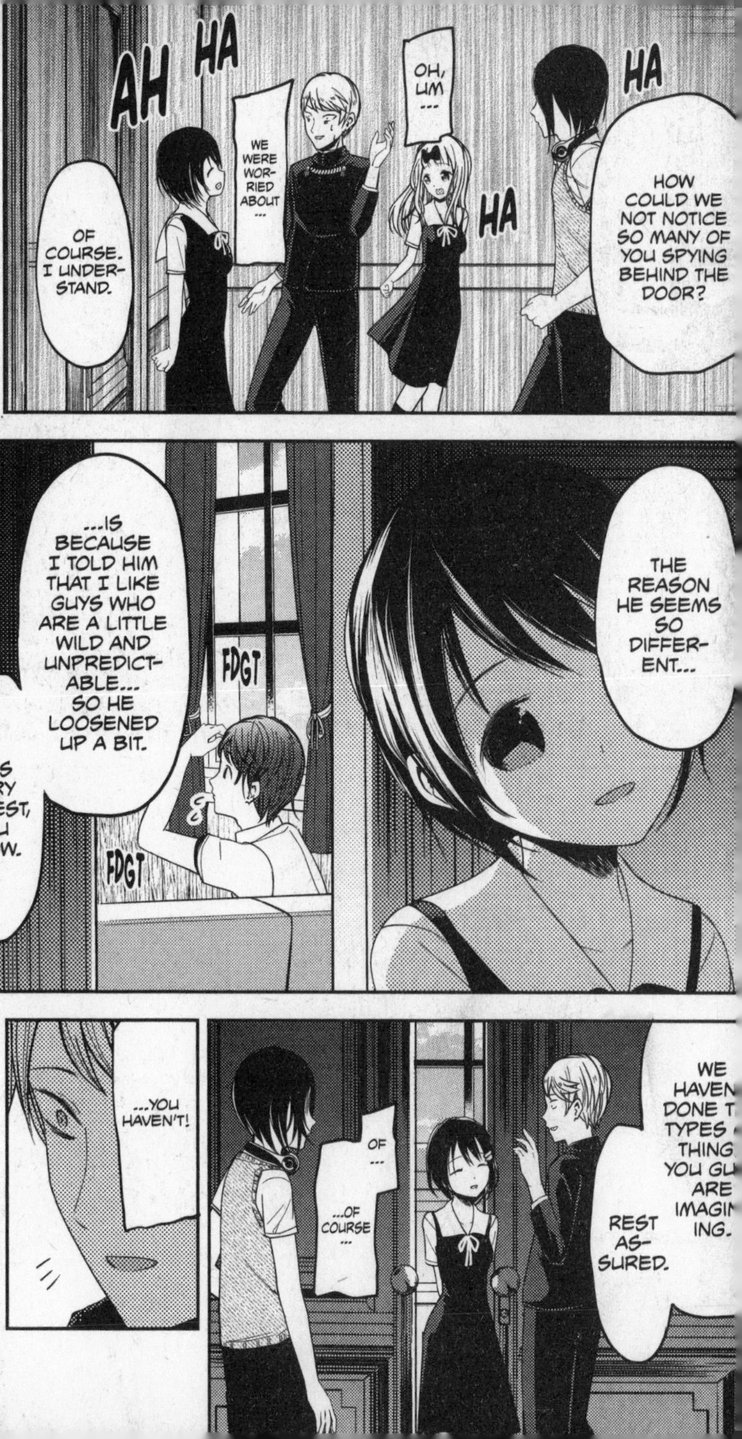
HA
HOW COULD WE NOT NOTICE SO MANY OF YOU SPYING BEHIND THE DOOR?
OH, UM ...
HA
WE WERE WOR-RIED ABOUT ...
AH HA
OF COURSE. I UNDER-STAND.
THE REASON HE SEEMS SO DIFFER-ENT...
...IS BECAUSE I TOLD HIM THAT I LIKE GUYS WHO ARE A LITTLE WILD AND UNPREDICT-ABLE... SO HE LOOSENED UP A BIT.
FDGT
HE'S VERY HONEST, YOU KNOW.
FDGT
WE HAVEN DONE T TYPES THING YOU GU ARE IMAGIN ING.
REST AS-SURED.
OF ...
...OF COURSE ...
...YOU HAVEN'T!

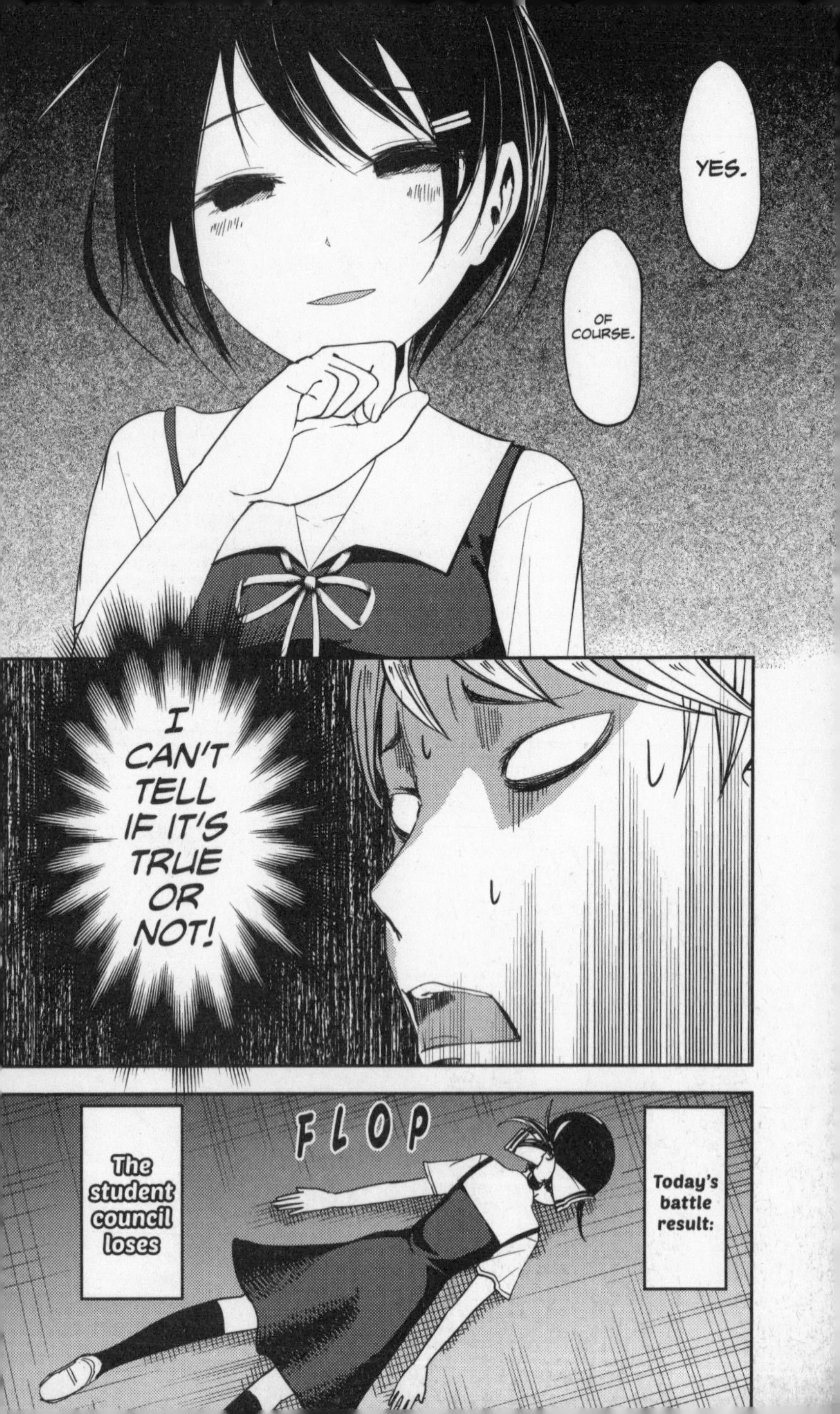
YES.
OF COURSE.
I CAN'T TELL IF IT'S TRUE OR NOT!
Today's battle result:
FLOP
The student council loses

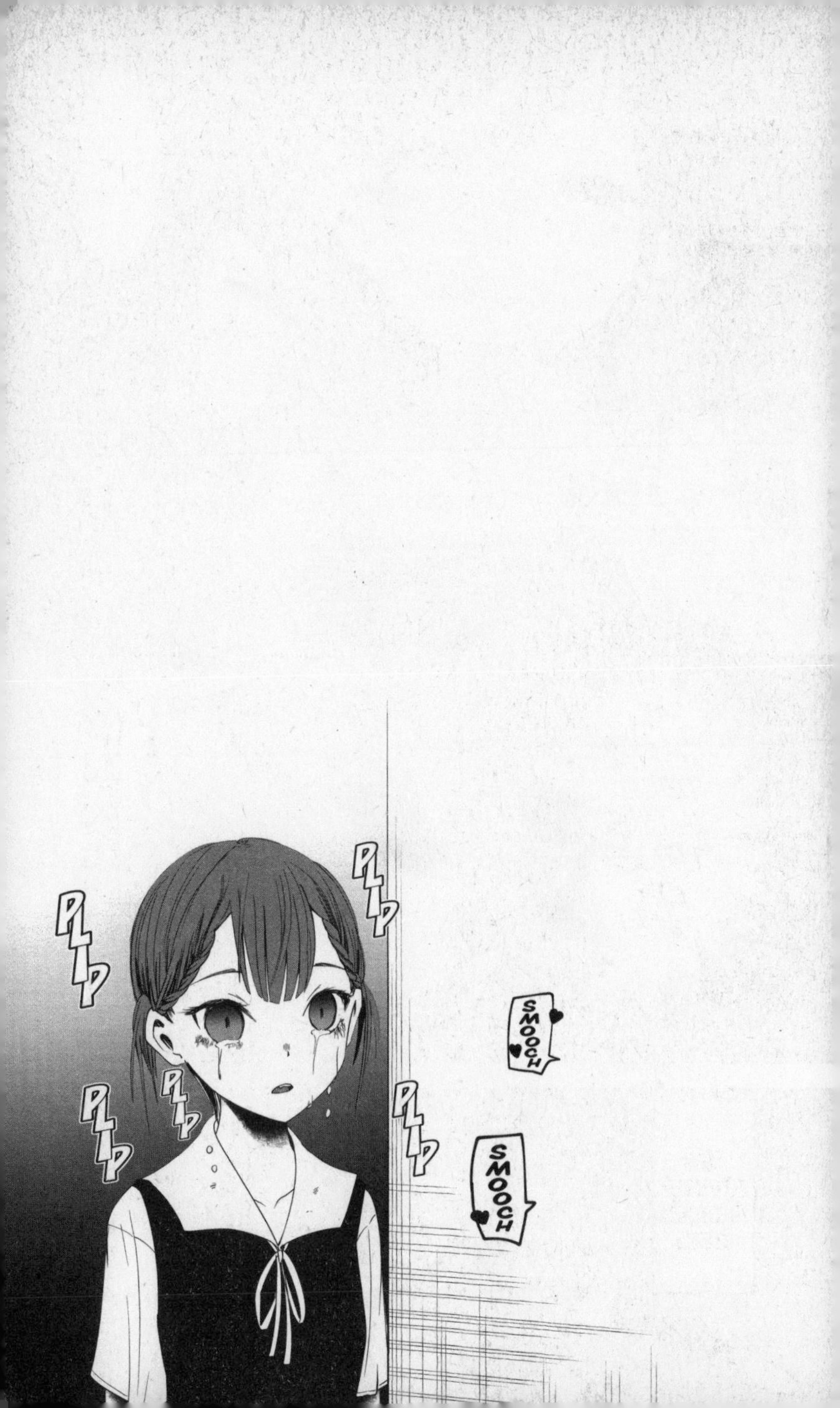
PLIP
SMOOCH
PLIP
SMOOCH
PLIP
PLIP
PLIP

KAGUYA-SAMA
LOVE IS WAR

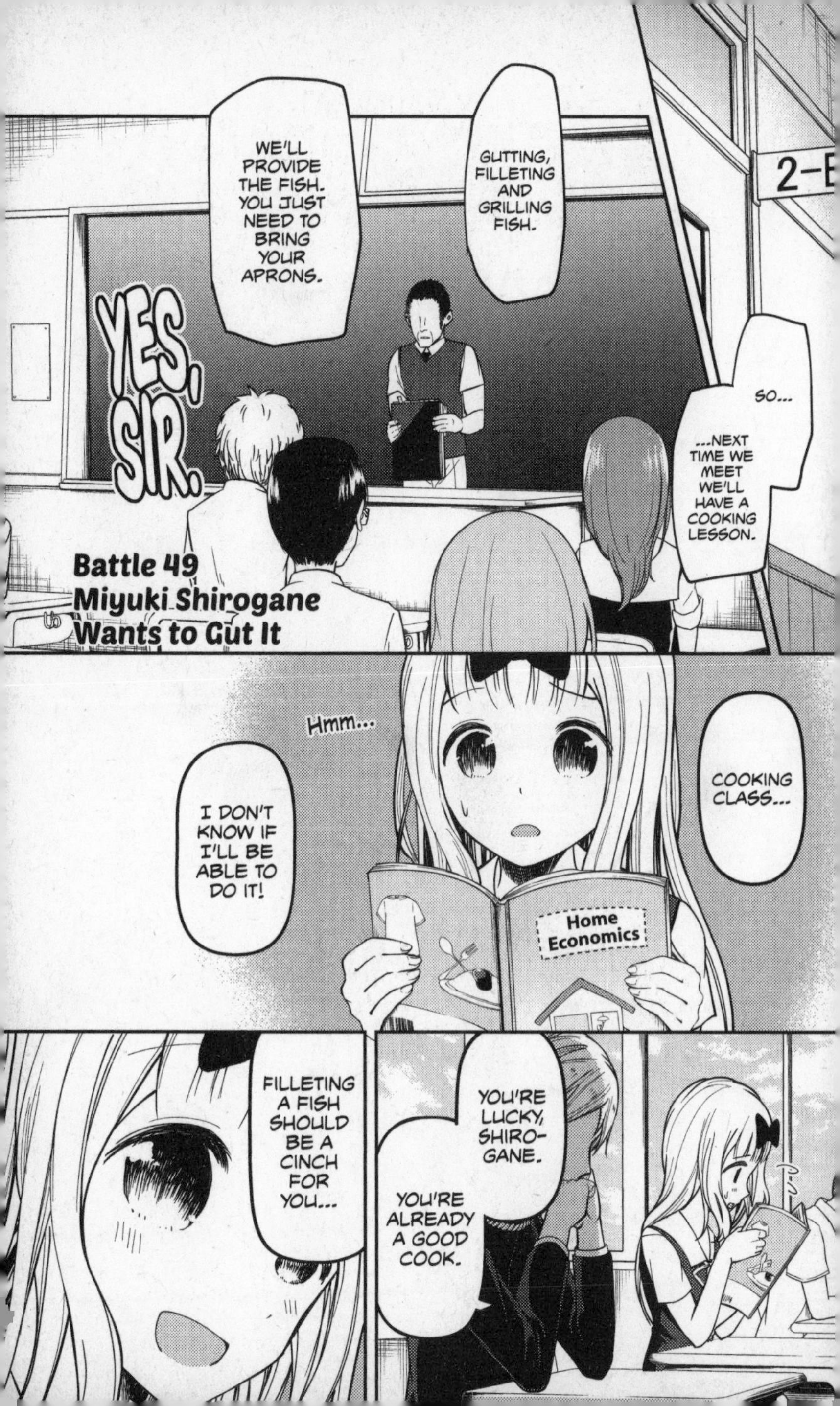
SO...
...NEXT TIME WE MEET WE'LL HAVE A COOKING LESSON.
GUTTING, FILLETING AND GRILLING FISH.
WE'LL PROVIDE THE FISH. YOU JUST NEED TO BRING YOUR APRONS.
YES, SIR.
Battle 49
Miyuki Shirogane Wants to Gut It
COOKING CLASS...
Hmm...
I DON'T KNOW IF I'LL BE ABLE TO DO IT!
Home Economics
YOU'RE LUCKY, SHIROGANE.
YOU'RE ALREADY A GOOD COOK.
FILLETING A FISH SHOULD BE A CINCH FOR YOU...

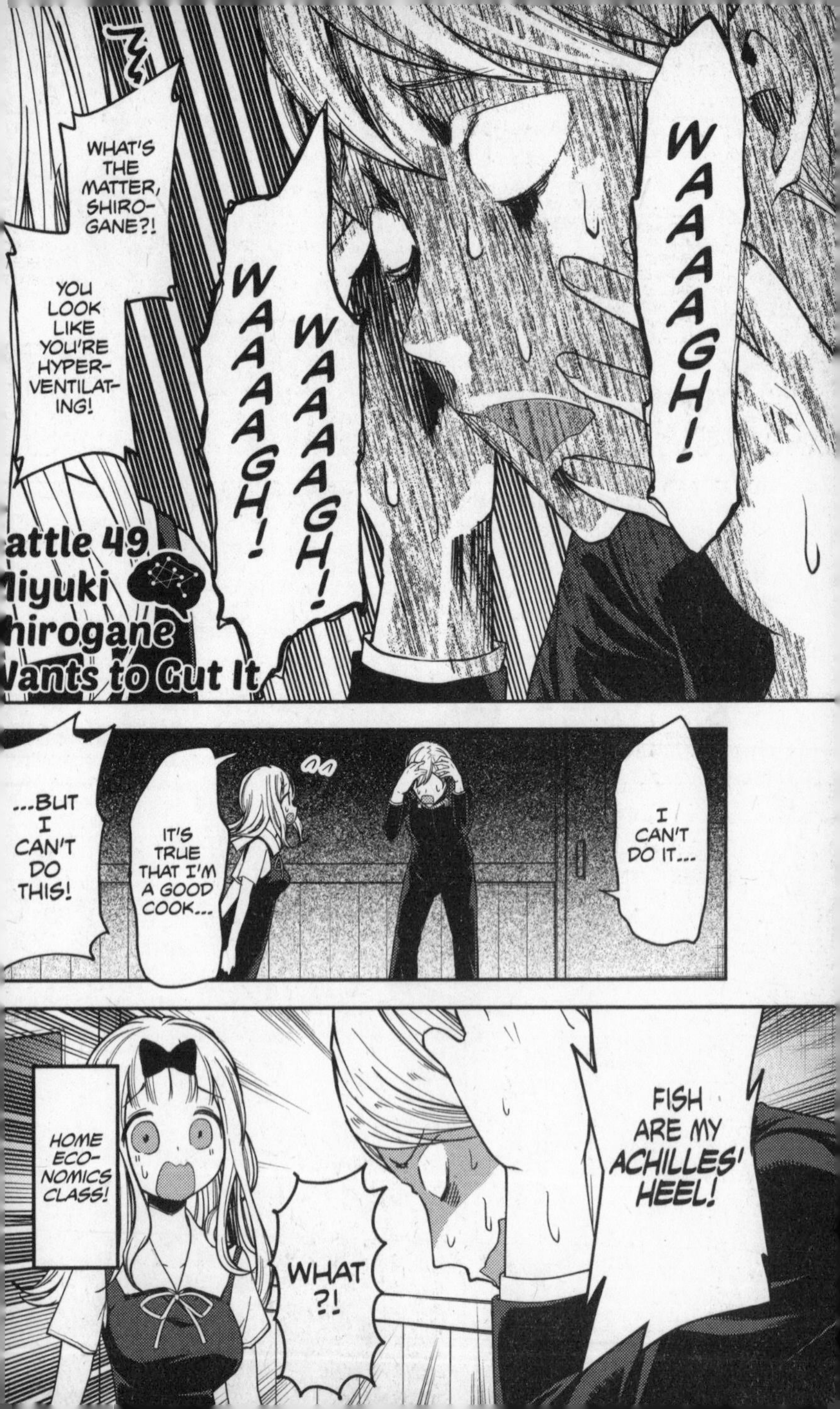
WAAAAGH!
WAAAAGH!
WAAAAGH!
WHAT'S THE MATTER, SHIRO-GANE?!
YOU LOOK LIKE YOU'RE HYPER-VENTILAT-ING!
attle 49
liyuki
hirogane
Vants to Gut It
I CAN'T DO IT...
IT'S TRUE THAT I'M A GOOD COOK...
...BUT I CAN'T DO THIS!
FISH ARE MY ACHILLES' HEEL!
WHAT?!
HOME ECO-NOMICS CLASS!

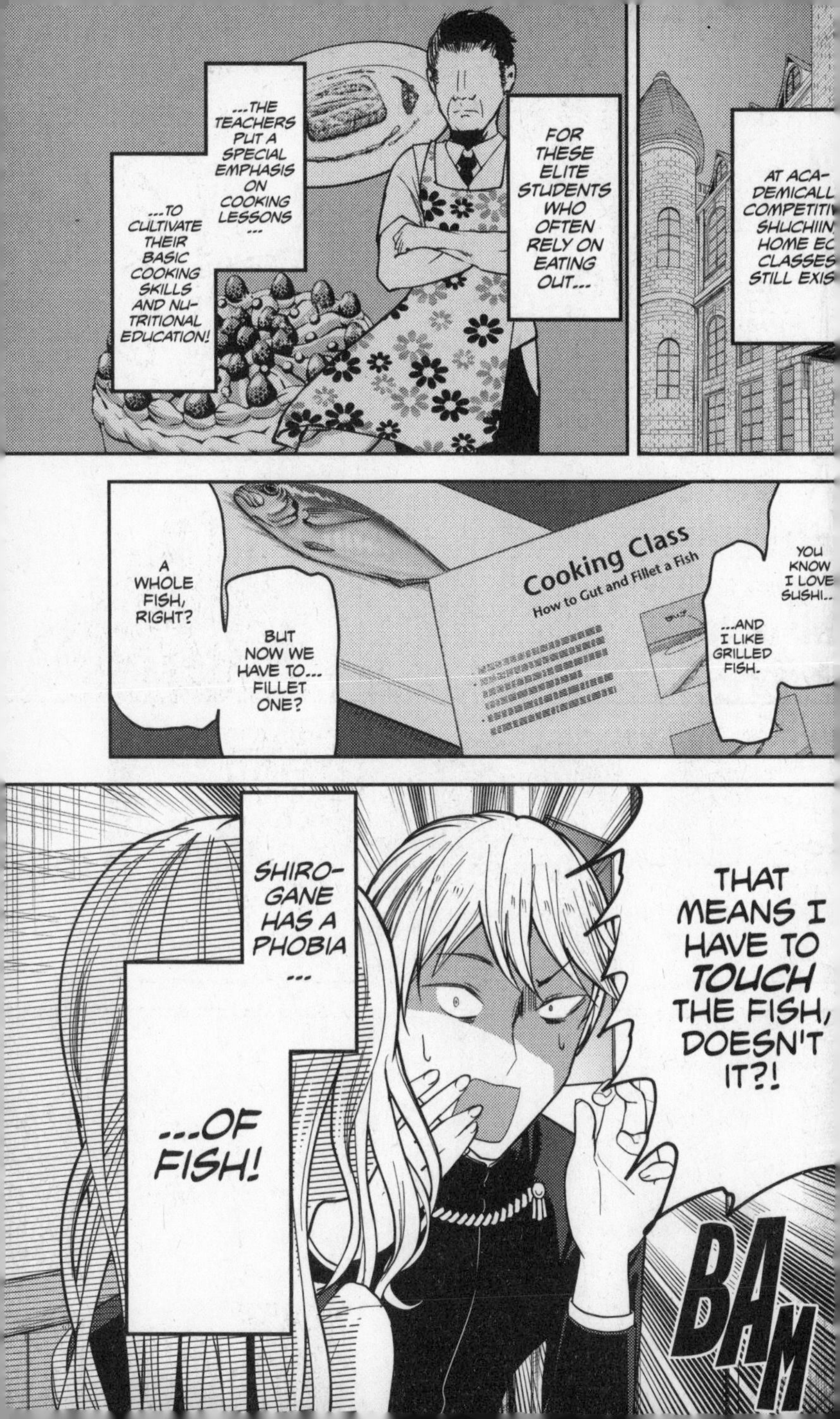
AT ACA-DEMICALL COMPETITIV SHUCHIIN, HOME EC CLASSES STILL EXIS
FOR THESE ELITE STUDENTS WHO OFTEN RELY ON EATING OUT...
...THE TEACHERS PUT A SPECIAL EMPHASIS ON COOKING LESSONS...
...TO CULTIVATE THEIR BASIC COOKING SKILLS AND NUTRITIONAL EDUCATION!
YOU KNOW I LOVE SUSHI...
...AND I LIKE GRILLED FISH.
Cooking Class
How to Gut and Fillet a Fish
A WHOLE FISH, RIGHT?
BUT NOW WE HAVE TO... FILLET ONE?
THAT MEANS I HAVE TO *TOUCH* THE FISH, DOESN'T IT?!
BAM
SHIRO-GANE HAS A PHOBIA...
...OF FISH!

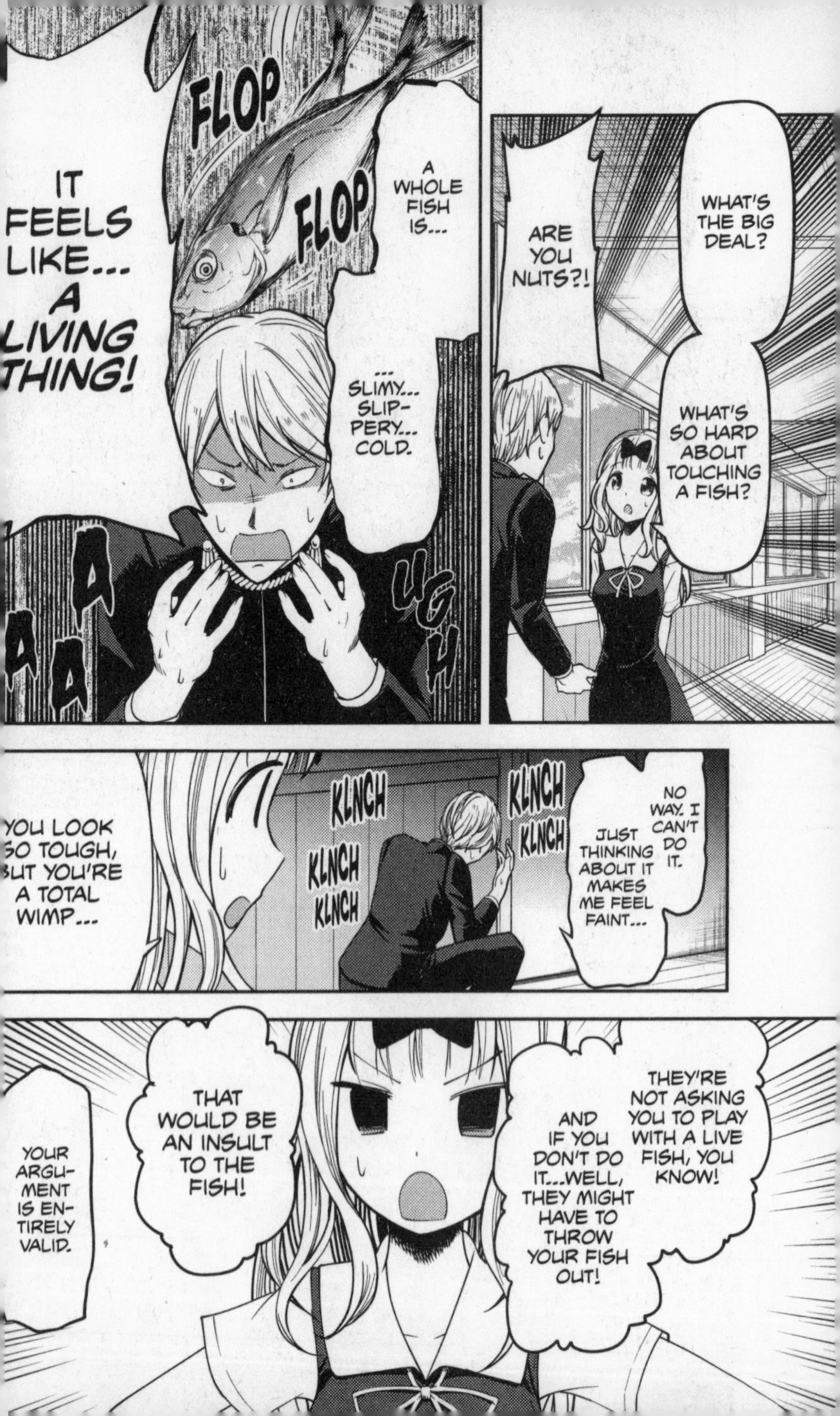
WHAT'S THE BIG DEAL?
WHAT'S SO HARD ABOUT TOUCHING A FISH?
ARE YOU NUTS?!
A WHOLE FISH IS...
FLOP
FLOP
...SLIMY... SLIPPERY... COLD.
IT FEELS LIKE... A LIVING THING!
UGH
AAAA
NO WAY. I CAN'T DO IT.
JUST THINKING ABOUT IT MAKES ME FEEL FAINT...
KLNCH KLNCH
KLNCH
KLNCH KLNCH
YOU LOOK SO TOUGH, BUT YOU'RE A TOTAL WIMP...
THEY'RE NOT ASKING YOU TO PLAY WITH A LIVE FISH, YOU KNOW!
AND IF YOU DON'T DO IT...WELL, THEY MIGHT HAVE TO THROW YOUR FISH OUT!
THAT WOULD BE AN INSULT TO THE FISH!
YOUR ARGUMENT IS ENTIRELY VALID.

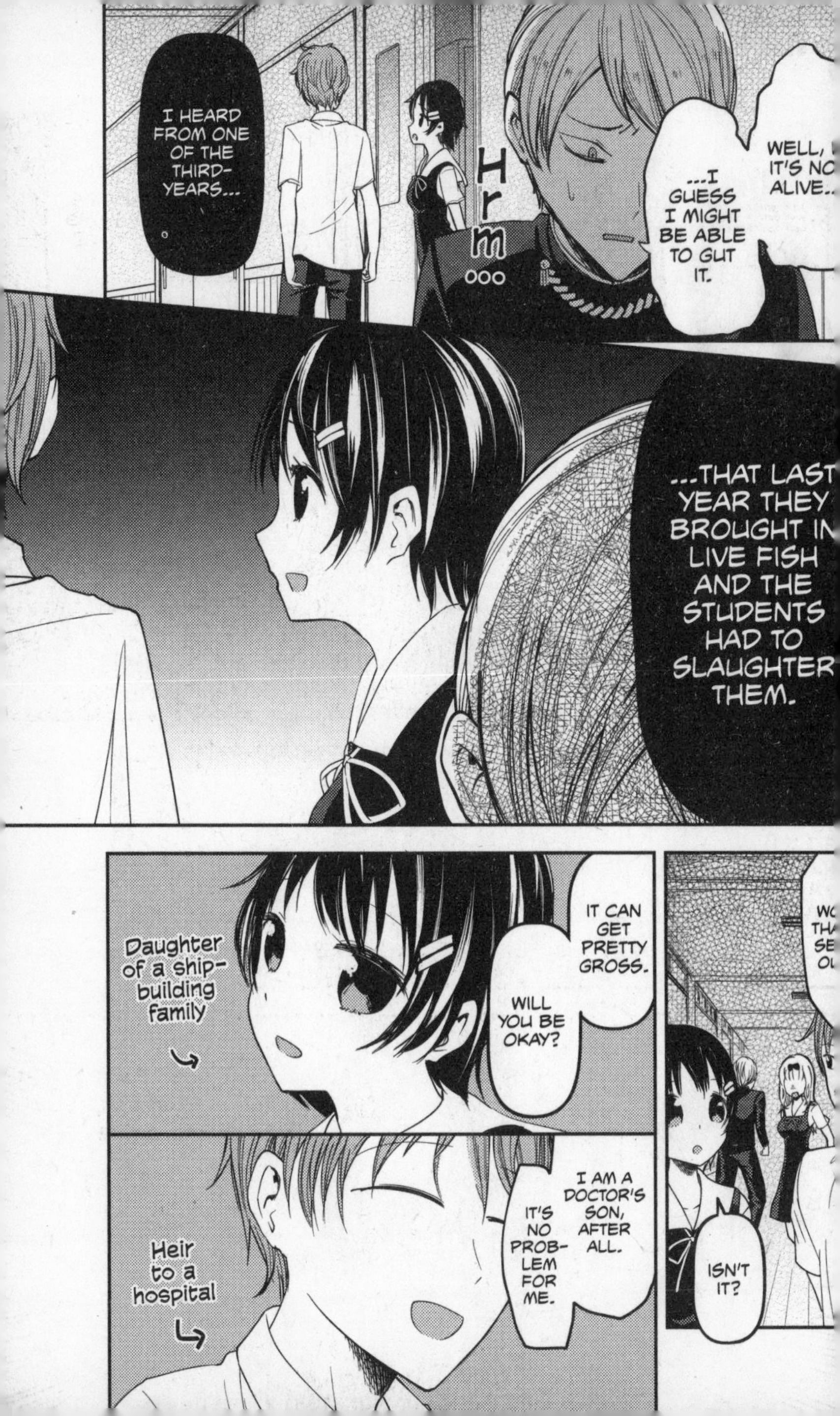
WELL, IT'S NO ALIVE...
...I GUESS I MIGHT BE ABLE TO GUT IT.
Hrm
I HEARD FROM ONE OF THE THIRD-YEARS...
...THAT LAST YEAR THEY BROUGHT IN LIVE FISH AND THE STUDENTS HAD TO SLAUGHTER THEM.
WO THA SE OU
ISN'T IT?
IT CAN GET PRETTY GROSS.
WILL YOU BE OKAY?
Daughter of a ship-building family
I AM A DOCTOR'S SON, AFTER ALL.
IT'S NO PROB-LEM FOR ME.
Heir to a hospital

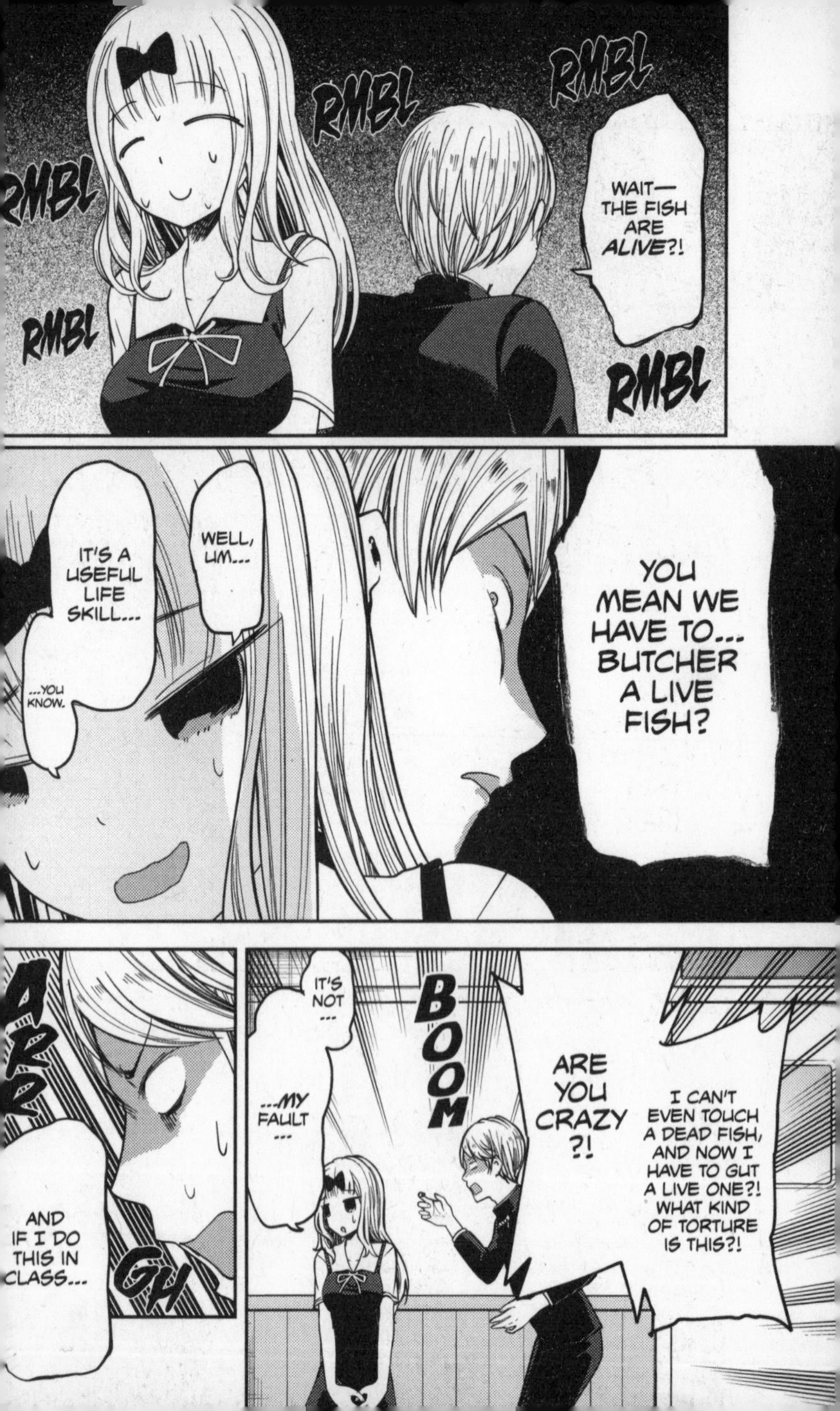
RMBL
WAIT— THE FISH ARE ALIVE?!
RMBL
RMBL
RMBL
RMBL
YOU MEAN WE HAVE TO... BUTCHER A LIVE FISH?
WELL, UM...
IT'S A USEFUL LIFE SKILL...
...YOU KNOW.
I CAN'T EVEN TOUCH A DEAD FISH, AND NOW I HAVE TO GUT A LIVE ONE?! WHAT KIND OF TORTURE IS THIS?!
ARE YOU CRAZY?!
BOOM
IT'S NOT...
...MY FAULT...
ARGH
AND IF I DO THIS IN CLASS...

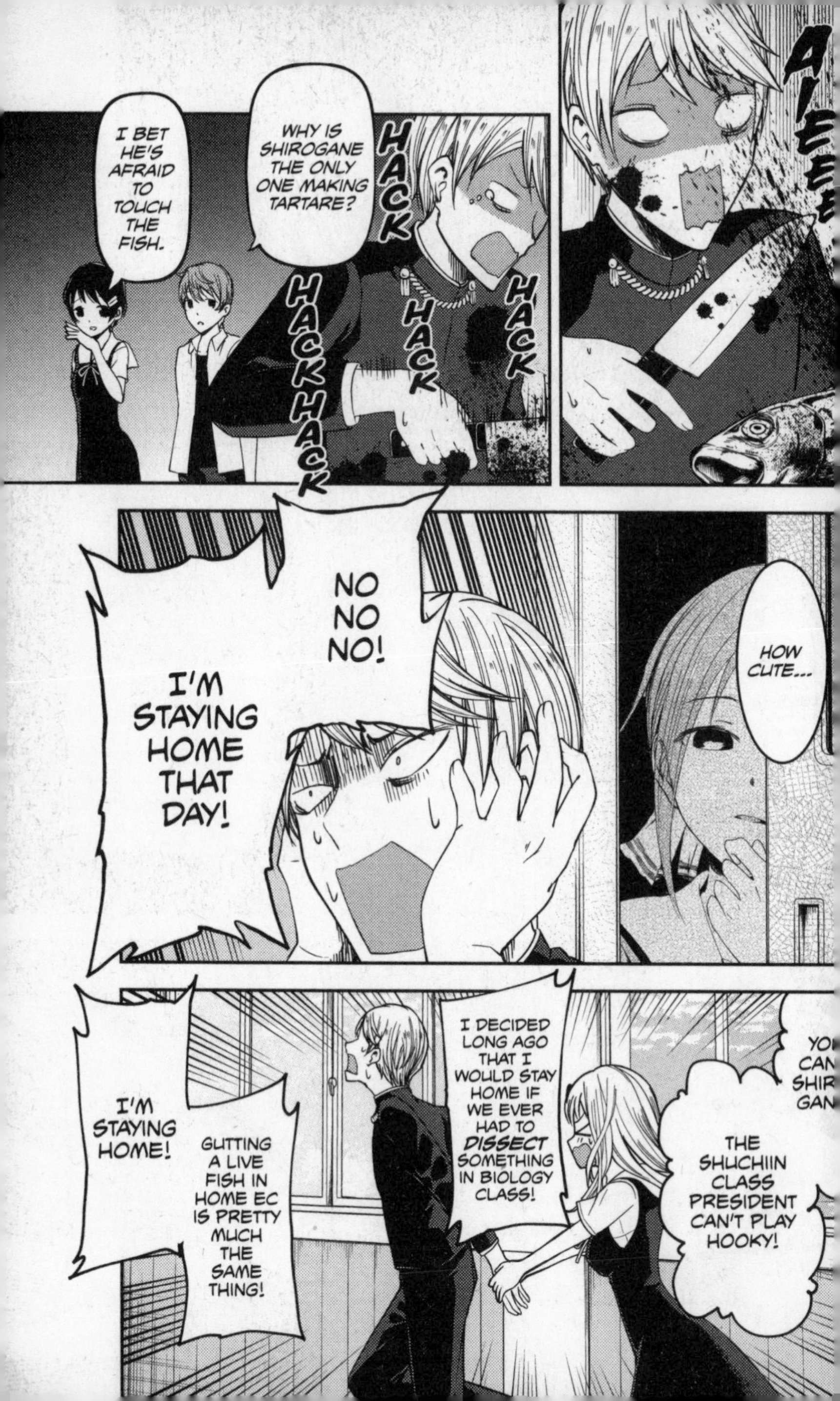
AIEEE
WHY IS SHIROGANE THE ONLY ONE MAKING TARTARE?
HACK HACK HACK HACK HACK
I BET HE'S AFRAID TO TOUCH THE FISH.
HOW CUTE...
NO NO NO!
I'M STAYING HOME THAT DAY!
THE SHUCHIIN CLASS PRESIDENT CAN'T PLAY HOOKY!
I DECIDED LONG AGO THAT I WOULD STAY HOME IF WE EVER HAD TO *DISSECT* SOMETHING IN BIOLOGY CLASS!
GUTTING A LIVE FISH IN HOME EC IS PRETTY MUCH THE SAME THING!
I'M STAYING HOME!

IT'S TRUE.

BUT ---

ARGH!

DON'T LET SOMETHING LIKE THIS RUIN YOUR RECORD!

YOU TOLD ME YOU'VE HAD PERFECT ATTENDANCE SINCE ELEMENTARY SCHOOL!

!

NOT THIS AGAIN!!

...HOW CAN I...?

IT'S JUST THAT I CAN'T TALK TO THE OTHERS ABOUT THIS...

SO...

WHY CAN'T YOU TALK TO THEM?!

KLNCH

IF YOU THINK I'M GOING TO HELP YOU EVERY TIME, YOU'VE GOT ANOTHER THINK COMING!

...FIGURE IT OUT ON YOUR OWN!

YOU NEED TO...

THAT'S NOT MY INTENTION.

SORRY.

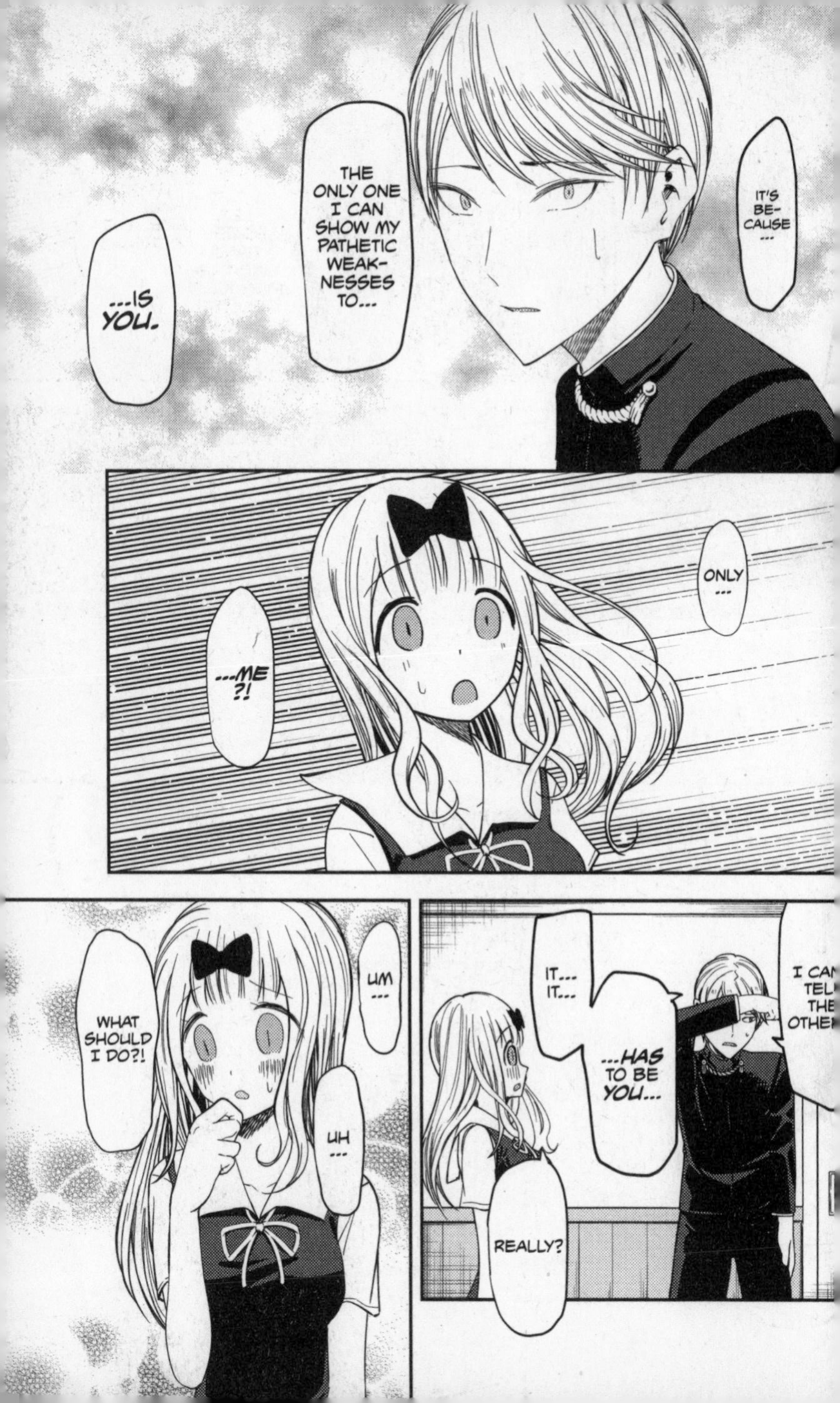
IT'S BE-CAUSE...
THE ONLY ONE I CAN SHOW MY PATHETIC WEAK-NESSES TO...
...IS YOU.
ONLY...
...ME?!
I CAN TELL THE
IT... IT...
...HAS TO BE YOU...
REALLY?
UM...
UH...
WHAT SHOULD I DO?!

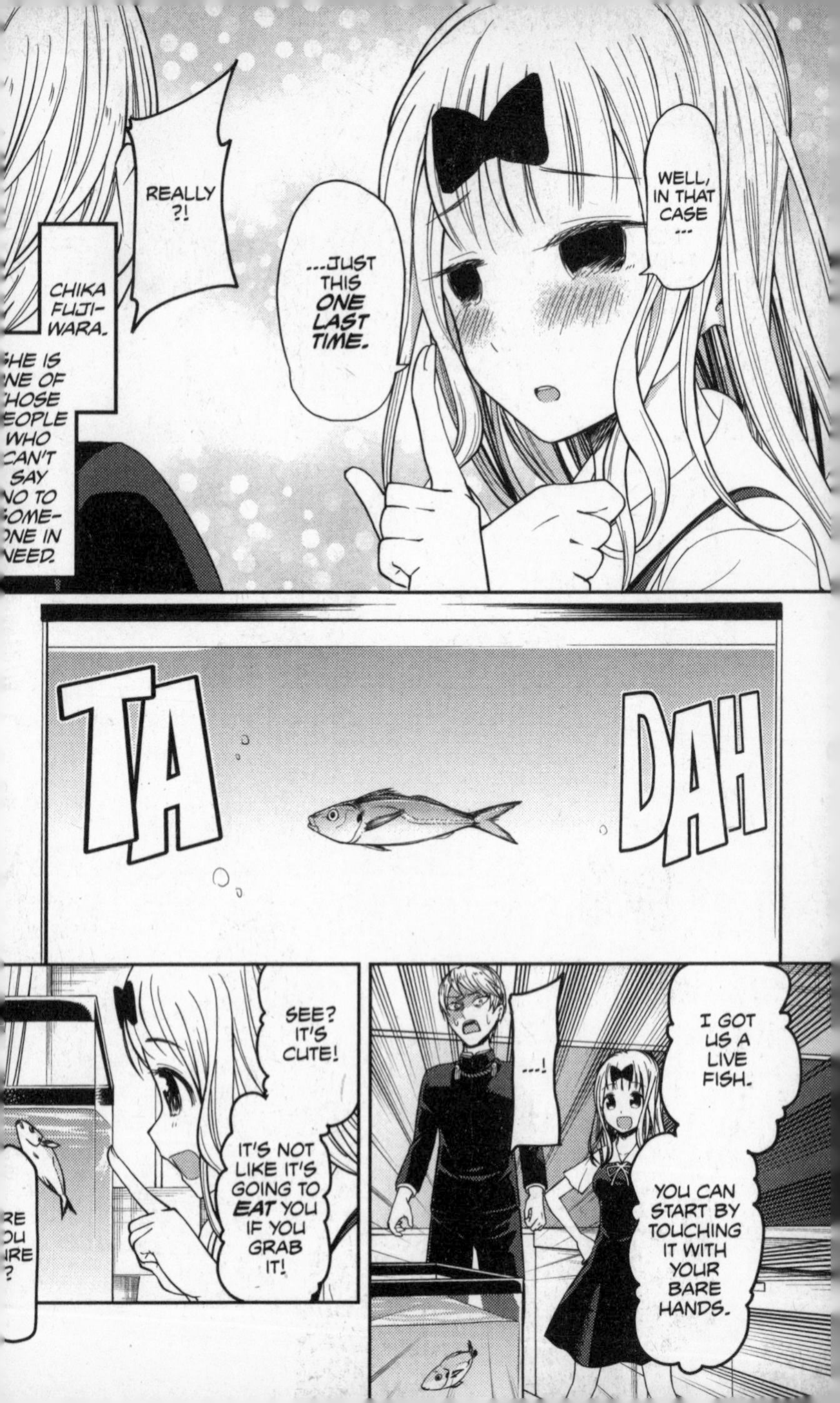
WELL, IN THAT CASE ...
...JUST THIS ONE LAST TIME.
REALLY ?!
CHIKA FUJIWARA.
HE IS NE OF HOSE EOPLE WHO CAN'T SAY NO TO OME- ONE IN NEED.
TA DAH
I GOT US A LIVE FISH.
...!
YOU CAN START BY TOUCHING IT WITH YOUR BARE HANDS.
SEE? IT'S CUTE!
IT'S NOT LIKE IT'S GOING TO EAT YOU IF YOU GRAB IT!
RE OU RE ?

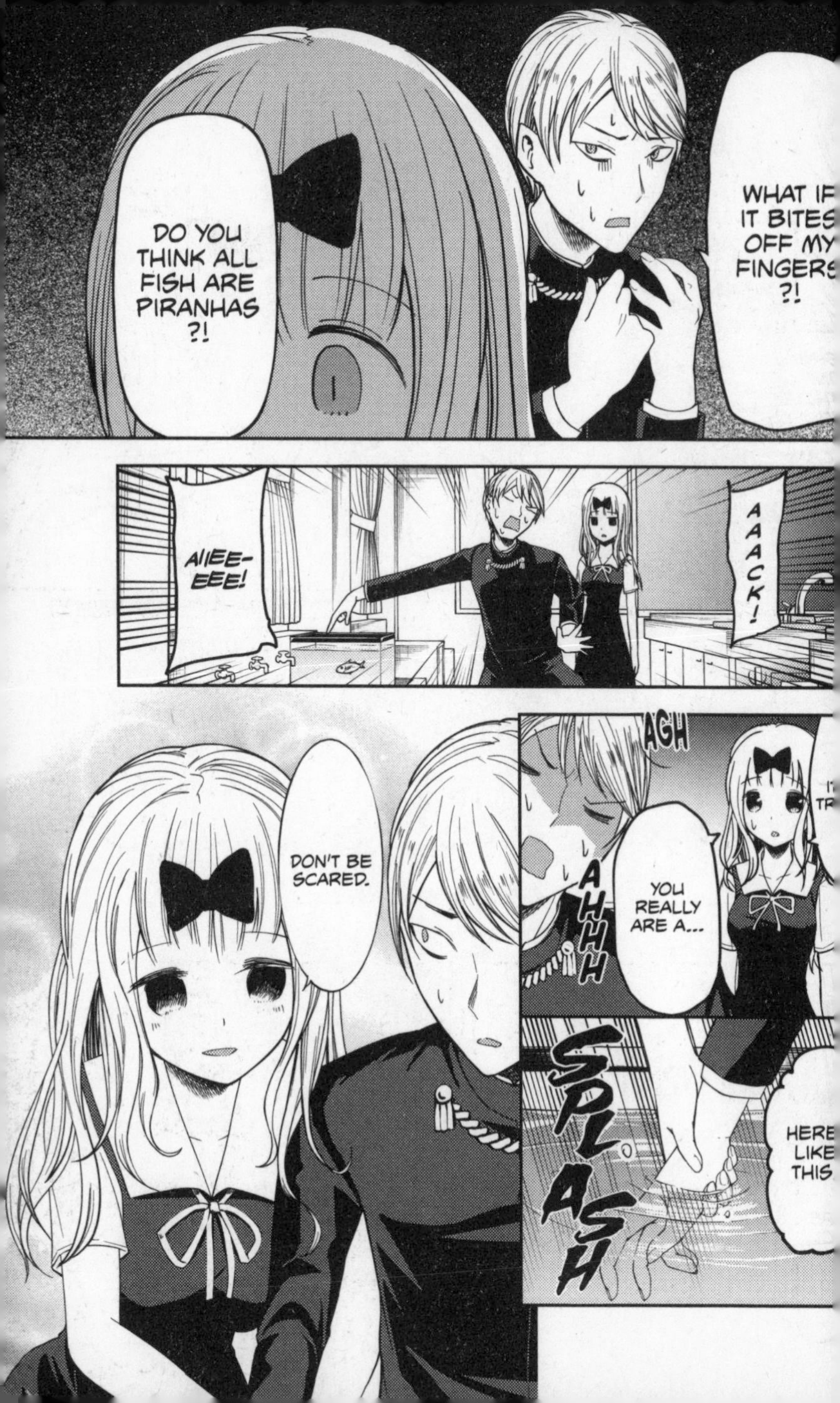
WHAT IF IT BITES OFF MY FINGERS ?!
DO YOU THINK ALL FISH ARE PIRANHAS ?!
AAAACK!
AIIEE-EEE!
AGH
YOU REALLY ARE A...
AHHH
HERE LIKE THIS
SPLASH
DON'T BE SCARED.

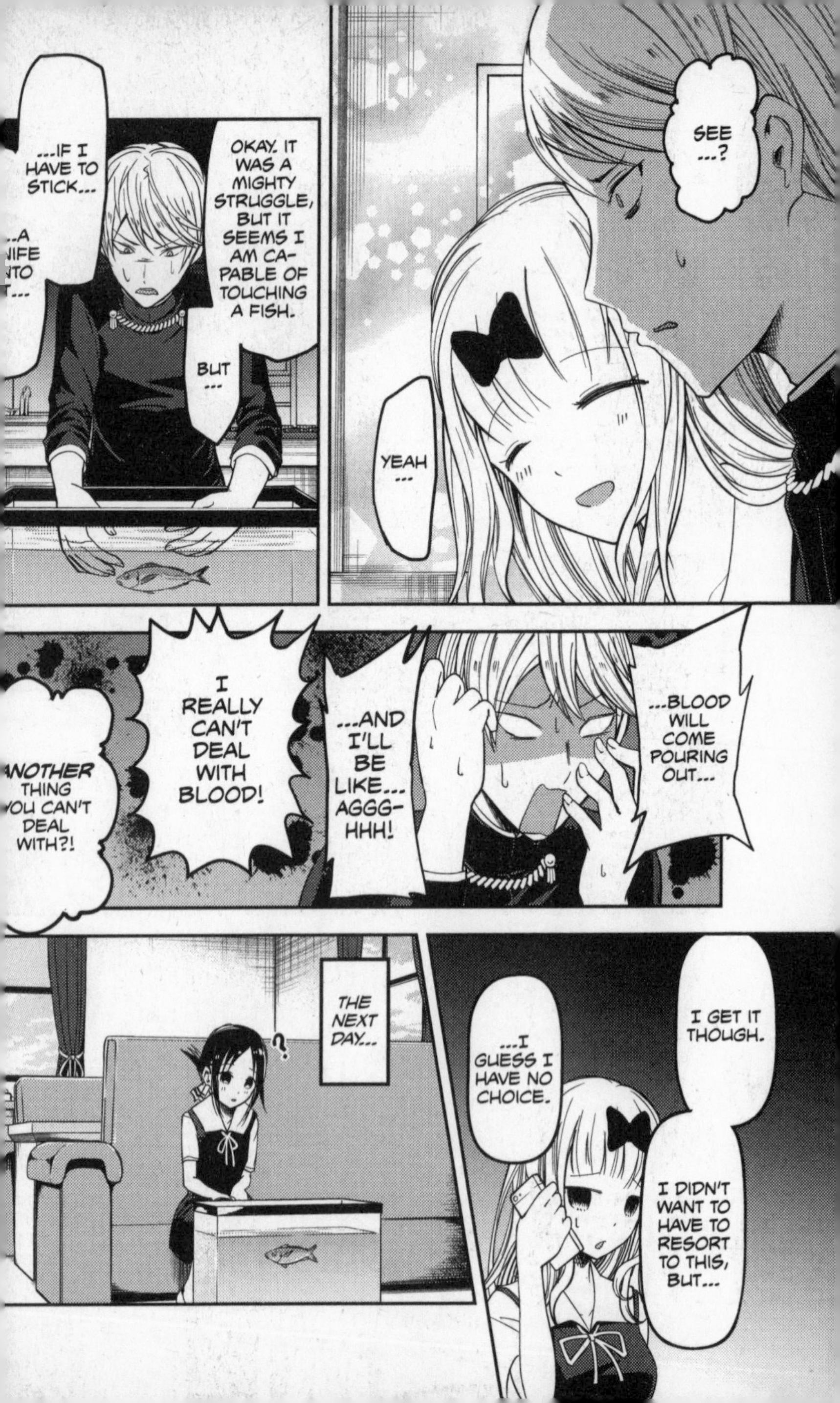
SEE ...?
YEAH ...
OKAY. IT WAS A MIGHTY STRUGGLE, BUT IT SEEMS I AM CAPABLE OF TOUCHING A FISH.
BUT ...
...IF I HAVE TO STICK...
...A NIFE NTO T ...
...BLOOD WILL COME POURING OUT...
...AND I'LL BE LIKE... AGGG-HHH!
I REALLY CAN'T DEAL WITH BLOOD!
NOTHER THING OU CAN'T DEAL WITH?!
I GET IT THOUGH.
...I GUESS I HAVE NO CHOICE.
I DIDN'T WANT TO HAVE TO RESORT TO THIS, BUT...
THE NEXT DAY...
?

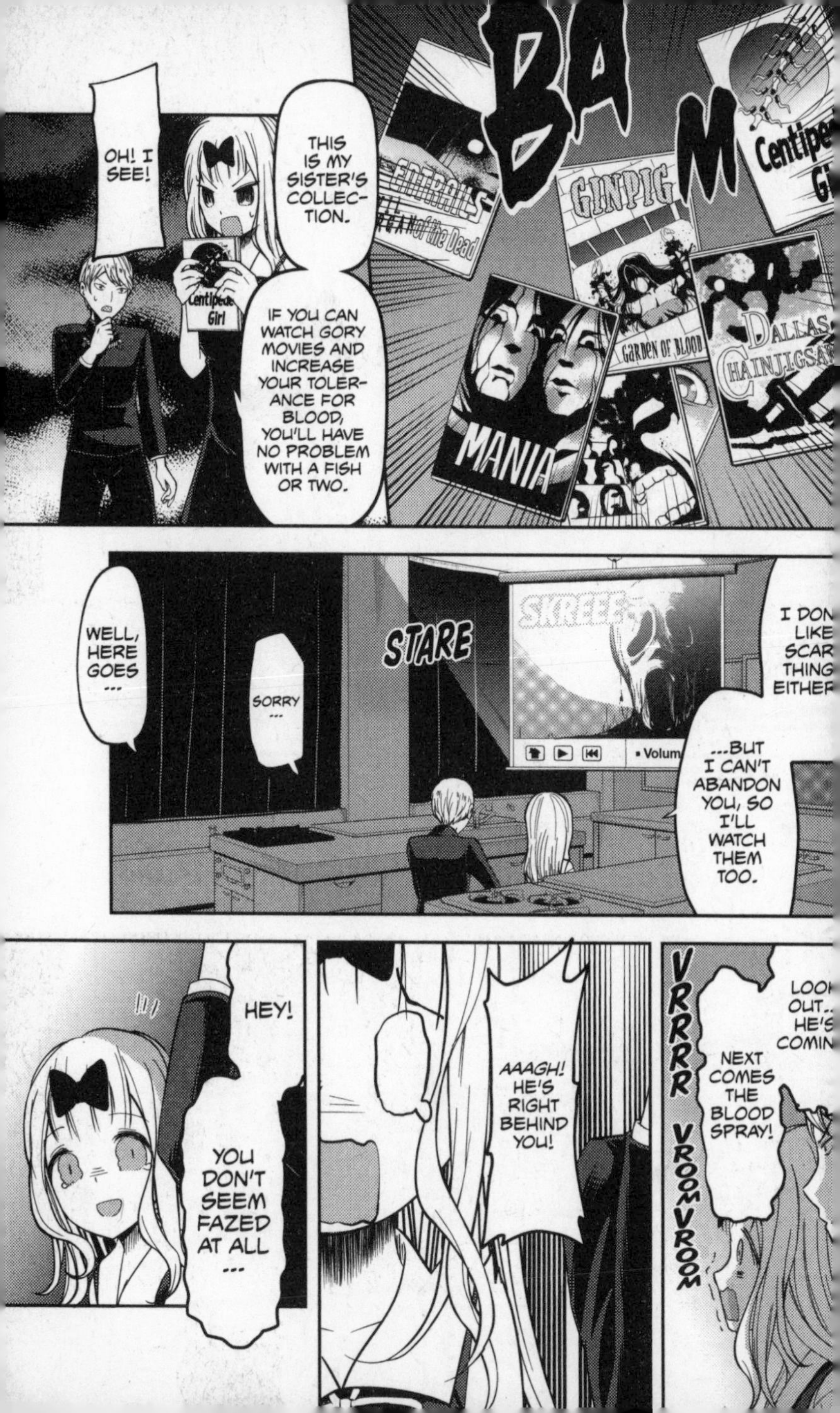
BAM
Centipede Girl
ENTRAILS
GINPIG
GARDEN OF BLOOD
DALLAS CHAINJIGSAW
MANIA
THIS IS MY SISTER'S COLLECTION.
IF YOU CAN WATCH GORY MOVIES AND INCREASE YOUR TOLERANCE FOR BLOOD, YOU'LL HAVE NO PROBLEM WITH A FISH OR TWO.
Centipede Girl
OH! I SEE!
I DON LIKE SCAR THING EITHER
...BUT I CAN'T ABANDON YOU, SO I'LL WATCH THEM TOO.
SKREEE
Volum
STARE
SORRY...
WELL, HERE GOES...
LOOK OUT... HE'S COMIN
VRRRR VROOMVROOM
NEXT COMES THE BLOOD SPRAY!
AAAGH! HE'S RIGHT BEHIND YOU!
HEY!
YOU DON'T SEEM FAZED AT ALL...

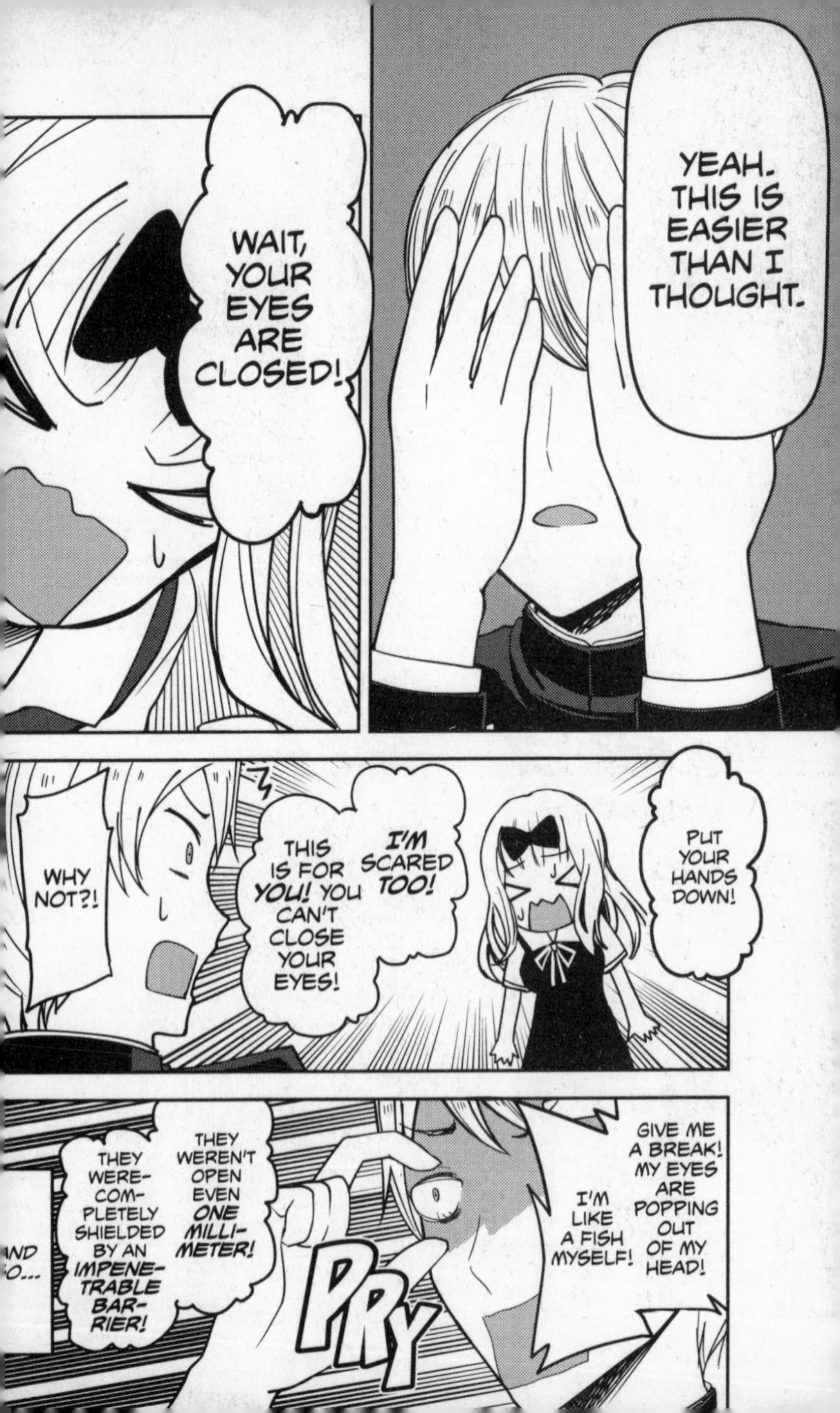
YEAH. THIS IS EASIER THAN I THOUGHT.
WAIT, YOUR EYES ARE CLOSED!
PUT YOUR HANDS DOWN!
I'M SCARED TOO!
THIS IS FOR YOU! YOU CAN'T CLOSE YOUR EYES!
WHY NOT?!
GIVE ME A BREAK! MY EYES ARE POPPING OUT OF MY HEAD!
I'M LIKE A FISH MYSELF!
PRY
THEY WEREN'T OPEN EVEN ONE MILLIMETER!
THEY WERE COMPLETELY SHIELDED BY AN IMPENETRABLE BARRIER!

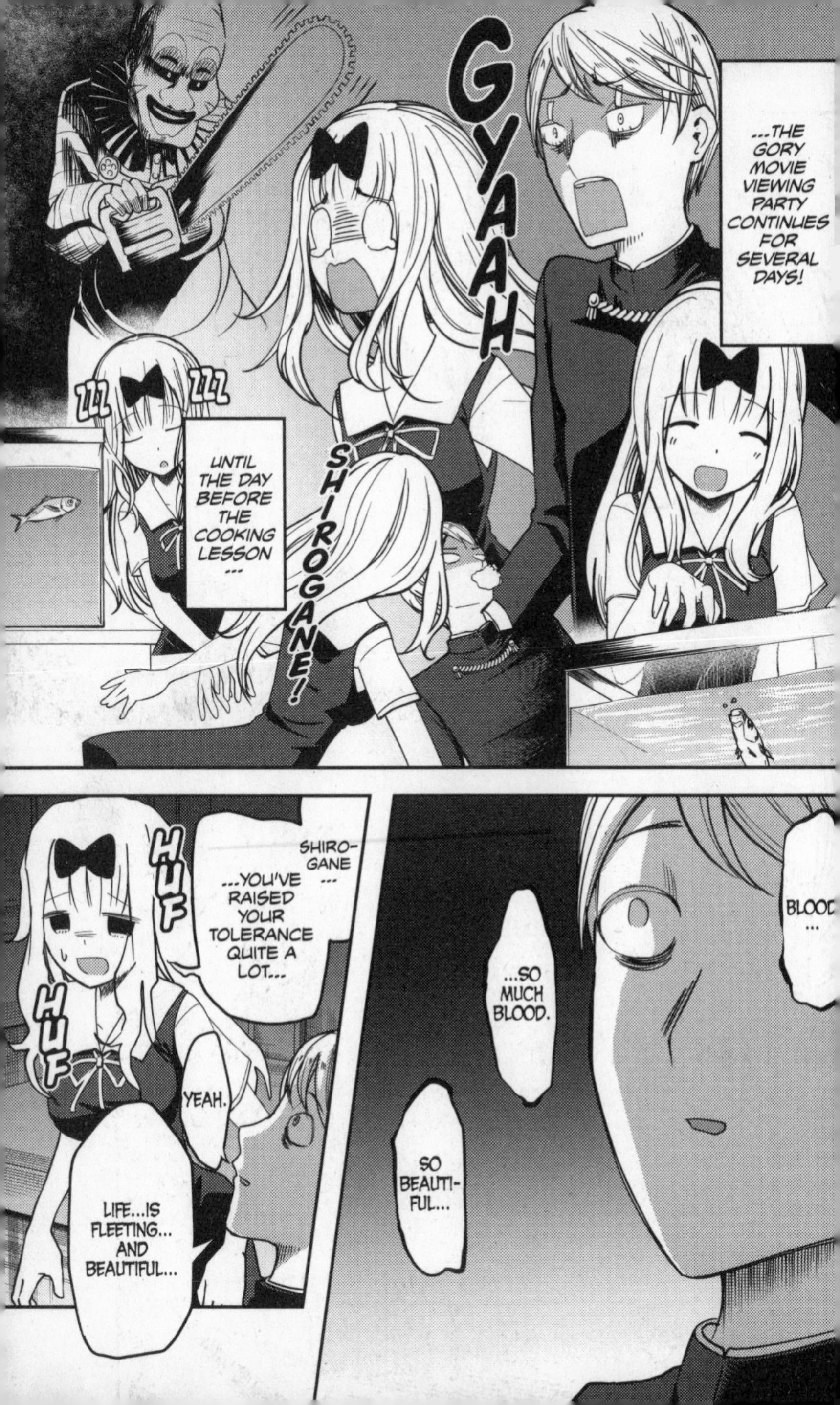
...THE GORY MOVIE VIEWING PARTY CONTINUES FOR SEVERAL DAYS!
GYAAH
SHIROGANE!
UNTIL THE DAY BEFORE THE COOKING LESSON ...
ZZZ
ZZZ
BLOOD ...
...SO MUCH BLOOD.
SO BEAUTI-FUL...
SHIRO-GANE ...
...YOU'VE RAISED YOUR TOLERANCE QUITE A LOT...
HUF
HUF
YEAH.
LIFE...IS FLEETING... AND BEAUTIFUL...

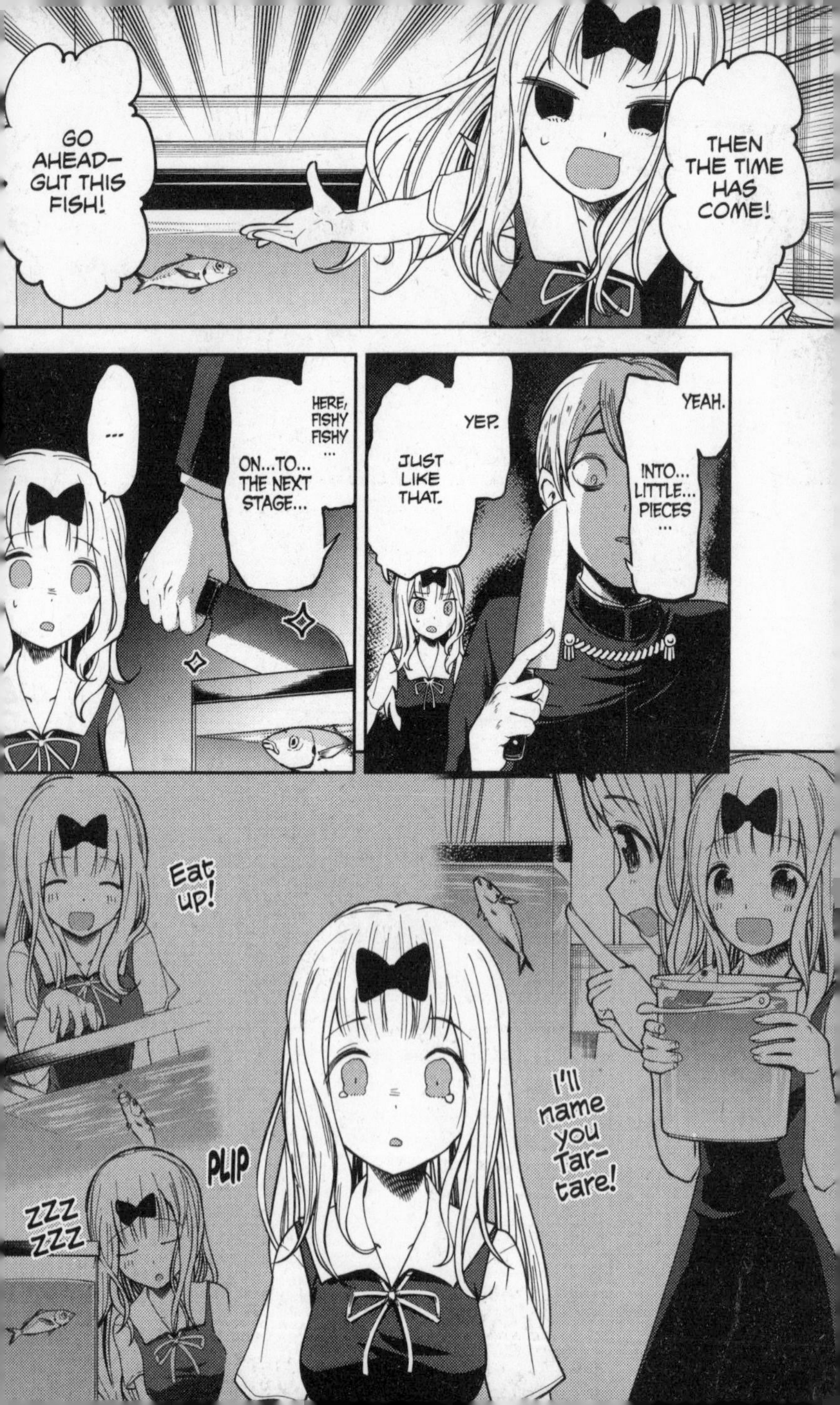
THEN THE TIME HAS COME!
GO AHEAD—GUT THIS FISH!
YEAH.
INTO... LITTLE... PIECES...
YEP.
JUST LIKE THAT.
HERE, FISHY FISHY...
ON...TO... THE NEXT STAGE...
...
I'll name you Tar-tare!
Eat up!
PLIP
ZZZ ZZZ

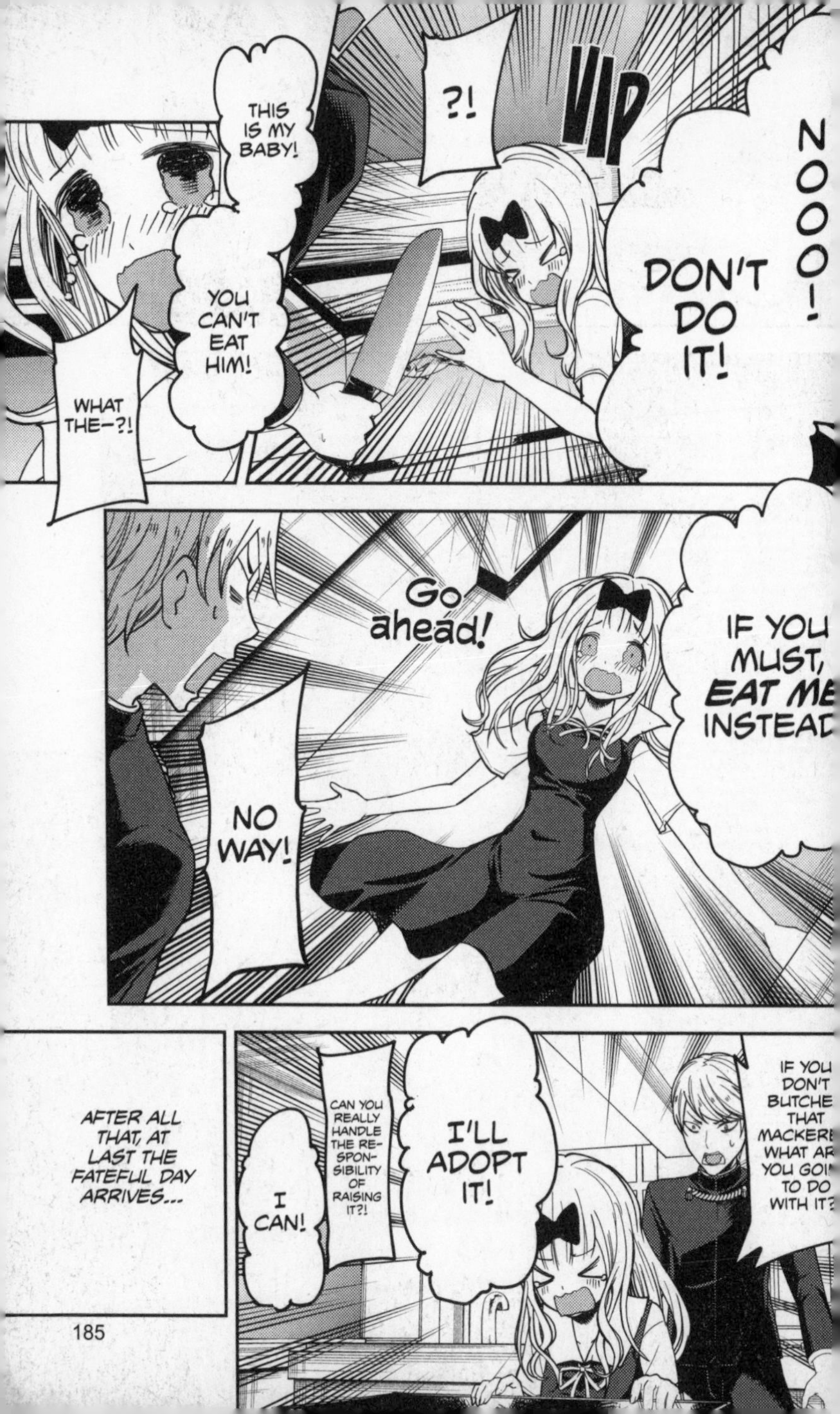
NOOOO!
DON'T DO IT!
VIP
?!
THIS IS MY BABY!
YOU CAN'T EAT HIM!
WHAT THE-?!
IF YOU MUST, *EAT ME* INSTEA
Go ahead!
NO WAY!
IF YOU DON'T BUTCHE THAT MACKER WHAT AR YOU GOI TO DO WITH IT?
I'LL ADOPT IT!
CAN YOU REALLY HANDLE THE RE-SPON-SIBILITY OF RAISING IT?!
I CAN!
AFTER ALL THAT, AT LAST THE FATEFUL DAY ARRIVES...

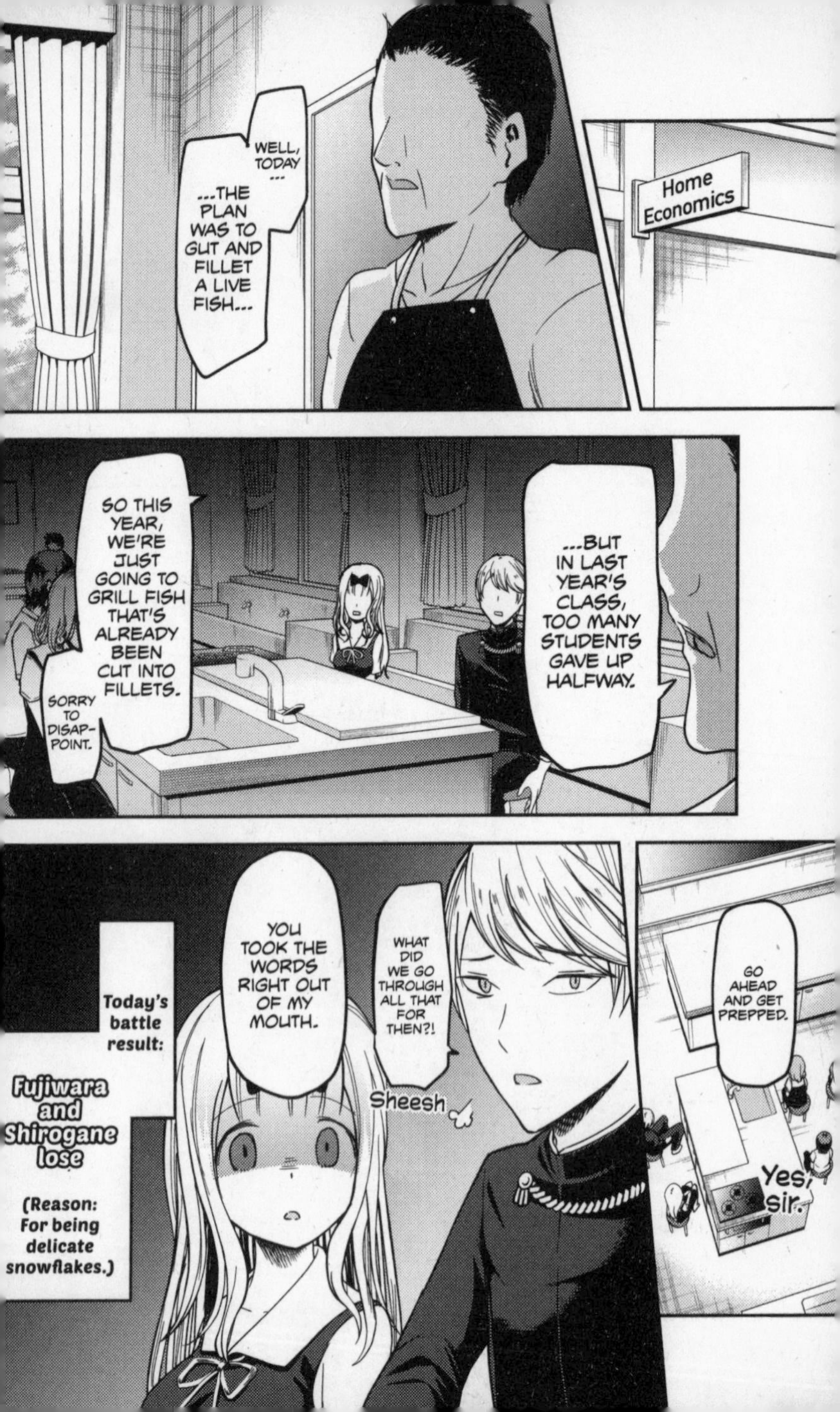
Home Economics
WELL, TODAY...
...THE PLAN WAS TO GUT AND FILLET A LIVE FISH...
...BUT IN LAST YEAR'S CLASS, TOO MANY STUDENTS GAVE UP HALFWAY.
SO THIS YEAR, WE'RE JUST GOING TO GRILL FISH THAT'S ALREADY BEEN CUT INTO FILLETS.
SORRY TO DISAPPOINT.
GO AHEAD AND GET PREPPED.
Yes, sir.
WHAT DID WE GO THROUGH ALL THAT FOR THEN?!
YOU TOOK THE WORDS RIGHT OUT OF MY MOUTH.
Sheesh
Today's battle result:
Fujiwara and Shirogane lose
(Reason: For being delicate snowflakes.)

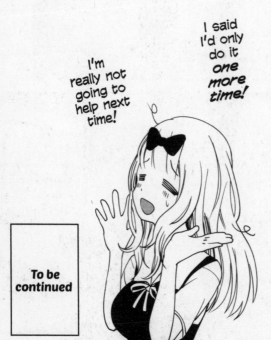

I said I'd only do it *one more time!*
I'm really not going to help next time!

To be continued

KAGUYA-SAMA
LOVE IS WAR

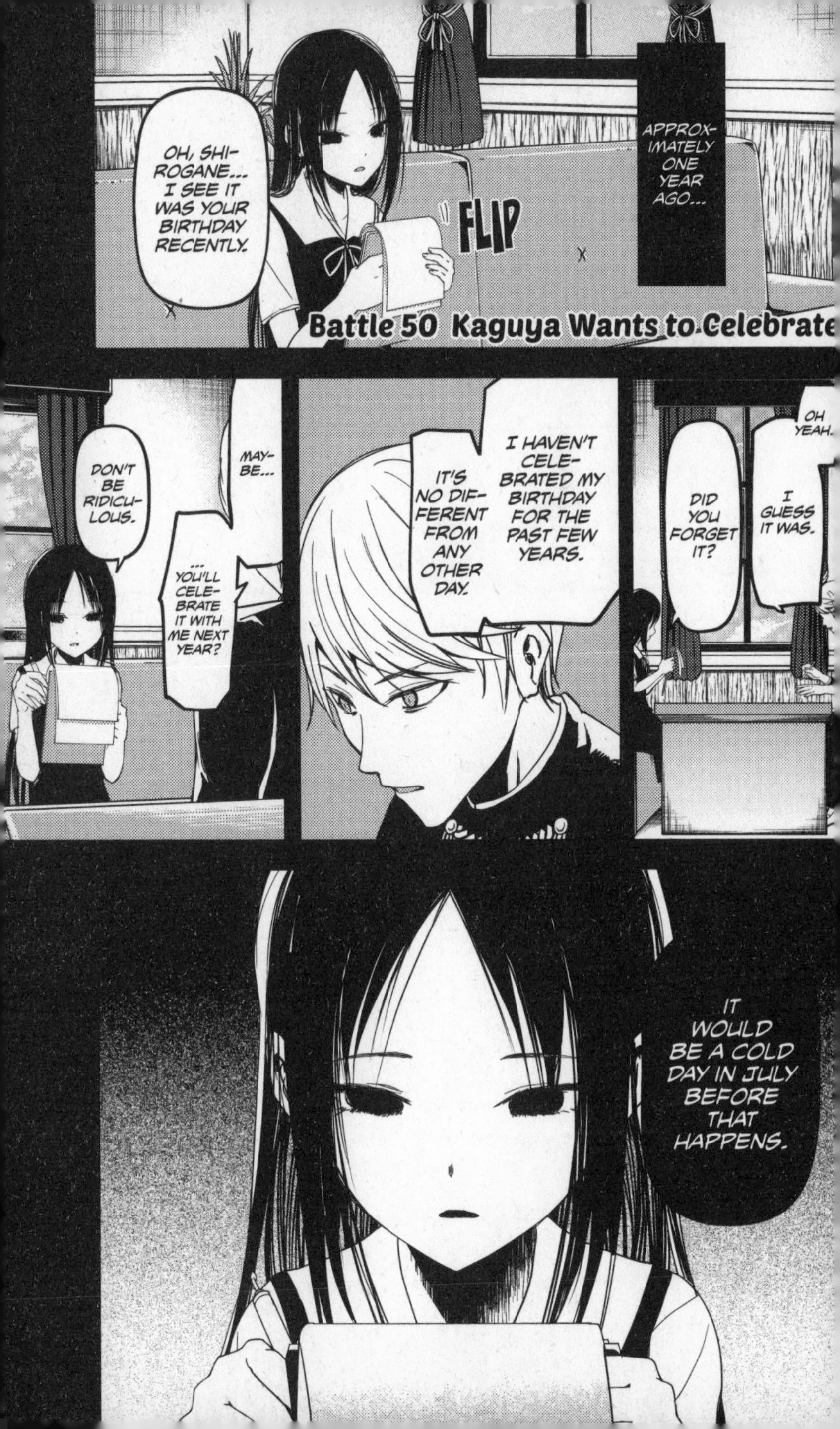
APPROXIMATELY ONE YEAR AGO...
OH, SHIROGANE... I SEE IT WAS YOUR BIRTHDAY RECENTLY.
FLIP
Battle 50 Kaguya Wants to Celebrate
OH YEAH.
I GUESS IT WAS.
DID YOU FORGET IT?
I HAVEN'T CELEBRATED MY BIRTHDAY FOR THE PAST FEW YEARS.
IT'S NO DIFFERENT FROM ANY OTHER DAY.
MAYBE...
...YOU'LL CELEBRATE IT WITH ME NEXT YEAR?
DON'T BE RIDICULOUS.
IT WOULD BE A COLD DAY IN JULY BEFORE THAT HAPPENS.

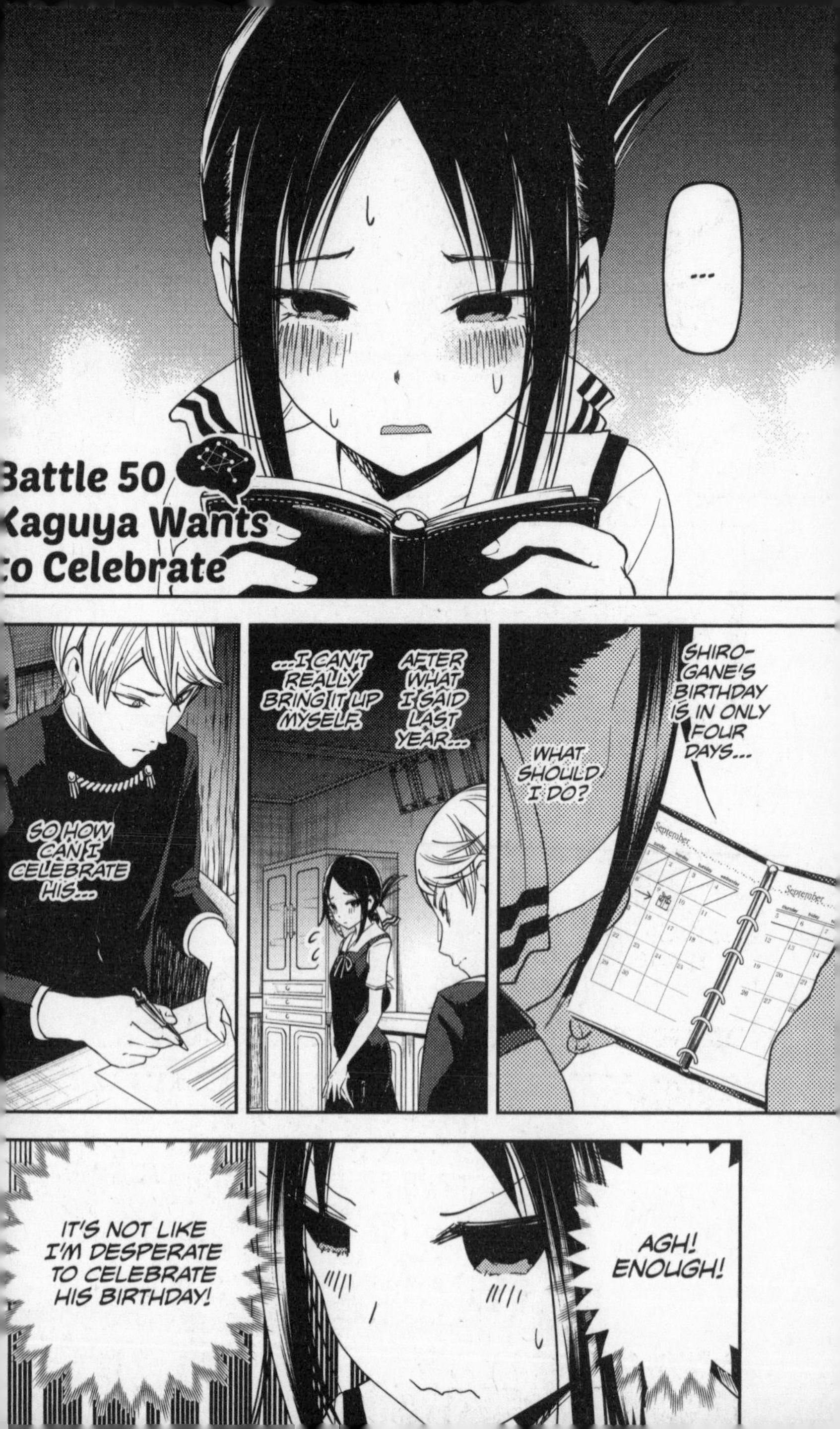
...
Battle 50 Kaguya Wants to Celebrate
SHIROGANE'S BIRTHDAY IS IN ONLY FOUR DAYS...
WHAT SHOULD I DO?
September
AFTER WHAT I SAID LAST YEAR...
...I CAN'T REALLY BRING IT UP MYSELF.
SO HOW CAN I CELEBRATE HIS...
AGH! ENOUGH!
IT'S NOT LIKE I'M DESPERATE TO CELEBRATE HIS BIRTHDAY!

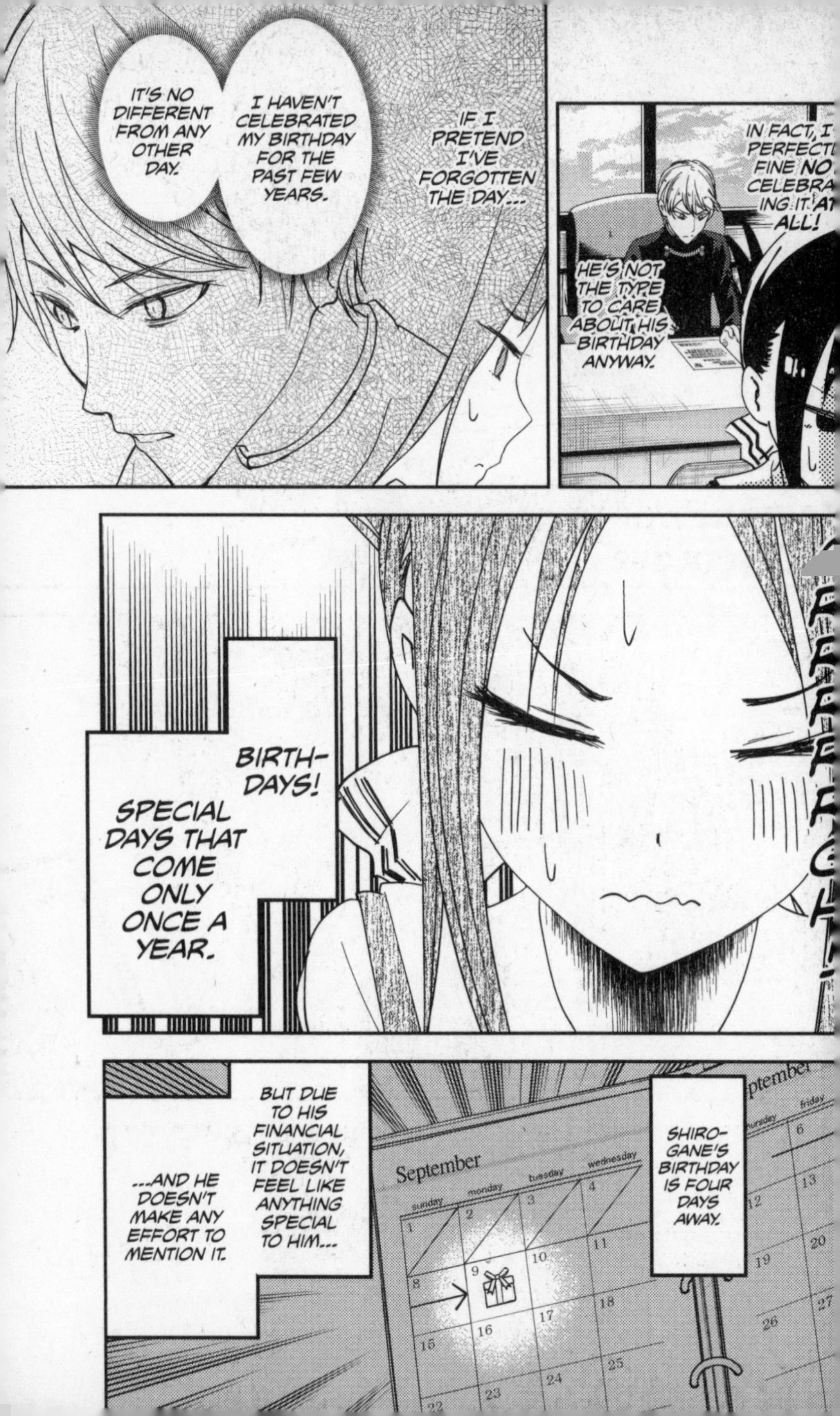
IN FACT, I PERFECT FINE NO CELEBRA ING IT AT ALL!
HE'S NOT THE TYPE TO CARE ABOUT HIS BIRTHDAY ANYWAY.
IF I PRETEND I'VE FORGOTTEN THE DAY...
I HAVEN'T CELEBRATED MY BIRTHDAY FOR THE PAST FEW YEARS.
IT'S NO DIFFERENT FROM ANY OTHER DAY.
BIRTH-DAYS!
SPECIAL DAYS THAT COME ONLY ONCE A YEAR.
SHIRO-GANE'S BIRTHDAY IS FOUR DAYS AWAY.
BUT DUE TO HIS FINANCIAL SITUATION, IT DOESN'T FEEL LIKE ANYTHING SPECIAL TO HIM...
...AND HE DOESN'T MAKE ANY EFFORT TO MENTION IT.
September

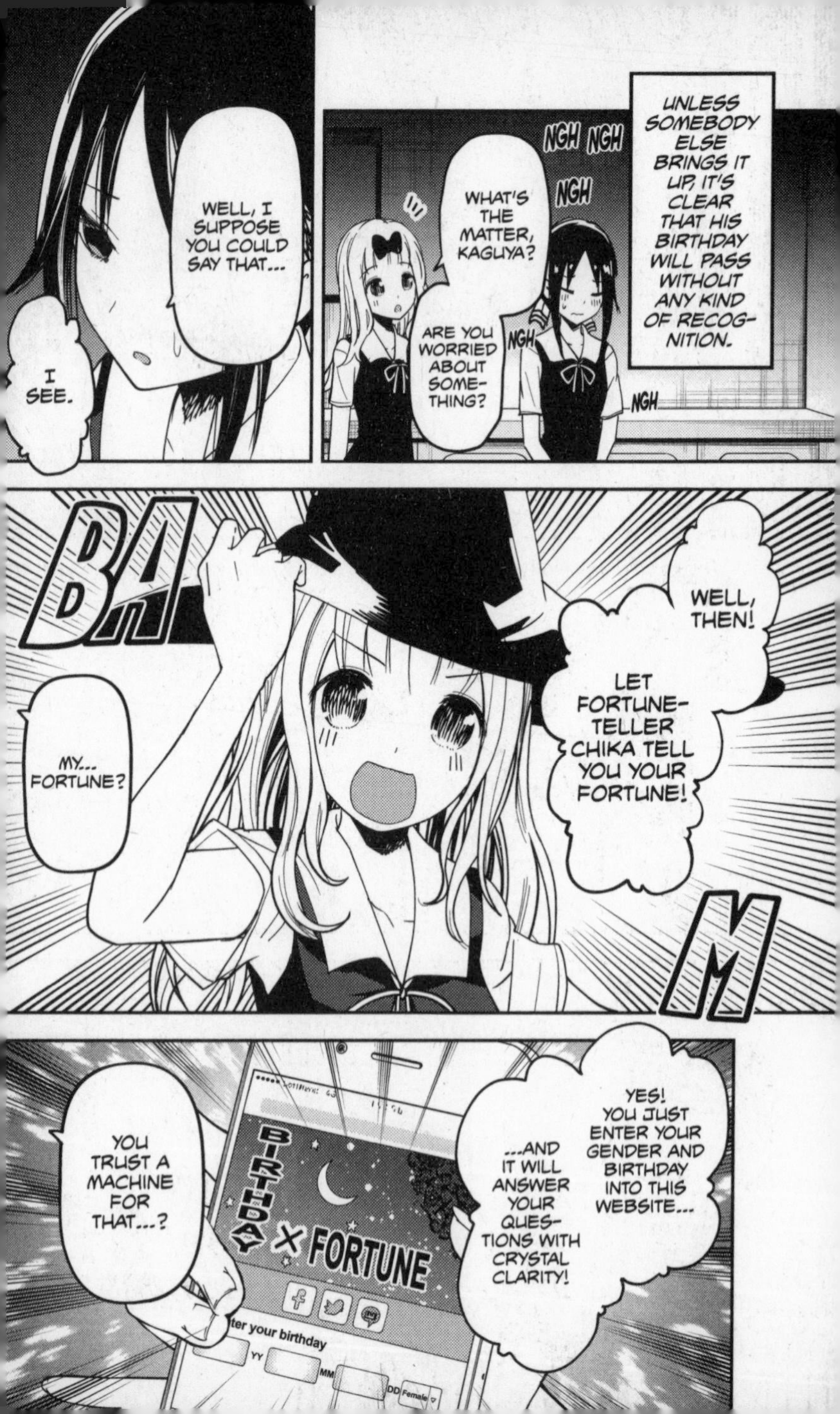
UNLESS SOMEBODY ELSE BRINGS IT UP, IT'S CLEAR THAT HIS BIRTHDAY WILL PASS WITHOUT ANY KIND OF RECOGNITION.
NGH NGH
NGH
WHAT'S THE MATTER, KAGUYA?
ARE YOU WORRIED ABOUT SOME-THING?
NGH
NGH
WELL, I SUPPOSE YOU COULD SAY THAT...
I SEE.
BAM
WELL, THEN!
LET FORTUNE-TELLER CHIKA TELL YOU YOUR FORTUNE!
MY... FORTUNE?
YES! YOU JUST ENTER YOUR GENDER AND BIRTHDAY INTO THIS WEBSITE...
...AND IT WILL ANSWER YOUR QUES-TIONS WITH CRYSTAL CLARITY!
BIRTHDAY × FORTUNE
ter your birthday
YY
MM
DD
Female
YOU TRUST A MACHINE FOR THAT...?

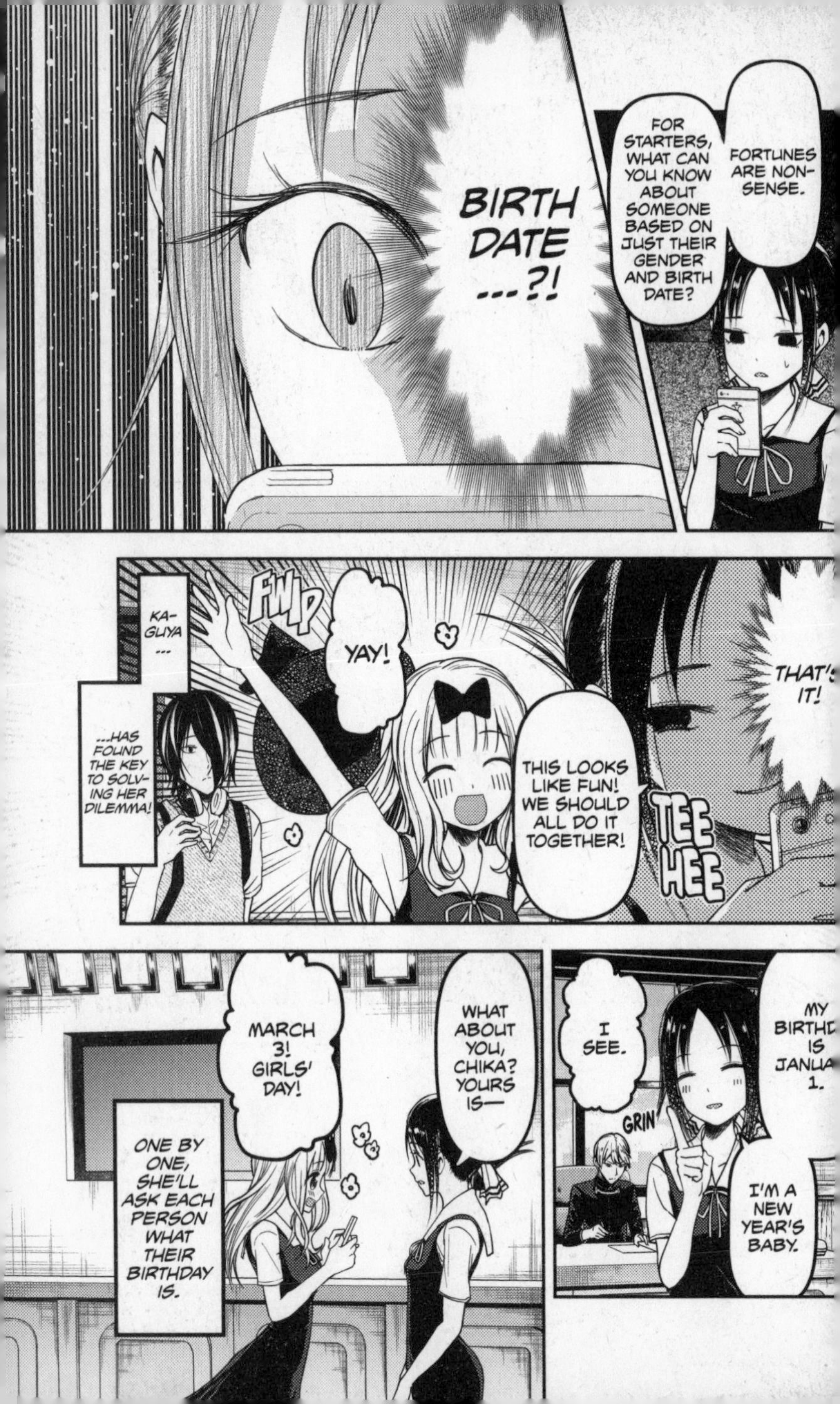
FORTUNES ARE NON-SENSE.
FOR STARTERS, WHAT CAN YOU KNOW ABOUT SOMEONE BASED ON JUST THEIR GENDER AND BIRTH DATE?
BIRTH DATE ...?!
THAT'S IT!
TEE HEE
THIS LOOKS LIKE FUN! WE SHOULD ALL DO IT TOGETHER!
YAY!
FWIP
KA-GUYA ...
...HAS FOUND THE KEY TO SOLV-ING HER DILEMMA!
MY BIRTHD IS JANUA 1.
I SEE.
GRIN
I'M A NEW YEAR'S BABY.
WHAT ABOUT YOU, CHIKA? YOURS IS—
MARCH 3! GIRLS' DAY!
ONE BY ONE, SHE'LL ASK EACH PERSON WHAT THEIR BIRTHDAY IS.

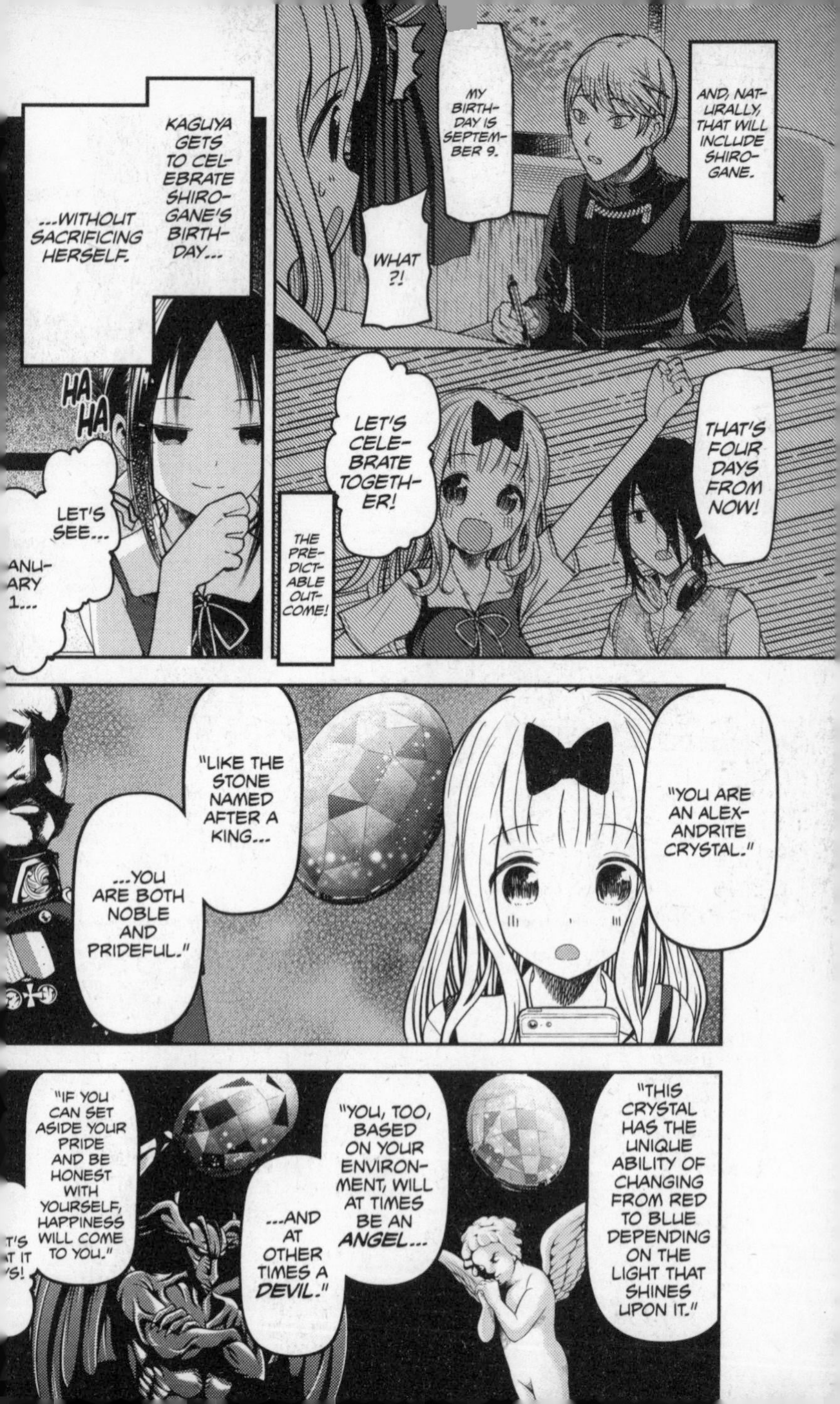
AND, NATURALLY, THAT WILL INCLUDE SHIROGANE.
MY BIRTHDAY IS SEPTEMBER 9.
WHAT?!
THAT'S FOUR DAYS FROM NOW!
LET'S CELEBRATE TOGETHER!
THE PREDICTABLE OUTCOME!
KAGUYA GETS TO CELEBRATE SHIROGANE'S BIRTHDAY...
...WITHOUT SACRIFICING HERSELF.
HA HA
LET'S SEE...
ANUARY 1...
"YOU ARE AN ALEXANDRITE CRYSTAL."
"LIKE THE STONE NAMED AFTER A KING...
...YOU ARE BOTH NOBLE AND PRIDEFUL."
"THIS CRYSTAL HAS THE UNIQUE ABILITY OF CHANGING FROM RED TO BLUE DEPENDING ON THE LIGHT THAT SHINES UPON IT."
"YOU, TOO, BASED ON YOUR ENVIRONMENT, WILL AT TIMES BE AN ANGEL...
...AND AT OTHER TIMES A DEVIL."
"IF YOU CAN SET ASIDE YOUR PRIDE AND BE HONEST WITH YOURSELF, HAPPINESS WILL COME TO YOU."

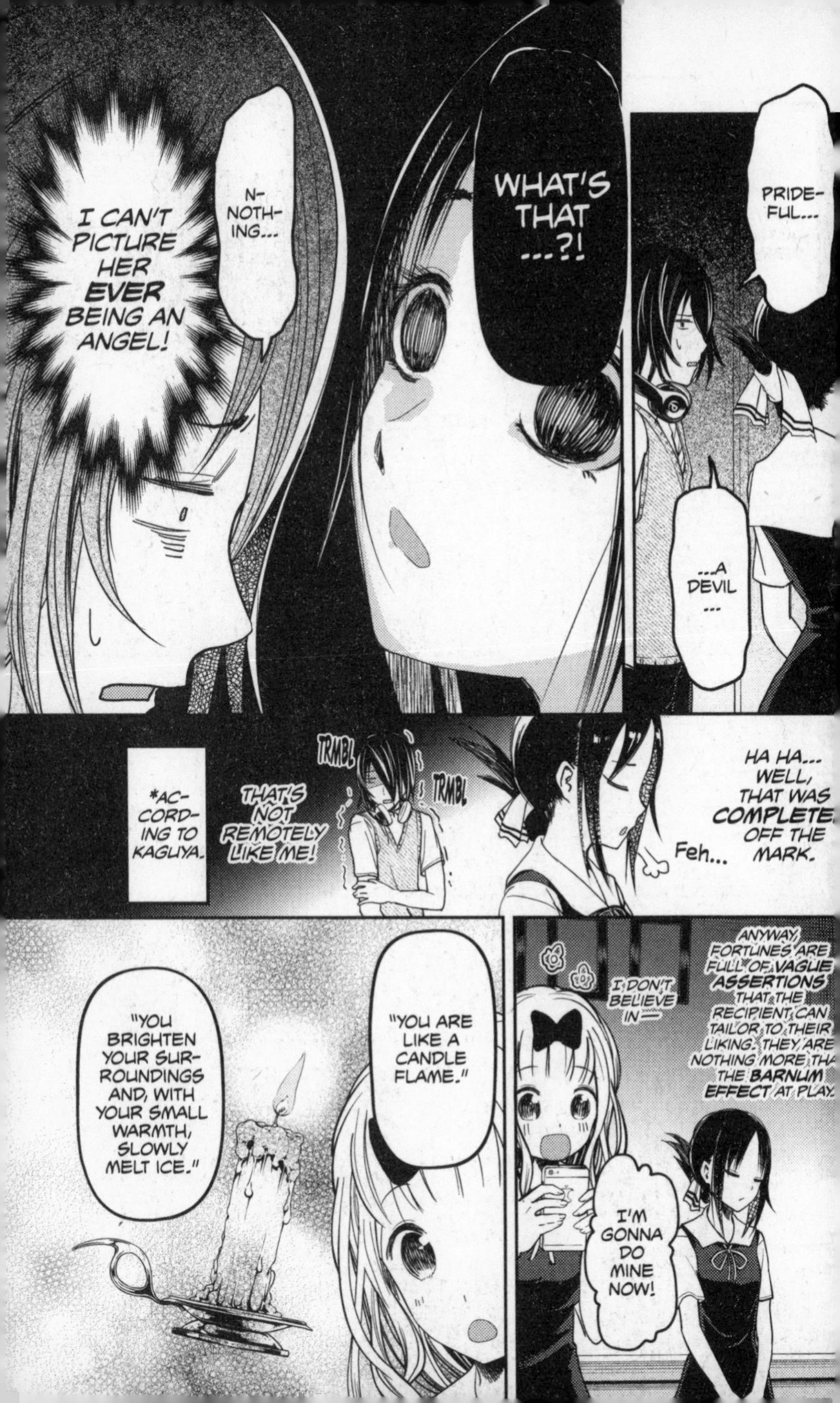
PRIDE-FUL...
...A DEVIL...
WHAT'S THAT...?!
N-NOTH-ING...
I CAN'T PICTURE HER EVER BEING AN ANGEL!
HA HA... WELL, THAT WAS COMPLETE OFF THE MARK.
Feh...
TRMBL
TRMBL
THAT'S NOT REMOTELY LIKE ME!
*AC-CORD-ING TO KAGUYA.
ANYWAY, FORTUNES ARE FULL OF VAGUE ASSERTIONS THAT THE RECIPIENT CAN TAILOR TO THEIR LIKING. THEY ARE NOTHING MORE THA THE BARNUM EFFECT AT PLAY.
I DON'T BELIEVE IN—
I'M GONNA DO MINE NOW!
"YOU ARE LIKE A CANDLE FLAME."
"YOU BRIGHTEN YOUR SUR-ROUNDINGS AND, WITH YOUR SMALL WARMTH, SLOWLY MELT ICE."

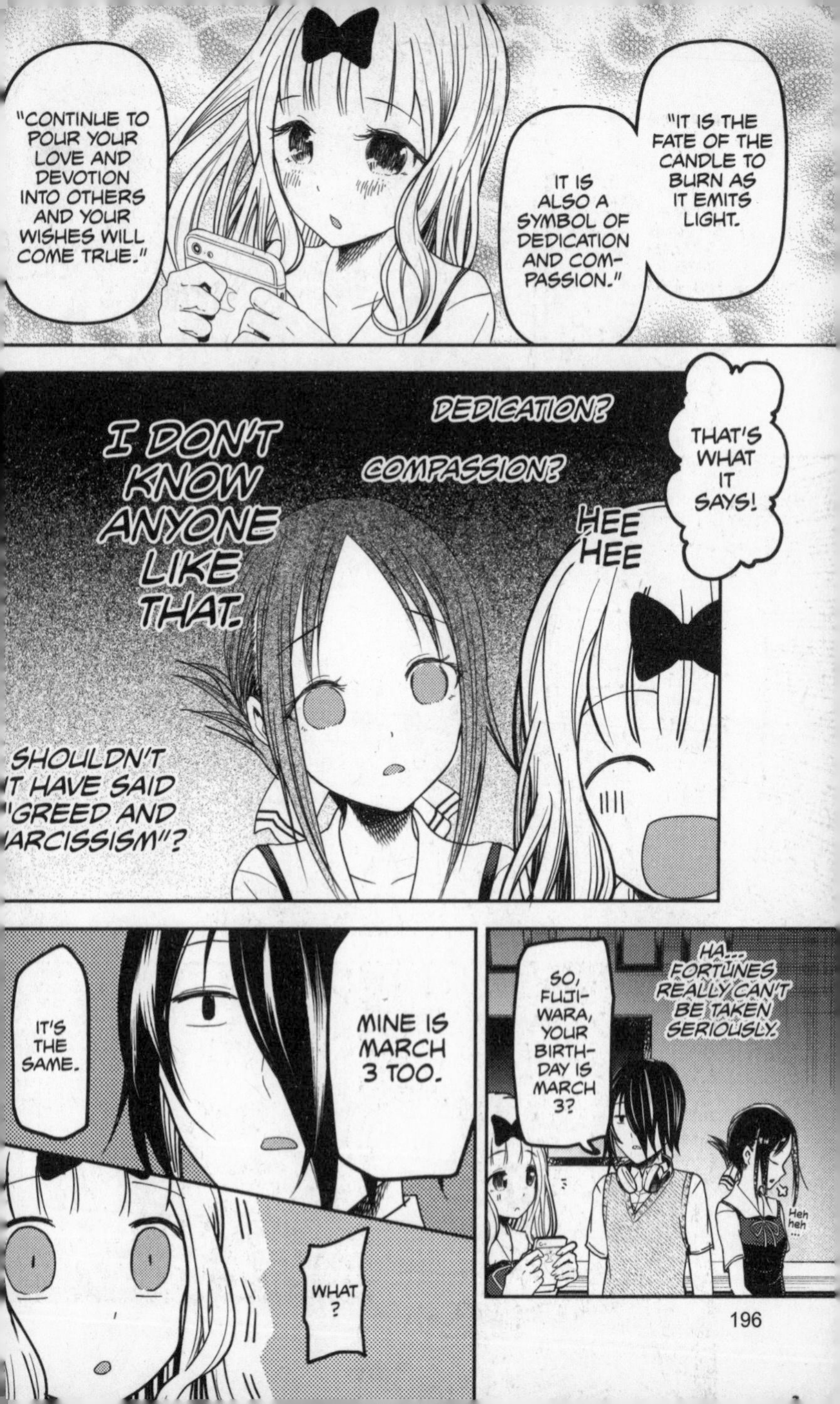

"IT IS THE FATE OF THE CANDLE TO BURN AS IT EMITS LIGHT.
IT IS ALSO A SYMBOL OF DEDICATION AND COM-PASSION."
"CONTINUE TO POUR YOUR LOVE AND DEVOTION INTO OTHERS AND YOUR WISHES WILL COME TRUE."
THAT'S WHAT IT SAYS!
HEE HEE
DEDICATION?
COMPASSION?
I DON'T KNOW ANYONE LIKE THAT.
SHOULDN'T
T HAVE SAID
"GREED AND
ARCISSISM"?
HA... FORTUNES REALLY CAN'T BE TAKEN SERIOUSLY.
SO, FUJI-WARA, YOUR BIRTH-DAY IS MARCH 3?
Heh heh...
MINE IS MARCH 3 TOO.
IT'S THE SAME.
WHAT?

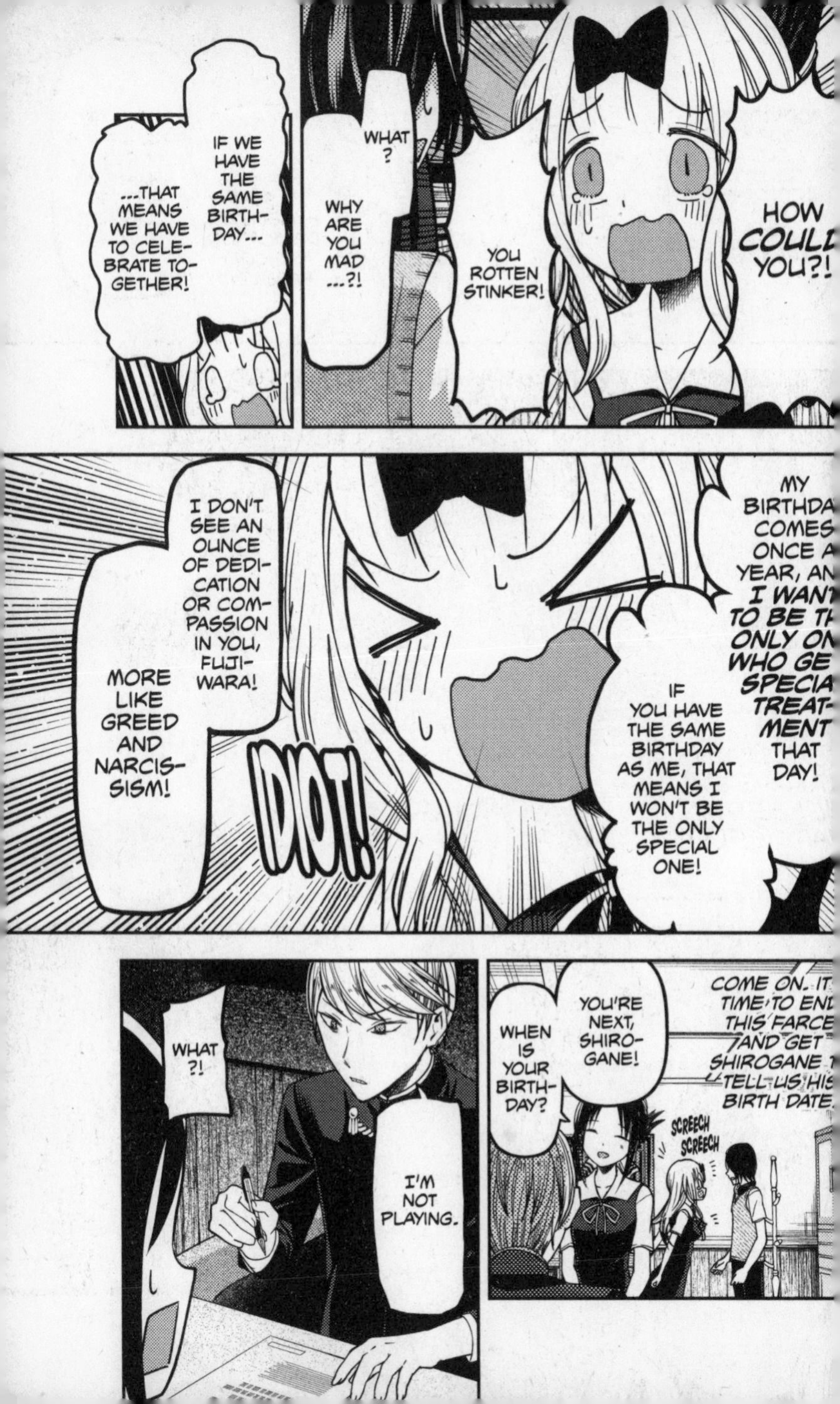
HOW COULD YOU?!
YOU ROTTEN STINKER!
WHAT?
WHY ARE YOU MAD...?!
IF WE HAVE THE SAME BIRTHDAY...
...THAT MEANS WE HAVE TO CELEBRATE TOGETHER!
MY BIRTHDA COMES ONCE A YEAR, AN I WANT TO BE TH ONLY ON WHO GE SPECIA TREATMENT THAT DAY!
IF YOU HAVE THE SAME BIRTHDAY AS ME, THAT MEANS I WON'T BE THE ONLY SPECIAL ONE!
IDIOT!
I DON'T SEE AN OUNCE OF DEDICATION OR COMPASSION IN YOU, FUJIWARA!
MORE LIKE GREED AND NARCISSISM!
COME ON. IT TIME TO END THIS FARCE AND GET SHIROGANE T TELL US HIS BIRTH DATE.
SCREECH SCREECH
YOU'RE NEXT, SHIROGANE!
WHEN IS YOUR BIRTHDAY?
WHAT?!
I'M NOT PLAYING.

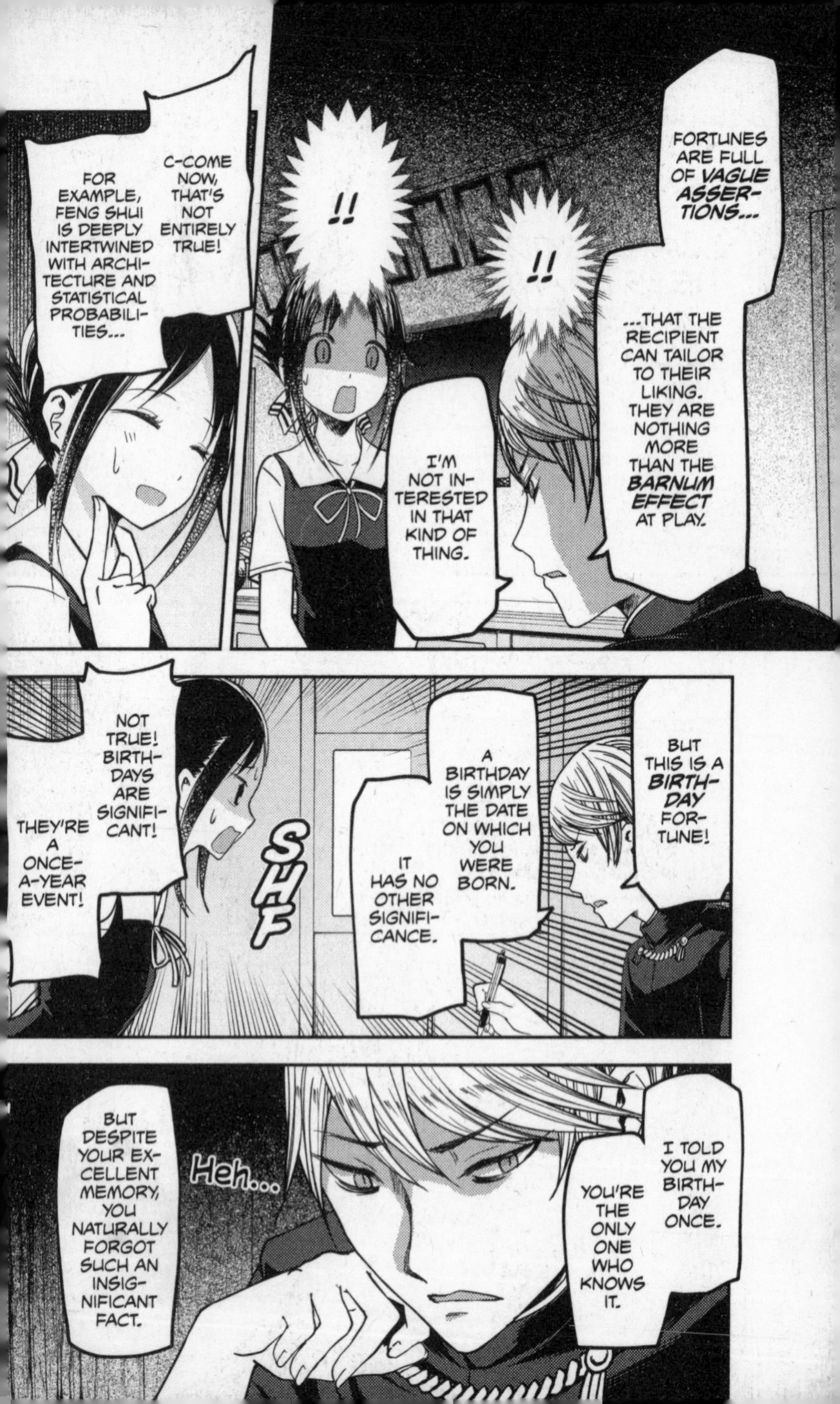
FORTUNES ARE FULL OF VAGUE ASSERTIONS...
...THAT THE RECIPIENT CAN TAILOR TO THEIR LIKING. THEY ARE NOTHING MORE THAN THE BARNUM EFFECT AT PLAY.
!!
I'M NOT INTERESTED IN THAT KIND OF THING.
!!
C-COME NOW, THAT'S NOT ENTIRELY TRUE!
FOR EXAMPLE, FENG SHUI IS DEEPLY INTERTWINED WITH ARCHITECTURE AND STATISTICAL PROBABILITIES...
BUT THIS IS A BIRTHDAY FORTUNE!
A BIRTHDAY IS SIMPLY THE DATE ON WHICH YOU WERE BORN.
IT HAS NO OTHER SIGNIFICANCE.
SHF
NOT TRUE! BIRTHDAYS ARE SIGNIFICANT!
THEY'RE A ONCE-A-YEAR EVENT!
I TOLD YOU MY BIRTHDAY ONCE.
YOU'RE THE ONLY ONE WHO KNOWS IT.
Heh...
BUT DESPITE YOUR EXCELLENT MEMORY, YOU NATURALLY FORGOT SUCH AN INSIGNIFICANT FACT.

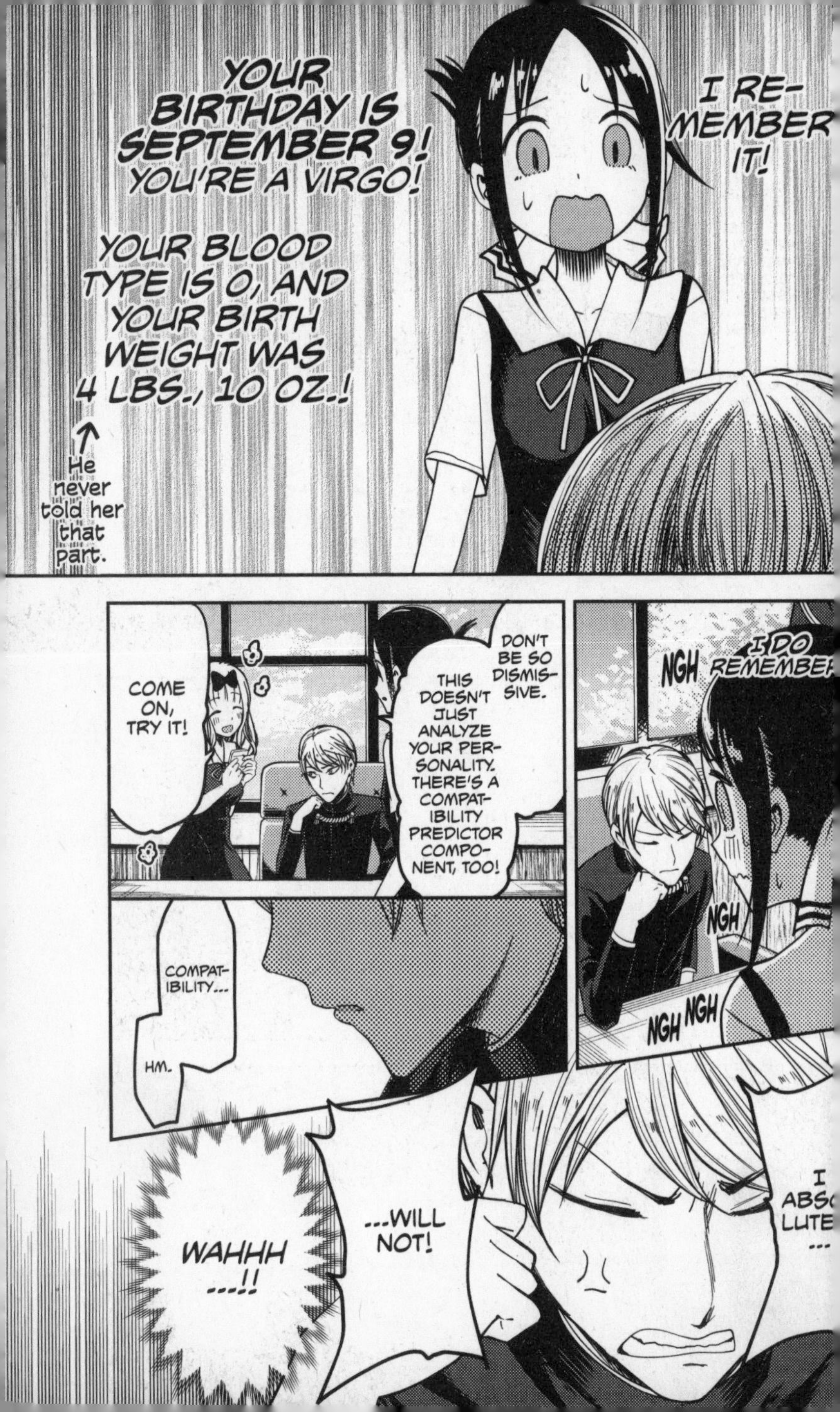

I RE-MEMBER IT!
YOUR BIRTHDAY IS SEPTEMBER 9! YOU'RE A VIRGO!
YOUR BLOOD TYPE IS O, AND YOUR BIRTH WEIGHT WAS 4 LBS., 10 OZ.!
He never told her that part.
NGH
I DO REMEMBE
NGH
NGH NGH
DON'T BE SO DISMIS-SIVE.
THIS DOESN'T JUST ANALYZE YOUR PER-SONALITY. THERE'S A COMPAT-IBILITY PREDICTOR COMPO-NENT, TOO!
COME ON, TRY IT!
COMPAT-IBILITY...
HM.
I ABSO LUTE ...
...WILL NOT!
WAHHH ...!!

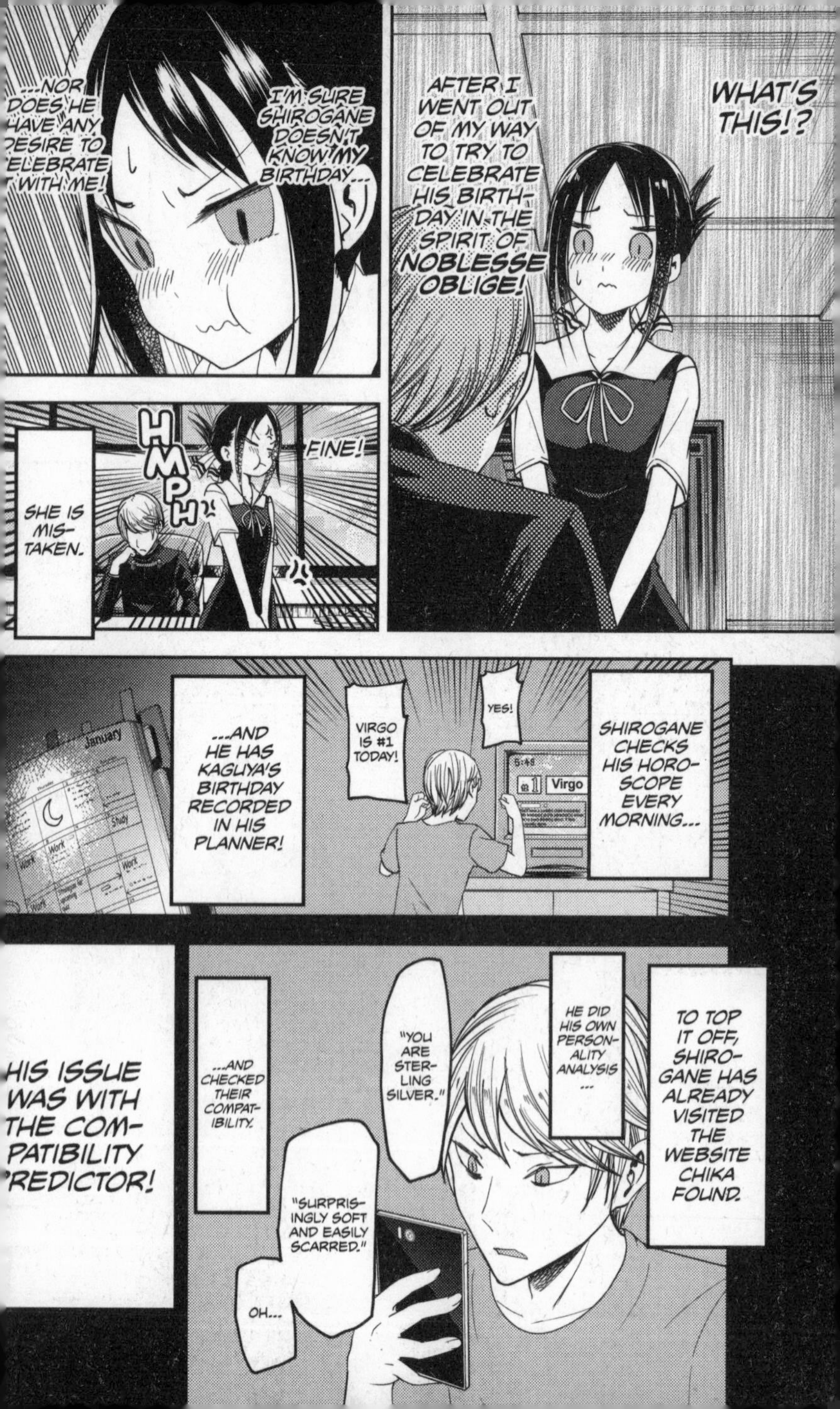
WHAT'S THIS!?
AFTER I WENT OUT OF MY WAY TO TRY TO CELEBRATE HIS BIRTHDAY IN THE SPIRIT OF NOBLESSE OBLIGE!
I'M SURE SHIROGANE DOESN'T KNOW MY BIRTHDAY...
...NOR DOES HE HAVE ANY DESIRE TO CELEBRATE IT WITH ME!
HMPH!
FINE!
SHE IS MISTAKEN.
SHIROGANE CHECKS HIS HOROSCOPE EVERY MORNING...
YES!
1 Virgo
VIRGO IS #1 TODAY!
...AND HE HAS KAGUYA'S BIRTHDAY RECORDED IN HIS PLANNER!
January
Study
Work
Work
Work
Work
TO TOP IT OFF, SHIROGANE HAS ALREADY VISITED THE WEBSITE CHIKA FOUND.
HE DID HIS OWN PERSONALITY ANALYSIS...
"YOU ARE STERLING SILVER."
...AND CHECKED THEIR COMPATIBILITY.
"SURPRISINGLY SOFT AND EASILY SCARRED."
OH...
HIS ISSUE WAS WITH THE COMPATIBILITY PREDICTOR!

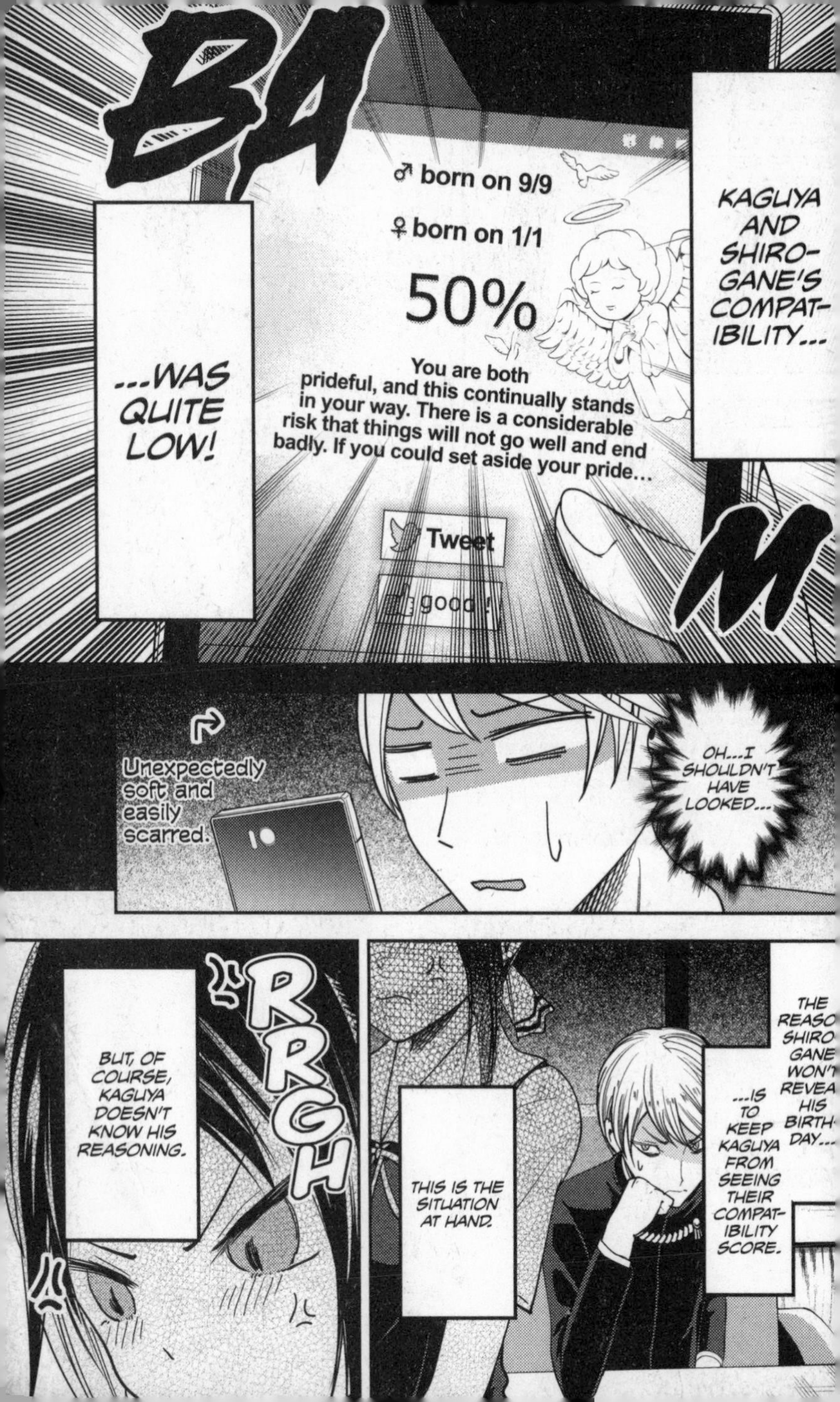
KAGUYA AND SHIRO-GANE'S COMPAT-IBILITY...
BA
M
♂ born on 9/9
♀ born on 1/1
50%
You are both prideful, and this continually stands in your way. There is a considerable risk that things will not go well and end badly. If you could set aside your pride...
Tweet
good!
...WAS QUITE LOW!
OH...I SHOULDN'T HAVE LOOKED...
Unexpectedly soft and easily scarred.
THE REASO SHIRO GANE WON'T REVEA HIS BIRTH DAY...
...IS TO KEEP KAGUYA FROM SEEING THEIR COMPAT-IBILITY SCORE.
THIS IS THE SITUATION AT HAND.
RRGH
BUT, OF COURSE, KAGUYA DOESN'T KNOW HIS REASONING.

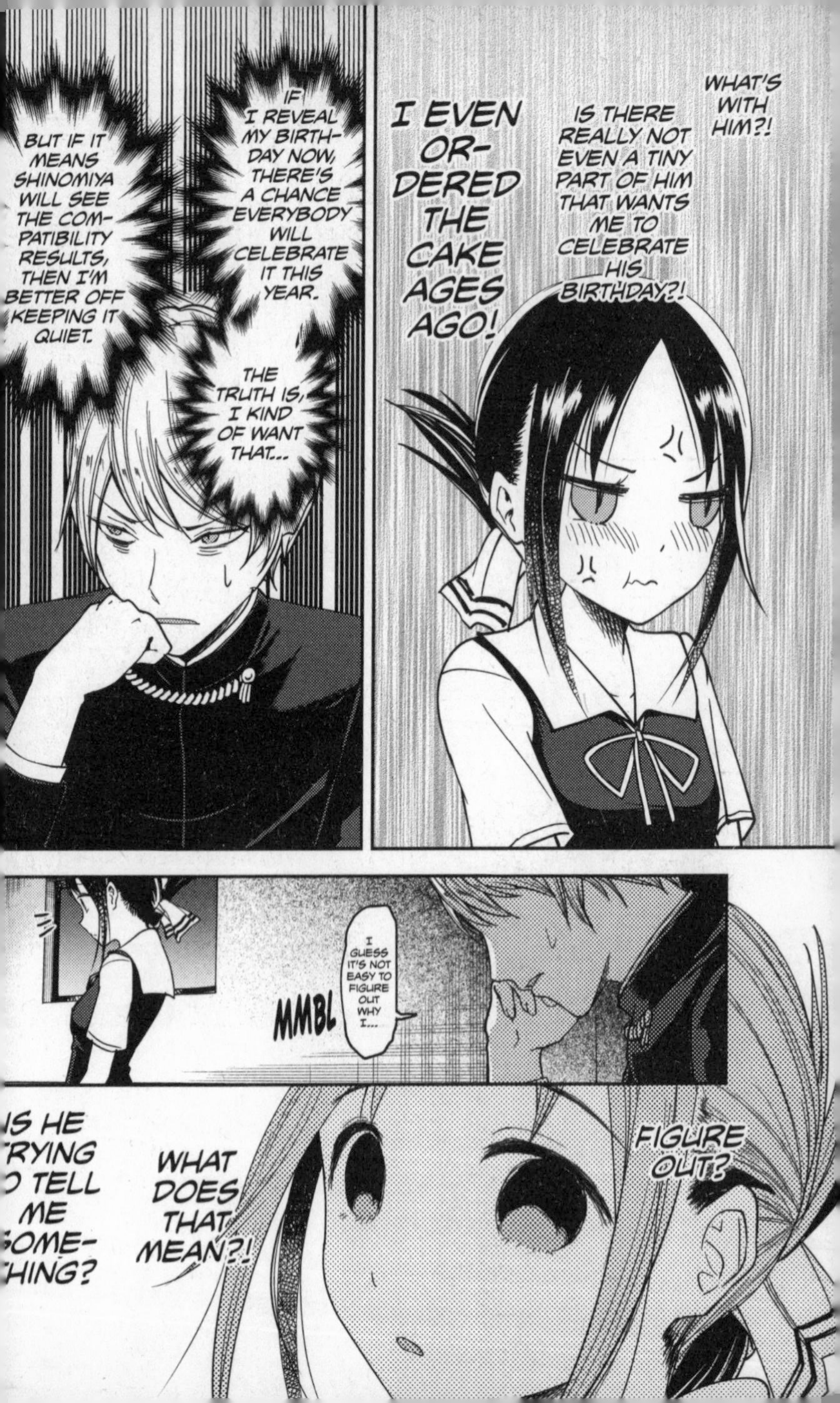
WHAT'S WITH HIM?!
IS THERE REALLY NOT EVEN A TINY PART OF HIM THAT WANTS ME TO CELEBRATE HIS BIRTHDAY?!
I EVEN OR-DERED THE CAKE AGES AGO!
IF I REVEAL MY BIRTH-DAY NOW, THERE'S A CHANCE EVERYBODY WILL CELEBRATE IT THIS YEAR.
THE TRUTH IS, I KIND OF WANT THAT...
BUT IF IT MEANS SHINOMIYA WILL SEE THE COM-PATIBILITY RESULTS, THEN I'M BETTER OFF KEEPING IT QUIET.
I GUESS IT'S NOT EASY TO FIGURE OUT WHY I...
MMBL
FIGURE OUT?
WHAT DOES THAT MEAN?!
IS HE TRYING TO TELL ME SOME-THING?

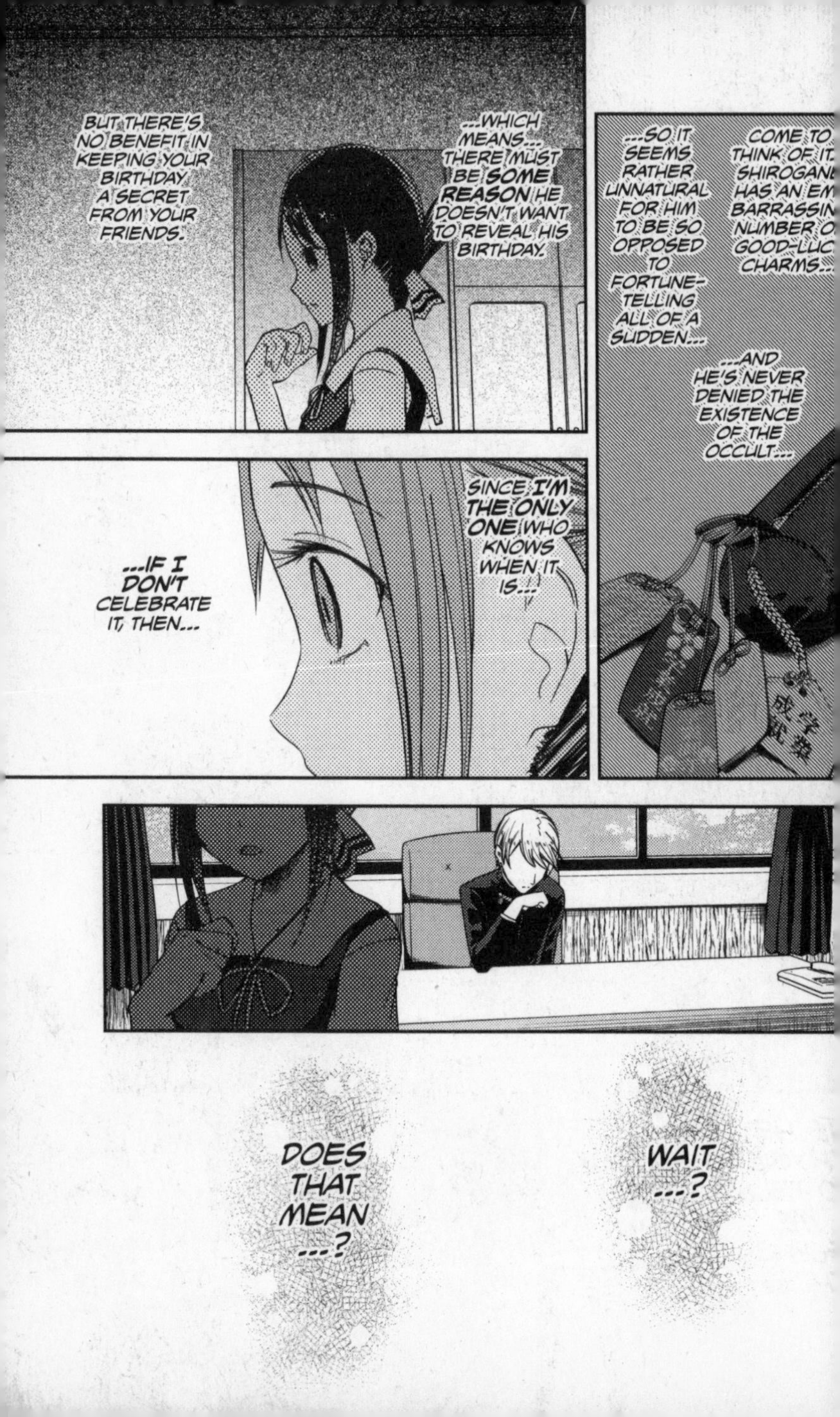
COME TO THINK OF IT, SHIROGAN HAS AN EM BARRASSIN NUMBER O GOOD-LUC CHARMS...
...SO IT SEEMS RATHER UNNATURAL FOR HIM TO BE SO OPPOSED TO FORTUNE-TELLING ALL OF A SUDDEN...
...AND HE'S NEVER DENIED THE EXISTENCE OF THE OCCULT...
BUT THERE'S NO BENEFIT IN KEEPING YOUR BIRTHDAY A SECRET FROM YOUR FRIENDS.
...WHICH MEANS... THERE MUST BE **SOME REASON** HE DOESN'T WANT TO REVEAL HIS BIRTHDAY.
SINCE **I'M THE ONLY ONE** WHO KNOWS WHEN IT IS...!
...IF I **DON'T** CELEBRATE IT, THEN...
WAIT ...?
DOES THAT MEAN ...?

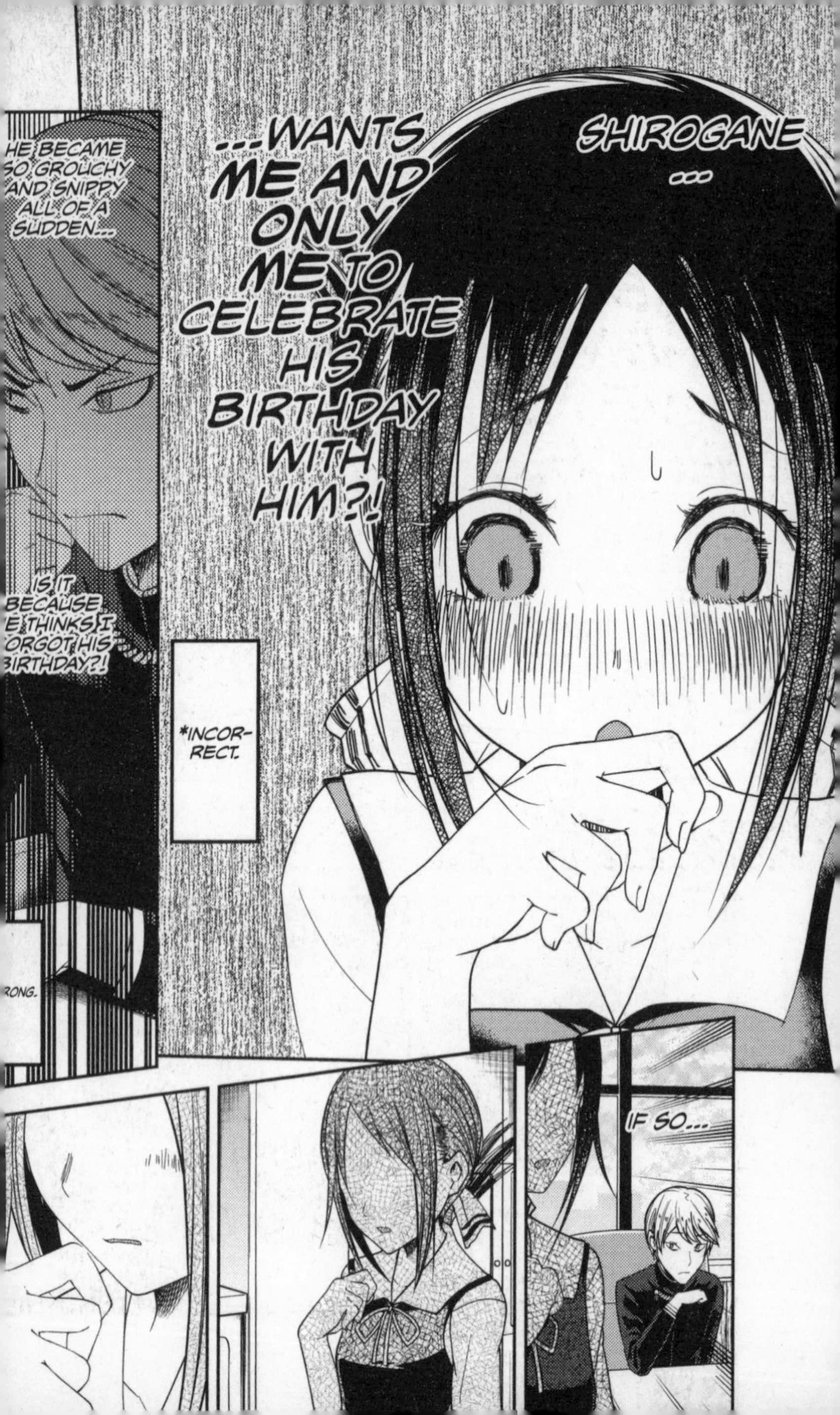
SHIROGANE ...
...WANTS ME AND ONLY ME TO CELEBRATE HIS BIRTHDAY WITH HIM?!
HE BECAME SO GROUCHY AND SNIPPY ALL OF A SUDDEN...
IS IT BECAUSE E THINKS I ORGOT HIS BIRTHDAY?!
*INCOR-RECT.
RONG.
IF SO...

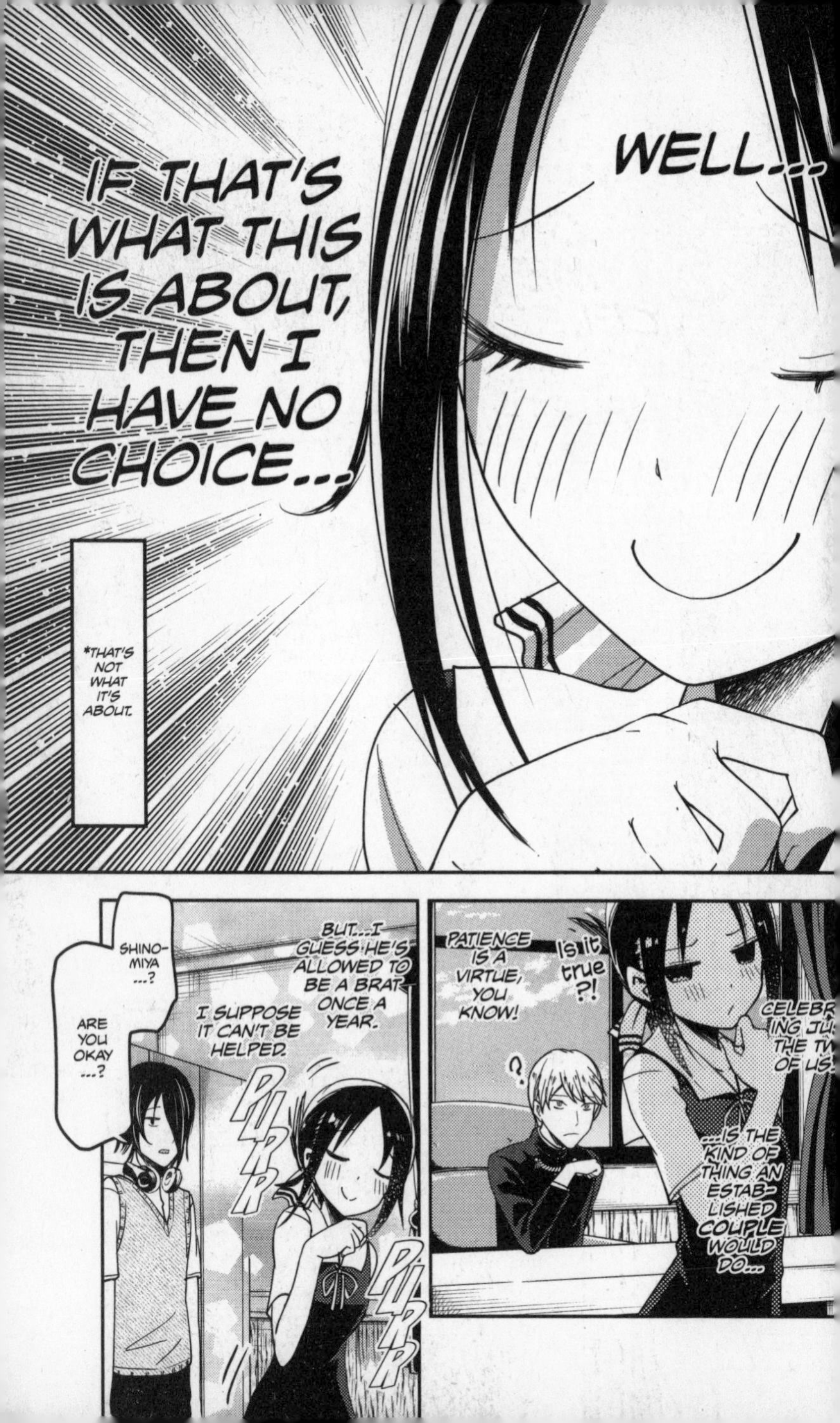

WELL...
IF THAT'S WHAT THIS IS ABOUT, THEN I HAVE NO CHOICE...
*THAT'S NOT WHAT IT'S ABOUT.
CELEBR ING JU THE TW OF US.
...IS THE KIND OF THING AN ESTAB-LISHED COUPLE WOULD DO...
Is it true?!
PATIENCE IS A VIRTUE, YOU KNOW!
?
BUT...I GUESS HE'S ALLOWED TO BE A BRAT ONCE A YEAR.
I SUPPOSE IT CAN'T BE HELPED.
PURR
PURR
SHINOMIYA...?
ARE YOU OKAY...?

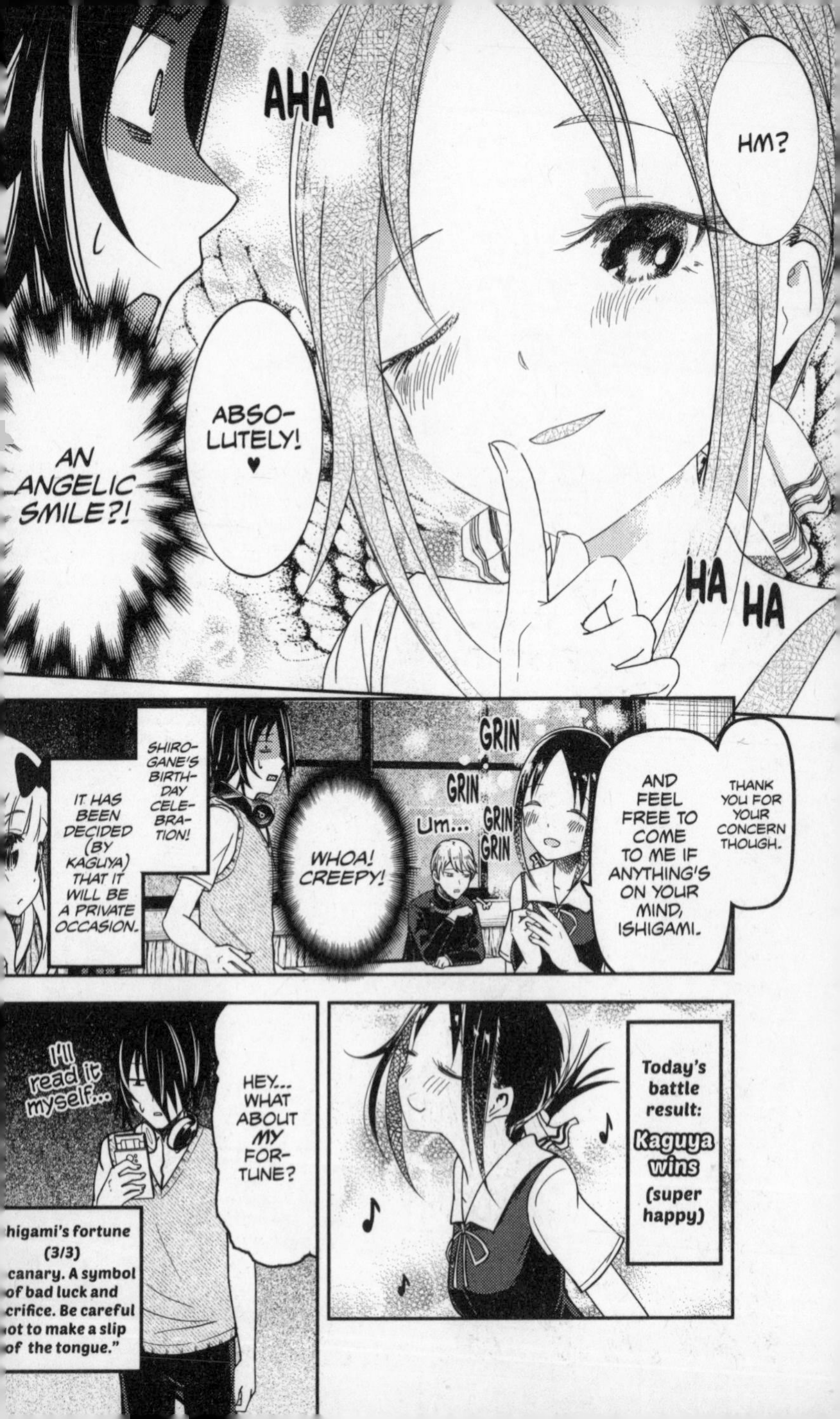
HM?
AHA
HA HA
ABSO-LUTELY! ♥
AN ANGELIC SMILE?!
THANK YOU FOR YOUR CONCERN THOUGH.
AND FEEL FREE TO COME TO ME IF ANYTHING'S ON YOUR MIND, ISHIGAMI.
GRIN GRIN GRIN GRIN
Um...
WHOA! CREEPY!
SHIROGANE'S BIRTHDAY CELEBRATION!
IT HAS BEEN DECIDED (BY KAGUYA) THAT IT WILL BE A PRIVATE OCCASION.
Today's battle result: Kaguya wins (super happy)
HEY... WHAT ABOUT *MY* FORTUNE?
I'll read it myself...
higami's fortune (3/3)
canary. A symbol of bad luck and crifice. Be careful ot to make a slip of the tongue.”

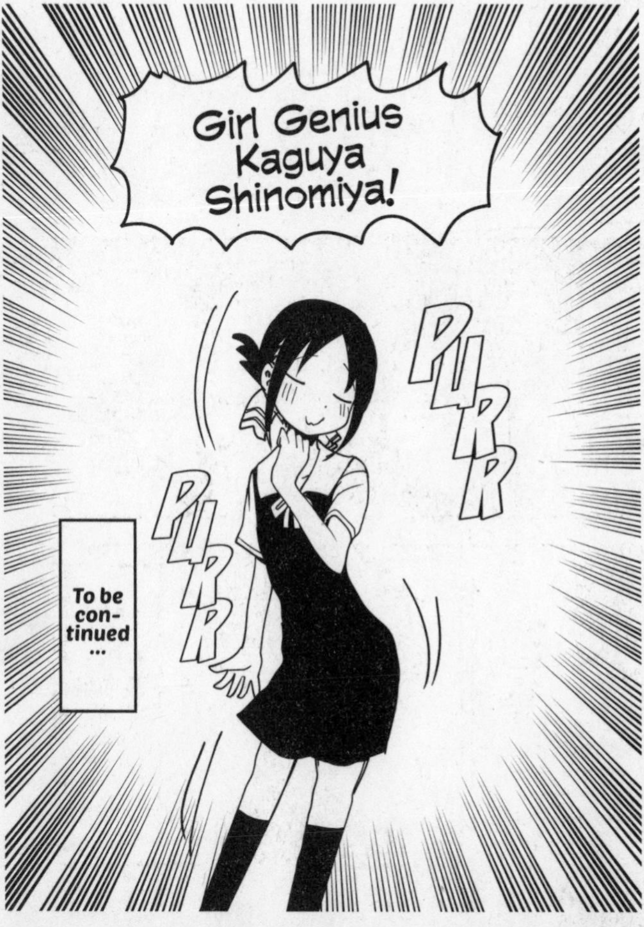
Girl Genius Kaguya Shinomiya!
PURR
PURR
To be continued...

THE ESSENCE OF LOVE IS FEAR. WHEN ONE LOSES ONE'S FEAR, LOVE LOSES TS COLOR.

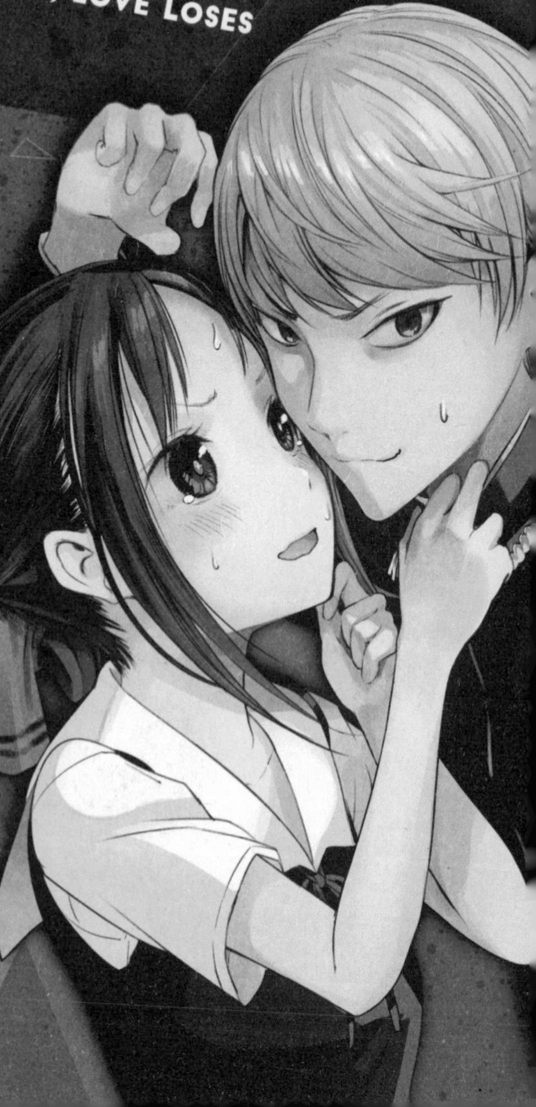

Aka Akasaka

Aka Akasaka got his start as an assistant to Jinsei Kataoka and Kazuma Kondou, the creators of *Deadman Wonderland*. His first serialized manga was an adaptation of the light novel series *Sayonara Piano Sonata*, published by Kadokawa in 2011. *Kaguya-sama: Love Is War* began serialization in *Miracle Jump* in 2015 but was later moved to *Weekly Young Jump* in 2016 due to its popularity.

Regarding the *Kaguya-sama: Love Is War* under-the-cover cartoon hiatus

The *Kaguya-sama: Love Is War* front under-the-cover cartoon that was originally planned for this volume is on hiatus due to author Aka Akasaka's feigned illness. We extend our deepest apologies to the many readers who were looking forward to this feature.

The author is working on regaining his health as soon as possible, but the truth is that his bed is just so warm and comfy that he can't be bothered to get the work done. In this period of cold weather, he is following a strict regimen of not working too hard.

Though this may be a cause of concern or worry for our readers, we ask for your continued support during this not-difficult time.

Sorry!

From the Editorial Department

Regarding the *Kaguya-sama: Love Is War* under-the-cover cartoon hiatus

The *Kaguya-Sama Love Is War* back under-the-cover cartoon that was originally planned for this volume is on hiatus due to author Aka Akasaka's feigned illness. We extend our deepest apologies to the many readers who were looking forward to this feature.

The author is working on regaining his health as soon as possible, but the truth is that it's so much work to come up with text and images to put under the cover that I'm wondering why I ever started this in the first place. Why didn't anybody stop me? Does everyone hate me? Are people secretly contemptuous of me behind their smiling faces? That's a frightening thought... This is stressful...and scary... And now I'm indulging in the worst kind of obsessive thinking and will need some time to recover.

Though this may be a cause of concern or worry for our readers, we ask for your continued support during this not-difficult time.

Sorry!

From the Editorial Department

KAGUYA-SAMA
LOVE IS WAR

SHONEN JUMP MANGA EDITION

5

STORY AND ART BY
AKA AKASAKA

Translation/Emi Louie-Nishikawa
English Adaptation/Annette Roman
Touch-Up Art & Lettering/Stephen Dutro
Cover & Interior Design/J. Shikuma
Editor/Annette Roman

KAGUYA-SAMA WA KOKURASETAI~TENSAITACHI NO REN'AI ZUNO SEN~
© 2015 by Aka Akasaka
All rights reserved.
First published in Japan in 2015 by SHUEISHA Inc., Tokyo.
English translation rights arranged by SHUEISHA Inc.

Printed in Canada

Published by VIZ Media, LLC
P.O. Box 77010
San Francisco, CA 94107

10 9 8 7 6 5 4 3 2 1
First printing, November 2018

viz.com

shonenjump.com

COMING NEXT VOLUME

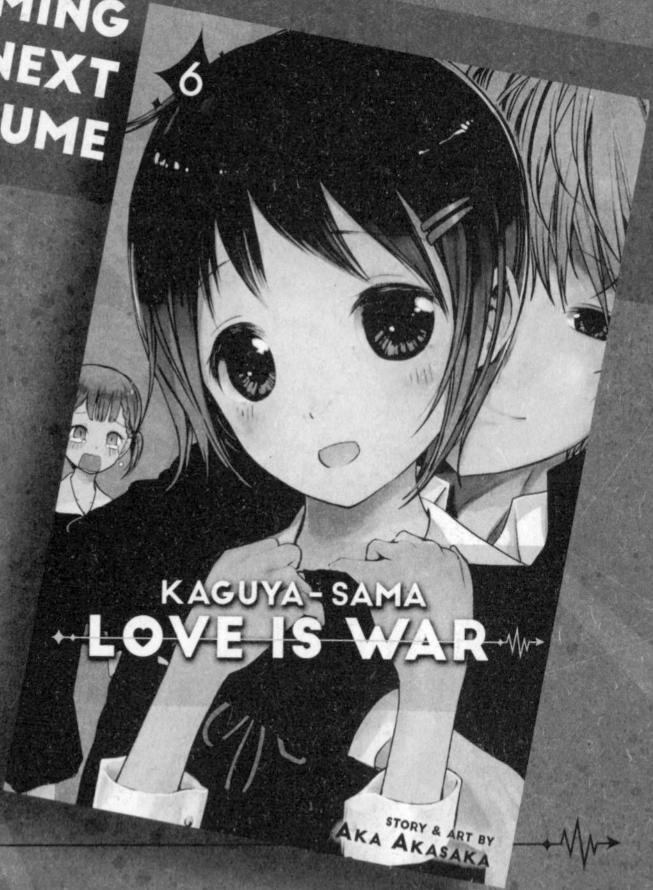
6
KAGUYA-SAMA
LOVE IS WAR
STORY & ART BY
AKA AKASAKA

6

Will Kaguya figure out what Miyuki wants for his birthday and present him with the perfect cake too? Is treasurer Yu flunking out of school and beyond help...or can the one he fears most get him back on track? Then the romantic autumn moon-viewing festival leads to some stellar night moves. The student council plays a role-playing game in which at least one member doesn't get to play out their fantasy. Ai assumes an alter ego to prove she can get Miyuki to fall in love with her in just one day. And Miyuki's time as student council president is up!

We play many roles in life.

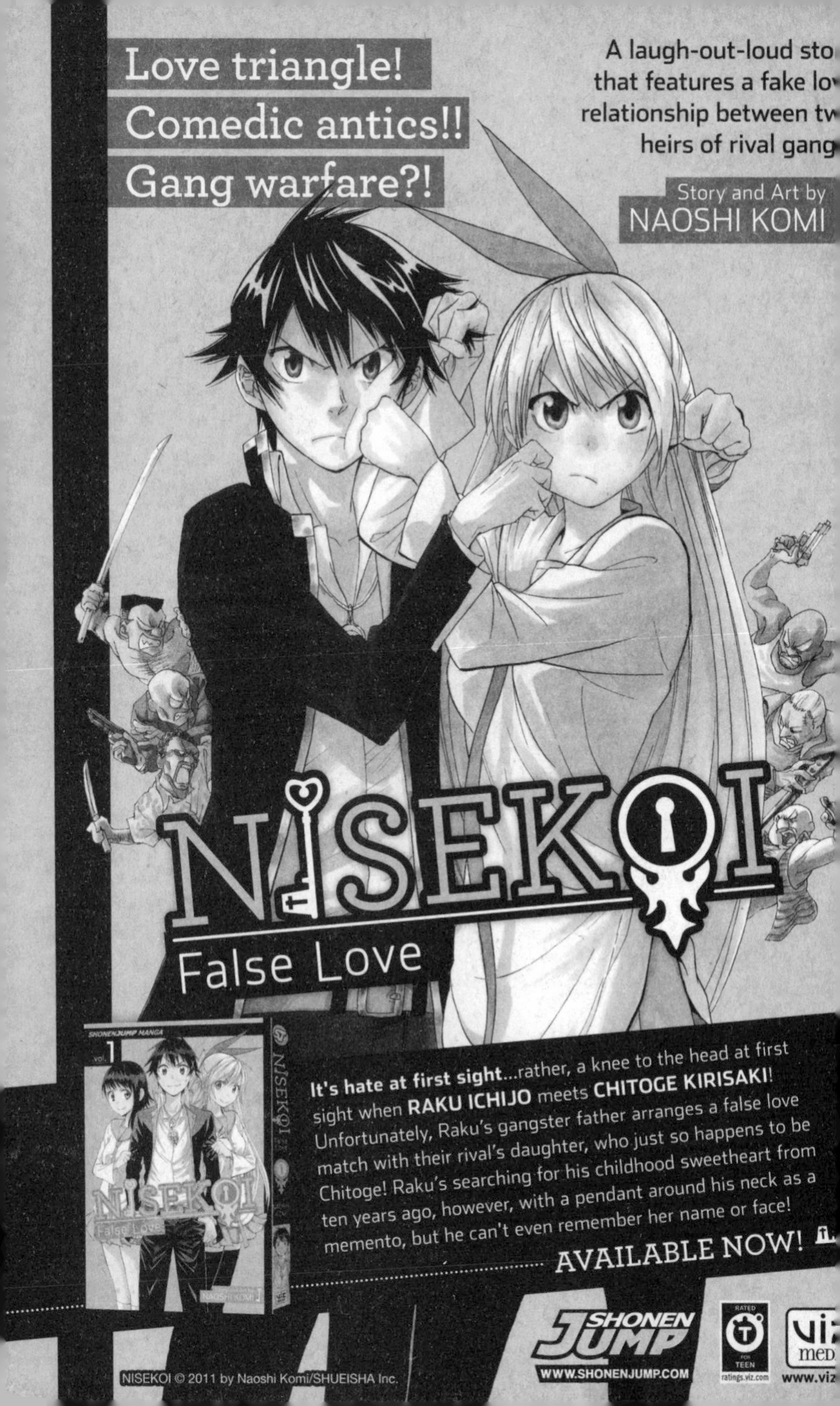
Love triangle!
Comedic antics!!
Gang warfare?!
A laugh-out-loud sto
that features a fake lo
relationship between tw
heirs of rival gang
Story and Art by
NAOSHI KOMI
NISEKOI
False Love
SHONENJUMP MANGA
vol. 1
NISEKOI
False Love
NAOSHI KOMI
It's hate at first sight...rather, a knee to the head at first sight when RAKU ICHIJO meets CHITOGE KIRISAKI! Unfortunately, Raku's gangster father arranges a false love match with their rival's daughter, who just so happens to be Chitoge! Raku's searching for his childhood sweetheart from ten years ago, however, with a pendant around his neck as a memento, but he can't even remember her name or face!
AVAILABLE NOW!
SHONEN JUMP
WWW.SHONENJUMP.COM
RATED T FOR TEEN
ratings.viz.com
www.viz
NISEKOI © 2011 by Naoshi Komi/SHUEISHA Inc.

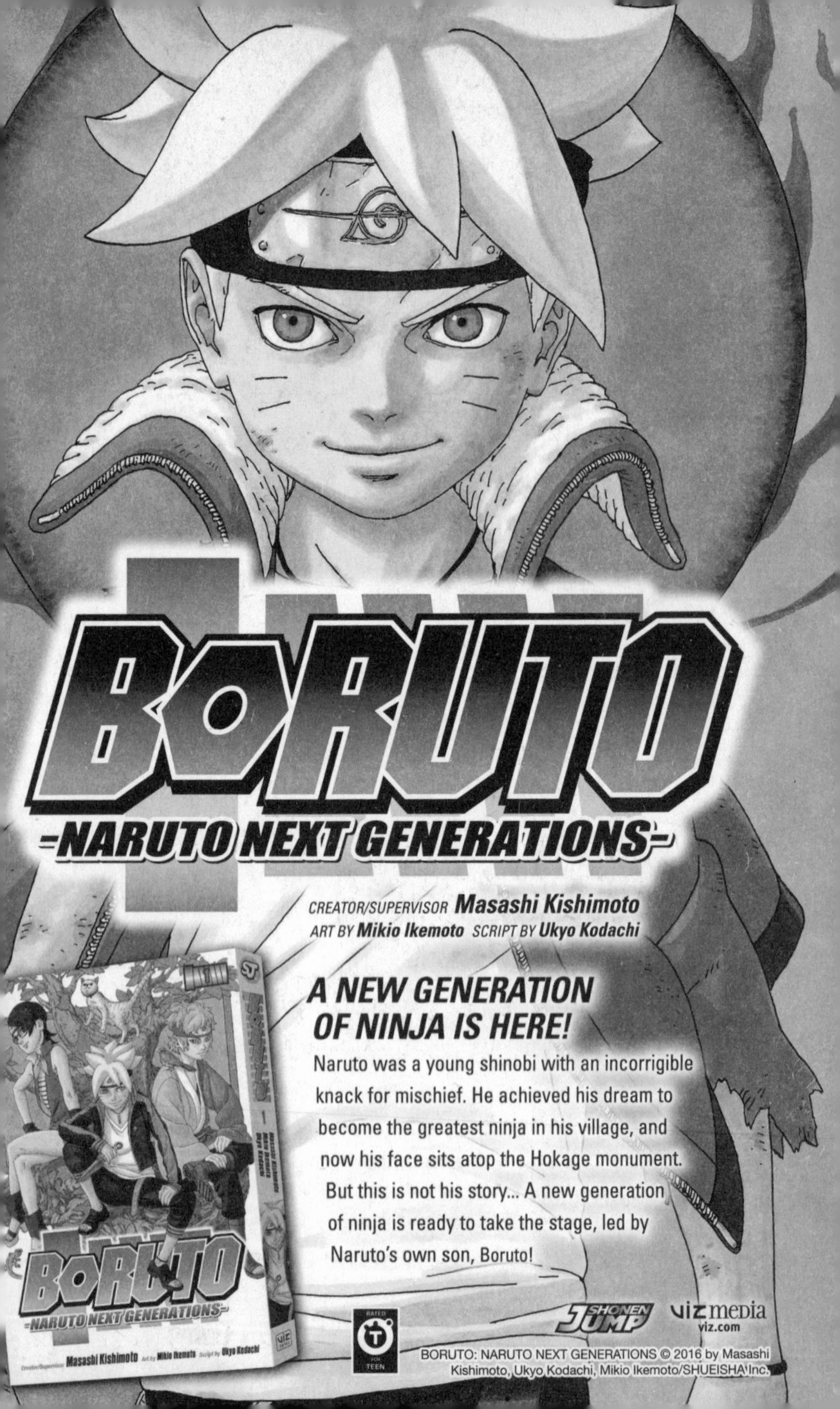
BORUTO
-NARUTO NEXT GENERATIONS-
CREATOR/SUPERVISOR Masashi Kishimoto
ART BY Mikio Ikemoto SCRIPT BY Ukyo Kodachi
A NEW GENERATION OF NINJA IS HERE!
Naruto was a young shinobi with an incorrigible knack for mischief. He achieved his dream to become the greatest ninja in his village, and now his face sits atop the Hokage monument. But this is not his story... A new generation of ninja is ready to take the stage, led by Naruto's own son, Boruto!
BORUTO
-NARUTO NEXT GENERATIONS-
Masashi Kishimoto Mikio Ikemoto Ukyo Kodachi
RATED T FOR TEEN
SHONEN JUMP
VIZ media
viz.com
BORUTO: NARUTO NEXT GENERATIONS © 2016 by Masashi Kishimoto, Ukyo Kodachi, Mikio Ikemoto/SHUEISHA Inc.

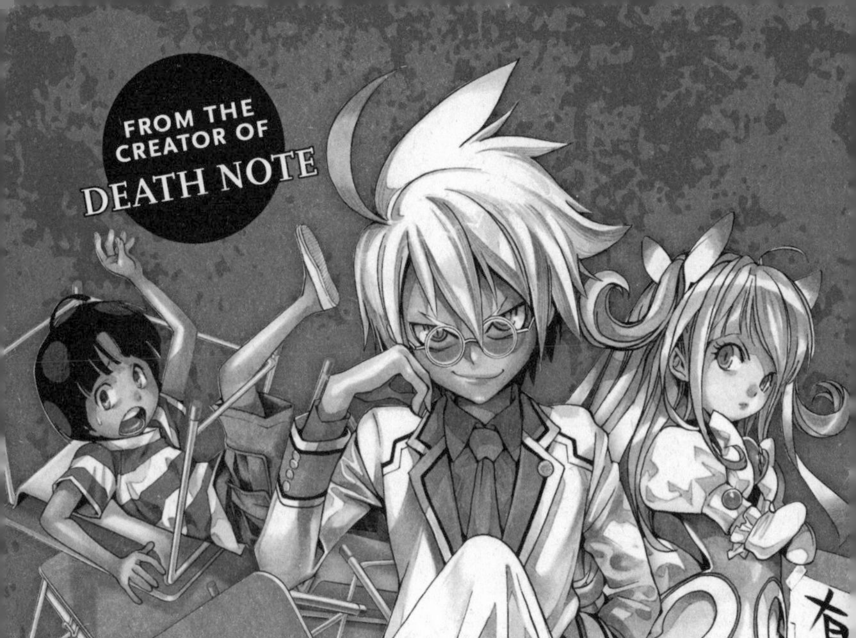
FROM THE CREATOR OF
DEATH NOTE

YOU'RE READING THE WRONG WAY!

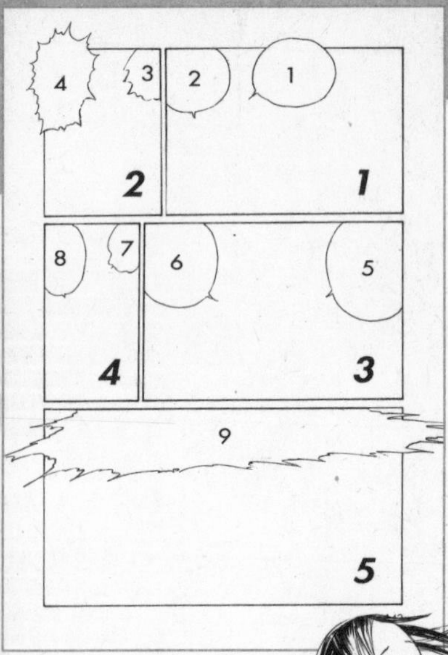

1
2
3
4
5
6
7
8
9
1
2
3
4
5

KAGUYA-SAMA: LOVE IS WAR reads from right to left, starting in the upper-right corner. Japanese is read from right to left, meaning that action, sound effects and word-balloon order are completely reversed from English order.

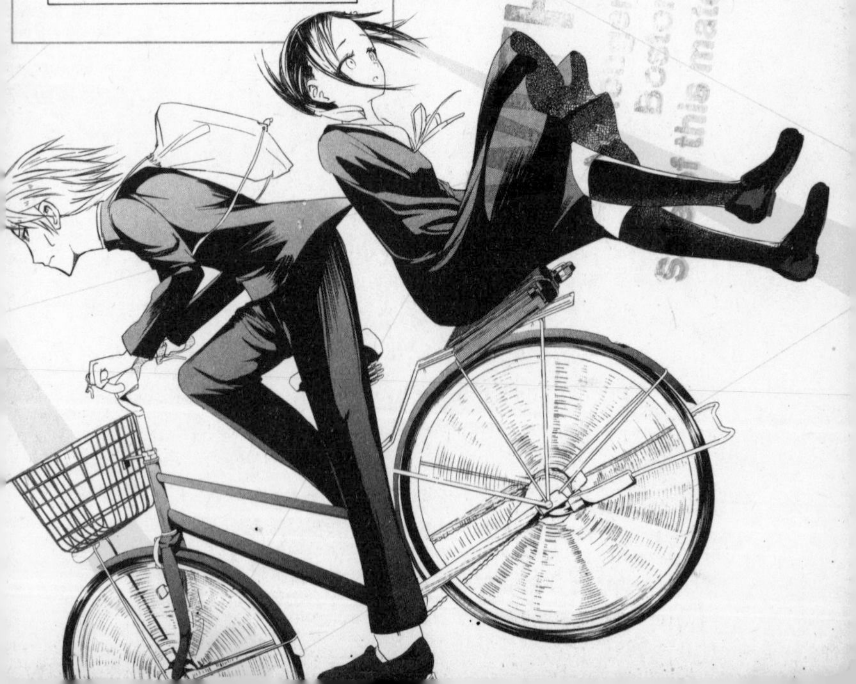